CPM in Construction Management

CPM in Construction Management

JAMES J. O'BRIEN
Professional Engineer

Third Edition

McGRAW-HILL BOOK COMPANY
New York   St. Louis   San Francisco   Auckland
Bogotá   Hamburg   London   Madrid   Mexico
Montreal   New Delhi   Panama   Paris   São Paulo
Singapore   Sydney   Tokyo   Toronto

Library of Congress Cataloging in Publication Data

O'Brien, James Jerome, 1929–
  CPM in construction management.

  1. Construction industry—Management.   2. Critical
path analysis.   I. Title.   II. Title: C.P.M. in
construction management.
HD9715.A202   1983   690′.068   84-854
ISBN 0-07-047663-2

67890 DOC/DOC 898

ISBN 0-07-047663-2

The editors for this book were Joan Zseleczky and Lester Strong,
the designer was Naomi Auerbach, and the production supervisor
was Sally Fliess. It was set in Century Schoolbook
by University Graphics, Inc.
Printed and bound by R. R. Donnelley & Sons Company.

This book is dedicated to my mother, Emma O'Brien Fulforth, with love, and with appreciation for her unfailing encouragement (which was particularly appreciated in regard to this book).

CONTENTS

PREFACE

The original purpose of this book, in 1965, was to present and discuss the Critical Path Method (CPM) and its use in the construction industry. At that point in time, CPM was a young but proven technique—usually considered to be optional. When the second edition was published in 1971, the network approach to scheduling was becoming a regular requirement in construction contracts. This current edition, published after 25 years of experience in the application of CPM, describes highlights of that experience and its significance in today's practical use of CPM.

The basic strength of CPM continues to be its ability to represent logical planning factors in network form. One reviewer noted: "Perhaps the most ironic aspect of the Critical Path Method is that after you understand it, it is self-evident. Just as an Algebra student can apply the rules without full appreciation of the power of the mathematical concepts, so can the individual apply CPM or its equivalent without fully appreciating the applicability of the method."

The book first describes the development of CPM and its practical use in the construction industry. The basic technique is described in sufficient depth for the reader to apply it to practical construction situations.

The "John Doe" case study is used throughout the book in order first to describe basic CPM network techniques, and then to illustrate special functions such as cost control, resource planning, and project monitoring. Uses of CPM in project management in nonconstruction areas, such as design and procurement, are also described. Optimum methods of specifying the use of CPM are described in sufficient detail that they can be incorporated directly into construction specifications.

Since the second edition, CPM has become widely utilized as an analytical tool in the evaluation, negotiation, resolution, and/or litigation of construction claims. This aspect is thoroughly explored in the current edition. Legal precedents are provided for the use of CPM during litigation.

Current computer programs and capabilities for a wide range of computer uses of CPM are presented, and a number of case studies are also offered.

The approaches and procedures suggested by the first two editions are, almost without exception, still valid. This book explains and records the experiences of the first 25 years of the use of CPM, and looks forward to the optimum method of applying CPM in future construction projects.

While network techniques are basic and logical, assimilation of the network concept does take time. Further, an effort is required to build an experience level which in turn builds confidence. It is the goal of this book to be a useful element in the development of that conceptual experience and confidence on the part of new users of CPM techniques.

Recognizing as we do the growing roles of women in and their contributions to the fields of construction and management, every effort has been made to achieve a gender-neutral presentation of the material contained in this book. However, in cases where copyrighted sources have been quoted, the generic terms "he" and "his" have been retained, as has the word "manpower" instead of the term "work force" we have used elsewhere. Likewise, there is as yet no widely accepted and familiar gender-neutral equivalent for the term "manhole," so for purposes of clarity we have retained it throughout.

James J. O'Brien

ACKNOWLEDGMENTS

The first edition of this book was typed and proofread by Carmen H. O'Brien. The second edition was typed and proofread by Rita F. Gibson. The third edition has been a team effort under the direction of Rita F. Gibson, with word processor input by Kathy Wollschlager and proofreading by Kathy Wollschlager, Jessica Snyder, Julie Becica, Patti Smith, and others. New illustrations were by the OKA drafting room under the direction of Ben Lewitt and Jim Holt. Tom Petruzzi, with the cooperation of McDonnell Automation, provided the John Doe computer runs. Other OKA staff providing assistance included Patti Mihalik, Fred Andersen, and Marian Kapischke. The author was the final proofreader and, therefore, takes credit for any remaining errors.

INTRODUCTION

The Critical Path Method (CPM) was developed specifically for the planning of construction. The choice was fortuitous, since construction accounts for more than 10 percent of the annual gross national product. Almost every activity and every person is affected to some degree by new construction or the need for it. Most projects are started well after the need has been established, seeming to follow the whimsy, "If I'd wanted it tomorrow, I'd have asked for it tomorrow."

The construction industry is a heterogeneous mix of companies, ranging in size from the large top hundred to one-person operations. Most, however, face similar situations and, to some degree, similar pressures. Many of these factors are either beyond control or difficult to control, such as weather, unions, accidents, capital demands, work loading, and new problems in project approvals that have arisen with the increase in public awareness about pollution and ecological needs. CPM does not offer clairvoyance, but it does assemble all the information available to the project managing team.

Initially, CPM use placed the spotlight on construction and the contractor. The owner, architect, engineer, and public agencies involved were like the backer, producer, and director of a Broadway show. Without them, the show cannot go on; any lack of competence, motivation, or interest on the part of any one of the team members can delay a project. However, the contractor is the performer who ultimately makes or breaks the construction show.

The typical contractor is a planner, generally using instinctive methods rather than formal scheduling. Contractors had little choice prior to 1957, since there were no comprehensive, disciplined procedures for planning and scheduling construction projects. Nevertheless, construction people have always been good schedulers, often scheduling on an hour-to-hour basis.

One of the keys to the success of CPM is that it utilizes the planner's knowledge, experience, and instincts in a logical method first to plan and, then, to schedule. CPM can save time through better planning, and in construction, time is money.

TRADITIONAL PLANNING

The Egyptians and Romans worked construction miracles in their day. Surviving ruins attest to the brilliance of their architecture, but little is known of their construction planning and scheduling. It can be supposed that they solved many scheduling programs by the "use a bigger whip" philosophy. Project management has other roots reaching back into the days before the pyramids. Historical project managers included Noah, Solomon, and the unknown architect who designed the Tower of Babel. History records much about the construction details, but little about the methods of control. In the mid-nineteenth century, at least one writer discussed a work-versus-time graphical representation very similar to today's bar charts. However, it remained for Henry L. Gantt and Frederick W. Taylor in the early 1900s to popularize their graphical representations of work versus time. Their "Gantt charts" were the basis for today's bar graphs or bar charts. The work of Taylor and Gantt was the first scientific consideration of the problem of work scheduling. Although this work was originally aimed at production scheduling, it was readily accepted for planning construction and recording its progress. The bar graph was, and is, an excellent graphical representation of activity. It is easily read and understood by all levels of management and supervision.

If the bar graph is so well suited to construction activity, why look for another planning aid? The reason lies in the fact that the bar graph is limited in what it can retain. In the preparation of a bar chart, the scheduler is almost necessarily influenced by desired completion dates, often actually working backward from the completion dates. The resultant mixture of planning and scheduling is often no better than wishful thinking.

If a bar graph is carefully prepared, the scheduler goes through the same thinking process that the CPM planner does. However, the bar

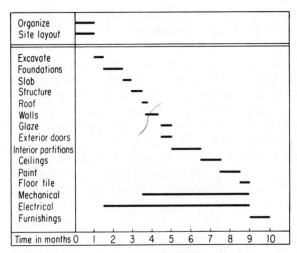

Figure 1.1 Bar chart, small office building.

graph cannot show (or record) the interrelations and interdependencies which control the progress of the project. At a later date, even the originator is often hard-pressed to explain the plan using the bar graph. Figure 1.1 is a simplified bar chart of the construction of a small one-story office building. Suppose that, after this 10-month schedule has been prepared, the owner asks for a 6-month schedule. By using the same time for each activity, the bar chart can be changed as shown in Figure 1.2. Although this looks fine, it is not based upon logical planning; it is merely a juggling of the original bar graph.

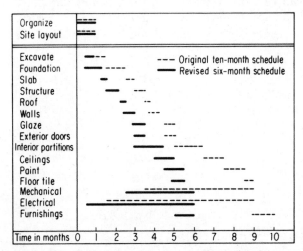

Figure 1.2 Revised bar chart, small office building.

The overall construction plan is usually prepared by the general contractor. This is sensible since the schedules of the other major contractors depend upon the general contractor's schedule. Note that in Figures 1.1 and 1.2 the general contractor's work is broken down in some detail, while the mechanical and electrical work are each shown as a continuous line starting early and ending late. In conformance with the bar graph "schedule," the general contractor often pushes the subcontractors to staff the project as early as possible with as many mechanics as possible, while the subcontractors would like to come on the project as late as possible with as few mechanics as possible. The general contractor often complains that the subcontractor is delaying the project through his or her lack of interest in the project progress. At the same time, the subcontractor often complains that the general contractor is not turning working areas over to him or her and that he or she, the sub, will have to go into a crash effort to save the schedule. As in most things, the truth of the matter is somewhere between the extremes. CPM offers the means to resolve these differences with specific information rather than generalities.

The bar chart often suffers from a morning-glory complex: It blooms early in the project but is nowhere to be found later on. We can suppose some general reasons for this disappearing act: Prior to the construction phase, the architect, the engineer, the owner, or all of them are trying to visualize the project schedule in order to set realistic completion dates. Most specifications require the submission of a schedule in bar-graph form by the contractor soon after the award of the contract. When the project begins to take shape in the field, the early bar-chart plans become as useful as last year's calendar because the bar graph does not lend itself to planning revisions.

Although progress can be plotted directly on the schedule bar chart, the S curve has become popular for measuring progress. The usual S curve consists of two plots (see Figure 1.3): scheduled dollar expenditures versus

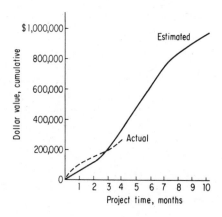

Figure 1.3 Typical S curve.

time, and actual expenditures versus time. Similar S curves can be prepared for worker-hours, equipment and material acquisitions, concrete yardage, etc. While this presentation can be interesting, it does not necessarily give a true indication of project completion. For instance, a low-value critical activity could delay the project completion far out of proportion to its value.

Misuse of bar charts does not prove that they should be discarded. To throw out bar charts is like throwing out the baby with the bath water.

HISTORY OF CPM

In 1956, the E. I. du Pont de Nemours Company set up a group at its Newark, Delaware, facility to study the possible application of new management techniques to the company's engineering functions. One of the first areas considered was the planning and scheduling of construction projects. The group had a UNIVAC I computer at its disposal and decided to evaluate the potential of computers in scheduling construction work. Mathematicians worked out a general approach, theorizing that if the computer was fed information on the sequence of work and the length of each activity, it could generate a schedule of work.

In early 1957, the Univac Applications Research Center, under the direction of Dr. John W. Mauchly, joined the effort with James E. Kelley, Jr., of Remington Rand (UNIVAC) and Morgan Walker of Du Pont in direct charge at Newark. The original conceptual work was revised and the resulting routines became the basic CPM. It is interesting that no fundamental changes have been made in this first work.

In December 1957, a test group was set up to apply the new technique, then called the *Kelley-Walker method.* The test team (made up of six engineers, two area engineers, a process engineer, and an estimator) and a normal scheduling group were assigned to plan the construction of a $10 million chemical plant in Louisville, Kentucky.

As a control, the new scheduling team worked independently of the normal scheduling group. This is the only documented case of a comprehensive comparative CPM application. The test group had not been part of the development of CPM method, but was given a 40-hour workshop course on the technique before starting the test.

The network diagram for the project was restricted to include only the construction steps. The project was analyzed starting at the completion of its preliminary design. The entire project was subdivided into major areas of scope, and each of these areas was analyzed and broken down into the individual work activities. These activities were diagramed into a network of more than 800 activities, of which 400 represented construction activities and 150 represented design or material deliveries. The ability of the first team was such that a larger-capacity computer program had to be developed to support them. By March 1958, the first part of the network scheduling was complete. At that time, a change in corporate outlook, plus certain design changes, caused a 40 percent change in the plan of the project. Both planning groups were authorized to modify the plan and recompute schedules. The revisions, which took place during April 1958, required only about 10 percent of the original effort for the CPM test team. This was substantially better than the normal scheduling group required.

One significant factor involved the determination of critical delivery items. The normal scheduling group arbitrarily assigned critical categories. The CPM group determined these from their network analysis. From this analysis it was determined that only seven items would be critical, and of these, three were not included in the normal scheduling group's list.

The initial test scheduling was considered successful in all respects. In July 1958, a second project, valued at $20 million, was selected for test scheduling. This was also successfully scheduled. Since the first two projects were of such duration that the complete validity of the system could not be established, a shorter project, also at Du Pont in Louisville, was selected for scheduling. The process selected was a shutdown and overhaul operation involving neoprene. Since one of the materials in the process was self-detonating, little or no maintenance was possible during downtime. This particular maintenance effort had been done many times before, and was considered to be a difficult test of the CPM approach. In the first CPM plan, the average shutdown time for the turnaround was cut from 125 to 93 hours. In later CPM applications, this was further improved to a minimum approach of 78 hours. The total time reduction of almost 40 percent far exceeded any expectations.

Parallel Development

The development of CPM was enhanced by an interest shown by the U.S. Navy Polaris program. That program developed its own network system known as *Performance Evaluation and Review Technique*, or *PERT*. The Du Pont work is considered antecedent material for the PERT development.

The Polaris Fleet Ballistic Missile, or FBM, system was initiated in early 1957. To manage the program, a Special Projects Office (SPO) was established under the direction of Admiral Raborn. This SPO is generally credited with having developed the PERT system. One of the key people involved in the development of PERT was Willard Fazar, who was in charge of the program evaluation branch of the plans and programs division. He noted that in the fall of 1957, it was clear that the various management tools available for management of the Polaris program did not provide certain information essential to effective program evaluation. In particular, they did not furnish the following:

1. Appraisal of the validity of existing plans in terms of meeting program objectives

2. Measurement of progress achieved against program objectives

3. Measurement of potential for meeting program objectives

The search for a better management system continued through the fall of 1957. At this time, the Navy was cognizant of the development of CPM at Du Pont (see Ref. 8).

In January 1958, the SPO initiated a special study to determine whether or not computers could be used in planning and controlling the Polaris program. On January 27, 1958, the SPO directed the following group to undertake the task of formulating a PERT technique: C. E. Clark, D. Malcomb, and J. H. Roseboom of Booz, Allen, and Hamilton, R. Young and E. Lennen of the Missile System Division of Lockheed, and W. Fazar of the Navy SPO.

In February 1958, a task statement was issued outlining the goal of the group, which was to determine whether or not improved methods of planning and evaluating research and development work could be devised for application to the Polaris program, which involved 250 prime contractors and more than 9000 subcontractors.

The PERT program was evolved, including development of detailed procedures and mechanics. These two phases were reported in formal documents. The PERT method, as described in the phase II report, was designed to provide the following:

1. Increased orderliness and consistency in planning and evaluating

2. An automatic mechanism for identifying potential trouble spots

3. Operational flexibility for a program by allowing for a simulation of schedules

4. Rapid handling and analysis of integrated data, allowing expeditious corrections

The PERT system was programed at the Naval Ordnance Research Calculator (NORC) located at the Naval Proving Grounds, Dalgren, Virginia. Implementation of the system began in the propulsion component, followed by an extension to the flight control and ballistic shell components, and finally to the reentry body and guidance component. During the latter part of 1958, about 1 year after the start of the PERT research, the system was operational. This was outstanding considering the typical

36 percent time overrun for developing other weapons systems. Following its success in the Polaris program, PERT became popular and was incorporated voluntarily in many aerospace proposals in 1960 and 1961. In some proposals, PERT was added principally as window dressing to make the proposal more attractive to the government. But thanks to the basic soundness of PERT and to the acumen of the engineering staffs involved, PERT often stayed on as a useful planning tool even though it had entered some companies through the "back door," so to speak.

1960–1965: Networks Develop

1955 to 1960 was clearly the time of true conceptual design and testing. In the 5 years which followed, an almost evangelical enthusiasm spurred the conversion of the conceptual into practical utilization. Many public seminars were given, achieving great project engineer exposure to the techniques.

Development was spurred especially by three factors: First, the originating Du Pont group disseminated information on the planning technique to Du Pont customers as part of their overall service policy. Second, the Remington Rand Company, in further computer applications, assisted many of their computer clients in the application of CPM to planning problems. Third, the originating team went into private practice and actively developed the concept and the techniques of applying CPM to a broad range of projects and problems.

The construction industry in general (and the petrochemical industry in particular) was the greatest single area of activity in terms of CPM applications. This was a fortunate circumstance because CPM had no general sponsorship from any particular agency or group. It had to develop and grow upon its own merits. According to a 1965 survey, only 3 percent of the nation's contractors made active use of CPM. Since most of the CPM users were larger contractors, about 20 percent of the nation's major construction was actively scheduled with CPM. Of those contractors using CPM, 90 percent were satisfied with the investment in time and effort it required. Actual dollars-and-cents savings in scheduling time and costs were hard to identify, but the CPM users in contracting believed that the savings exceeded 10 percent in many cases.

PERT owed much of its origins to the earlier work by Kelley and Walker. Ironically, after a courtesy review of their own work as converted into PERT, Kelley and Walker were astute enough to claim the term "critical path" as the new caption for their Kelley-Walker ("main chain") technique.

CPM enthusiasts saw PERT as a competitor and as a factor fragmenting the enthusiastic, but limited, market for network techniques.

This feeling was further compounded in 1962 when then Secretary of Defense MacNamara drafted an executive regulation stating, in effect, that the existence of two different network-based scheduling systems was confusing—and that henceforth, all Department of Defense organizations would utilize PERT. At the time, this appeared to enhance the development of PERT as a system, at the expense of CPM.

PERT was applied to part of the Atlas E and to all the Atlas F site activation programs. It was also used in the Titan I, Titan II, and Minuteman site activation programs. Although the application varied from site to site and program to program, the approach used in Titan I is considered representative. Site activation PERT networks were developed for each site and limited to events which would occur on that site. Within the site network, individual networks were developed for each site. The networks were arranged so that they were compatible with networks prepared by Corps of Engineers contractors as well as planned delivery schedules. The Corps of Engineers Ballistic Missile Coordinating Office (CEBMCO) used a network monitoring system to monitor the current status of the Titan complexes. The cost of this monitoring system was about 0.5 percent of the site construction cost.

While large weapons systems and space systems accounted for the largest number of PERT networks, and the greatest expenditures on PERT, a number of other agencies picked up the new technique. The Atomic Energy Commission (AEC) used PERT to plan and control the development of new components for atomic weapons.

The National Aeronautics and Space Administration (NASA) made broad use of PERT and a form of PERT termed "NASA-PERT" (actually an activity-on-arrow CPM-type network) in their planning for the space program.

Also, firms such as RCA and General Electric, which had recognized the potential of networking in the late 1950s, applied network techniques to their space projects in the early 1960s.

1965–1970: Development Continues; Systems Evolve

The concept period of the 1950s, and the training and development of the 1960 to 1965 period, continued in the latter part of the 1960s. Although not apparent at the time, acceptance of network techniques broadened as the result of a number of independent factors:

1. The size of programs such as the Apollo program demanded some integrated project control system, and NASA-PERT (or CPM) offered the best vehicle for this type of a system.

2. Evolution of network scheduling as a device for controlling a single project was extrapolated into a program control system, in which a number of projects could be integrated and controlled simultaneously.

3. The logical basis of the network approach, irrespective of its computer-oriented identity, resulted in an increasing acceptance of its usefulness.

4. Academicians, particularly in civil engineering curricula, recognized the validity of network scheduling as a project control approach, and were incorporating it into the undergraduate curriculum. Graduating engineers were predisposed to use networks.

The Corps of Engineers, the Navy, and NASA were already utilizing network systems. Other agencies, such as the AEC, the Veterans Administration, and the General Services Administration, followed in their footsteps.

The initial development of CPM included a sophisticated cost-optimization approach developed by Kelley and Walker. This was actually included as part of the basic CPM algorithm for the computer program, combining information on crash and normal costs for each activity, and estimating an optimal completion time for the overall project. From a theoretical viewpoint, the system is most interesting. But to date, the difficulties in collecting the supporting cost and time information have precluded its wide use.

The Kelley-Walker group (Mauchly Associates) also developed over several years a computerized approach to using CPM networks for scheduling manpower, also termed "work force." This approach was called *Resource Planning and Scheduling Method,* or *RPSM.* Concurrently, the CEIR computer consulting organization (now part of Control Data) worked in collaboration with Du Pont to develop the *Resource Allocation and Manpower Planning System,* or *RAMPS.* Although used on a very limited basis, these extensions were well tested in field applications.

Current computer capabilities have resulted in a number of approaches and proprietary systems. Although today's computer technology has greatly facilitated the efficiencies of these computer program systems, the basic principles have not changed.

By 1962, the PERT team had released PERT/Cost. This combined cost reporting with the PERT network and became required in many aerospace and defense contracts. The system is technically correct, although it is based on a rather simple premise that the combined cost of the various components completed in a project when extended will give a meaningful prediction of the completion date of the overall project. Most of the difficulties encountered in using the system have occurred in collecting costs which can be meaningfully combined with the network. The difficulties in reconciling an internal accounting system with the special PERT/Cost breakdown has led the government to a new approach designated *Cost/Schedule Control Systems criteria,* or *CSCS.*

International Business Machines Corporation (IBM), NASA, the Navy, and others have prepared their own versions of PERT and PERT/Cost. IBM and McDonnell Automation combined forces to prepare a coordinated version of PERT and PERT/Cost designated *Project Management System,* or *PMS.*

Although substantial technology was applied in the programing and testing of computer systems for PERT and PERT/Cost, applications tended to simplify the theoretical approaches.

Variations on both CPM and PERT were developed by many organizations, usually seeking special systems to respond to special requirements. Variations on PERT included SPERT, GERT, MERT, and other systems whose acronyms designated the changes entailed.

CPM was recast into precedence networks (PDM) which were substantially different in appearance but provided essentially the same calculated result.

Professor John Fondahl of Stanford University, who was established in the early 1960s as an expert on noncomputerized solutions to CPM and PERT networks, was one of the early supporters of the precedence method, terming it "circle and connection arrow technique." Professor Fondahl's study for the Navy's Bureau of Yards and Docks included descriptive material and gave the technique early impetus, particularly in regard to Navy projects.

An IBM brochure credits the H. B. Zachry Company of San Antonio with the development of the precedent form of CPM. In cooperation with IBM, Zachry developed computer programs which handled precedence network computations on the IBM 1130 and IBM 360. This was particularly significant, since in 1964 Phillips and Moder indicated the availability of only one computerized approach to precedence networks versus sixty for CPM and PERT.

Project Control Systems (PCS)

In the 1965 to 1970 period, networking tools evolved into *Project Control Systems, PCS.* This organization into a systems approach was for the purpose of managing either larger programs or multiproject programs.

PCS approaches were developed from 1965 to 1970 for many projects, including the World's Fair in New York City, Expo 67 in Montreal, construction for the State University of New York, the Apollo launch complex at Cape Kennedy, the San Francisco transit system, and others. But this availability of tremendous amounts of project information, however important and meaningful, presented a new problem to management. Previously, although decisions had been made based on sparse and limited information, the executive mind was essentially uncluttered by facts. Now, with project and resource information flowing in, managers further had to determine what data were important and what could be disregarded in order to reach or establish alternatives for decisions.

Networks 1970–1980

This decade was highlighted by several diverse new influences which encouraged the acceptance and utilization of the PCS approach. First, engineering school curricula added both network techniques and computer applications to their undergraduate curricula during that period, resulting in a more natural utilization of the once new techniques by recent engineering graduates.

Second, the decade saw the evolution of construction management, and better management control is an important corollary to the utilization of construction management.

Another characteristic of the 1970 to 1980 decade was a dramatic increase in construction litigation, particularly litigation citing delay as a cause of damages. Schedules and their utilization have become important both to plaintiff and defendant. The existence and proper utilization of a CPM plan can be a significant factor in either supporting a contractor's claim, or defending the role of the owner–construction manager in coordinating a project.

Finally, the dramatic evolution in computer compatibility has not only made basic network systems more available but has also provided an economical support for the implementation of network systems which not only track a schedule, but correlate the schedule with cost and resources.

SUMMARY

The basis for the CPM network approach remains essentially unchanged from its earliest formulation, and has survived every test, extension, improvement, change in format, and manipulation it has undergone. Although network techniques are basic and logical, assimilation of the concept does take time and experience.

The principal danger in the continuing extension of and experimentation on network techniques is that the basic framework (the network) might be obscured or lost. Thus far, the semanticists have not been able to accomplish this, nor have many deliberately tried. On the contrary, the strength and effectiveness of the network approach have tended to delay the development of extensions. Extensions, by the very nature of their complexity, tend to run headlong into the law of diminishing returns.

REFERENCES

1. James E. Kelley and Morgan R. Walker, "Critical Path Planning and Scheduling," *Proceedings of the Eastern Joint Computer Conference,* pp. 160–173, Dec. 1–3, 1959; see also James E. Kelley, "Critical-Path Planning and Scheduling: Mathematical Basis," *Operations Research,* vol. 9, no. 3, pp. 296–320. 1961.
2. Hayward and Robinson, *Preliminary Analysis of the Construction Scheduling Problem,* internal paper, Engineering Department, Du Pont Company, December 1956.
3. James E. Kelley, "Computers and Operations Research in Road Building," *Operations Research, Computers and Management Decisions,* Symposium Proceedings, Case Institute of Technology, January 31–February 1 and 2, 1957.
4. John Fondahl, *A Noncomputer Approach to the Critical Path Method for the Construction Industry,* 2d ed., Stanford University, Stanford, CA, 1962.
5. D. G. Malcolm et al., *A Network Flow Computation for Project Cost Curves,* Rand Paper P-1947, Rand Corporation, March 1960
6. J. S. Kane, "Origin of CPM and PERT," in H. L. Wattel (ed.). *The Dissemination of New Business Techniques: Network Scheduling and Control Systems (CPM/PERT),* Hofstra University Yearbook of Business, series 1, vol. 2, pp. 50–54, Hofstra University, Hempstead, NY, 1964.
7. D. G. Malcomb, J. H. Roseboom, C. E. Clark, and W. Fazar, "Application of a Technique for Research and Development Program Evaluation," *Operations Research,* vol. 7, no. 5, pp. 646–699, 1959.
8. W. Fazar, "The Origin of PERT," *The Controller,* vol. 30, pp. 598 ff., December 1962.
9. *PERT Summary Report: Phase I,* Special Projects Office, Bureau of Naval Ordnance, Navy Department, 1958.
10. *PERT Summary Report: Phase II,* Special Projects Office, Bureau of Naval Ordnance, Navy Department, 1958.
11. "Corps Keeps Electronic Finger on Titan Base Work," *Engineering News-Record,* vol. 168, no. 5, pp. 22–23, February 1, 1962.

2

FUNDAMENTALS
OF CPM

The backbone of the Critical Path Method is a graphical model of a project. The basic component of this model is the *arrow*. Each arrow represents one *activity* in the project. The tail of the arrow represents the starting point of the activity and the head represents the completion. The arrow is not a vector, nor is it drawn to scale; it may be curved or bent as required. However, it cannot be interrupted, as it is a separate entity.

Typical activity

Start ———————————————➤ Finish

ARROW DIAGRAM

The arrows are arranged to show the plan or logical sequence in which the activities of the project are to be accomplished. This is done by answering three questions with each arrow:

1. What arrows (activities) must *precede* this one?
2. What arrows (activities) can be *concurrent* with this one?
3. What arrows (activities) must *follow* this one?

The resulting logical flow chart is a network of arrows, usually referred to as either the *arrow diagram* or the network. As an example, consider a routine checkup of your car as a project. Assume that you want the following work done:

Rotate tires

Lubricate

Change oil

Wax and polish

Drain antifreeze

CPM is often referred to as a "decision maker." This is a misnomer since CPM, being inanimate, can make no decisions. However, the use of CPM encourages decisions since the user must make decisions in order to draw the arrow diagram.

In this example, a decision is required before any arrows can be drawn. The mechanic must decide whether to do the hoist work first or last. Assume that this mechanic decided to do the hoist work first. Accordingly, the first arrow would be

Hoist car

Following this, all arrows start which could logically follow hoisting of the car. From the work list, these would be rotate tires, lubricate, and change oil.

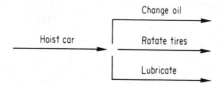

When the activity "lower car" is added, note that the general work list is not broken down into enough detail to show the mechanic's work plan. Adding this activity after the hoist work:

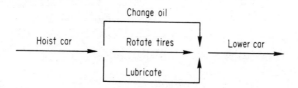

What does this really say? The diagram states that the activities cannot start until the hoist is raised and must finish before the hoist is lowered. However, something is missing. The activity "rotate tires" indicates that the mechanic must get the spare tire out while the car is on the hoist. This is not logical, and certainly not what the mechanic might be expected to do. Also, it is usual practice for the mechanic to loosen the tire lug nuts before raising the wheels clear of the ground. Change

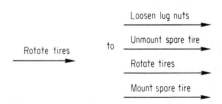

This part of the network would then become

For "lubricate," the first network indicates that the oiling and checking of items under the hood (battery, alternator, radiator, brake fluid, etc.) must occur while the car is up on the hoist. To do this, the mechanic would need stilts or a ladder. Change

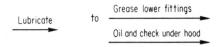

This part of the network would then become

| Hoist car | Grease lower fittings | Lower car | Oil and check under hood |

Similarly,

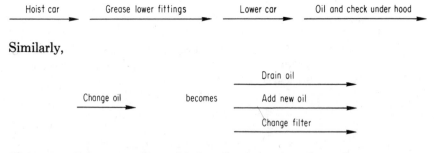

This part of the network would then become

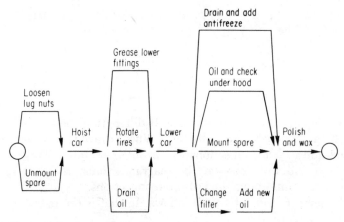

Figure 2.1 Arrow diagram, car checkup.

Combining these portions of the network and adding the two activities not shown before, "drain antifreeze" and "polish and wax car," the arrow diagram representing this everyday operation is shown in Figure 2.1.

Preparation of the arrow diagram focuses attention on one activity or group of related activities at a time. The reason is obvious: Only one arrow at a time is drawn. The very simplicity of this reasoning gives strength to the technique. No one can thoughtfully consider all details of a multi-million dollar project simultaneously; but using the arrow diagram to record thoughts spotlights and plans one area at a time. As each area is completed, thoughts and plans are recorded by the arrow diagram.

LOGIC DIAGRAMS

The logic diagram is the most important single feature of the CPM method. Logic diagrams have long been used by mathematicians, and it was a happy circumstance that mathematician Kelley utilized the logic diagram to convey the basic plan sequence to the computer. Although the selection was made because of the basic limitations of a computer (in comparison with the abilities of the human brain), the introduction of the logic diagram to reflect the intended sequence of a plan has had a dramatic impact on the planning process.

There are a number of abstract logical rules which are useful in the preparation of a network. If activities A, B, and C occur in series, their network representation is

If the statement is that B and C follow A, the above is one solution. A more correct one would be

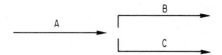

Examine the latter solution. In what way does it differ from the first? It shows B and C as independent activities. When drawing network sequences, do not add logical connections which were not stated. This is perhaps an obvious caution; however, the diagramer must constantly guard against subtle, unintentional logical interconnections.

If activity C follows B and activity D follows A, what is the network expression? It may seem to be

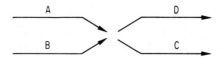

However, no connection between C and A or B and D was stated. Therefore, the proper relation is

Now, if both A and B precede both C and D, the network expression is

However, this is not correct if A and B precede C, but only B precedes D. Starting this diagram as

means B is not shown as a precedent to C. And starting the diagram as

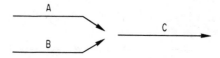

means B is not shown precedent to D. The problem is that the arrow B cannot be broken into two parts. The arrow diagram is not permitted to speak with a "forked tongue." The dilemma is solved by introducing the *logical connection*. This is an arrow which represents logic flow but no work. To differentiate from regular arrows, show these no-work connections as dotted arrows. In this example, the logical connection (or *logical restraint*) is as follows:

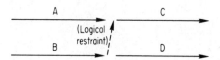

The network now shows that C follows A and B, but that D follows only B. The concept of the logical connection is common sense, but is indispensable to CPM.

Now consider a network example with two parallel chains of activities. One of these chains is made up of activities A, B, and C in series. The other is made up of X, Y, and Z, also in series. A and X are the starting activities; C and Z are the terminal activities. This gives

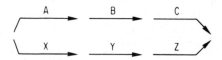

Now add an activity M originating at the project start. If activity M must precede C and Y, the result is

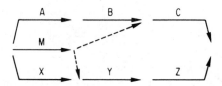

The point is that any number of logical restraints can originate from the finish of an activity. Similarly, any number can lead into the start of an activity. In the network

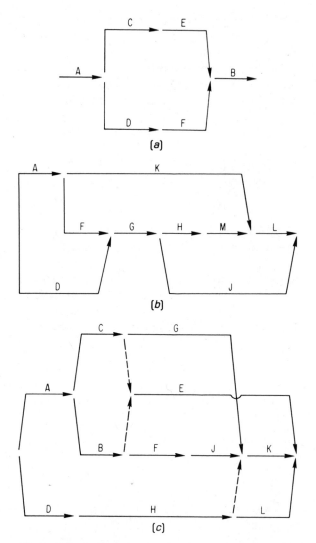

Figure 2.2 Logic network examples. (*a*) Activities *C* and *D* both follow *A*; activity *E* follows *C*; activity *F* follows *D*; *E* and *F* precede *B*. (*b*) *A* and *D* start at the origin; *J* follows *F* but precedes *K*; *C* follows *A* but precedes *G*; *H* follows *D* but precedes *L*. (*c*) *G* follows *F* but precedes *H*; *G* follows *D* but precedes *J*; *M* follows *H* but precedes *L*; *K* follows *A* but precedes *L*; *F* follows *A*; *A* and *D* start at the same time; *J* and *L* terminate at the same time.

adding terminal activity E, which follows A but is independent of C, is not accomplished by

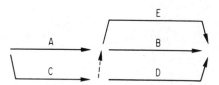

This is typical when unintentional logical connections are made. To keep E independent of C, add another logical restraint after A:

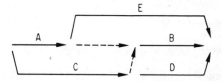

This might be termed a *logic splitter* or *logic spreader*. Logic cannot back up from B against the arrowhead, which functions as a check valve.

Figure 2.2 offers more examples.

LOGICAL LOOP

If activities A, B, C, and D are in series and activity E following C precedes B,

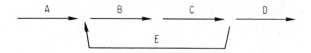

The portion B, C, E is a *logical loop*. It's a case of "which comes first, the chicken or the egg." Since a loop is illogical, it has no place in a logical network. It might seem unlikely that anyone would draw a loop. However, in large complex networks, it is quite common for loops to be inadvertently inserted. Figure 2.3 shows the site layout for a hospital project. Because the existing hospital was in a prime location, the new building was to be constructed immediately behind the old one. However, an annex building had to be demolished before new construction started. Since this service annex included the kitchen-cafeteria area, a temporary kitchen-cafeteria had to be established in the existing building until a new kitchen-cafeteria in the building to be constructed was ready for occupancy. At that time, the temporary kitchen-cafeteria was to be vacated.

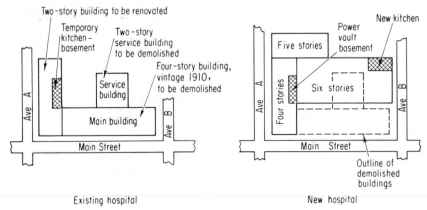

Existing hospital   New hospital

Figure 2.3 Hospital site layout.

This is easily shown in arrow-diagram form:

| Establish temporary kitchen | Demolish service annex | Foundations for new building | Complete new kitchen | Move into new kitchen | Dismantle temporary kitchen |

However, a factor not noticed until the preparation of the arrow diagram was the location of the electrical power distribution vault for the new building. This was to be the place in the old building occupied by the temporary kitchen. Adding this information to the network resulted in the following loop:

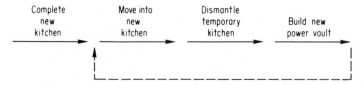

The situation was pointed out to the owner and the architect. Since the power vault was not needed until a year later, a new vault location was designed and constructed. Through the use of the CPM plan, a costly and inconvenient time loss was foreseen and avoided.

NONCONSTRUCTION EXAMPLES

There are any number of nonconstruction projects which could be planned by means of CPM. Some actual projects include

1. Shipbuilding
2. City planning

3. Refinery maintenance
4. Architectural design
5. Staffing a new plant
6. Research project
7. Embarkation of a construction battalion
8. Cooking a meal
9. Procedure for state approval of a new school
10. Bringing a show to Broadway
11. Preparing a corporate budget
12. Preparing a city budget
13. City approval of plans
14. Purchasing a new house
15. Purchasing a car
16. Manufacturing one car
17. Family camping trip activity list

While there is no one correct activity list for a family camping trip, this example assumes a family consisting of a father, a mother, and two children aged nine and eleven. A typical list might be:

Prepare budget	Select site
Collect site information	Make equipment list

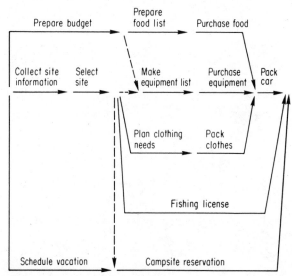

Figure 2.4 Family camping trip.

Purchase equipment   Purchase fishing license

Purchase food   Schedule vacation

Prepare food list   Plan clothing list

Park car   Pack clothing

Make camp site reservations

Figure 2.4 presents one plan that could be used to coodinate these activities.

SUMMARY

In this chapter the concept of the network approach was discussed, as well as the premise that CPM can encourage decision making but cannot make decisions itself. The preparation of arrow and logic diagrams helps the planner to understand a project by clearly defining the activities required to complete it. CPM is particularly applicable to construction work, but its usefulness is by no means limited to the construction field.

3

NETWORK CONSTRUCTION

Chapter 2 discussed the concept of the CPM network and the fundamentals of its construction. This chapter covers the practical mechanics of network construction. Since CPM is a logical and organized planning system, it is important that the physical layout of the network reflect this same logical organization. The thought required to separate its parts into practical subdivisions contributes to the overall plan The network is often used to present the plan to strangers to the project. If the physical layout is clear, concise, and well arranged, first impressions will be good. However, CPM analysis is a two-way street: It exposes poor planning just as readily as it enhances a competent effort. Figure 3.1 shows two networks with the same information. Both are logically correct. However, the top network was drawn directly from a problem description without careful attention being given to its physical layout. The bottom network is a rearrangement of the top network. This example has only twelve activities. In a project network, the differences between network layouts and the possible resulting confusion would be multiplied a hundredfold.

FORM AND FORMAT

The network is usually drawn on reproducible paper or linen. In preparing it, trial layouts should be sketched out before drawing it in finished form.

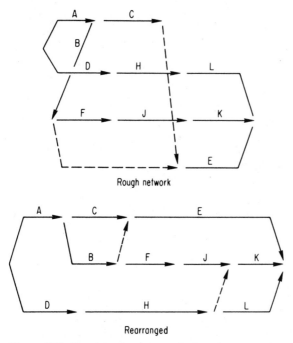

Rough network

Rearranged

Figure 3.1   Rough and rearranged networks.

These sketches are usually done on a blackboard, nonreproducible paper, vellum, or grid paper.

Grid paper with nonreproducing squares is helpful in laying out a network. It can be used for the freehand sketch phase or the finished network.

Because the early networks were modest in size, the drawing size was not a problem. As networks became larger, the first tendency was to increase the size of the drawing. This "the bigger the better" philosophy was similar to the mammoth B-19 bomber which didn't fly much better than the dodo bird. Like the B-19, a huge network is unwieldy and difficult to handle. Accordingly, the tendency is to leave it rolled up and unused. One of the bigger networks of this Dead Sea scroll type was 4 feet high by 30 feet long. It was rolled out like a wall-to-wall carpet when in use (which was rarely, because it meant rearranging the office furniture). This network may not have been the largest made as a single sheet; however, if a bigger one did exist, it must have been mounted on a roadside billboard.

There may be times when special considerations make a long roll-out drawing a practical method of presentation. For most work, however, it is better to break down larger networks onto a number of sheets. The selection of the scope to be contained on each sheet is important. The sheet should not be crowded, but it should be well used. In subdividing the project so that it can be presented on a number of sheets, keep the practical use of the network in mind. For instance, if all the foundation work for a building appears on one sheet, the field office will find the network easier to use, since current field status can be located on one network sheet, or two, at a time.

There is no fixed rule in regard to the optimum sheet size. A sheet of about 34 by 44 inches is used by the Corps of Engineers. A larger size can be used for drawing and then reduced in reproduction for better handling. Since this method introduces additional cost and time delay in reproduction of the network, it should not be used unless necessary.

Many of the early diagrams were drawn with random direction lines (Figure 3.2) or wide-sweeping curves (Figure 3.3). The clarity of hindsight obscures whatever reasons there might have been for this free-and-easy

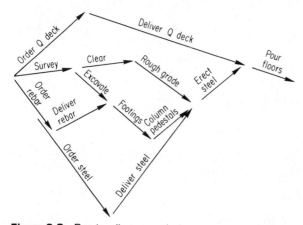

Figure 3.2   Random line example.

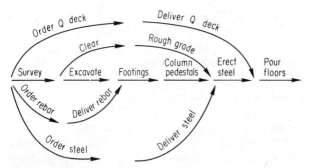

Figure 3.3   Sweeping curve example.

method originally. However, it is mentioned here since people continually rediscover these techniques and still try to use them.

EVENTS

The intersection of two or more activity arrows is termed an *event*. An event has a zero time dimension. However, *all* activities leading into an event must be completed before *any* of the activities leading out of the event can be started. This is just a restatement of the rules of network logic.

Certain key events are called *milestones*. These represent important intermediate goals within the network. For instance, "ready to advertise for bids" (Figure 3.4) is an important event. It represents an instant in time but has no time dimension of its own. To reach this particular event,

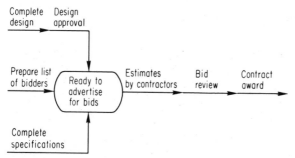

Figure 3.4 Example of milestone event: ready to advertise for bids.

all activities pertaining to the design and specifications for the project must be completed. No action can be taken toward getting a contract until the logic flow has passed through this event.

On the CPM diagram, important events can be identified by name. However, event titles are not emphasized; instead, events are assigned numbers. Since each activity is bounded by a starting and completion event, the event can be identified by these numbers.

$$\text{Starting event} \xrightarrow{\text{Typical activity}} \text{Completion event}$$

The number assigned to the starting event is referred to as the i; the number assigned to the completion event is the j. (These designations were used by the founders of CPM and have remained in general use, probably because of their brevity.) Thus, the typical activity looks like

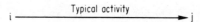

The *i-j* number for an activity can be used as an abbreviated name for the activity. A number of rules must be followed in assigning event numbers to a network:

Rule 1 Each activity must have a unique *i-j* description. But there are often cases where two or more activities span the same events. For instance, between events 1 and 4 could be the following:

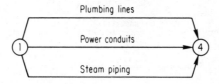

A list of these activities would read

i-j		*Description*
1-4	....	Plumbing lines
1-4	....	Power conduits
1-4	....	Steam piping

This confusing situation is corrected by adding logical restraints, originally called *dummies*. The term "dummy" was used because the connection says nothing new; it was added only so that unique event numbers could be introduced. The more proper term *restraint* is used now.

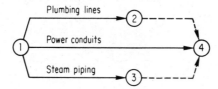

The activity list now reads

i-j		*Description*
1-2	....	Plumbing lines
1-3	....	Steam piping
1-4	....	Power conduits
2-4	....	Restraint
3-4	....	Restraint

Rule 2 When event numbers are assigned, the number at the head (or j end) of the arrow should be greater than the event number at the tail (or i end). That is, $j > i$.

In early computer programs, the ability of the computer to calculate the network often depended upon this rule, as well as upon the consecutive numbering of events. But almost all computer programs will now handle nonconsecutive event numbers. Many will also handle random* numbering (random numbering can be $j > i$, $j < i$, or both in a network). Random numbering is not only a convenience, it is often almost a necessity. For instance, consider the partial network

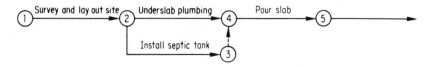

Assume that the network continues for perhaps fifty more event numbers. Now, suppose it is discovered that the activity "clear and grade," which should follow activity 1-2, survey and lay out site, and precede both 2-3, install septic tank, and 2-4, underslab plumbing, was forgotten. Without random numbering, the network would have to be renumbered as follows:

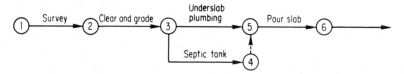

Since there would now be fifty-one event numbers, fifty of these would have to be changed (all except event 1). With random numbering allowed, the revised network could be

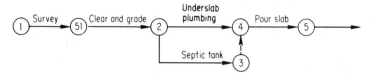

No event numbers would have to be changed and only one would have to be added. Since many of today's networks have in excess of 1000 events, random numbering is very important when activities must be added to the network.

Since random numbering is available, why even try to follow rule 2,

---

*Random is used here in its literal sense: "without direction, rule, or method."

which might be called the traditional *rule for event numbering?* There are two reasons: First, numbering in the j greater than i manner makes it easier to locate events on the diagram. Second, logical loops are identified. Using the example of a loop and numbering the events,

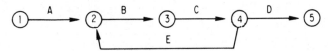

The fact that $4 > 2$ or $i > j$ for activity E indicates a loop. Reverse the positions of 2 and 4:

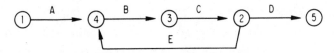

Then $j > i$ for activity E but not for activities B and C.

The event numbers should not be added until the network has been completed and is ready for its first computation. They should be assigned in a regular fashion. There are two basic ways of doing this, the horizontal (Figure 3.5a) and vertical (Figure 3.5b) methods. Both are acceptable. In the *horizontal method,* event numbers are assigned along a chain of activities until a junction event (a meeting of more than one activity) is reached. This routine is repeated until all chains into the junction event are numbered. In *vertical event numbering* the numbers are assigned up and down vertically but still observe the j greater than i rule.

The vertical numbering system localizes numbers in areas of the diagram. This makes it easier to locate a particular activity.

The horizontal numbering system results in logical groupings of activities, so that the i-j list (or printout) has groupings of activities which are logically related. But horizontal numbering can produce networks in which it is difficult to locate an event number.

Similarly, the use of random numbers can make it difficult to locate a particular event on the network.

The number of digits in the event is limited by the computer program to be used. Older programs were often three-digit-oriented. Since the average ratio of activities to events is about 1:5, the three-digit concept limits the network size to about 1500 activities.

Today's major programs can accept five digits. This would permit a network of 150,000 activities. And now many programs can accept alphabetics, so that the maximum network size is essentially unlimited. With the capacity for many event numbers, event numbers can be assigned by area or function (such as purchasing material or equipment, shop drawing review, etc.). This can cause confusion when the computer sorts by i-j

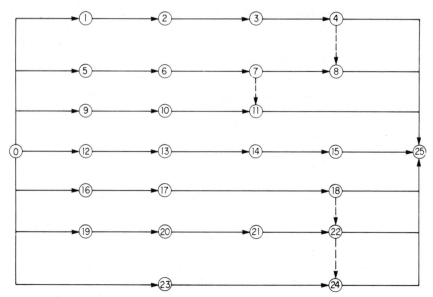

Figure 3.5a Horizontal numbering.

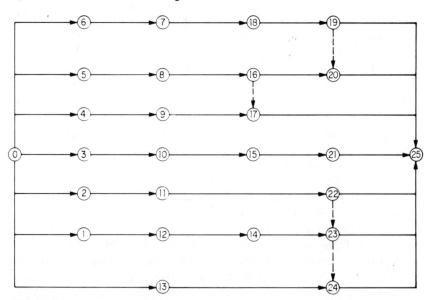

Figure 3.5b Vertical numbering.

numbers, since sorting rules vary—sometimes producing unexpected results.

In drafting the network, it is optional whether the event is circled or not:

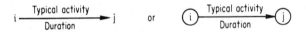

There is no significance to the event numbers except their value in identifying the activities. To the one who assigns these numbers, this is obvious. However, people not familiar with CPM often try to read unintended significance into the event numbers.

Activity descriptions should be written on the horizontal. To do this, a part of each arrow (except dummies) must be drawn on the horizontal (Figure 3.6). A comparison of the three cases shown in Figures 3.2, 3.3, and 3.6 will demonstrate the advantages of horizontal activity titles.

Another temptation for the drafter is to code activities rather than put their full titles on them. The example network shown in Figure 3.7 is coded; compare this with Figure 3.6. A coded network is easier to prepare than a titled one, but is almost useless since even the diagramer cannot read it directly.

In arranging a network, center the significant activities on the sheet. They will function as the backbone of the network. This places visual emphasis on the important areas and minimizes crossover of arrows. Figure 3.8 illustrates this technique. In the past, some specifications have

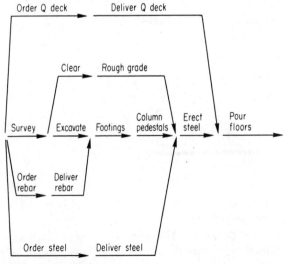

Figure 3.6 Horizontal format.

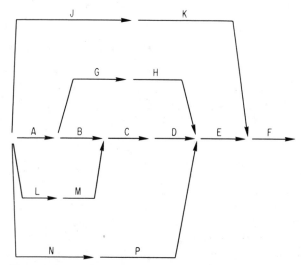

Figure 3.7 Untitled (coded) network.

Do this:

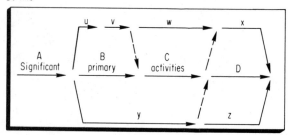

Rather than this:

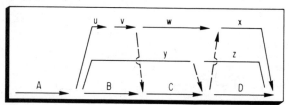

Figure 3.8 Significant primary activities.

required that the critical path be this network backbone. This is not a valid requirement though, because the critical activities are not yet identified when the network is being prepared. However, activities which are usually critical can be identified from experience; these have been termed *significant*.

The arrow size and spacing are quite important. If the arrows are too long and widely spread apart, the diagram will become too large and unwieldy. If, on the other hand, the arrow arrangement is too tight, the network will be difficult to read. Also, a crowded network cannot be readily revised or amended.

The arrow length is usually 2 to 3 inches. Of course this cannot be applied as a mandatory rule. In the example

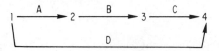

activity 1-4 must be the sum of the lengths of 1-2, 2-3, and 3-4. A minimum vertical distance of 2 to 3 inches between arrows leaves room for changes.

Backward arrows should be avoided. These are confusing because they are drawn against the time flow of the network. Backward arrows also increase the possibility of introducing unintended logical loops. In the example shown in Figure 3.9, the first network did not show a requirement that the hydro testing and insulation must precede the start of lath because part of the piping is enclosed by lath and plaster. The restraint arrow added to show this logic is a backward arrow.

Crossovers are a problem. It is inevitable that some lines of logic must cross over others. Many crossovers can be eliminated by careful layout (see Figure 3.8), but there will always be some to contend with. There is no one method for showing these crossovers. It is important, however, that the lines should not be allowed to intersect. In the example shown in Figure 3.10, the intersection of activities 12-14 and 9-16 illustrated in the lower left-hand corner is not proper since it implies a logical crossroads which does not exist. One solution to this problem is to use a pipeline

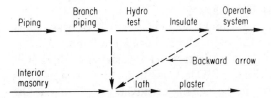

Figure 3.9 Section of network with backward arrow.

technique (Figure 3.10, upper left-hand corner). The crossover is shown in the same manner that a pipe crossing is shown on piping drawings. Another solution is to show a broken arrow (Figure 3.10, upper right-hand corner). Any good crossover technique may be used, but the same tech-

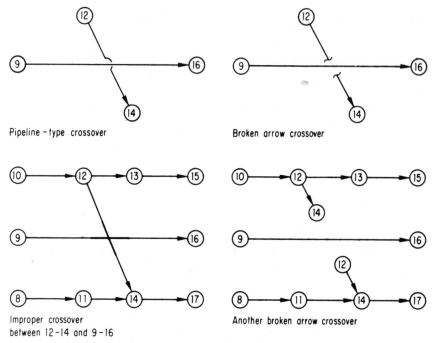

Figure 3.10 Arrow crossover techniques.

nique should be used consistently so that the network user can become accustomed to it. A second version of the broken arrow is shown in the lower right-hand corner of Figure 3.10. In this case, the parts of the broken arrow are in line. On large networks, it may not be practical to maintain this straight-line relation.

The broken arrow may connect events on different sheets of a multisheet network. This flexibility is necessary for the preparation of large networks. However, coupled with backward arrows, this can lead to unintended loops. The best safety check against loops is the use of the traditional event numbering $j > i$. To make this check effective, the events should not be numbered until the network has been completed.

At the project start, a number of activities usually originate. The result often looks like a traffic jam (Figure 3.11). A useful technique sometimes used in this instance is called the *bus bar*. The advantage of this at the project start or the project finish is that it reduces unproductive congestion of the network. Some network purists object to this technique because it violates the rule against the intersection of arrows at points which are not events. But the decision to use or not to use a special technique must be made by the diagramer. His or her criterion in making the decision should be the clarity of the resulting network. If the technique is

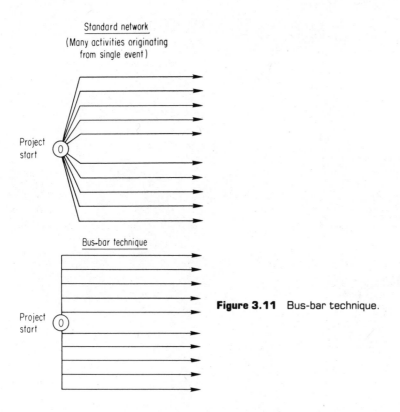

Standard network
(Many activities originating
from single event)

Project start

Bus-bar technique

Project start

Figure 3.11 Bus-bar technique.

clever but confuses the user, it is a case of "the operation was a success but the patient died."

PROBLEM CONNECTED WITH MULTISHEET NETWORKS

A difficult factor in multisheet networks is where to cut off the arrows on one sheet to start the next. For ease in drawing and to facilitate its use, the network should be interrupted at the point where the least number of arrows must be cut. Assume that the portion of the network shown in Figure 3.12 is to be on the end of one sheet and the start of the next. If the network is split as shown in Figure 3.13, it is more difficult for the drafter. More significantly, it does not present a clear picture to field workers or other users of the diagram. In Figure 3.14, the network is split at the end of foundation work and prior to steel erection. Splitting the network at an important event meets the needs of both the diagramer and the user of the diagram.

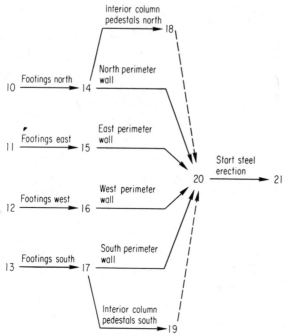

Figure 3.12 Multisheet network example.

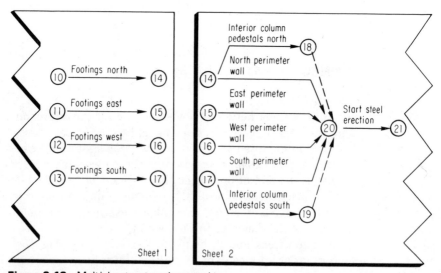

Figure 3.13 Multisheet network example.

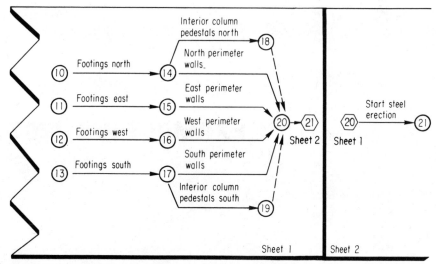

Figure 3.14 Multisheet network example.

Figure 3.14 illustrates another useful technique. When connecting events from sheet to sheet, the connecting event is highlighted with a hexagon. The number of the sheet to which that event connects is written outside the hexagon.

SUMMARY

This chapter discussed the practical mechanics of network construction. Primarily, the network layout must be logical and organized. A confused diagram exposes confused planning. The drawing size should be reasonable, using multiple sheets if necessary. The activity descriptions should be on horizontal lines. Avoid wide-sweeping lines or random lines. Center significant chains of activities to form a network backbone. Space the arrows so that additions may be made. Crossovers of logic lines can take a number of forms but the form used should be consistent.

i-j event numbers are abbreviated activity designations and must be unique for each activity. The careful assignment of event numbers makes the network easier to use and avoids unintended logical loops.

4

EXAMPLE PROJECT

To demonstrate a basic network, the construction of a combination plant-office-warehouse for a small industrial firm, the John Doe Company, will be planned. A plan of the entire complex is shown in Figure 4.1 and a perspective of the building and exterior elevations is shown in Figure 4.2. Figure 4.3 shows a site plan section of the electrical service and sewer. The floor plan for the plant is shown in Figure 4.4; that for the office in Figure 4.5; and that for the warehouse in Figure 4.6. The list of activities is broken down by building area where applicable. Exterior elevation views of the buildings are shown in Figure 4.2 and interior sections are shown in Figures 4.7 and 4.8.

ACTIVITY LIST

The site is in a low area, overgrown with scrub timber and bushes; the soil is a sand and gravel mixture overlaid by clay. Cast-in-place piles will be driven to about 30 feet for the plant and warehouse foundations. The office building will be on spread footings. As there is no water supply available, a well and 50,000-gallon elevated water tower will be installed. Sewage and power trunk lines are 2000 feet away. Power connections will

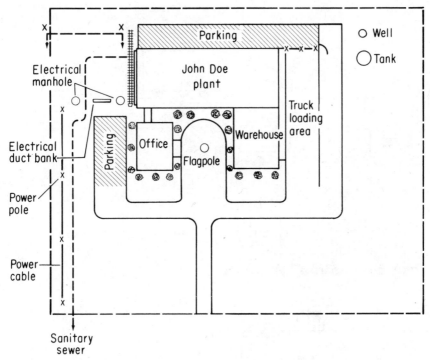

Figure 4.1 Site plan, John Doe project.

be by overhead pole line up to 200 feet from the building; from that point in, the power line will run underground. The sewer will pass under part of the power line. The activities representing the above work are:

Survey and layout	Drill well
Clear site	Install well pump
Rough grade	Install underground water supply
Drive and pour piles	Excavate for sewer
Excavate plant and warehouse	Install sewer
Pour pile caps	Set pole line
Excavate office building	Excavate for electrical manholes
Pour spread footings	Install electrical manholes
Pour grade beams	Energize power feeder
Install power feeder	

The plant and warehouse structures are to be structural steel, with high-tensile bolted connections. The plant will have an overhead crane-

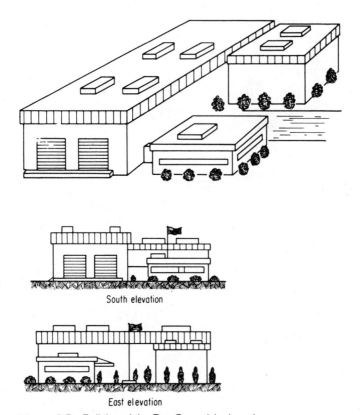

South elevation

East elevation

Figure 4.2 Building, John Doe Co., with elevations.

way running the length of the building; the warehouse will have a monorail. The roof system will be bar joists and precast concrete planks covered with 20-year built-up roofing. The siding of both buildings will be transite with translucent upper panels to admit light. Both buildings will have concrete floor slabs, which are to be poured on compacted sand. The activities representing this work are:

Erect structural steel	Apply built-up roofing
Bolt up steel	Compact slab subgrade
Erect craneway	Install underslab plumbing
Erect monorail track	Pour floor slabs
Install underslab conduit	Erect bar joists
Erect roof planks	Erect siding

When the plant and warehouse shells are erected, interior partitions (offices, bathrooms, etc.) will be made of concrete block. The interior ceil-

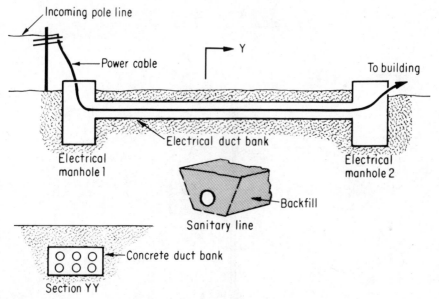

Figure 4.3   Electrical duct bank section XX (see Figure 4.1).

ings are to be wood beam and dry wall; the loading docks will be reinforced concrete. The railroad siding must be brought in from a spur line
¼ mile away. This adds the following activities:

Masonry partitions
Office ceilings
Piping systems
Power conduit
Branch conduit
Install electrical load center
Install power panel boxes
Install power panel insides
Monorail
Paint interior
Pull wire
Electrical fixtures
Floor tile (offices)
Grade and ballast
Railroad siding

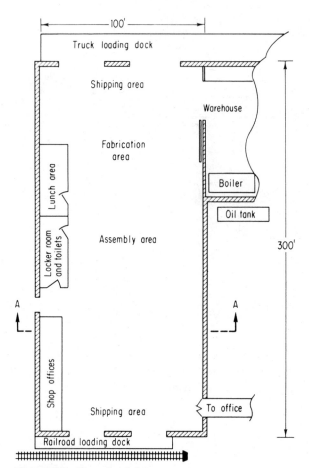

Figure 4.4 Plant floor plan.

Form and pour truck loading dock
Form and pour railroad loading dock
Install boiler
Install fuel tank
Plumbing fixtures
Crane
Heating and ventilating units (roof)
Ceramic tile (lavatory and lunchroom)
Exterior doors
Interior doors
Ductwork

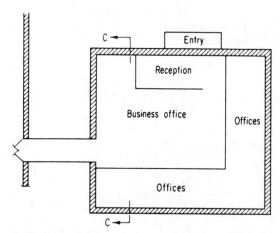

Figure 4.5 Office floor plan.

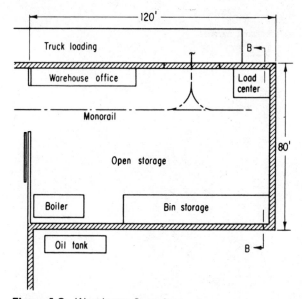

Figure 4.6 Warehouse floor plan.

The office building is designed as a precast concrete structure with masonry walls. The roof system is designed as precast planks with built-up roofing. The partitions are to be metal lath with plaster. The ceiling is to be hung. The building will have a self-contained air-conditioning unit. These activities include:

Erect precast structure   Roofing
Erect roof   Exterior masonry (cavity wall)

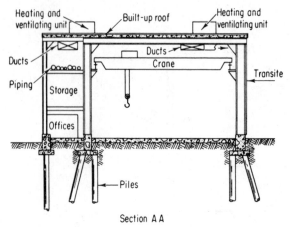

Section A A

Figure 4.7 Interior Section AA (see Figure 4.4).

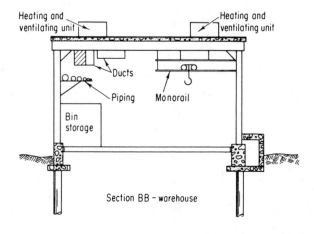

Section BB – warehouse

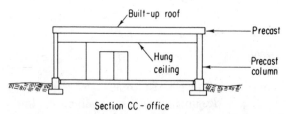

Section CC – office

Figure 4.8 Interior sections BB and CC (see Figures 4.5 and 4.6).

46

Windows and glaze	Interior doors
Paint interior	Plumbing fixtures
Paint exterior	Ceramic tile (lavatory)
Lighting panel	Lath
Wiring	Trim and millwork
Flooring	Hung ceiling
Exterior doors	Plaster

The project outside work includes:

Fine grade

Flagpole

Access road

Perimeter fence

Seed, plant shrubs and trees

Pave parking area

Area lighting

NETWORK LOGIC

The first rough arrow diagram usually becomes the activity list. For a number of reasons, this owner elects to proceed in a definite fashion. To expedite the project, the site preparation and utilities work is to be put out as a separate package to be accomplished before the foundation contractor moves on the site. The foundation contract is to include pile driving, excavation, and all concrete for the plant, warehouse, and office. Since the owner expects to finance the building from current income, the warehouse and plant areas must be completed before any work starts on the office building. Steel erection is to start after the slabs are poured. The office will be temporarily located in the warehouse while the office building is in construction. Figure 4.9 represents the site preparation and utilities portion of the project. Note that the events have been numbered according to the traditional $j > i$ and by the horizontal method.

EVENT 0—The project start:

0-1 *Clear site:* Necessary before any survey work can start.

1-2 *Survey and layout:* Cannot start before the site is cleared; otherwise, many of the survey stakes would be lost in the clearing operation.

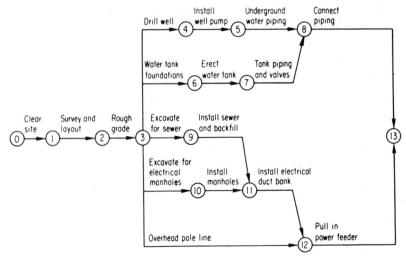

Figure 4.9 CPM network, site preparation and utilities.

2-3   *Rough grade:* Cannot start until the area has been laid out. This activity ties up the whole site with earth-moving equipment.

3-4   *Drill well:* Cannot start until the rough-grading operation is completed.

4-5   *Install well pump:* Cannot be done until well is completed and cased.

5-8   *Underground water piping:* Although this might be started earlier, the site contractor prefers to work from the pump toward the building site.

3-6   *Water tank foundations:* After the rough grading, these simple foundations can be installed.

6-7   *Erect water tank:* Obviously the water tank cannot be erected until its foundations are poured.

7-8   *Tank piping and valves:* Cannot be fabricated and erected until the tank is completed.

8-13   *Connect piping:* The water piping cannot be linked up until both sections are completed.

3-9   *Excavate for sewer:* Can be started after rough grading.

9-11   *Install sewer and backfill:* Immediately follows the sewer excavation, working from the low point uphill.

3-10   *Excavate for electrical manholes:* Can start after rough grading.

10-11   *Install electrical manholes:* Cannot start until the excavation is completed.

11-12 *Install electrical duct bank:* Is started after the electrical man-holes are complete. The start of this also depends upon the completion of the sewer line since that line is deeper than the duct bank.

3-12 *Overhead pole line:* Can be started after the site is rough-graded.

12-13 *Pull in power feeder:* Can start after both the duct bank and the overhead pole line are ready to receive the cable.

EVENT 13—The site preparation and utilities work are complete. Figure 4.10 represents the foundation and concrete work for the John Doe Project:

13-14 *Building layout:* Necessary before foundation work can start.

14-15 *Drive and pour piles:* After layout, this is the first step in the plant and warehouse foundation work.

15-16 *Excavate:* Follows piling. This is fine grading to finish grade.

16-17 *Pour pile caps:* Starts after the fine grading.

17-18 *Form and pour grade beams:* These are poured across the exterior pile caps in this project.

18-21 *Form and pour railroad loading dock:* This dock is essentially an extension of the grade beams.

18-22 *Form and pour truck loading dock:* This dock at the opposite end of the building also backs on the grade beams.

18-19 *Backfill and compact:* Cannot start until the grade beams are ready to contain the fill.

19-20 *Underslab plumbing:* Cannot be installed until the backfill is complete.

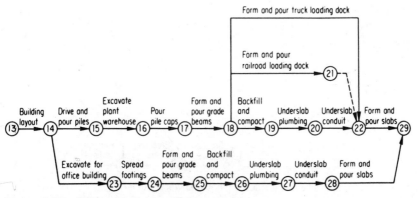

Figure 4.10 CPM network, foundation contract.

20-22   *Underslab conduit:* Is installed after the plumbing because the plumbing lines are deeper.

22-29   *Form and pour slabs:* The loading dock sides and underslab preparation must be completed before the slabs are poured.

14-23   *Excavate for office building:* Can start after the building layout work is complete.

23-24   *Spread footings:* Can be placed after the excavation is done.

24-25   *Form and pour grade beams:* Are poured on top of the spread footings.

25-26   *Backfill and compact:* Is done after the grade beams are finished.

26-27   *Underslab plumbing:* Is installed in the backfill.

27-28   *Underslab conduit:* Is installed on top of the plumbing lines.

28-29   *Form and pour slabs:* Can be done after the underslab preparations are complete.

EVENT 29—The foundations and concrete contract are completed. Figure 4.11 represents the erection of the framework for the plant and warehouse, and also the closings-in of these buildings.

29-30   *Erect structural steel:* Follows the completion of foundations.

30-31   *Plumbing and bolt steel:* Of course, this cannot be done until the steel has been erected.

31-32   *Erect craneway and crane:* Can be done after the steel is bolted up; and to make rigging easier, is planned before the installation of the bar joists system.

31-33   *Erect monorail track:* Although this is not as difficult to erect as the craneway, it is convenient to erect it before the bar joists.

33-34   *Erect bar joists:* Can start after structural steel and major rigging.

34-35   *Erect roof planks:* Cannot be done until the bar joists system is complete.

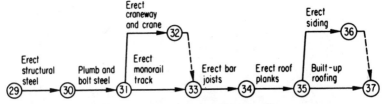

Figure 4.11   CPM network, close-in, plant and warehouse.

35-37 *Built-up roofing:* Goes on top of the roof planks.

35-36 *Erect siding:* Follows the roof planking for safety reasons and because the flashing detail makes it more practical.

EVENT 37—The building is closed in, and interior work can start. Figure 4.12 represents the interior work for the plant and warehouse. At this point the general, mechanical, and electrical contractors can each initiate activities.

37-38 *Set electrical load center:* Is located on the slab in the warehouse. This is package unit.

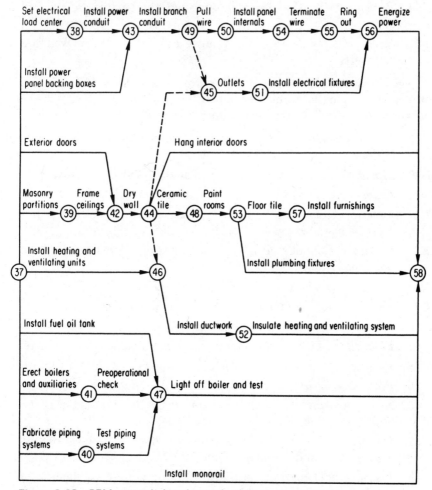

Figure 4.12 CPM network, interior work, plant and warehouse.

37-43   *Power panel backing boxes:* Can be mounted on the masonry walls and structural steel.

38-43   *Power conduit:* Main runs start after the electrical load center is set in place.

43-49   *Install branch conduit:* These runs follow the installation of the main conduit runs and the backing boxes for the power panels.

49-50   *Pull wire:* Follows completion of the conduit system.

50-54   *Panel internals:* Are installed after the panel wires are pulled in.

54-55   *Terminate wires:* These are terminated after the panel internals are in place.

55-56   *Ringout:* After the wiring is connected, the circuits are checked out.

45-51   *Room outlets:* Start after branch conduit and dry wall are complete.

Logical restraints 49-45 and 44-45 operate as spreaders. If 44-45 were not there, "ceramic tile" would depend on "branch conduit." If 49-45 were not there, "pull-wire" would depend upon "dry wall."

51-56   *Install electrical fixtures:* Follows the completion of the room outlets.

37-39   *Masonry partitions:* Start as soon as the building is closed in.

39-42   *Frame ceiling:* Is supported upon the masonry partitions.

37-42   *Exterior doors:* Can be hung after the building is closed in but must be installed prior to the dry wall.

42-44   *Dry wall:* Cannot start until the building is weathertight and the partitions framed out.

44-58   *Hang interior doors:* Can follow dry wall installation.

44-48   *Ceramic tile:* Can follow dry wall.

48-53   *Paint rooms:* Follows the dry wall and ceramic tile installation.

53-57   *Floor tile:* Should be held off until the room painting is complete.

57-58   *Furnishings:* Are installed last.

53-58   *Plumbing fixtures:* Are installed after painting.

37-46   *Install heating and ventilating units:* Can be installed after the built-up roofing, as they are on the roof.

46-52   *Ductwork:* Can be installed after the heating and ventilating units and room dry wall are complete.

52-58   *Insulate heating and ventilating ducts:* Cannot be done until the ductwork is in place.

37-41   *Erect boiler and auxiliaries:* Is in the warehouse and is best done after the warehouse is closed in. The unit is small enough to move through the regular shipping door opening.

41-47   *Preoperational check:* Is a routine check after the boiler is installed.

37-40   *Fabricate piping systems:* Can be done after the building is closed in.

40-47   *Test piping:* Follows completion of the piping systems.

37-47   *Install fuel oil tank:* Is planned to start after the building siding is on so that the excavation will not interfere with the siding work.

47-58   *Light off the boiler:* Cannot be done until the piping systems are tested, boiler checked out, and fuel oil tank ready.

37-58   *Install monorail:* Can be done any time between the close-in and completion of the building.

Figure 4.13 represents the structure and interior work for the office building. At the owner's request, this follows the completion of the plant and warehouse, which occurs by event 58.

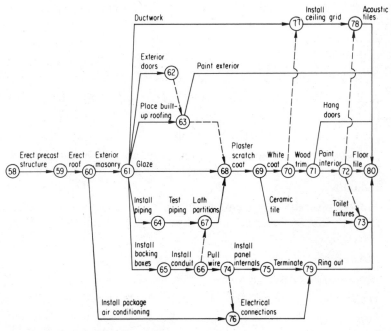

Figure 4.13 CPM network, office building.

58-59   *Erect precast:* Is the first operation in the office building, since the foundations were prepared previously.

59-60   *Erect roof:* Naturally must follow the erection of the structure. Since it uses the same crane rigging, it follows closely.

60-61   *Exterior masonry:* Follows the roof erection.

60-76   *Package air conditioning:* Can be set as soon as the roof is completed.

61-77   *Ductwork:* Can commence when the building is closed in. If started earlier, this operation would interfere with the masonry scaffolds.

61-63   *Built-up roofing:* Follows masonry so that the roofers are not mopping tar on the masons. This might be called "preferential logic," since this operation could physically commence at event 60.

61-62   *Exterior doors:* Installation must wait for the door bucks which go up with the masonry.

61-68   *Glazing:* Is done in the windows which went up with the exterior masonry.

61-64   *Piping installation:* Can start after the exterior masonry is closed in.

61-65   *Install backing boxes:* As they mount on the masonry and structure, can start after the masonry is placed.

63-80   *Paint exterior:* Starts after the roofing is on and the doors are installed.

64-67   *Test piping:* Follows the piping installation.

65-66   *Install conduit:* Follows backing boxes since this is smaller branch conduit rather than main feeders.

66-74   *Pull wire:* Is done after the conduit is in place.

67-68   *Lath partitions:* Follow the piping tests and the conduit installation since portions of these systems are embedded in or behind the lath.

68-69   *Plaster scratch coat:* Cannot start until the building is weathertight ("glaze," "roofing," and "exterior doors") and the lath is installed.

69-70   *Plaster white coat:* Follows the scratch coat.

69-73   *Ceramic tile:* Also follows the scratch coat.

70-71   *Wood trim:* Is placed after the plaster white coat.

71-72   *Paint interior:* Follows the wood trim.

72-80   *Floor tile:* Follows the painting in order to protect the tile.

73-80 *Lavatory fixtures:* Are installed after the interior painting and ceramic tile in order to protect the fixtures.

74-75 *Install electrical panel internals:* Follows the pulling of wires.

75-79 *Terminate wires:* Follows the installation of panel internals.

76-79 *Electrical connections (air conditioning):* Follow the air-conditioning equipment installation and the electrical panel installation.

77-78 *Install ceiling grid:* Is preceded by ductwork and the plaster white coat.

78-80 *Acoustic tiles:* Can be installed after the ceiling grid is installed and interiors painted.

79-80 *Ringout:* Of electrical systems; comes after systems are complete.

Figure 4.14 represents the site work which starts when the structural work is completed (event 37). Note that random numbering was used for this diagram since all digits up to 80 had been used in previous sections of the diagram. The following can all commence when the structural contractor moves off the site.

37-93 *Area lighting*

37-92 *Access road*

37-91 *Grade and ballast railroad siding*

37-90 *Pave parking areas*

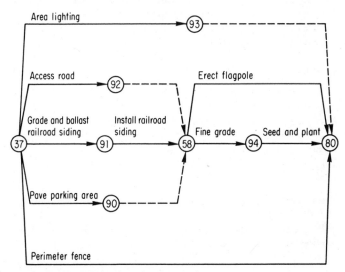

Figure 4.14 CPM network, site work.

37-80 *Perimeter fence*

91-58 *Railroad siding:* Follows grading and ballast of the bed.

The access road, parking, and railroad siding have to be ready by the completion of the plant and warehouse (event 58). The final activities for the office building include:

58-80 *Erect flagpole*

58-94 *Fine grade*

94-80 *Seed and plant*

In preparing the six sections of the CPM description of the John Doe project, the standard routine of considering the overall project by its several physical components has been followed.

This family of individual networks can be effective. If drawing space is a limitation, these could be sheets 1 through 6 of one network.

LOGIC CHANGES—EXAMPLES

If the initial logic is incorrect, or the situation changes, the network is changed by adding to, deleting from, or revising the logic network. For instance:

EXAMPLE 1: What changes to the John Doe network would be required to run the office building in parallel with the plant and warehouse?

SOLUTION: To run the office building in parallel with the plant warehouse, only two activities need to be changed:

28-29 Connects directly to the start of the office. To do this, change 28-29 to 28-99.

58-59 Must be unconnected from the warehouse completion. Change 58-59 to 99-59.

EXAMPLE 2: If the sewer passes under the water tank location, what work sequence changes are necessary?

SOLUTION: If the sewer passes under the water tank foundations, activity 9-11, install sewer, would have to precede 3-6, tank foundations. Do not do this with restraint 11-3 or you will have a loop. First add a spreader restraint between event 3 and the start of "tank foundations."

EXAMPLE 3: If the plant building underslab plumbing were deeper than the office building sewer, how would this restriction be shown?

SOLUTION: If the plant plumbing is deeper than the office sewer, a restraint activity 20-26 might be in order.

EXAMPLE 4: If the electrical load center were to be masonry-enclosed, show the changes required.

SOLUTION: To show the electrical load center enclosed, a restraint from event 38 to the start of masonry partitions would be necessary. To do this, activity 37-39 would have to be preceded by a dummy to avoid a loop.

EXAMPLE 5: If the boiler were too large for the building doors, how would the necessary logical changes be shown?

SOLUTION: If the boiler were too large for the building doors, activity 35-36, erect siding, would have to be amended to leave an opening for the boiler in the warehouse section. Then an activity 47-42 would have to be added to close in the building before dry wall is erected.

EXAMPLE 6: If the primary power feeder were to be pulled in by the building contractor, what changes would be necessary?

SOLUTION: If the power feeder were to be pulled in by the building contractor, activity 12-13 would have to be replaced with a restraint 12-13. Also, an activity 37-56, power feeder, would have to be added.

EXAMPLE 7: If "boiler test" depends upon regular power, what changes are required in the diagram?

SOLUTION: If "boiler test" (activity 47-58) depends upon power availability, a restraint from 56-58 completion to event 47 is necessary. To do this, activity 56-58 must be followed by a restraint to avoid a loop.

In the examples above, note the necessity to test the changed logic for loops. This is especially true when the revised logic requires a connection from a lower number j to a higher number i. It is permissible to violate the $j > i$ rule when necessary, but doing so increases the opportunity for loops.

SUMMARY

In this chapter a sample light industrial project was planned with CPM. The activities involved in each section of the project were defined; then the CPM network for each section was drawn. In describing the network construction, an index or dictionary approach was used. This can be very useful in CPM but is not often employed because of the additional effort required.

5

EVENT TIME
COMPUTATIONS

The preparation of the arrow diagram furnishes a number of advantages, including:

1. A disciplined method of preparing a plan

2. A method of considering the project in detail

3. A graphic record of the plan, also useful in exchanging opinions and constructive criticism about that plan

One thing the arrow diagram lacks thus far is the dimension of time. It might be said that the portion of CPM described up till now has been qualitative but not quantitative.

TIME ESTIMATES

The time dimension used for CPM analysis is *project time.* Any convenient unit can be used, but it must be consistent throughout the network. The unit usually used is days. However, on a short-term project, such as a refinery maintenance shutdown, shifts, half-shifts, or hours may be used. In city planning, where the activity descriptions are fairly broad, weeks may be used. Full-time units are usually used in CPM. For instance, if any activity is expected to take 3 days and 6 hours, 4 days would be used.

To estimate the time duration required for an activity, the estimator assumes a normal work crew carrying out that activity. This normal crew may be composed of the optimum number of members, but it could be larger or smaller. The assumed crew size should be the one which the estimator expects to be used.

One method of estimating activity durations is to estimate worker-hour requirements for the activity and divide that figure by the assumed size of the work crew. Worker-hour requirements are usually not available by activity. This is to be expected since almost all construction estimates are prepared by taking off the work quantities by physical category. An activity will often include more than one work category but rarely includes all major categories.

For the application of basic CPM, this is not the problem it might appear to be. It is, of course, not possible to make an accurate time estimate for the entire project on an off-the-cuff basis. However, when the project is properly broken down into its discrete activities, very accurate time estimates can be made informally if the estimator is experienced in the type of project being planned. The project is like a steer: The meat can't be consumed on the hoof, but the breakdown of the project into activities is like making bite-size hamburgers of it. This apparently casual approach to time estimates is not easily accepted, particularly by engineers. However, experience confirms the validity of the approach.

The project time estimate for the activity is usually referred to as the *activity duration* and is shown below the arrow:

$$i \xrightarrow[\text{Duration}]{\text{Typical activity}} j \quad \text{or} \quad i \xrightarrow[\boxed{\text{Duration}}]{\text{Typical activity}} j$$

There are situations where it is not practical to forecast the time requirement. For instance, in subgrade work, unusual situations may develop or weather conditions may be a big factor. In any case, the estimator makes the best judgment of the probable time factor. In this situation it is quite proper to add some contingency time. The more uncertain the conditions, the more contingency time that should be included. Here again, the breakdown of the overall project into well-defined activities helps to reduce the contingency time required. Where a unique new structural or architectural system is planned, the architect-engineer is usually reluctant to place a time estimate on his or her activities. In this case, a bracket approach is useful. The first tack is to ask how long the activity might take, starting with a high figure like 10 months and working down. Then start with a low figure and work up from the minimum time it could take. The result in almost all cases will be a reasonable time range within which the activity could be accomplished. Within this range, a specific time estimate can then be selected.

If a time estimate is not established, the work will tend to fill the time apparently available for it (a paraphrase of Parkinson's law*). However, the type of project to be planned must be considered in setting estimates. The maximum time required per activity should usually not exceed 10 working days. (However, in city planning allowances may include time durations up to 26 weeks in order to give the planners maximum latitude in their schedule.)

The addition of time to the arrow does *not* make it a vector and the arrow is *not* drawn to scale. (There are certain uses of time-scaled networks, but these should not be drawn for the initial network.)

From the network showing the site preparation for the John Doe project (Figure 4.9), the first nine activities are:

0-1	Clear site
1-2	Survey and layout
2-3	Rough grade
3-9	Excavate for sewer
9-11	Install sewer and backfill
3-10	Excavate for electrical manholes
10-11	Install electrical manholes
11-12	Install electrical duct bank
3-12	Overhead pole line

An estimation of the time required for these activities, based on materials and takeoffs, is:

	Activity	Quantity	Project time, days
0-1	Clear site	Four acres @ 2 dozer days per acre by four dozers.	2
1-2	Survey and layout	Set control traverse—1½ days; layout, grade, and line—½ day.	2
2-3	Rough grade	One acre, move 1000 yards, two dozers @ 250 cubic yards per day.	2

*By permission from C. Northcote Parkinson, *Parkinson's Law,* Riverside Editions, Houghton Mifflin Company, Boston, 1957.

	Activity	Quantity	Project time, days
3-9	Excavate for sewer	Approximate cross section at deep end (10-foot depth) is 12 square yards by 667 yards in length. Averaging, approximately 4000 cubic yards, clamshell with 2-yard bucket @ 100 cubic yards per hour.	5
9-11	Install sewer and backfill	2000 feet @ 60 feet per hour—33 hours.	4
3-10	Excavate for two electrical manholes	@ 2 hours per manhole, say.	1
10-11	Install two electrical manholes	800 square feet forms total @ 100 square feet per team-hour—8 hours. Crew setup time—4 hours; pour concrete—4 hours; strip—8 hours.	4
11-12	Install electrical duct	800-foot conduit @ 2 feet per hour—400 worker-hours per 10-person crew. Concrete follows by 1 day.	6
3-12	Overhead line	1800 feet, set 24 poles—one crew, 3 days; string wire—3 days.	6

Informal time estimates for these are:

	Activity	Brief description	Assumed crew size	Project time, days
0-1	Clear site	Four acres, four bulldozers	5	3
1-2	Survey and layout	Four acres, benchmarks available	3	2
2-3	Rough grade	One acre, two dozers	3	2
3-9	Excavate for sewer	Average depth 5 feet, 2000 feet long	5	10
9-11	Install sewer and backfill		5	5
3-10	Excavate for electrical manholes	Two manholes, 5 feet deep	2	1
10-11	Install electrical manholes	Poured in place	4	5
11-12	Install electrical duct	200-feet-long by 5-feet-deep 4-inch conduit, straight run	7	3
3-12	Overhead line	1800 feet	4	6

These lists were prepared independently:

Activity		Informal estimate, days	Formal estimate, days
0-1	Clear site	3	2
1-2	Survey	2	2
2-3	Rough grade	2	2
3-9	Excavate for sewer	10	5
9-11	Install sewer	5	4
3-10	Excavate electrical manholes	1	1
10-11	Install electrical manholes	5	4
11-12	Electrical duct bank	3	6
3-12	Overhead pole line	6	6

The results are quite close. As in bar charts, there was a tendency to work backward from the answer; however, there is a significance in the comparison. The formal estimation of project time really is not formal. Although the estimating information can be well documented, it is almost always in terms of dollars or worker-hours. To get project time from either money or worker-hours, the size of the work crew and the equipment to be used must be assumed.

MATRIX MANUAL COMPUTATION

Now that activity time durations are assigned, how do we use them? The first computed network solutions were computer-generated. The first manual solutions were by matrix. This was a natural step since mathematicians often use a graphic grid to solve problems. Figure 5.1 shows the portion of the network with assigned-time estimates. Figure 5.2 is the matrix (grid) for this small portion. The matrix is prepared by listing the starting events in the left-hand vertical column. The last event is not listed in this column, since no activity originates from it. The concluding events are listed on the top horizontal line of the matrix. Since no activity

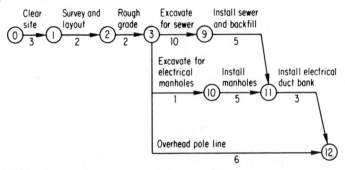

Figure 5.1 Activity time assignments, site preparation.

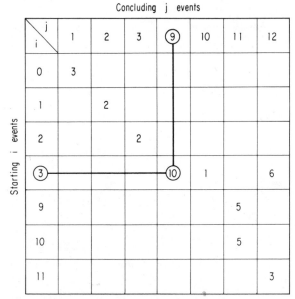

Figure 5.2   Matrix solution to Figure 5.1.

concludes at the first event, it is not listed on this line. The duration for an activity is listed at the intersection of the i and j values. For instance, 10 is the duration for activity 3-9 (the i-j and duration are circled on Figure 5.2).

Although the matrix served its purpose in early work, there is an easier and more direct solution. When James Kelley of the original CPM group was asked why members of the group had not seen this easier solution immediately, he explained with an illustration of the difference between a mathematician and an engineer: If both are confronted with the problem of how to move a pan of water from the kitchen table to the stove, both will solve it by lifting the pan from the table directly to the stove. Now, if the next day, the engineer finds the pan of water on the floor, he will again move it directly to the stove. The mathematician will not. He will move the pan from the floor to the table, *then* from the table to the stove. Why? Because the mathematician has already solved the table-to-stove problem.

Similarly, having used the matrix approach before, it was natural for the CPM mathematicians to utilize this in solving the network manually. The CPM matrix did work, and still does. The same is true for the model T Ford. The disadvantages of the matrix in CPM are:

1. *Data must be transferred* from the diagram to the matrix. This is time-consuming and can result in mistakes because of error in the transfer.

2. *The matrix is unwieldy.*   The matrix must be $(m - 1) \times (m - 1)$, where m equals the number of events in the network. Thus for our small sample network, the matrix must be 93 spaces times 93 spaces (8649 squares).

3. *The matrix will not accept random numbers.*   The diagram must be numbered $j > i$ and this can be inconvenient.

4. *The time estimates become divorced from the diagram logic.*   This makes the solution entirely mechanical.

However, the matrix approach continues as the basis for computer solutions (algorithms) of the CPM network.

INTUITIVE MANUAL COMPUTATION

The manual CPM computation now in use was probably developed concurrently by several persons. There is a famous phrase used by almost all college professors at some time or other in explaining a mathematical solution: "*Intuitively* we can understand this next step. . . ." However, in this case, the computation *is* based upon common sense and *is* intuitively obvious. Since the matrix was still in use by the CPM originating team in late 1960, the intuitive solution probably originated in 1961. The mental block that probably deterred the mathematicians from arriving at it is that the intuitive solution is logical rather than mathematical.

EARLY EVENT TIMES T_E

Look at the first activity in Figure 5.1,

If the project is started at event 0, what is the earliest time for reaching event 1? According to estimate, 3 days would finish clearing the site. The *early time* T_E for event 1 is then 3 days. How early could event 2 be reached? The answer is of course $3 + 2$, or at the end of the fifth project day. To keep track of these results, show them in a box just over the event:

The earliest schedule for reaching event 3 is the sum of the times required to accomplish the first three activities, $3 + 2 + 2$, or 7. Now look at event 9. Do not go back to originating event to determine the T_E (early event time) for this event. Add the duration to the T_E for event 3, and the result is a T_E of 17 for event 9. To go on to event 11, two logic paths lead into this event:

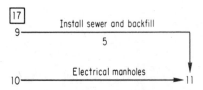

The earliest time for reaching event 11 is along path 3-9-11. This is T_E for event 9 plus the duration, or $17 + 5$, or 22. Note this *without* enclosing it in a box, and then investigate the path through events 3-10-11:

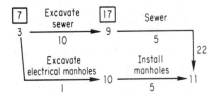

For event 10, the T_E is $7 + 1$, or 8. For event 11 along path 3-10-11, the early event time would be $8 + 5$, or 13. The activities along path 0-1-2-3-10-11 can be accomplished in as early a time as 13 days. Along path 0-1-2-3-9-11 it would take 22 days. What is T_E for event 11? The earliest time for reaching event 11 is the end of the twenty-second project day. Accordingly, discard the 13-day solution, and select the longer 22-day answer as T_E for event 11:

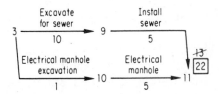

T_E is always the larger value when there is a choice between two or more values.

A caution is in order here. Remember that the event numbers have no significance other than identification. It is unfortunately easy to add them in accidentally as durations or to use the event number rather than the T_E. This is particularly the case with one- or two-digit event numbers. To

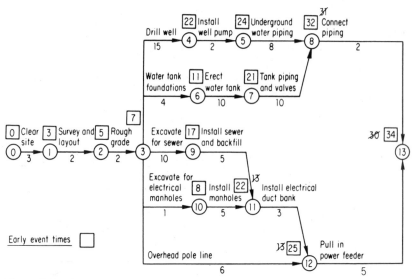

Figure 5.3 Early event times, site preparation.

avoid this error, circle the event numbers or use three-digit event numbers, or both.

Figure 5.3 is the entire site preparation network with times assigned and early event times noted. The T_E at event 12 is the choice of the time along path 11-12 (22 + 3 = 25) or along path 3-12 (7 + 6 = 13). The T_E at event 12 is the longer time, or 25. The early event time at event 13 along this lower path is 25 + 5, or 30.

Now observe the two upper paths. The path through events 3-4-5-8 totals 25 days. This, added to the T_E at event 3, gives an early time along this path to event 8 of 7 + 25, or 32. Along the path through events 3-6-7-8, the activities total 24 days. This 24 + 7 is 31 days, which is less than 32. Thus the T_E at event 8 is 32. The early time to event 13 along this upper path is 34 days. Since this is larger than 30 days, the T_E for this network is 34.

The result is 34 days, but what is the significance? Based upon our logical sequence and time estimates, the shortest time in which this work could be completed is 34 working days, or about 7 weeks.

LATE EVENT TIMES T_L

The *late event time* T_L for an event is defined as the latest time at which an event may be reached without delaying the computed project duration.

Keep in mind that "late" in this context is late in terms of this computed completion time rather than a desired or prescribed completion time. To determine late event times, work backward through the network. From Figure 5.3, the final event 13 has two activities (8-13 and 12-13) leading into it:

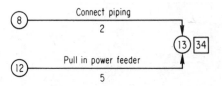

By definition, the late event time at event 13 is 34 days, since the late event time for the terminal event equals the early event time for that event. If event 13 is to be reached by time 34, event 8 must start no later than 34 less the duration of activity 8-13 (34 − 2). Thus the late event time for event 8 is 32. The late event time for event 12 is 34 − 5, or 29.

In showing the late event times T_L on the diagram, put them in circles to differentiate them from the T_E values. Figure 5.4 shows the late event times for this network. In determining T_L values, there is a choice between values when two or more arrow tails converge. On Figure 5.4 this occurs

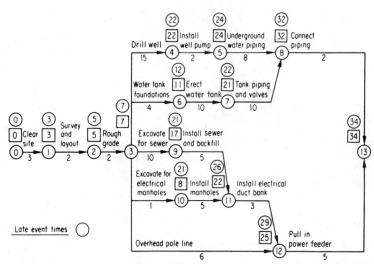

Figure 5.4 Late event times, site preparation.

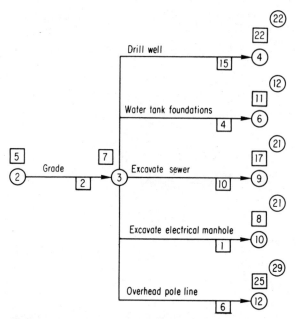

Figure 5.5   Network at event 3.

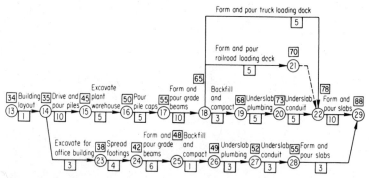

Figure 5.6   Foundation network with early event times.

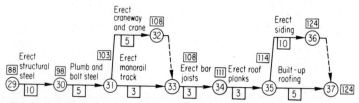

Figure 5.7   Close-in of plant and warehouse with early event times.

only at event 3 where the tails of five arrows converge. Figure 5.5 is an enlargement of the network at event 3. From Figure 5.5:

Activity	Late event time	Duration, days	Late event time along this path from event 3
3-4	22	15	7
3-6	12	4	8
3-9	21	10	11
3-10	21	1	20
3-12	29	6	23

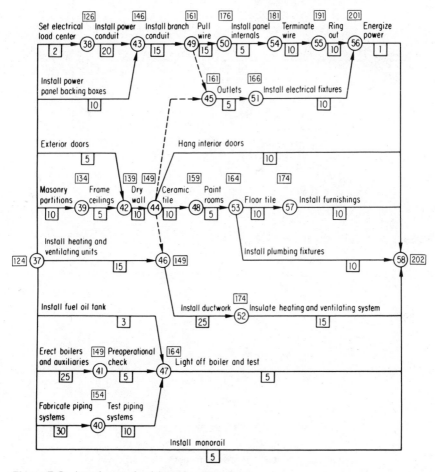

Figure 5.8 Interior work with early event times.

From the table, path backward from event 4 results in the "earlier" late event time at event 3. T_L is always the earlier value whenever there is a convergence of two or more arrow tails. Accordingly, T_L at event 3 is time 7. As a check, the late event time for the originating event should always be zero.

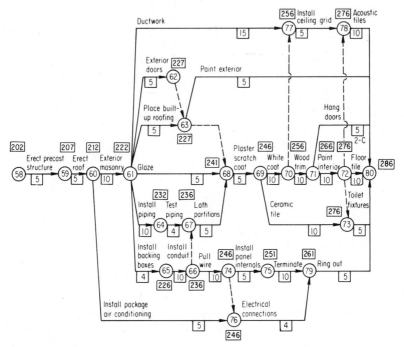

Figure 5.9 Office building with early event times.

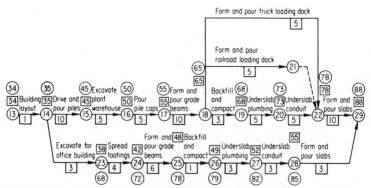

Figure 5.10 Foundation structure portion with both early (□) and late (O) event times.

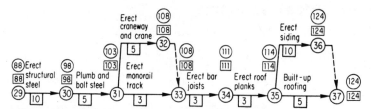

Figure 5.11 Close-in of plant and warehouse with early (□) and late (○) event times.

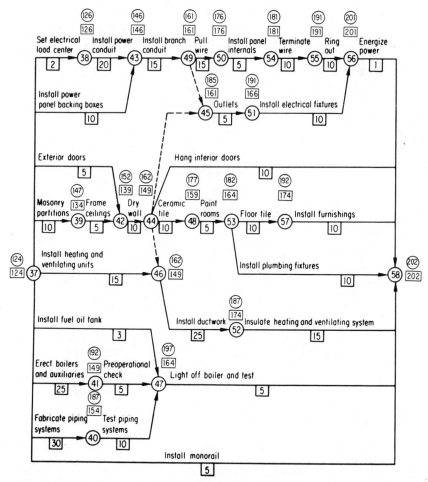

Figure 5.12 Interior work with early (□) and late (○) event times.

EARLY EVENT TIMES—JOHN DOE PROJECT

The early event times for the balance of the John Doe Project are shown in Figures 5.6 through 5.9.

LATE EVENT TIMES—JOHN DOE PROJECT

Both late and early event times are shown in Figures 5.10 through 5.13.

SUMMARY

The assignment of project time to the CPM network activities was discussed. It was demonstrated that the informal assignment of time estimates can be accurate. The matrix noncomputer solution of the CPM diagram was discussed in broad terms. The recommended manual solution

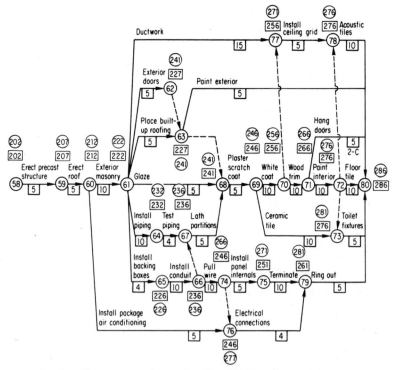

Figure 5.13   Office building with early (□) and late (○) event times.

of the diagram was described by using an intuitive and direct approach, which can be summarized by three paradoxical rules:

1. The early event time is the latest of the possibilities at a convergence of arrows (head end).

2. The late event time is the earliest of the possibilities at a convergence of arrows (tail end).

3. The shortest project time is the result of the longest path, which is the critical path.

6

ACTIVITY TIME COMPUTATION

In Chapter 5, the computation of event times was described. The event times, early and late, are fundamental information. Nonetheless, the network events are not too descriptive. Look at event 3 in Figure 5.5; how would you describe this event? You would probably term it "completion of grading." But how would you indicate that it marks the logical starting point for five other activities? Certain key events, or milestones, are easily identified and are of interest. Among these would be complete foundations, start steel erection, start lath, complete plaster, start piping, etc. However, construction is work-oriented, and activity descriptions better define the CPM plan. Accordingly, activity time information is the more useful format.

ACTIVITY START AND FINISH TIMES

The source of this information is the event time calculations. Look at the typical activity:

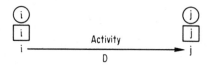

Each activity must be bounded by two events. What is the earliest time that an activity can start? It can start when the T_E for its starting (or i) event has been reached. That is,

Early start = ES = T_E (event i) = $\boxed{i}$

If the early start (ES) is known, what is the earliest time that this activity can be completed? The answer is the start time plus the job duration D:

Early finish = EF = ES + duration = ES + D

After determining the early times for an activity, what are the late times? The late finish is of course the T_L for the finishing (or j) event; that is,

Late finish = LF = T_L (event j) = $\bigcirc\!\!\!\!j$

After late finish, the late start is obviously

Late start = LS = LF − D

Certain information about activities can be summarized before any calculations are made. For instance, from Figure 5.3, the first nine activities offer this information:

Activity	Duration, days	Description
0-1	3	Clear site
1-2	2	Survey and layout
2-3	2	Rough grade
3-4	15	Drill well
3-6	4	Water tank foundations
3-9	10	Excavate sewer
3-10	1	Excavate electrical manholes
3-12	6	Pole line
4-5	2	Well pump

After the event times are computed, the following additional information from Figure 5.4 can be listed:

Activity	Duration, days	Description	ES	LF
0-1	3	Clear site	0	3
1-2	2	Survey and layout	3	5
2-3	2	Rough grade	5	7
3-4	15	Drill well	7	22
3-6	4	Water tank foundations	7	12
3-9	10	Excavate sewer	7	21
3-10	1	Excavate electrical manholes	7	21
3-12	6	Pole line	7	29
4-5	2	Well pump	22	24

Now, adding duration to the ES column and subtracting it from the LF gives:

Activity	Duration, days	Description	ES	EF	LS	LF
0-1	3	Clear site	0	3	0	3
1-2	2	Survey and layout	3	5	3	5
2-3	2	Rough grade	5	7	5	7
3-4	15	Drill well	7	22	7	22
3-6	4	Water tank foundations	7	11	8	12
3-9	10	Excavate sewer	7	17	11	21
3-10	1	Excavate electrical manholes	7	8	20	21
3-12	6	Pole line	7	13	23	29
4-5	2	Well pump	22	24	22	24

CRITICAL ACTIVITIES

The early CPM team referred to the critical path as the "main chain." This term was dropped in favor of "critical path," which was used by the early PERT group. The critical path determines the length of the project. This is the longest path into the last event, since it establishes the latest T_E for that last event. Accordingly, the longest chain or path of activities through the network is the critical path.

The critical path is not always obvious. Look at the network for the interior work for the John Doe plant (Figure 4.12). You might guess at the critical path based upon experience, but, without a project time estimate for each activity, you cannot identify it.

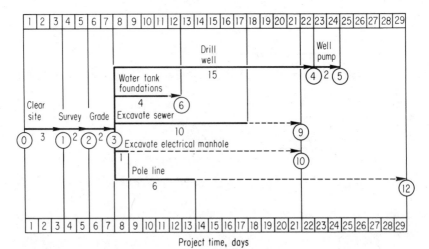

Figure 6.1 Plot of activity times to time scale.

Figure 6.1 is a plot of this activity information on a time scale. Note that the activities 0-1, 1-2, 2-3, 3-4, and 4-5 show a solid connection. These activities are on the path of critical events (0-1-2-3-4-5, etc.). Look at the activity times for activity 4-5. The ES is 22 and the LF is 24. The time span between them is 24 − 22, or 2. Since the time span available equals the duration for activity 4-5, this activity *must* start on its ES and finish on its EF if the project is to finish by time 34. Note that for these critical activities early start equals late start and early finish equals late finish.

In Figure 5.4, the critical path goes through events 0-1-2-3-4-5-8-13. There are three conditions which each *critical activity* must meet:

1. The early and late event times at the activity start must be equal:

$$\boxed{i} = \bigcirc\!\!\!\!\;i$$

2. The early and late event times at the activity completion must be equal:

$$\boxed{j} = \bigcirc\!\!\!\!\;j$$

3. The difference between the ES and LF must equal the duration.

The first two conditions are easy to recognize when the network is manually computed with T_E and T_L right on the diagram. People often forget to test for the third rule. Add an activity 3-5 to the network and call it "deliver pipe." The delivery cannot start until the site is rough-graded (event 3), and it is needed before piping installation starts (event 5). If this delivery takes a week (duration = 5),

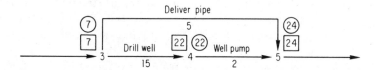

Activity 3-5 meets the first two conditions, but 24 − 7, or 17, is greater than an activity duration of 5; accordingly, activity 3-5 is not critical even though it spans two critical events.

Note that there can be any number of critical paths through the network. One path can spread out into a number of paths. A number of critical paths can converge into one. However, the critical path(s) must be a continuous chain of activities. It (they) cannot be intermittent. Also, there must be at least one critical path from the first to the last event of the project.

FLOAT

In preparing the CPM diagram for a channel improvement project, the Corps of Engineers planners were certain that the critical path would be through the pile-driving activities. Pile driving had always been critical in the past. However, they had reckoned without their own foresight. Based upon past experience, the Corps construction group had devised a scheme which enabled them to utilize two pile-driving rigs instead of one in the limited space available. This cut pile driving off the critical path. It was replaced by a land acquisition situation handled by the Corps real estate group. Their time estimate was also based upon experience. The diagram in this case served as a communication medium to advise all cognizant Corps groups of new planning factors.

Since activity 3-5, deliver pipe, is not critical, what differentiates it from a critical activity? Since it has an available working time span of 17 ($24 - 7$) and a duration of 5, there is a latitude in scheduling this activity equal to $17 - 5$, or 12. We call this characteristic *float:*

$$\text{Float} = F = (LF - ES) - D$$

Since $EF = ES + D$, then

$$\text{Float} = (LF - ES) - D = LF - (ES + D)$$

$$= LF - EF$$

Also, since $(LF = LS + D)$ and $(EF = ES + D)$, then

$$\text{Float} = LF - EF = (LS + D) - (ES + D)$$

$$= LS - ES$$

Getting away from formulas, it is reasonable that the difference between the early and late starts should equal the scheduling flexibility or float. Also, the difference between the late and early finishes furnishes the same values.

Again in the network shown in Figure 5.4, the total float for all activities, by using each of the previously mentioned formulas, is:

FORMULA: $F = LF - ES - D$

Activity	LF	−	ES	−	Duration	=	Float
0-1	3		0		3		0
1-2	5		3		2		0
2-3	7		5		2		0
3-4	22		7		15		0
3-6	12		7		4		1

Activity	LF	−	ES	−	Duration	=	Float
3-9	21		7		10		4
3-10	21		7		1		13
3-12	29		7		6		16
4-5	24		22		2		0

FORMULA: $F = LF - EF$

Activity	LF	−	EF	=	Float
5-8	32		32		0
6-7	22		21		1
7-8	32		31		1
8-13	34		34		0

FORMULA: $F = LS - ES$

Activity	LS	(LF − D)	−	ES	=	Float
9-11	21			17		4
10-11	21			8		13
11-12	26			22		4
12-13	29			25		4

Case 1 shown in Figure 6.2 is a time scale plot of activities 3-9, 9-11, 11-12, and 12-13. Note that the total float for each of these activities is 4. Does this mean that each of these activities has 4 days of float to use? The answer is a qualified yes. Yes, if none of the prior activities in this same

Activity	ES	EF	LS	LF	Float, days
3-9	7	17	11	21	4
9-11	17	22	21	26	4
11-12	22	25	26	29	4
12-13	25	30	29	34	4

chain has used the float. In case 2 shown in Figure 6.2, assume that activity 3-9 used the 4 days of float. That is, it started at time 11 instead of the ES of 7. The result is a solid link of activities following 3-9. When total float is used up by any one activity or series of activities, all succeeding activities become critical.

Case 3 shown in Figure 6.2 illustrates the use of total float by different activities in the chain. Activity 3-9 starts 2 days after its early start, which reduces the float to 2 days. Activity 11-12 delays its start until the late start and no float remains.

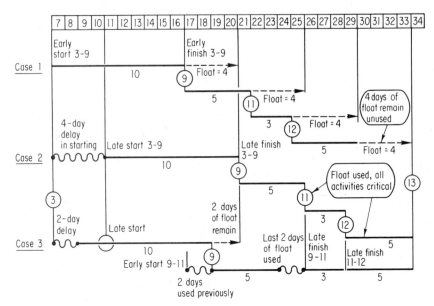

Figure 6.2 Plot of activity times to time scale. Case 1, activities start early; case 2, activities start late (4 days of float used prior to 3-9); case 3, activities use float (2 days prior to 3-9, 2 days after 9-11).

Look at the float picture in the broader view. The T_E for event 3 is 7; the T_L for event 13 is 34. The difference, or 27 days, is the time span within which the four activities must be accomplished. Adding the durations of these four activities gives:

Activity		Duration, days
3-9	....	10
9-11	....	5
11-12	....	3
12-13	....	5
Total	....	23

The available time span from event 3 to event 13 (27 days) less the total time for the activities in this chain (23 days) is 4 days float. This is another illustration of the shared aspect of float.

Free Float

The originators of the Critical Path Method defined a variety of floats including: total float, free float, and independent float. The measure of float described previously is known as "total float." It is the most widely used version and the most practical. Of the three types originally defined, only two appear to have any practical use: total float and free float.

Free float is defined as that float which, if used, will not delay the early start of any succeeding activity. The definition appears to offer a very useful identification. The formula, compared with the total float formula, is as follows:

$$\text{\textcircled{j}} - \boxed{i} - D = \text{total float}$$

$$\boxed{j} - \boxed{i} - D = \text{free float}$$

Looking past the formula, though, free float loses its luster. For example, take Figure 6.3, which is part of the initial John Doe network between event 3 and event 13. All of these activities have total float.

However, as a string of activities emerges from a junction event such as event 3, the early start for all activities has been controlled by the selection of the longest of all paths leading into that junction event. In this example, the critical path from event 0 to event 3 has determined that the early start time is 7. For a string of activities with more than 1, such as 3-9 or 3-10, in which the early finish for the j event is determined only by the early-start figure coming out of the junction point, the formula necessarily produces a free float of 0. It is only when the string of activities joins another junction event, at which a new early-start figure is determined by the longest path leading into the new juncture, that the free float formula produces a figure. It produces this figure because one or more other paths coming into the junction point establish an early start for that key junction which is greater than the early finish time of the series of activities under study.

Free float is really a comparative value of floats in parallel paths. All of the activities shown in Figure 6.3 have float, and the lowest float value is 4. Thus, the free float values are 0 for the lowest relative float path (3-9-11-12-13). However, the free float is also 0 on the activity 3-10 which initiates the path 3-10-11, but is 9 on the second activity because this is the last activity before a junction point.

The free float for activity 3-12, which has only a single activity in the string, is dependent upon the early event time at event 12, which is established by the longer path 3-9-11-12, and therefore has a free float value.

Free float is, therefore, deceptive since it shows a 0 value for the parallel path with the lowest total float, and also for any series of initial activities whose early finishes are not dependent upon another chain. In some cases, it will equal the total float value where reentering a critical path string of activities. It may be less than total float, but it will never be more.

Many programs still print out free float even though it is virtually never used. Other times, the program may continue to generate free float

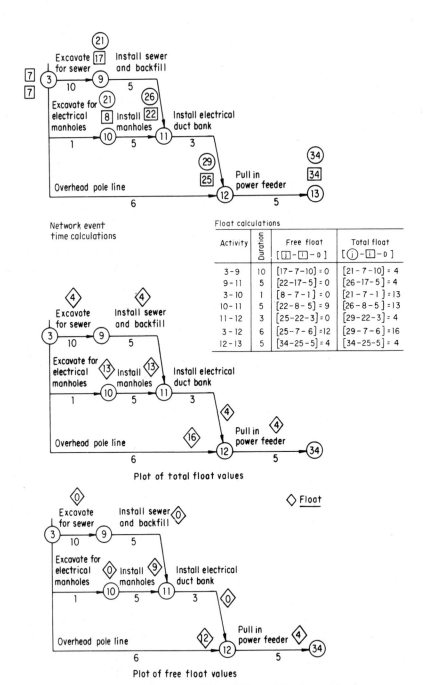

Figure 6.3 Free float compared with total float, John Doe project.

but the printout is blanked off by a request. A computer printout showing free float is usually a sign of an obsolescent program.

Time Scale Network

Figure 6.1, which demonstrated the critical activities, was the front end of a plot of the site work activities plotted according to a time scale. If all the activities are plotted according to a time scale, the result is a graphical calculation of the network (see Figure 6.4 for a time scale network of the John Doe project). The activities are plotted in solid line to scale, with dotted connections to the event connection point. The dotted section is equal to the float in the chain of activities.

In plotting a network where a computer or manual calculation has not been made, all activities are plotted by early start. Float will appear as dotted lines following the last activity in a series. If the network has been calculated, either manually or by computer, the preferred plot is by late start. The early-start plot gives the CPM calculation, but experience confirms that activities do not start at the earliest point. Accordingly, an early-start plot will be patently incorrect at each update. And if the network is to be updated correctly, each review will require a time-consuming redraft. On the other hand, if the graphical plot is to a late start, redraft-

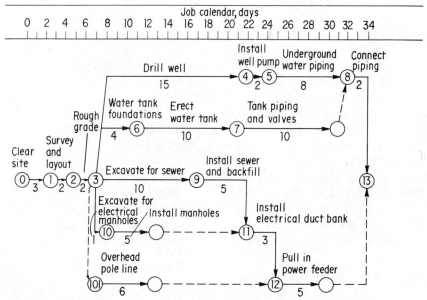

Figure 6.4 Time scale network, John Doe project (plotted to early times).

ing will not be required unless a major change in approach is decided upon. In fact, if the sequence and durations go unchanged, the graphical network (late-start plot) can remain correct by a simple shift of the horizontal time scale.

COMPUTATION TIME

How long does it take to compute a network manually, and how large a network can be hand-computed? These questions cannot be given specific answers because networks vary in characteristics. The John Doe networks have about 130 activities. (A rule of thumb: The number of activities in a network is about equal to 1.6 times the number of events.) All the networks, except the plant and warehouse interior, would be described as noncomplex. In networks of this type, manal computation of perhaps 500 activities is practical. In fact, manual calculation (forward pass only) is recommended for networks of 2000 to 3000 activities prior to computer calculation. This provides the overall time frame, and often picks up obvious errors. The availability of the computer is a factor. You could hand-compute the John Doe networks faster than you could transfer data to computer data input sheets for one run. However, if you expect several runs, the computer is much faster. If a computer is available, you should probably use it for networks above 100 to 200 activities if you expect reruns.

The plant interior network might be described as semicomplex. If you have a complex, tightly interconnected network, a network of 100 or 200 activities can be tedious to compute.

Thus, there is no specific limit to hand computation. You will have to set your own limits based upon your own situation and experience.

In an early application, a construction company could not arrange computer time for the computation of a large network. They decided to compute it by hand using two clerks. Toward the end of the first week, the network was almost computed when several estimate revisions were made. The clerks gave up, and the network never was computed. This is one advantage the computer offers. It has no personality, so it cannot get discouraged. In this example, note the 2 worker-weeks required to hand-compute the network. This incident occurred in the early CPM era and the clerks were computing by matrix. Using the intuitive approach, they could have done the computation in 1 day without discouragement.

CALENDAR TIME

Project time is fine for manual computation. However, when the information is put to use in an actual project, calendar dates are important. A

M	T	W	T	F	M	T	W	T	F	M	T	W	T	F
	July					September					November			
	1	2	3			1	2	3	4		2	3	4	5	6
	1	2	3			44	45	46	47		86	87	88	89	90
6	7	8	9	10	7	8	9	10	11	9	10	11	12	13
–	4	5	6	7	–	48	49	50	51	91	92	–	93	94
13	14	15	16	17	14	15	16	17	18	16	17	18	19	20
8	9	10	11	12	52	53	54	55	56	95	96	97	98	99
20	21	22	23	24	21	22	23	24	25	23	24	25	26	27
13	14	15	16	17	57	58	59	60	61	100	101	102	–	103
27	28	29	30	31	28	29	30			30				
18	19	20	21	22	62	63	64			104				
	August					October					December			
3	4	5	6	7				1	2		1	2	3	4
23	24	25	26	27				65	66		105	106	107	108
10	11	12	13	14	5	6	7	8	9	7	8	9	10	11
28	29	30	31	32	67	68	69	70	71	109	110	111	112	113
17	18	19	20	21	12	13	14	15	16	14	15	16	17	18
33	34	35	36	37	72	73	74	75		114	115	116	117	118
24	25	26	27	28	19	20	21	22	23	20	22	23	24	25
38	39	40	41	42	76	77	78	79	80	119	120	121	–	–
31					26	27	28	29	30	28	29	30	31	
43					81	82	83	84	85	122	123	124	125	

Figure 6.5   John Doe project calendar.

project calendar which converts project days into calendar dates is very useful. Figure 6.5 is the project calendar for the John Doe project. It assumes a July 1 start date and skips weekends and holidays. For activity 4-5, install well pump, the ES is 22 and the LF is 24. From the project calendar, the ES is July 31 and the LF is August 4.

The activity times list is equivalent to the following list of calendar times:

Activity	Duration, days	Description	ES*	EF*	LS*	LF*	Float, days
0-1	3	Clear site	7-1	7-3	7-1	7-3	0
1-2	2	Survey	7-3	7-8	7-3	7-8	0
2-3	2	Rough grade	7-8	7-10	7-8	7-10	0

Activity	Duration, days	Description	ES*	EF*	LS*	LF*	Float, days
3-4	15	Drill well	7-10	7-31	7-10	7-31	0
3-6	4	Water tank foundations	7-10	7-16	7-13	7-17	1
3-9	10	Excavate sewer	7-10	7-24	7-16	7-30	4
3-10	1	Excavate electrical manholes	7-10	7-13	7-29	7-30	13
3-12	6	Pole line	7-10	7-20	8-3	8-11	16
4-5	2	Well pump	7-31	8-4	7-31	8-4	0

*Numbers in column refer to calendar dates, i.e., "7-1 means "July 1," etc.

While this calendar-oriented information is more useful, the addition of as many as eight more digits per line does make it more difficult to read the activity list. Since early start and late finish are the two dates usually referred to, often the EF and LS columns are omitted in the calendar-dated summary of activity times. Using the float column is the fastest method for picking out the critical path.

If a project starts on July 29 instead of July 1, must you construct a new calendar? The difference in project days between July 1 and 29 is 20 − 1, or 19. Look up the date for project day 10 under 19 + 10, or 29, and the date is August 11. Thus one project calendar can be used for a number of projects.

SUMMARY

This chapter discussed the use of event times to compute activity times, specifically early start, early finish, late start, and late finish. The three rules for identifying a critical activity were stated. Float time was defined.

CPM BY COMPUTER

While networks of considerable size can be hand-computed, it would be shortsighted to disregard the use of computers in CPM computation. Just as you wouldn't use a 10-yard bucket to excavate for a residential septic tank, you wouldn't apply a computer to a small CPM plan. But you wouldn't use hand shovels to dig the Panama Canal, so don't have a closed mind about using computers to handle large CPM plans.

If an in-house computer with CPM program is available, the tendency is to computerize all networks. Even in that circumstance it is good practice to do a forward pass (early event times) to check the network.

The usual break point, at which it is practical to hand-compute, is 250 activities. This number reduces in a complex network to perhaps 100 activities, and may increase to 1000 activities for a simple network.

The absence of various outputs/edits (described in this chapter) as required by a specification may make a hand calculation unacceptable. Further, if the network is to be updated on a regular basis, manual calculation becomes inconvenient. And still further, the expression of time in project days, while useful in the abstract, is less desirable than the projection of the information in calendar dates.

CPM INPUT

Since computers cannot read, the network information must be converted to a form which can be put into the machine. The first step is the preparation of data sheets. Figure 7.1 is the first of the actual data sheets used to prepare the John Doe project for its computation.

To perform the CPM calculation, the computer needs only the i, j, and duration for each activity. From this it can mathematically reconstruct the network, just as you could from an activity list. The activity descriptions are put in for your convenience. The computer merely stores them and puts them back into the output.

The data takeoff is a chore, but an important one. It is relatively easy to forget an activity or to transcribe an incorrect event number. By reversing the i and the j, a logical loop can be created. The likelihood of error is reduced if the classical $j > i$ rule is used in assigning event numbers. In transferring the data from the network to the input sheets, it is recommended that you work in the order of consecutive event numbers. This will reduce the chance of error or omission.

I	J	NORMAL DURATION	CONTRACT	WORK CATEGORY	JOB DESCRIPTION
0	1	3		1	1 CLEAR SITE
1	2	2		1	2 SURVEY AND LAYOUT
2	3	2		1	1 ROUGH GRADE
3	4	15		1	7 DRILL WELL
3	6	4		1	3 WATER TANK FOUNDATIONS
3	9	10		1	1 EXCAVATE FOR SEWER
3	10	1		1	1 EXCAVATE ELECTRICAL MANHOLES
3	12	6		1	4 OVERHEAD POLE LINE
4	5	2		1	5 INSTALL WELL PUMP
5	8	8		1	5 UNDERGROUND WATER PIPING
6	7	10		1	6 ERECT WATER TOWER
7	8	10		1	5 TANK PIPING AND VALVES
8	13	2		1	5 CONNECT WATER PIPING
9	11	5		1	5 INSTALL SEWER AND BACKFILL
10	11	5		1	4 INSTALL ELECTRICAL MANHOLES
11	12	3		1	4 ELECTRICAL DUCT BANK
12	13	5		1	4 PULL IN POWER FEEDER
13	14	1		2	2 BUILDING LAYOUT
14	15	10		2	7 DRIVE AND POUR PILES
14	23	3		2	1 EXCAVATE FOR OFFICE BUILDING
15	16	5		2	1 EXCAVATE FOR PLANT
16	17	5		2	3 POUR PILE CAPS PLANT-WAREHSE
17	18	10		2	3 FORM AND POUR GRADE BEAMS P-W
18	19	3		2	1 BACKFILL AND COMPACT P-W
18	21	5		2	3 FORM AND POUR RR LOAD DOCK PW
18	22	5		2	3 FORM AND POUR TK LOAD DOCK PW
19	20	5		2	5 UNDERSLAB PLUMBING P-W
20	22	5		2	4 UNDERSLAB CONDUIT P-W
21	22	0			Dummy
22	29	10		2	3 FORM AND POUR SCABS A-W
23	24	4		2	3 SPREAD FOOTINGS OFFICE
24	25	6		2	3 FORM AND POUR GRADE BEAMS OFF
25	26	1		2	1 BACKFILL AND COMPACT OFFICE

Figure 7.1   First data sheet for John Doe project.

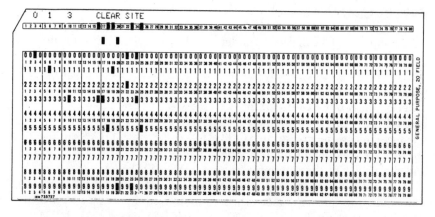

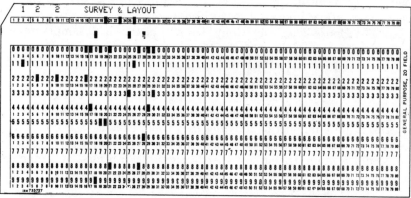

Figure 7.2   IBM CPM input cards. First two activities, John Doe project.

The next step is to transfer the CPM input from the data sheets to punched cards or to key it directly to a disk or tape. The vertical columns on the data sheet represent the specific card column in which the i, j, duration, or description is to be placed (see Figure 7.2). These specific assignments will vary with the program being used.

The input is always placed as far to the right as possible. The Key-punch or key-disk operator places one horizontal line of data in the appropriate spaces on one IBM card. This is another area where errors are easily introduced. To avoid errors, the key-in operator checks the input on a verifier or visually on a cathode ray tube (CRT).

An experienced operator can key in about 300 activities per hour. Since verification for accuracy takes about the same amount of effort, the average key-in plus verify rate is 150 activities per hour.

CPM COMPUTATION

The computer is a mindless wonder which needs a program to direct its operations. During early CPM development, the Navy Special Projects Office (SPO) developed MIS-LESS for its Polaris PERT program. This program was copied and modified by others, and provided the basis for a generic family of CPM programs. These programs preceded the introduction of the COBOL (Common Business Oriented Language) computer language and were written in FORTRAN (FORmula TRANslation) language. The selection of hardware depended upon the size of the program and the ability of the computer to handle FORTRAN.

Computer hardware manufacturers often provided a library of computer software to complement their computer equipment. IBM provided their Project Control System (PCS), which included a basic CPM program widely utilized by the construction industry. (PCS is often referred to as "The House That Jack Built" because of the small sample project used to demonstrate its output formats.)

Early computer manufacturer/equipment orientation resulted in the CPM programs being structured to match the capabilities of the computer. Conversely, the limitations of the second- or third-generation equipment directly limited the capabilities of many of the CPM programs in terms of total number of activities they could handle, their node numbering (i.e., many allowed only three digits), the number of code fields they could contain, the size of their activity descriptions, and other of their network characteristics. Current CPM programs are catalogued and discussed in Chapter 17.

One item not necessarily included in the CPM or PERT program (although an important program element) is an efficient routine for checking errors. This first step, if included, will stop the computation before it starts working on incorrect data. This can save the cost of many dry runs. An error check looks for dangling activities (either an i or a j end unconnected), duplicate activities, and loops. The first two are not difficult to locate, but loops are another matter. One method of checking for them is to watch for a project duration greater than the total duration of all the project activities when added together. This does not indicate a loop's location, but can indicate the presence of one. However, the method will fail if a loop is made up of dummy activities with zero time duration. In that case, computer running time in excess of the estimated time is an indication of the presence of a loop.

When the error check has been completed, the actual CPM computation commences. The first step is to clear the computer memory and then read in the program, from punched cards, tape, or disk. Next, the CPM input is read in and the computation starts. The computation time varies with the type of computer used and the size of the network; between 5 and 30 minutes is an average time range.

CPM OUTPUT

When the computer completes its computation, the results are automatically placed on punched cards, a tape, or a disk, or on a typewritten or printed list. These can be sorted in various orders.

The most common output is an *i-j* one; in this output, the activities are arranged in consecutive order of the *i* or starting events. The *i-j* list is most useful in working with CPM networks. If information is desired on a specific activity, it can easily be found in the listing. The *i-j* list functions as an index or dictionary of activities. The *i-j* listing for the John Doe project is shown in Figure 7.3.

I	J	DUR-ATION			DESCRIPTION	START		FINISH		TOTAL FLOAT
						EAR	LAT	EAR	LAT	
0	1	3	1	1	CLEAR SITE			3	3	0
1	2	2	1	2	SURVEY AND LAYOUT	3	3	5	5	0
2	3	2	1	1	ROUGH GRADE	5	5	7	7	0
3	4	15	1	7	DRILL WELL	7	7	22	22	0
3	6	4	1	3	WATER TANK FOUNDATIONS	7	8	11	12	1
3	9	10	1	1	EXCAVATE FOR SEWER	7	11	17	21	4
3	10	1	1	1	EXCAVATE ELECTRICAL MANHOLES	7	20	8	21	13
3	12	6	1	4	OVERHEAD POLE LINE	7	23	13	29	16
4	5	2	1	5	INSTALL WELL PUMP	22	22	24	24	0
5	8	8	1	5	UNDERGROUND WATER PIPING	24	24	32	32	0
6	7	10	1	6	ERECT WATER TOWER	11	12	21	22	1
7	8	10	1	5	TANK PIPING AND VALVES	21	22	31	32	1
8	13	2	1	5	CONNECT WATER PIPING	32	32	34	34	0
9	11	5	1	5	INSTALL SEWER AND BACKFILL	17	21	22	26	4
10	11	5	1	4	INSTALL ELECTRICAL MANHOLES	8	21	13	26	13
11	12	3	1	4	ELECTRICAL DUCT BANK	22	26	25	29	4
12	13	5	1	4	PULL IN POWER FEEDER	25	29	30	34	4
13	14	1	2	2	BUILDING LAYOUT	34	34	35	35	0
14	15	10	2	7	DRIVE AND POUR PILES	35	35	45	45	0
14	23	3	2	1	EXCAVATE FOR OFFICE BUILDING	35	65	38	68	30
15	16	5	2	1	EXCAVATE FOR PLANT WAREHOUSE	45	45	50	50	0
16	17	5	2	3	POUR PILE CAPS PLANT-WAREHSE	50	50	55	55	0
17	18	10	2	3	FORM + POUR GRADE BEAMS P-W	55	55	65	65	0
18	19	3	2	1	BACKFILL AND COMPACT P-W	65	65	68	68	0
18	21	5	2	3	FORM + POUR RR LOAD DOCK P-W	65	73	70	78	8
18	22	5	2	3	FORM + POUR TK LOAD DOCK P-W	65	73	70	78	8
19	20	5	2	5	UNDERSLAB PLUMBING P-W	68	68	73	73	0

Figure 7.3   John Doe output with *i-j* sort, computer CPM output.

I	J	DUR-ATION			DESCRIPTION	START		FINISH		TOTAL FLOAT
						EAR	LAT	EAR	LAT	
20	22	5	2	4	UNDERSLAB CONDUIT P-W	73	73	78	78	0
21	22	0			DUMMY	70	78	70	78	8
22	29	10	2	3	FORM + POUR SLABS P-W	78	78	88	88	0
23	24	4	2	3	SPREAD FOOTINGS OFFICE	38	68	42	72	30
24	25	6	2	3	FORM + POUR GRADE BEAMS OFF	42	72	48	78	30
25	26	1	2	1	BACKFILL + COMPACT OFFICE	48	78	49	79	30
26	27	3	2	5	UNDERSLAB PLUMBING OFFICE	49	79	52	82	30
27	28	3	2	4	UNDERSLAB CONDUIT OFFICE	52	82	55	85	30
28	29	3	2	3	FORM + POUR OFFICE SLAB	55	85	58	88	30
29	30	10	3	6	ERECT STRUCT STEEL P-W	88	88	98	98	0
30	31	5	3	6	PLUMB STEEL AND BOLT P-W	98	98	103	103	0
31	32	5	3	6	ERECT CRANE WAY AND CRANE P-W	103	103	108	108	0
31	33	3	3	6	ERECT MONORAIL TRACK P-W	103	105	106	108	2
32	33	0			DUMMY	108	108	108	108	0
33	34	3	3	6	ERECT BAR JOISTS P-W	108	108	111	111	0
34	35	3	3	6	ERECT ROOF PLANKS P-W	111	111	114	114	0
35	36	10	3	7	ERECT SIDING P-W	114	114	124	124	0
35	37	5	3	7	BUILT UP ROOFING P-W	114	119	119	124	5
36	37	0			DUMMY	124	124	124	124	0
37	38	2	3	4	SET ELECTRICAL LOAD CENTER PW	124	124	126	126	0
37	42	5	3	6	ERECT EXTERIOR DOORS P-W	124	147	129	152	23
37	43	10	3	4	POWER PANEL BACKFILL BOXES P-	124	136	134	146	12
37	39	10	3	7	MASONRY PARTITIONS P-W	124	137	134	147	13
37	46	15	3	5	INSTALL H + V UNITS P-W	124	147	139	162	23
37	40	30	3	5	FABRICATE PIPING P-W	124	157	154	187	33
37	41	25	3	5	ERECT BOILER + AUXILIARY P-W	124	167	149	192	43
37	47	3	3	5	INSTALL FUEL TANK P-W	124	194	127	197	70

Figure 7.3 (*Continued*)

The computer output should be checked for errors. This is quite important since the CPM data are susceptible to error in their transfer from network to data sheet to punched card. Failure to make such a check of the computer output has caused embarrassment more than once. In one instance, the head of a school board received a telegram starting "Good news!" which went on to advise him that his project end date had improved by 3 weeks. This was followed several hours later by a telegram which should have been in red ink (to match the consultant's face). It noted that an error in the run had been overlooked and the project date had really been delayed by 1 week. The computer can be programed to locate many mechanical errors. However, it will not object to a statement that the moon is made of blue cheese, and it cannot pass on the practicality of CPM results. The human factor is indispensable. This, by the way, is an area of advantage for manual computation. While the human

I	J	DUR-ATION			DESCRIPTION	START		FINISH		TOTAL FLOAT
						EAR	LAT	EAR	LAT	
37	58	5	3	7	INSTALL MONORAIL WAREHOUSE	124	197	129	202	73
37	80	10	5	7	PERIMETER FENCE	124	276	134	286	152
37	90	5	5	7	PAVE PARKING AREA	124	197	129	202	73
37	91	5	5	1	GRADE + BALLAST RR SIDING	124	187	129	192	63
37	92	10	5	7	ACCESS ROAD	124	192	134	202	68
37	93	20	5	4	AREA LIGHTING	124	266	144	286	142
38	43	20	3	4	INSTALL POWER CONDUIT P-W	126	126	146	146	0
39	42	5	3	8	FRAME CEILINGS P-W	134	147	139	152	13
40	47	10	3	5	TEST PIPING SYSTEMS P-W	154	187	164	197	33
41	47	5	3	5	PREOPERATIONAL BOILER CHECK	149	192	154	197	43
42	44	10	3	8	DRYWELL PARTITIONS P-W	139	152	149	162	13
43	49	15	3	4	INSTALL BRANCH CONDUIT P-W	146	146	161	161	0
44	45	0			DUMMY	149	186	149	186	37
44	46	0			DUMMY	149	162	149	162	13
44	48	10	3	7	CERAMIC TILE	149	167	159	177	18
44	58	10	3	8	HANG INTERIOR DOORS P-W	149	192	159	202	43
45	51	5	3	4	ROOM OUTLETS P-W	161	186	166	191	25
46	52	25	3	7	INSTALL DUCTWORK P-W	149	162	174	187	13
47	58	5	3	5	LIGHTOFF BOILER AND TEST	164	197	169	202	33
48	53	5	3	7	PAINT ROOMS P-W	159	177	164	182	18
49	45	0			DUMMY	161	186	161	186	25
49	50	15	3	4	PULL WIRE P-W	161	161	176	176	0
50	54	5	3	4	INSTALL PANEL INTERNALS P-W	176	176	181	181	0
51	56	10	3	4	INSTALL ELECTRICAL FIXTURES	166	191	176	201	25
52	58	15	3	7	INSULATE H + V SYSTEM P-W	174	187	189	202	13
53	57	10	3	7	FLOOR TILE P-W	164	182	174	192	18
53	58	10	3	5	INSTALL PLUMBING FIXTURES P-W	164	192	174	202	28

computer may make many small errors, he or she is not likely to miss a big mistake; for instance, in a hand calculation, a loop just cannot slip by—but it takes the computer every time. One quick check that can be made of the computer output is to trace the critical path on the CPM network. To assist in this, a listing of activities in order of *total float* is useful. The critical activities are listed first and then float in ascending order. This listing is also useful for a fast review of the project by management. Figure 7.4 shows the sort by total float for the John Doe project.

Another popular listing is the *early-start* sort. In this, the activities are listed in order of early start (ES) times. It exhibits the activities in the order in which they *could* start. The activities for each date are listed, starting with the critical and low-float activities. Figure 7.5 shows the early-start sort for the John Doe project.

Figure 7.6 shows the John Doe project listed by work category (earth-

I	J	DUR-ATION			DESCRIPTION	START		FINISH		TOTAL FLOAT
						EAR	LAT	EAR	LAT	
54	55	10	3	4	TERMINATE WIRES P-W	181	181	191	191	0
55	56	10	3	4	RINGOUT P-W	191	191	201	201	0
56	58	1	3	4	ENERGIZE POWER	201	201	202	202	0
57	58	10	3	7	INSTALL FURNISHING P-W	174	192	184	202	18
58	59	5	4	6	ERECT PRECAST STRUCT. OFFICE	202	202	207	207	0
58	94	5	5	1	FINE GRADE	202	276	207	281	74
58	80	5	5	7	ERECT FLAGPOLE	202	281	207	286	79
59	60	5	4	6	ERECT PRECAST ROOF OFFICE	207	207	212	212	0
60	61	10	4	7	EXTERIOR MASONRY OFFICE	212	212	222	222	0
60	76	5	4	5	INSTALL PACKAGE AIR CONDITR	212	272	217	277	60
61	62	5	4	8	EXTERIOR DOORS OFFICE	222	236	227	241	14
61	63	5	4	7	BUILT UP ROOFING OFFICE	222	236	227	241	14
61	77	15	4	7	DUCTWORK OFFICE	222	256	237	271	34
61	68	5	4	7	GLAZE OFFICE	222	236	227	241	14
61	64	10	4	5	INSTALL PIPING OFFICE	222	222	232	232	0
61	65	4	4	4	INSTALL ELEC BACKING BOXES	222	222	226	226	0
62	63	0			DUMMY	227	241	227	241	14
63	68	0			DUMMY	227	241	227	241	14
63	80	5	4	7	PAINT OFFICE EXTERIOR	227	281	232	286	54
64	67	4	4	5	TEST PIPING OFFICE	232	232	236	236	0
65	66	10	4	4	INSTALL CONDUIT OFFICE	226	226	236	236	0
66	67	0			DUMMY	236	236	236	236	0
66	74	10	4	4	PULL WIRE OFFICE	236	256	246	266	20
67	68	5	4	7	LATH PARTITIONS OFFICE	236	236	241	241	0
68	69	5	4	7	PLASTER SCRATCH AND BROWN	241	241	246	246	0
69	70	10	4	7	PLASTER WHITE COATS	246	246	256	256	0
69	73	10	4	7	CERAMIC TILE OFFICE	246	271	256	281	25

Figure 7.3 (*Continued*)

work, surveying, concrete, electrical, mechanical, structural and rigging, subcontracts, and carpentry).

These and other sorts can be useful; however, don't get carried away by the capability of generating great amounts of data. This is more likely to alienate field people than to impress them. CPM can function at only half-power if those in the field do not actively participate in the preparation and use of the CPM information. To work effectively with the field people, find out what information they want and the form in which they want it. One field superintendent asked, "Will CPM shorten my scheduling work?" We lunged into the trap with a "yes"; then he noted that it would take him a considerable length of time just to page through the 2-inch stack of paper which was the early-start sort for his project. From his constructive criticism, we began furnishing him only the listing of work for the next two months in both early-start and late-start formats. He was

I	J	DUR-ATION			DESCRIPTION	START		FINISH		TOTAL FLOAT
						EAR	LAT	EAR	LAT	
70	77	0			DUMMY	256	271	256	271	15
70	71	10	4	8	WOOD TRIM OFFICE	256	256	266	266	0
71	72	10	4	7	PAINT INTERIOR OFFICE	266	266	276	276	0
71	80	5	4	8	HANG DOORS OFFICE	266	281	271	286	15
72	80	10	4	7	FLOOR TILE OFFICE	276	276	286	286	0
72	78	0			DUMMY	276	276	276	276	0
72	73	0			DUMMY	276	281	276	281	5
73	80	5	4	5	TOILET FIXTURES OFFICE	276	281	281	286	5
74	76	0			DUMMY	246	277	246	277	31
74	75	5	5	5	INSTALL PANEL INTERNALS OFFICE	246	266	251	271	20
75	79	10	4	4	TERMINATE WIRES OFFICE	251	271	261	281	20
76	79	4	4	4	AIR CONDITIONING ELEC CONNECT	246	277	250	281	31
77	78	5	4	8	INSTALL CEILING GRID OFFICE	256	271	261	276	15
78	80	10	4	7	ACOUSTIC TILE OFFICE	276	276	286	286	0
79	80	5	4	4	RINGOUT ELECT.	261	281	266	286	20
90	58	0			DUMMY	129	202	129	202	73
91	58	10	5	7	INSTALL RR SIDING	129	192	139	202	63
92	58	0			DUMMY	134	202	134	202	68
93	80	0			DUMMY	144	286	144	286	142
94	80	5	5	7	SEED + PLANT	207	281	212	286	74
					E N D					

right. Why did he need CPM information for the next year, when we were furnishing a new computer run once each month? For management, the early-start sort is usually too detailed, and they cannot see the forest for the trees. A sort of critical and near-critical activities is sufficient to give the project status in clear and concise terms.

Another caution about computed CPM information: It will be no better than the network information inputted into it. A soil mechanics professor had a similar caution about soil strength formulas. He advised against formulas integrating, differentiating, and extrapolating field information to the nth degree. His premise was that there is an inherent danger in cloaking rough field data in polished mathematical formulas.

In one refinery application, the field was unresponsive even to the abbreviated early-start sort. One of the plant engineers had an inspiration and, with scissors, cut out the description list (less all the computed activ-

I	J	DUR-ATION			DESCRIPTION	START		FINISH		TOTAL FLOAT
						EAR	LAT	EAR	LAT	
0	1	3	1	1	CLEAR SITE			3	3	0
1	2	2	1	2	SURVEY AND LAYOUT	3	3	5	5	0
2	3	2	1	1	ROUGH GRADE	5	5	7	7	0
3	4	15	1	7	DRILL WELL	7	7	22	22	0
4	5	2	1	5	INSTALL WELL PUMP	22	22	24	24	0
5	8	8	1	5	UNDERGROUND WATER PIPING	24	24	32	32	0
8	13	2	1	5	CONNECT WATER PIPING	32	32	34	34	0
13	14	1	2	2	BUILDING LAYOUT	34	34	35	35	0
14	15	10	2	7	DRIVE AND POUR PILES	35	35	45	45	0
15	16	5	2	1	EXCAVATE FOR PLANT WAREHOUSE	45	45	50	50	0
16	17	5	2	3	POUR PILE CAPS PLANT-WAREHSE	50	50	55	55	0
17	18	10	2	3	FORM + POUR GRADE BEAMS P-W	55	55	65	65	0
18	19	3	2	1	BACKFILL AND COMPACT P-W	65	65	68	68	0
19	20	5	2	5	UNDERSLAB PLUMBING P-W	68	68	73	73	0
20	22	5	2	4	UNDERSLAB CONDUIT P-W	73	73	78	78	0
22	29	10	2	3	FORM + POUR SLABS P-W	78	78	88	88	0
29	30	10	3	6	ERECT STRUCT STEEL P-W	88	88	98	98	0
30	31	5	3	6	PLUMB STEEL AND BOLT P-W	98	98	103	103	0
31	32	5	3	6	ERECT CRANE WAY AND CRANE P-W	103	103	108	108	0
32	33	0			DUMMY	108	108	108	108	0
33	34	3	3	6	ERECT BAR JOISTS P-W	108	108	111	111	0
34	35	3	3	6	ERECT ROOF PLANKS P-W	111	111	114	114	0
35	36	10	3	7	ERECT SIDING P-W	114	114	124	124	0
36	37	0			DUMMY	124	124	124	124	0
37	38	2	3	4	SET ELECTRICAL LOAD CENTER PW	124	124	126	126	0
38	43	20	3	4	INSTALL POWER CONDUIT P-W	126	126	146	146	0
43	49	15	3	4	INSTALL BRANCH CONDUIT P-W	146	146	161	161	0

Figure 7.4   John Doe output, total-float sort (partial).

ity times and i-j numbers). When the output was reduced to a plain list, the field people were willing to work with it.

There is often a psychological barrier to anything associated with a computer. In some cases, this is justified. Several computer types have come up with their own version of breakthroughs in network analysis. For instance, at least three different computer-oriented groups have advocated methods of generating a computer output similar to CPM without drawing a diagram. Such a computed result is naturally suspect. First, if those in the field have strong reservations about the computed results of an arrow diagram, how then would they react to a computed schedule not based upon a diagram or their tangible plan? Second, if the CPM computation must be carefully checked for errors, what can the diagramless computer output be checked against?

I	J	DUR-ATION			DESCRIPTION	START		FINISH		TOTAL FLOAT
						EAR	LAT	EAR	LAT	
49	50	15	3	4	PULL WIRE P-W	161	161	176	176	0
50	54	5	3	4	INSTALL PANEL INTERNALS P-W	176	176	181	181	0
54	55	10	3	4	TERMINATE WIRES P-W	181	181	191	191	0
55	56	10	3	4	RINGOUT P-W	191	191	201	201	0
56	58	1	3	4	ENERGIZE POWER	201	201	202	202	0
58	59	5	4	6	ERECT PRECAST STRUCT. OFFICE	202	202	207	207	0
59	60	5	4	6	ERECT PRECAST ROOF OFFICE	207	207	212	212	0
60	61	10	4	7	EXTERIOR MASONRY OFFICE	212	212	222	222	0
61	64	10	4	5	INSTALL PIPING OFFICE	222	222	232	232	0
61	65	4	4	4	INSTALL ELEC BACKING BOXES	222	222	226	226	0
64	67	4	4	5	TEST PIPING OFFICE	232	232	236	236	0
65	66	10	4	4	INSTALL CONDUIT OFFICE	226	226	236	236	0
66	67	0			DUMMY	236	236	236	236	0
67	68	5	4	7	LATH PARTITIONS OFFICE	236	236	241	241	0
68	69	5	4	7	PLASTER SCRATCH AND BROWN	241	241	246	246	0
69	70	10	4	7	PLASTER WHITE COATS	246	246	256	256	0
70	71	10	4	8	WOOD TRIM OFFICE	256	256	266	266	0
71	72	10	4	7	PAINT INTERIOR OFFICE	266	266	276	276	0
72	80	10	4	7	FLOOR TILE OFFICE	276	276	286	286	0
72	78	0			DUMMY	276	276	276	276	0
78	80	10	4	7	ACOUSTIC TILE OFFICE	276	276	286	286	0
3	6	4	1	3	WATER TANK FOUNDATIONS	7	8	11	12	1
6	7	10	1	6	ERECT WATER TOWER	11	12	21	22	1
7	8	10	1	5	TANK PIPING AND VALVES	21	22	31	32	1
31	33	3	3	6	ERECT MONORAIL TRACK P-W	103	105	106	108	2
3	9	10	1	1	EXCAVATE FOR SEWER	7	11	17	21	4
9	11	5	1	5	INSTALL SEWER AND BACKFILL	17	21	22	26	4

It is possible to generate an output without a diagram to support it. As an expedient in high-rise work, we have prepared the basic CPM plan for one floor and then regenerated it to suit the total number of similar floors. The same method was effective in a dormitory renovation with eight similar wings. However, in both cases, we prepared a finished CPM diagram to support these computations.

Proponents of diagramless schedules see the arrow-diagram preparation as drudgery. Granted that an effort must be put forth to prepare the diagram; but the value of doing so far outweighs the effort. The diagram offers a graphical representation of the planners' thoughts. What do the proponents of these computerized techniques offer in place of this graphical view of the project? In preparing the computer input, the preceding and succeeding activities for each activity must be specified. This means

I	J	DUR-ATION			DESCRIPTION	START		FINISH		TOTAL FLOAT
						EAR	LAT	EAR	LAT	
11	12	3	1	4	ELECTRICAL DUCT BANK	22	26	25	29	4
12	13	5	1	4	PULL IN POWER FEEDER	25	29	30	34	4
35	37	5	3	7	BUILT UP ROOFING P-W	114	119	119	124	5
72	73	0			DUMMY	276	281	276	281	5
73	80	5	4	5	TOILET FIXTURES OFFICE	276	281	281	286	5
18	21	5	2	3	FORM + POUR RR LOAD DOCK P-W	65	73	70	78	8
18	22	5	2	3	FORM + POUR TK LOAD DOCK P-W	65	73	70	78	8
21	22	0			DUMMY	70	78	70	78	8
37	43	10	3	4	POWER PANEL BACKFILL BOXES P-	124	136	134	146	12
3	10	1	1	1	EXCAVATE ELECTRICAL MANHOLES	7	20	8	21	13
10	11	5	1	4	INSTALL ELECTRICAL MANHOLES	8	21	13	26	13
37	39	10	3	7	MASONRY PARTITIONS P-W	124	137	134	147	13
39	42	5	3	8	FRAME CEILINGS P-W	134	147	139	152	13
42	44	10	3	8	DRYWALL PARTITIONS P-W	139	152	149	162	13
44	46	0			DUMMY	149	162	149	162	13
46	52	25	3	7	INSTALL DUCTWORK P-W	149	162	174	187	13
52	58	15	3	7	INSULATE H + V SYSTEM P-W	174	187	189	202	13
61	62	5	4	8	EXTERIOR DOORS OFFICE	222	236	227	241	14
61	63	5	4	7	BUILT UP ROOFING OFFICE	222	236	227	241	14
61	68	5	4	7	GLAZE OFFICE	222	236	227	241	14
62	63	0			DUMMY	227	241	227	241	14
63	68	0			DUMMY	227	241	227	241	14
70	77	0			DUMMY	256	271	256	271	15
71	80	5	4	8	HANG DOORS OFFICE	266	281	271	286	15
77	78	5	4	8	INSTALL CEILING GRID OFFICE	256	271	261	276	15
3	12	6	1	4	OVERHEAD POLE LINE	7	23	13	29	16
44	48	10	3	7	CERAMIC TILE	149	167	159	177	18

Figure 7.4 (*Continued*)

that the planner must mentally visualize an arrow diagram without the aid of paper and pencil and without the benefits of the record furnished by the diagram. The planner is also likely to miss many of the subtle connections which the arrow diagram brings to light. While such efforts to do without diagrams are sincere and apparently offer useful results to those who advocate them, they would appear to have limited application.

An extension of the diagramless computer output is the generation of a diagram by a computer based upon the CPM output. This innovation is discussed in a later chapter.

COMPUTER FACILITIES

If you own or lease a computer which can handle CPM, your computation situation presents no problem. If you do not, however, what do you do if you want to machine-compute a CPM network? There are a number of possibilities. First, you might consider renting time at a computer service center, preferably one experienced in CPM computation. Rates are based upon the running time for the networks, usually at a cost of $50 to $150 per calculation on-line hour. In selecting a service center, the following considerations are pertinent:

1. Its experience in CPM

2. The capability of the programs it has available, including those for error check

3. The cost per 1000 activities it charges

4. Its proximity to your own location

5. The number and variety of sorts it includes in the base cost

I	J	DUR-ATION	CONTRACT	WORK CATEGORY	DESCRIPTION	START		FINISH		TOTAL FLOAT
						EAR	LAT	EAR	LAT	
13	14	1	2	2	BUILDING LAYOUT	34	34	35	35	0
3	6	4	1	3	WATER TANK FOUNDATIONS	7	8	11	12	1
16	17	5	2	3	POUR PILE CAPS PLANT-WAREHSE	50	50	55	55	0
17	18	10	2	3	FORM + POUR GRADE BEAMS P-W	55	55	65	65	0
18	21	5	2	3	FORM + POUR RR LOAD DOCK P-W	65	73	70	78	8
18	22	5	2	3	FORM + POUR TK LOAD DOCK P-W	65	73	70	78	8
22	29	10	2	3	FORM + POUR SLABS P-W	78	78	88	88	0
23	24	4	2	3	SPREAD FOOTINGS OFFICE	38	68	42	72	30
24	25	6	2	3	FORM + POUR GRADE BEAMS OFF	42	72	48	78	30
28	29	3	2	3	FORM + POUR OFFICE SLAB	55	85	58	88	30
3	12	6	1	4	OVERHEAD POLE LINE	7	23	13	29	16
10	11	5	1	4	INSTALL ELECTRICAL MANHOLES	8	21	13	26	13
11	12	3	1	4	ELECTRICAL DUCT BANK	22	26	25	29	4
12	13	5	1	4	PULL IN POWER FEEDER	25	29	30	34	4
20	22	5	2	4	UNDERSLAB CONDUIT P-W	73	73	78	78	0
27	28	3	2	4	UNDERSLAB CONDUIT OFFICE	52	82	55	85	30
37	38	2	3	4	SET ELECTRICAL LOAD CENTER PW	124	124	126	126	0
37	43	10	3	4	POWER PANEL BACKFILL BOXES P-	124	136	134	146	12
37	93	20	5	4	AREA LIGHTING	124	266	144	286	142
38	43	20	3	4	INSTALL POWER CONDUIT P-W	126	126	146	146	0
43	49	15	3	4	INSTALL BRANCH CONDUIT P-W	146	146	161	161	0
45	51	5	3	4	ROOM OUTLETS P-W	161	186	166	191	25
49	50	15	3	4	PULL WIRE P-W	161	161	176	176	0
50	54	5	3	4	INSTALL PANEL INTERNALS P-W	176	176	181	181	0
51	56	10	3	4	INSTALL ELECTRICAL FIXTURES	166	191	176	201	25
54	55	10	3	4	TERMINATE WIRES P-W	181	181	191	191	0
55	56	10	3	4	RINGOUT P-W	191	191	201	201	0

Figure 7.5 John Doe output, early-start sort (partial).

I	J	DUT-ATION	CONTRACT	WORK CATEGORY	DESCRIPTION	START		FINISH		TOTAL FLOAT
						EAR	LAT	EAR	LAT	
56	58	1	3	4	ENERGIZE POWER	201	201	202	202	0
61	65	4	4	4	INSTALL ELEC BACKING BOXES	222	222	226	226	0
65	66	10	4	4	INSTALL CONDUIT OFFICE	226	226	236	236	0
66	74	10	4	4	PULL WIRE OFFICE	236	256	246	266	20
75	79	10	4	4	TERMINATE WIRES OFFICE	251	271	261	281	20
76	79	4	4	4	AIR CONDITIONING ELEC CONNECT	246	277	250	281	31
79	80	5	4	4	RINGOUT ELECT.	261	281	266	286	20
4	5	2	1	5	INSTALL WELL PUMP	22	22	24	24	0
5	8	8	1	5	UNDERGROUND WATER PIPING	24	24	32	32	0
7	8	10	1	5	TANK PIPING AND VALVES	21	22	31	32	1
8	13	2	1	5	CONNECT WATER PIPING	32	32	34	34	0
9	11	5	1	5	INSTALL SEWER AND BACKFILL	17	21	22	26	4
19	20	5	2	5	UNDERSLAB PLUMBING P-W	68	68	73	73	0
26	27	3	2	5	UNDERSLAB PLUMBING OFFICE	49	79	52	82	30
37	46	15	3	5	INSTALL H + V UNITS P-W	124	147	139	162	23
37	40	30	3	5	FABRICATE PIPING P-W	124	157	154	187	33
37	41	25	3	5	ERECT BOILER + AUXILIARY P-W	124	167	149	192	43
37	47	3	3	5	INSTALL FUEL TANK P-W	124	194	127	197	70
40	47	10	3	5	TEST PIPING SYSTEMS P-W	154	187	164	197	33
41	47	5	3	5	PREOPERATIONAL BOILER CHECK	149	192	154	197	43
47	58	5	3	5	LIGHTOFF BOILER AND TEST	164	197	169	202	33
53	58	10	3	5	INSTALL PLUMBING FIXTURES P-W	164	192	174	202	28
60	76	5	4	5	INSTALL PACKAGE AIR CONDITR	212	272	217	277	60
61	64	10	4	5	INSTALL PIPING OFFICE	222	222	232	232	0
64	67	4	4	5	TEST PIPING OFFICE	232	232	236	236	0
73	80	5	4	5	TOILET FIXTURES OFFICE	276	281	281	286	5
74	75	5	5	5	INSTALL PANEL INTERNALS OFFICE	246	266	251	271	20

Figure 7.6   John Doe output by work category (partial).

Another economical procedure is to rent time from a computer owner. This is often at nominal cost, but suitable programs and experienced personnel are usually a problem here.

You might consider leasing your own machine. A caution is in order: When you get your computer you have to keep it occupied—and it's a busy beaver.

CALENDAR DATES

The listings shown thus far in this chapter have been in terms of project days. Is a project calendar necessary to utilize computer outputs? No, the computer, in a relatively easy step, can calendar-date the output. Figure 7.7 shows part of the i-j listing with calendar dates rather than project

I	J	DUR-ATION	CONTRACT	WORK CATEGORY	DESCRIPTION	START EAR	START LAT	FINISH EAR	FINISH LAT	TOTAL FLOAT
0	1	3	1	1	CLEAR SITE			3	3	0
11	2	2	1	2	SURVEY AND LAYOUT	3	3	5	5	0
2	3	2	1	1	ROUGH GRADE	5	5	7	7	0
3	4	15	1	7	DRILL WELL	7	7	22	22	0
3	6	4	1	3	WATER TANK FOUNDATIONS	7	8	11	12	1
3	9	10	1	1	EXCAVATE FOR SEWER	7	11	17	21	4
3	10	1	1	1	EXCAVATE ELECTRICAL MANHOLES	7	20	8	21	13
3	12	6	1	4	OVERHEAD POLE LINE	7	23	13	29	16
10	11	5	1	4	INSTALL ELECTRICAL MANHOLES	8	21	13	26	13
6	7	10	1	6	ERECT WATER TOWER	11	12	21	22	1
9	11	5	1	5	INSTALL SEWER AND BACKFILL	17	21	22	26	4
7	8	10	1	5	TANK PIPING AND VALVES	21	22	31	32	1
4	5	2	1	5	INSTALL WELL PUMP	22	22	24	24	0
11	12	3	1	4	ELECTRICAL DUCT BANK	22	26	25	29	4
5	8	8	1	5	UNDERGROUND WATER PIPING	24	24	32	32	0
12	13	5	1	4	PULL IN POWER FEEDER	25	29	30	34	4
8	13	2	1	5	CONNECT WATER PIPING	32	32	34	34	0
13	14	1	2	2	BUILDING LAYOUT	34	34	35	35	0
14	15	10	2	7	DRIVE AND POUR PILES	35	35	45	45	0
14	23	3	2	1	EXCAVATE FOR OFFICE BUILDING	35	65	38	68	30
23	24	4	2	3	SPREAD FOOTINGS OFFICE	38	68	42	72	30
24	25	6	2	3	FORM + POUR GRADE BEAMS OFF	42	72	48	78	30
15	16	5	2	1	EXCAVATE FOR PLANT WAREHOUSE	45	45	50	50	0
25	26	1	2	1	BACKFILL + COMPACT OFFICE	48	78	49	79	30
26	27	3	2	5	UNDERSLAB PLUMBING OFFICE	49	79	52	82	30
16	17	5	2	3	POUR PILE CAPS PLANT-WAREHSE	50	50	55	55	0
27	28	3	2	4	UNDERSLAB CONDUIT OFFICE	52	82	55	85	30

days. In Chapter 6 it took two moves to find the ES and LF dates (July 31 and August 4) for activity 4-5. In Figure 7.7 we find this in one move. [Note that the computer-generated date is August 3, since this program (MSCS) assumes the start date to be in the a.m. after the calculated p.m. date.]

Figure 7.8 shows a computer-generated universal calendar which is similar in concept to the John Doe calendar shown in Figure 6.5. It can be generated on a 5-day-per-week, 6-day-per-week, or 7-day-per-week basis, with or without holidays.

To use this to determine project days between two dates, enter the table at each date, and subtract the reference numbers to get net project days. Conversely, the table can be entered at any date and calendar days can be added (or subtracted) to identify a date separated from another date by a set number of days.

NETWORK REPORT /02
SORT BY I NODE/J NODE

JOHN DOE BASELINE CPM SCHEDULE
PREPARED BY O'BRIEN-KREITZBERG & ASSOC., INC.

DATA DATE 01JUL87
PAGE 1

I NODE	J NODE	ACTIVITY DESCRIPTION	ORG DUR	REM DUR	CNTR TYPE	WORK CAT.	SPEC SEC.	EARLY START	EARLY *FINISH	LATE START	LATE *FINISH	TOTAL FLOAT
00	01	CLEAR SITE	3.0	3.0	GC	1-1	0210	01JUL87	06JUL87	01JUL87	06JUL87	0.0
01	02	SURVEY AND LAYOUT	2.0	2.0	GC	1-2	0140	07JUL87	08JUL87	07JUL87	08JUL87	0.0
02	03	ROUGH GRADE	2.0	2.0	GC	1-1	0220	09JUL87	10JUL87	09JUL87	10JUL87	0.0
03	04	DRILL WELL	15.0	15.0	GC	1-7	0201	13JUL87	31JUL87	13JUL87	31JUL87	0.0
03	06	WATER TANK FOUNDATIONS	4.0	4.0	GC	1-3	0330	13JUL87	16JUL87	14JUL87	17JUL87	1.0
03	09	EXCAVATE FOR SEWER	10.0	10.0	GC	1-1	0250	13JUL87	24JUL87	17JUL87	30JUL87	4.0
03	10	EXCAVATE ELECTRICL MANHOLES	1.0	1.0	GC	1-1	0250	13JUL87	13JUL87	30JUL87	30JUL87	13.0
03	12	OVERHEAD POLE LINE	6.0	6.0	GC	1-4	0250	13JUL87	20JUL87	04AUG87	11AUG87	16.0
04	05	INSTALL WELL PUMP	2.0	2.0	PR	1-5	0250	03AUG87	04AUG87	03AUG87	04AUG87	0.0
05	08	UNDERGROUND WATER PIPING	8.0	8.0	PR	1-5	0250	05AUG87	14AUG87	05AUG87	14AUG87	0.0
06	07	ERECT WATER TOWER	10.0	10.0	PR	1-6	0250	17JUL87	30JUL87	20JUL87	31JUL87	1.0
07	08	TANK PIPING AND VALVES	10.0	10.0	PR	1-5	0250	31JUL87	13AUG87	03AUG87	14AUG87	1.0
08	13	CONNECT WATER PIPING	2.0	2.0	PB	1-5	0250	17AUG87	18AUG87	17AUG87	18AUG87	0.0
09	11	INSTALL SEWER AND BACKFILL	5.0	5.0	PB	1-5	0250	27JUL87	31JUL87	31JUL87	06AUG87	4.0
10	11	INSTALL ELECTRICAL MANHOLES	5.0	5.0	EL	1-4	0250	14JUL87	20JUL87	31JUL87	06AUG87	13.0
11	12	INST ELEC DUCTBANK	3.0	3.0	EL	1-4	0250	03AUG87	05AUG87	07AUG87	11AUG87	4.0
12	13	PULL IN POWER FEEDER	5.0	5.0	EL	1-4	0250	06AUG87	12AUG87	12AUG87	18AUG87	4.0
13	14	BUILDING LAYOUT	1.0	1.0	GC	2-2	0140	19AUG87	19AUG87	19AUG87	19AUG87	0.0
14	15	DRIVE AND POUR PILES	10.0	10.0	GC	2-7	0230	20AUG87	02SEP87	20AUG87	02SEP87	0.0
14	23	EXCAVATE FOR OFFICE BUILDNG	3.0	3.0	GC	2-1	0220	20AUG87	24AUG87	02OCT87	06OCT87	30.0
15	16	EXCAVATE FOR PLANT WHSE	5.0	5.0	GC	2-1	0220	03SEP87	10SEP87	03SEP87	10SEP87	0.0
16	17	POUR PILES CAPS PLANT WHSE	5.0	5.0	GC	2-3	0230	11SEP87	17SEP87	11SEP87	17SEP87	0.0
17	18	FORM+POUR GRADE BEAMS P-W	10.0	10.0	GC	2-3	0330	18SEP87	01OCT87	18SEP87	01OCT87	0.0

NETWORK REPORT   /02
SORT BY I NODE/J NODE

JOHN DOE BASELINE CPM SCHEDULE
PREPARED BY O'BRIEN-KREITZBERG & ASSOC., INC.

DATA DATE   PAGE   2
               01JUL87

I NODE	J NODE	ACTIVITY DESCRIPTION	ORG DUR	REM DUR	CNTR TYPE	WORK CAT.	SPEC SEC.	EARLY START	EARLY *FINISH	LATE START	LATE *FINISH	TOTAL FLOAT
18	19	BACKFILL AND COMPACT P-W	3.0	3.0	GC	2-1	0220	02OCT87	06OCT87	02OCT87	06OCT87	0.0
18	21	FORM+POUR RR LOAD DOCK P-W	5.0	5.0	GC	2-3	0330	02OCT87	08OCT87	14OCT87	20OCT87	8.0
18	22	FORM+POUR TK LOAD DOCK P-W	5.0	5.0	GC	2-3	0330	02OCT87	08OCT87	14OCT87	20OCT87	8.0
19	20	UNDERSLAB PLUMBING P-W	5.0	5.0	PB	2-5	1540	07OCT87	13OCT87	07OCT87	13OCT87	0.0
20	22	UNDERSLAB CONDUIT P-W	5.0	5.0	EL	2-4	1640	14OCT87	20OCT87	14OCT87	20OCT87	0.0
21	22	RESTRAINT	0.0	0.0		-		09OCT87	09OCT87	21OCT87	21OCT87	8.0
22	29	FORM+POUR SLABS P-W	10.0	10.0	GC	2-3	0330	21OCT87	03NOV87	21OCT87	03NOV87	0.0
23	24	SPREAD FOOTINGS OFFICE	4.0	4.0	GC	2-3	0330	25AUG87	28AUG87	07OCT87	12OCT87	30.0
24	25	FORM+POUR GRADE BEAMS OFF	6.0	6.0	GC	2-3	0330	31AUG87	08SEP87	13OCT87	20OCT87	30.0
25	26	BACKFILL+COMPACT OFFICE	1.0	1.0	GC	2-1	0220	09SEP87	09SEP87	21OCT87	21OCT87	30.0
26	27	UNDERSLAB PLUMBING OFFICE	3.0	3.0	PB	2-5	1540	10SEP87	14SEP87	22OCT87	26OCT87	30.0
27	28	UNDERSLAB CONDUIT OFFICE	3.0	3.0	EL	2-4	1640	15SEP87	17SEP87	27OCT87	29OCT87	30.0
28	29	FORM+POUR OFFICE SLAB	3.0	3.0	GC	2-3	0330	18SEP87	22SEP87	30OCT87	03NOV87	30.0
29	30	ERECT STRUCT STEEL P-W	10.0	10.0	GC	3-6	0510	04NOV87	18NOV87	04NOV87	18NOV87	0.0
30	31	PLUMB STEEL AND BOLT P-W	5.0	5.0	GC	3-6	0510	19NOV87	25NOV87	19NOV87	25NOV87	0.0
31	32	ERECT CRANE WAY AND CRN P-W	5.0	5.0	GC	3-6	1430	27NOV87	03DEC87	27NOV87	03DEC87	0.0
31	33	ERECT MONORAIL TRACK P-W	3.0	3.0	GC	3-6	1430	27NOV87	01DEC87	01DEC87	03DEC87	2.0
32	33	RESTRAINT	0.0	0.0		-		04DEC87	04DEC87	04DEC87	04DEC87	0.0
33	34	ERECT BAR JOISTS P-W	3.0	3.0	GC	3-6	0520	04DEC87	08DEC87	04DEC87	08DEC87	0.0
34	35	ERECT ROOF PLANKS P-W	3.0	3.0	GC	3-6	0340	09DEC87	11DEC87	09DEC87	11DEC87	0.0
35	36	ERECT SIDING P-W	10.0	10.0	GC	3-7	0740	14DEC87	28DEC87	14DEC87	28DEC87	0.0
35	37	BUILT UP ROOFING P-W	5.0	5.0	GC	3-7	0750	14DEC87	18DEC87	21DEC87	28DEC87	5.0
36	37	RESTRAINT	0.0	0.0		-		29DEC87	29DEC87	29DEC87	29DEC87	0.0

Figure 7.7 *i-j* listing with calendar dates (partial).

JOHN DOE CPM CALENDAR-5 DAY WORK WEEK! 8 HOLIDAYS-NEW YEAR'S,
PRESIDENTS,MEMORIAL,INDEPENDENCE,LABOR,VETERANS,THANKSGIVING,CHRISTMAS

DATES FOUND IN ( ) NON-WORK UNITS
WORK UNITS DISPLACED FROM 07/01/87

WU— 1	2	*	*	*	3	4	5	6	7
DATE- 07/01/87	07/02/87	(07/03/87)	(07/04/87)	(07/05/87)	07/06/87	07/07/87	07/08/87	07/09/87	07/10/87
FCU— 1	2	3	4	5	6	7	8	9	10

WU— *	*	8	9	10	11	12	*	*	13
DATE- (07/11/87)	(07/12/87)	07/13/87	07/14/87	07/15/87	07/16/87	07/17/87	(07/18/87)	(07/19/87)	07/20/87
FCU— 11	12	13	14	15	16	17	18	19	20

WU— 14	15	16	17	*	*	18	19	20	21
DATE- 07/21/87	07/22/87	07/23/87	07/24/87	(07/25/87)	(07/26/87)	07/27/87	07/28/87	07/29/87	07/30/87
FCU— 21	22	23	24	25	26	27	28	29	30

WU— 22	*	*	23	24	25	26	27	*	*
DATE- 07/31/87	(08/01/87)	(08/02/87)	08/03/87	08/04/87	08/05/87	08/06/87	08/07/87	(08/08/87)	(08/09/87)
FCU— 31	32	33	34	35	36	37	38	39	40

WU— 28	29	30	31	32	*	*	33	34	35
DATE- 08/10/87	08/11/87	08/12/87	08/13/87	08/14/87	(08/15/87)	(08/16/87)	08/17/87	08/18/87	08/19/87
FCU— 41	42	43	44	45	46	47	48	49	50

WU— 36	37	*	*	38	39	40	41	42	*
DATE- 08/20/87	08/21/87	(08/22/87)	(08/23/87)	08/24/87	08/25/87	08/26/87	08/27/87	08/28/87	(08/29/87)
FCU— 51	52	53	54	55	56	57	58	59	60

WU— *	43	44	45	46	47	*	*	*	48
DATE- (08/30/87)	08/31/87	09/01/87	09/02/87	09/03/87	09/04/87	(09/05/87)	(09/06/87)	(09/07/87)	09/08/87
FCU— 61	62	63	64	65	66	67	68	69	70

WU— 49	50	51	*	*	52	53	54	55	56
DATE- 09/09/87	09/10/87	09/11/87	(09/12/87)	(09/13/87)	09/14/87	09/15/87	09/16/87	09/17/87	09/18/87
FCU— 71	72	73	74	75	76	77	78	79	80

WU— *	*	57	58	59	60	61	*	*	62
DATE- (09/19/87)	(09/20/87)	09/21/87	09/22/87	09/23/87	09/24/87	09/25/87	(09/26/87)	(09/27/87)	09/28/87
FCU— 81	82	83	84	85	86	87	88	89	90

WU— 63	64	65	66	*	*	67	68	69	70
DATE- 09/29/87	09/30/87	10/01/87	10/02/87	(10/03/87)	(10/04/87)	10/05/87	10/06/87	10/07/87	10/08/87
FCU— 91	92	93	94	95	96	97	98	99	100

WU— 71	*	*	72	73	74	75	76	*	*
DATE- 10/09/87	(10/10/87)	(10/11/87)	10/12/87	10/13/87	10/14/87	10/15/87	10/16/87	(10/17/87)	(10/18/87)
FCU— 101	102	103	104	105	106	107	108	109	110

WU— 77	78	79	80	81	*	*	82	83	84
DATE- 10/19/87	10/20/87	10/21/87	10/22/87	10/23/87	(10/24/87)	(10/25/87)	10/26/87	10/27/87	10/28/87
FCU— 111	112	113	114	115	116	117	118	119	120

JOHN DOE CPM CALENDAR-5 DAY WORK WEEK1 8 HOLIDAYS-NEW YEAR'S,
PRESIDENTS,MEMORIAL,INDEPENDENCE,LABOR,VETERANS,THANKSGIVING,CHRISTMAS

DATA DATE 07/01/87

DATES FOUND IN ( ) NON-WORK UNITS
WORK UNITS DISPLACED FROM 07/01/87

WU---	85	86	*	*	87	88	89	90	91	*
DATE-	10/29/87	10/30/87	(10/31/87)	(11/01/87)	11/02/87	11/03/87	11/04/87	11/05/87	11/06/87	(11/07/87)
FCU--	121	122	123	124	125	126	127	128	129	130

WU---	*	92	93	*	94	95	*	96	97
DATE-	(11/08/87)	11/09/87	11/10/87	(11/11/87)	11/12/87	11/13/87	(11/14/87)	11/16/87	11/17/87
FCU--	131	132	133	134	135	136	137	138	139	140

WU---	98	99	100	*	*	101	102	103	*	104
DATE-	11/18/87	11/19/87	11/20/87	(11/21/87)	(11/22/87)	11/23/87	11/24/87	11/25/87	(11/26/87)	11/27/87
FCU--	141	142	143	144	145	146	147	148	149	150

WU---	*	*	105	106	107	108	109	*	*	110
DATE-	(11/28/87)	(11/29/87)	11/30/87	12/01/87	12/02/87	12/03/87	12/04/87	(12/05/87)	(12/06/87)	12/07/87
FCU--	151	152	153	154	155	156	157	158	159	160

WU---	111	112	113	114	*	*	115	116	117	118
DATE-	12/08/87	12/09/87	12/10/87	12/11/87	(12/12/87)	(12/13/87)	12/14/87	12/15/87	12/16/87	12/17/87
FCU--	161	162	163	164	165	166	167	168	169	170

WU---	119	*	*	120	121	122	123	*	*	*
DATE-	12/18/87	(12/19/87)	(12/20/87)	12/21/87	12/22/87	12/23/87	12/24/87	(12/25/87)	(12/26/87)	(12/27/87)
FCU--	171	172	173	174	175	176	177	178	179	180

WU---	124	125	126	127	*	*	*	128	129	130
DATE-	12/28/87	12/29/87	12/30/87	12/31/87	(01/01/88)	(01/02/88)	(01/03/88)	01/04/88	01/05/88	01/06/88
FCU--	181	182	183	184	185	186	187	188	189	190

WU---	131	132	*	*	133	134	135	136	137	*
DATE-	01/07/88	01/08/88	(01/09/88)	(01/10/88)	01/11/88	01/12/88	01/13/88	01/14/88	01/15/88	(01/16/88)
FCU--	191	192	193	194	195	196	197	198	199	200

WU---	*	138	139	140	141	142	*	*	143	144
DATE-	(01/17/88)	01/18/88	01/19/88	01/20/88	01/21/88	01/22/88	(01/23/88)	(01/24/88)	01/25/88	01/26/88
FCU--	201	202	203	204	205	206	207	208	209	210

WU---	145	146	147	*	*	148	149	150	151	152
DATE-	01/27/88	01/28/88	01/29/88	(01/30/88)	(01/31/88)	02/01/88	02/02/88	02/03/88	02/04/88	02/05/88
FCU--	211	212	213	214	215	216	217	218	219	220

WU---	*	*	153	154	155	156	157	*	*	*
DATE-	(02/06/88)	(02/07/88)	02/08/88	02/09/88	02/10/88	02/11/88	02/12/88	(02/13/88)	(02/14/88)	(02/15/88)
FCU--	221	222	223	224	225	226	227	228	229	230

WU---	158	159	160	161	*	*	162	163	164	165
DATE-	02/16/88	02/17/88	02/18/88	02/19/88	(02/20/88)	(02/21/88)	02/22/88	02/23/88	02/24/88	02/25/88
FCU--	231	232	233	234	235	236	237	238	239	240

Figure 7.8 Computer-generated universal calendar.

The project calendar may also be generated day for day (i.e., 365 days per year, or 366 in a leap year). The result will schedule work on holidays and weekends. While seemingly illogical, this calendar is useful for contracts where schedules (and extensions thereto) are expressed in calendar days.

SUMMARY

This chapter discussed the specific use of digital computers in computing the CPM network. The first step is the preparation of data sheets which arrange the activity information (*i-j*, duration, and description) in the proper columns for the key-punch operator. Next, information is punched on cards or keyed onto tape or a disk. The input is then checked in a verifier to reduce the chance of error. A variety of computer hardware and programs for CPM is available. The cost of running your network is one method of selecting the combination of computer and program to use.

The first step in computing the CPM network is to read in the program. The first phase of the program is the error check, which reviews the input for open events, duplicate activities, and loops. Of these, loops are the most difficult to locate. When the input has been reviewed for mechanical errors (and any errors have been corrected), the computer computes the event times and activity times. The time of computation varies with the complexity and length of the network as well as with the type of computer being used. For a small (fifty-activity) network, the running time might be a few seconds. For the average network (500 to 2000 activities) the running time is from a few minutes to half an hour.

The computer outputs its answers onto punched cards, a tape, a disk, or onto a typewritten or printed list. These can be sorted in various orders. The popular listings are *i-j*, early start, late start, total float, and special codes. The original computer output should be checked before special sorts and edits are made because the computer can only pick up mechanical errors. Tracing the critical path is a first check.

The quality of CPM output can be no better than that of what is input. Put more directly, "garbage in, garbage out."

PREPARATION OF
CPM NETWORK

Consider the use of CPM in an actual project: What size should a project be to be arrow-diagramed? A project of what dollar value and type is suitable for CPM treatment? When do you apply CPM to the project? How do you collect the information? How long does it take to prepare the CPM network? How do you prepare a network? What level of detail do you use?

APPLICABLE PROJECTS

The size of projects suitable to be diagramed is a matter of broad discretion. Arrow diagrams are obviously useful for huge projects such as the TVA's Bull Run Dam, which cost in excess of $165 million and required a network of over 12,000 arrows. More recently, two areas of the King Khalid Military City (KKMC), costing more than $200 million, had a network of more than 25,000 items.

At the opposite end of the size range, a very useful diagram was prepared to define the twenty-four separate reviews and approvals required by the State of Pennsylvania prior to the commencement of a public school design. The subject, size, and approach of a CPM analysis are limited only by the ingenuity of the user; the average diagram size is gradually increasing. Most of today's diagrams contain between 1000 and 3000 activities.

The dollar size of the project can also be a guide in determining which projects should be diagramed. In projects valued above $5 million, arrow-diagram planning is usually a must. Of course, there are exceptions to every rule. For instance, on large-volume earth-moving projects, network analysis may not be necessary. In some projects valued in the $500,000 to $1 million range, networks are useful. The primary considerations are the complexity of the project and the degree of coordination required to implement it.

While many projects may not appear to be amenable to network analysis, the use of CPM often defines planning factors which were previously vague and unidentified—and sometimes incorrect. The areas of application increase in direct proportion to the experience of the applier.

TIME OF APPLICATION (CONSTRUCTION PROJECTS)

A project should always be analyzed immediately after the award of the construction contract. This is an appropriate initiation point because it is the first time at which the successful contractor has been identified. But even though the contractor's contribution to the plan is vital, a useful diagram can be prepared much earlier. This earlier analysis is usually called the *preliminary plan* or *prebid plan* to differentiate it from the *working plan,* which is prepared after the contract award.

But CPM can also be applied at any time after construction has started. If, for example, 6 months after work has begun, a project is having schedule troubles, CPM can be applied for the balance of the project's duration. Thus CPM is useful at every stage of a project, from its first beginnings to its final completion.

INFORMATION COLLECTION: CONFERENCE, EXECUTIVE, CONSULTANT, AND STAFF PLANNING APPROACHES

Conference Approach

How is the actual network preparation initiated? There is no one correct method. Sometimes the *conference approach* is most effective. Key persons involved in the project take part in the conference. These should include people from the contractors' offices and field groups, as well as representatives from the owner or architect or both. The size of the group must be kept small enough to permit it to function as a working group, and those who attend should be prepared to work. "Visiting firemen" will only serve to dilute its effectiveness. The group must also have sufficient horsepower; that is, it must have the authority to make commitments on the sequence of work. If the decisions of the group are not upheld in the implementation of work, the network becomes worthless.

Once the planning group meets, its work routine is simple. The project is talked through from start to finish. As each portion is discussed, the arrows representing that portion are drawn. This first try at a diagram must be viewed and discussed by the group. For that reason, the first network is usually drawn in rough form on a blackboard. When the group reaches agreement on the work sequence of a given portion, the information is transferred from the blackboard to tracing paper or cloth.

Attention is focused on the phase of the project under discussion. In the preparation of the John Doe networks, a list of activities was utilized. In most cases, however, the conference group works directly on the network without preparing an activity list. Nor is the use of such a list recommended, since its preparation requires redundant project analyses. Nevertheless, when the group has used CPM before, there may be activity lists available from similar projects carried out in the past. These can be invaluable as checklists to ensure that all the activities required for the current project are being listed.

The CPM plan prepared must be the one which, by consensus, everyone in the work group expects to be used to implement the project. This is particularly important since the contractor is usually delegated broad powers in the scheduling of work. Since the owner is purchasing the contractor's experience and know-how, nothing in the CPM plan should preclude the use of this background.

There are cases, particularly in public projects, where a barely qualified contractor is awarded a contract. It is important that the CPM plan reflect this contractor's work plan (or lack of one) early in its own diagram. Perhaps an engineer or CPM consultant could devise a better work plan, but unless the contractor sincerely adopted its improvements, doing so would be a useless exercise.

On the other hand, expertise should be given recognition. In planning a refinery boiler overhaul, we had assembled key personnel concerned with the equipment, including the chief engineer, the process engineer, the area maintenance engineer, the inspection engineer, and so forth. One of the preshutdown activities was to be the fabrication of elaborate A frames. These frames were to hold the upper steam header in place while most of the old fireside tubes were taken out and replaced with new ones. A late-comer to the conference was the contractor who was to do the field work. He listened to the discussion about the erection of these temporary supports in the boiler. This erection would be difficult, and the disassembly of the A frames would require cutting torches. The contractor at first made no comment, then he remarked that we could plan it any way we wanted on paper, but he would do it his way in the field. When we told him that it was his plan we were interested in, he opened up. In the first place, he saw no need for the expensive, special A frames. Instead he planned to lay temporary timber beams across the top of the boiler. Slings hung from these beams would support the headers. This scheme would save time in installation and removal, as well as eliminate the cost of the special A frames. The plan was accepted immediately, and the contractor led the balance of the planning session.

An important ingredient for a successful conference is leadership. If the meeting is not directed, the conversation becomes a generalized and philosophical bull session. For example, a city planning commission had undertaken a 2-year study program to develop the city's long-range planning for the next 20 years. This involved planning the Community Renewal Program (CRP) rather than the actual renewal projects. In gross terms, the CRP involved three groups: physical planners, economists, and sociologists. The program had been under way for 6 months and each group had conducted preliminary studies. Each group seemed convinced that its own specialty controlled the future of the city. The physical planners said beautiful people live in a beautiful city. The sociologists said that well-adjusted people result in a well-adjusted city. Meanwhile, the economists said that a beautiful and well-adjusted city was not possible without a healthy economic base.

When we started the CPM planning sessions, the three groups had a 2-day debate on philosophies. There was no end in sight until we shifted from generalities to the preparation of the arrow diagram. Each group was able to define its plan until it touched on that of another group. At this point, there was usually a difference of opinion, and since an arrow can't have two heads and no tail, a decision had to be made. These decisions were on specific terms, so compromises could be made, and were. Small decisions are easier than big ones. Note that the diagram does not make decisions; people must. Also, the diagram cannot be drawn if decisions are delayed.

The direction in this group was provided by the planning group technical director, who arbitrated deadlocks, and the author of this book, who provided guidance in the preparation of the network. The two fruitless days were followed by 3 days of arrow-guided decision making which defined the scope of the study.

Executive Approach

The conference approach is not suitable for all projects. There are situations where there are too *many* key people to make it manageable. There are others where there are too *few* for a full-blown conference. In both situations, an *executive approach* is required. The planning group is limited to two or three people. A typical group would be the general contractor's superintendent and the project manager plus the staff CPM engineer or CPM consultant. With such a small group, the diagram preparation can go more quickly; of course, there is a commensurate loss in communication among key personnel.

The diagram is prepared as the project is talked through. A blackboard can be used for drawing the rough diagram; however, with the smaller group a long sheet of reproducible paper with a blue-line disappearing grid can also be used. This saves the step of transferring the information from the blackboard to the paper. There is rarely an initial network which would not be much improved if it were redrawn. Also, the rough diagram can be drawn two to three times as quickly as a finished network. This minimizes the time demands on the group.

There is an inherent danger in committing the plan to paper. This is the tendency of people to try to make the project suit the network, rather than to have the network suit the best planning. A network must be flexible; don't allow it to lock in your thinking. The network should be altered if better ideas are offered after the network has been prepared. This is, in fact, one of the prime advantages of CPM. Most people, understanding something clearly, assume that everyone else views it with the same clarity. The CPM plan is the communication medium which can demonstrate this clarity, or the lack of it, to the various planners of a project.

On a hospital project, the contractor's project superintendent (a grizzled up-through-the-ranks type), the project engineer, and the author prepared the first rough arrow diagram at the job site. It took us about 4 days to talk the project through. When we finished, the superintendent said, "Well, now I've built the job." He had been able to think the project through to completion in unaccustomed detail. The diagram had 1500 arrows, so that no activity described more than 1 percent of the project value and the average arrow covered about one-tenth of 1 percent.

Consultant Approach

A modified version of the executive approach is the *consultant approach*. It involves a CPM consultant or staff engineer talking the project through with the general contractor's superintendent and key people and then preparing the diagram. This method is the least demanding on the time of the people involved in the project. It can be effective but it must be applied with care. The primary problem is that project people do not accept the diagram as their plan as readily as a diagram which they helped to prepare.

A large diagram can be more than a little overwhelming (even to an experienced CPM planner). The project people must be properly oriented in CPM fundamentals if this approach is used. But it can be very effective when the project people have participated in at least one previous CPM-planned project and have developed confidence in CPM itself.

Staff Planning

Large contractors and industrial firms who use CPM often set up staff planning groups. Some cautions are in order here: A group of this type has a tendency to be out of touch with the needs of the project group, particularly the field portion of that group. It is not unusual to find field people servicing the planning group rather than the planning group fulfilling its mission of servicing the project group.

Planning groups often become paper mills to justify their existence. Again Parkinson's law* comes into play ("work expands so as to fill the time available for its completion"). In discussing his law, Professor Parkinson notes that the number of officials employed is unrelated to the quantity of work to be done. To support this statement he refers to the Royal Navy, which at one point showed a gain of 78 percent in land-locked Admiralty officials (from 2000 to 3569) while suffering a 32 percent reduction in fleet work force (from 146,000 to 100,000). The paradox is that the members of a paper-mill type of planning group have less time to devote to the working project groups, where their main energies should go.

SUBCONTRACTORS' PLANS

The work of some subcontractors is independent of the work of the general contractor after the site has been prepared for them. This subcontracting category would include operations such as structural steel erection, cooling tower erection, and tank erection. All these are essentially package units. However, major subcontract operations such as electrical, mechanical, heating, and plumbing work are entirely dependent upon the progress of the general contractor's work. It is not usually practical to prepare a separate network to show the subcontractors' work (except for the

---

*By permission from C. Northcote Parkinson, *Parkinson's Law,* Riverside Editions, Houghton Mifflin Company, Boston, 1957.

package units). Experiments in this regard have resulted in disjointed, disconnected failures unless the general work is also indicated on the diagram. But when the general work is so indicated, the subcontract network is no longer separate. Even if it were practical to draw the subcontractors' work on a separate network, the result would be self-defeating since the purpose of CPM is to show a coordinated plan of the work all the contractors are doing.

During the later stages of a project, the subcontracts often include much of the critical work. If the conference approach is used in planning the network, key subcontractor personnel can be included in the conference group. If the executive approach is used, the general contractor assumes a sequence of work and time estimates for the subcontractors' work. These assumptions are then reviewed with the applicable subcontractors and revised as necessary. It is quite important that subcontractors point out those areas where they need special consideration. For instance, a school kitchen-equipment subcontractor might need complete control of the kitchen area to install the equipment. The kitchen work being done by other subcontractors (electrical, plumbing, plaster, painting, quarry tile, etc.) would have to be coordinated to recognize this requirement for space. The general contractor often does not allot sufficient time for the subcontractors' work, because he or she is necessarily preoccupied with his or her own responsibilities. But through the use of a network, proper work sequences and time estimates can be made before the coordination problems ever get to the field. The diagram can be used to demonstrate to the general contractor that the subcontractor does not need workers on the job at certain times and could not use them effectively if they were there. Of course, this is a two-way street: The diagram may show the subcontractor that his or her work is critical during certain phases and must be staffed accordingly. One contractor, after his first exposure to CPM, categorized it as a new means of communication. This would appear to be an oversimplification, but communication is recognized as a major advantage of the method.

PREPARATION TIME

The time required to prepare the initial network is difficult to quantify. It is a function of several variables, including the nature of the project, the background those involved in the project have in CPM, and the degree of detail required in the network.

If the project is a familiar one, defining the activities involved is not too difficult. In the construction of a high-rise building, for instance, most of the major activities could be listed and sequenced (but not time-esti-

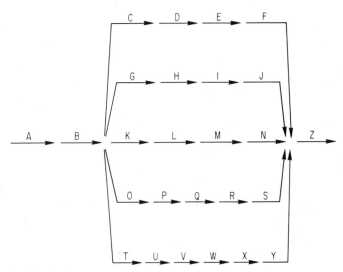

Figure 8.1 Noncomplex network (twenty-six activities).

mated) without recourse to the building plans. If the operation is unique and has never been previously accomplished, preparation of the logic network could require considerable study and discussion. If this were 1939 and Cal Tech were given the assignment to CPM-plan the design, fabrication, and testing of an atomic bomb, preparation of the network would necessarily be time-consuming.

Some operations have few interconnections between their constituent activities, while others have many interconnections that require a considerable degree of coordination. Figure 8.1 is an example of what we might call a noncomplex operation. An actual example might be the production of a prototype model for an appliance. Activity A might be market research, B the general design phase, C through Y individual-part fabrication, and Z assembly. Figure 8.2 is an example of a network showing an operation whose activities are very interconnected and require a high degree of coordination. Both networks have twenty-six activities. The preparation of a network such as that shown in Figure 8.1 would probably take considerably less time than the preparation of one like that shown in Figure 8.2. Network preparation time also varies in an almost linear manner with the degree of detail required through the first portion of the feasible range of detail (Figure 8.3). But as additional detail is required, there are fewer logical sequencing decisions required, and thus the rate of additional time needed falls off. Accordingly, the slope of the curve shown in Figure 8.3 decreases.

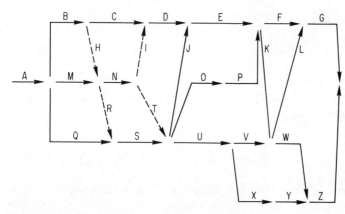

Figure 8.2 Complex network (twenty-six activities).

A question often encountered is, "How much longer does it take to plan an operation by network techniques?" Experience indicates that it takes no longer than planning by other means, although this is not always apparent. With CPM, planners have a tool which allows them to go further into detail than they could otherwise in the planning phase without losing perspective. Thus more complete planning is often accomplished with CPM since the planners have a method for retaining the details developed. To an onlooker, developing this more complete planning cycle appears to take longer than traditional methods. But the planning time required "per ounce of good planning effort" is about the same in both systems. Moreover, when monitoring actual field progress, CPM far outstrips traditional methods in speed, accuracy, and reliability. For replanning or evaluating new factors, CPM has no peer.

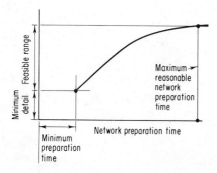

Figure 8.3 Network detail versus preparation time.

LEVEL OF DETAIL

The amount of detail to be included in the average arrow is a matter of judgment. The type, cost, and time duration of the project are major factors. Average cost per arrow is a good rule-of-thumb indicator.

If the project is the construction of a 10-mile length of highway, it could be represented by this network:

This is of course a gross oversimplification. A better representation is shown in Figure 8.4. While it may be reasonable to lay out and clear the entire route, it is doubtful that any contractor would want to leave 10 miles of drainage ditches open in any weather. To make the activity breakdown more realistic, a typical arrow can be broken down into these arrows:

Start   Continue   Complete
activity   activity   activity

This an example and should not suggest that an activity can be divided into only three sections. An activity can be broken down into any desired number of components. If the project is a forty-story high rise, the activity "exterior masonry" would probably be broken down into forty "exterior masonry" arrows. This is a judgment item whose importance cannot be overemphasized. If the segments activities are broken down into are too gross, the network will not reflect the plan in enough detail to be mean-

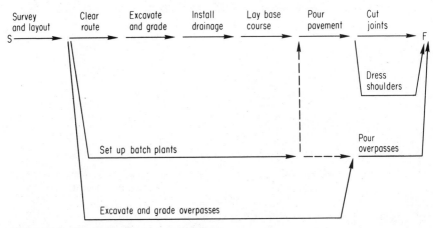

Figure 8.4 Basic plan for highway project.

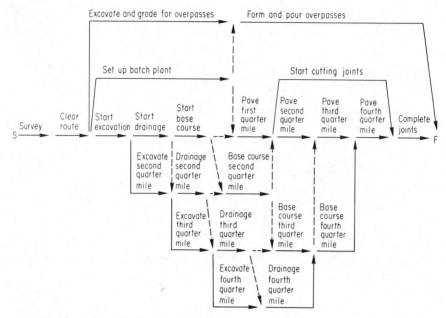

Figure 8.5   Network for 1 mile of highway.

ingful. The other extreme is too much detail, which results in concealment of significant planning factors (you literally can't see the plan for the arrows). There is no easy rule of thumb to guide one in this activity breakdown. The best way to develop one's judgment is to practice the preparation and use of arrow diagrams.

In the highway example, a reasonable planning unit would be a typical mile. Figure 8.5 shows a network for a typical mile of highway. (To keep the example simple, this network is much less detailed than an actual working network.) The plan for the 10-mile length would be ten of these networks suitably interconnected to show work crew and equipment transfers from one area to another.

In Figure 8.5 restraints are used as *logic spreaders* to avoid unintentional logical connections. Figures 8.6, 8.7, and 8.8 illustrate three examples of this important use of restraints.

SUBNETWORKS

There may be varying levels of useful networks. It is sometimes useful to enlarge on one portion of a network for study purposes. These detailed network studies are termed *subnetworks*. Figure 8.9 shows the subnet-

Without logic spreader: start of drainage work in the third quarter mile would depend upon completion of the quarter mile of base course.

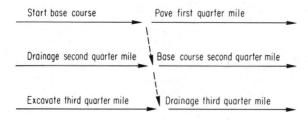

When we add the spreader after "drainage second quarter mile" the two sequences are held apart.

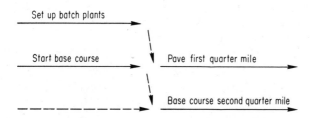

Figure 8.6 Logic spreader.

Without logic spreader: "base course second quarter mile" would depend upon the batch plant.

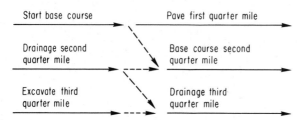

With the spreader: after "start base course," the two sequences are separated.

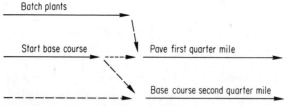

Figure 8.7 Logic speader.

Without spreader: "pave first quarter mile" would depend upon the excavation and grading for the overpasses.

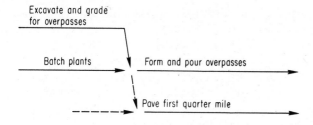

With the spreader: after "batch plants," overpass work is separated from paving.

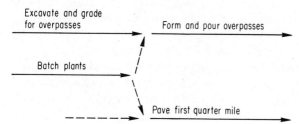

Figure 8.8 Logic spreader.

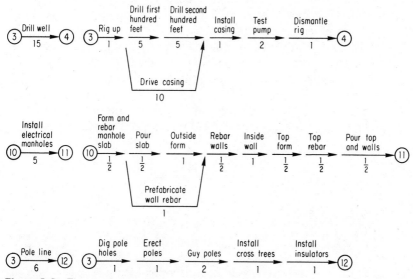

Figure 8.9 Three subnetworks.

works for three John Doe activities (drill well, 3-4; install electrical man-hole, 10-11; overhead pole line, 3-12).

In a high-rise apartment house, we prepared a detailed 150-arrow diagram for a typical floor. The diagram was too detailed for the field to use in forecasting a useful work schedule. Since the project was a forty-story building, the regeneration of this detailed network would have resulted in a diagram of more than 6000 arrows (allowing 10 arrows per floor for inter-connections). While this would not have been a record for network size, it would have given the superintendent a computer run almost 200 pages long to follow. This was, frankly, more detail than he needed and would have infringed upon his authority as a superintendent. CPM should be an aid to effective project supervision; it is not meant to replace supervision or to facilitate the use of less qualified people. The CPM plan depends upon a project's supervision personnel for its initial preparation. It should also allow a reasonable latitude for superintendents to schedule their people and equipment. CPM is a logical framework within which superintendents work. It is not a hard-and-fast hour-by-hour schedule which automates their every move.

If the detailed arrow diagram is not a working schedule, why prepare it? It is used to prepare sound time estimates for the activities in the network. For instance, Figure 8.10 gives the portion of a typical high-rise network representing the pouring of a floor slab. Two sets of forms were available. Through the use of a substantial system of shoring, the floors could be stripped the day after a pour. This reflected a possible 3-day cycle which appeared to be overly optimistic. Through the use of some equipment overtime for moving forms and shoring, a 2-day cycle was actually achieved. These seven arrows were replaced by one arrow "form and pour concrete." The seven arrows were replaced by eighteen arrows per floor (Figure 8.11), which permitted the network to remain at a reasonable size (1500 activities instead of 6000) and still furnish the same computed results.

Through familiarity with the typical floor, the superintendent knew which subnetwork-detailed activities were represented by the summarized

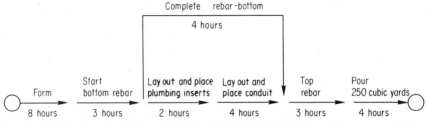

Figure 8.10 Three-day floor pour cycle; detailed network to estimate time cycle for high rise.

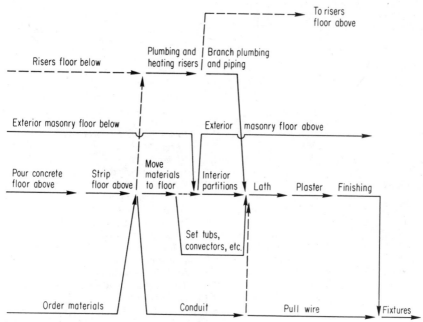

Figure 8.11 Summary of activities, one floor of high rise.

working network. However, if a new superintendent were to take over, a legend similar to the following would suffice:

Summarized network			*Typical floor*
1. Form and pour concrete	. . . .	1-1	Build forms
		1-2	Rebar
		1-3	Inserts and conduit
		1-4	Pour floor slab
2. Risers	. . . .	2-1	Install plumbing risers
		2-2	Install heating risers
3. Branch piping and heating	. . . .	3-1	Install plumbing branches
		3-2	Install heating branches
		3-3	Install convector boxes
		3-4	Install convectors
		3-5	Install pipe covering
4. Exterior masonry	. . . .	4-1	Install spandrel flashing
		4-2	Install shelf angles
		4-3	Exterior masonry
		4-4	Install window frames
		4-5	Install air-conditioner sleeves
		4-6	Balcony door bucks
5. Interior masonry	. . . .	5-1	Hall partitions
		5-2	Incinerator shafts
		5-3	Ventilation shafts

Summarized network		*Typical floor*	
		5-4	Elevator shaft
		5-5	Hall door bucks
6. Electrical conduit	. . . .	6-1	Power conduit from meter box
		6-2	Install meter box
		6-3	Backing boxes
		6-4	Install branch conduit
7. Electrical wiring	. . . .	7-1	Pull wire
		7-2	Install panel-box internals
		7-3	Terminate
		7-4	Ringout
		7-5	Install plates, trim, switches
8. Finish work	. . . .	8-1	Bathroom door saddles
		8-2	Ceramic wall tile
		8-3	Ceramic floor tile
		8-4	Install wood trim
		8-5	Prime paint walls
		8-6	Paint trim
		8-7	Finish paint walls
		8-8	Rubber cover baseboards
		8-9	Terazzo hall saddles
		8-10	Hall floor tile
		8-11	Room floor tiles
		8-12	Hang doors
9. Fixtures	. . . .	9-1	Install bathroom fixtures and trim
		9-2	Install medicine cabinets
		9-3	Install kitchen sinks
		9-4	Install bifold doors
		9-5	Install kitchen cabinets
		9-6	Install kitchen ranges and refrigerators
		9-7	Install electrical fixtures

Some items are not summarized by floor; typical of these are:

1. Clearing and excavation

2. Foundations

3. Install elevators

4. Basement work

5. Site work

6. Deliveries (including ordering, shop drawing reviews, etc.)

7. Installation of incinerators

8. Installation of boilers

9. Mailbox installation

10. Temporary heat (if required)

11. Piping tests

FORMAT

The layout of the working diagram is important, particularly when it is to be presented to persons (on either field or management level) who are not familiar with CPM.

While the working diagram for the high-rise apartment building (Figure 8.11) was logically correct, it did not convey a strong visual presentation of the project plan. Figure 8.12 shows a portion of the revised network. The logic is exactly the same; only the arrangement has changed. The vertical work (concrete superstructure, masonry, and risers) is vertically oriented, just as is the actual work it represents. The work on each floor is shown on ascending levels.

PREFERENTIAL LOGIC

When you prepare a network, there is an in-between logic called *preferential logic*. Theoretical or absolute logic is a black or white situation. For instance, "pour roof slab" must follow the lower superstructure. "Foundations" come after "excavation." In the planning of a project, there are certain work sequences which are based upon experience. If absolute logic is referred to as the logical *skeleton,* which is inflexible, then preferential logic could be considered the rest of the project *body.* The skeletal or absolute logic would be virtually the same for a specific set of project conditions. However, the preferential logic, which forms the logical body, can have an unlimited form and character. Preferential logic, then, is the area where the CPM planner's ingenuity can be best applied to the character of a specific project plan. Some examples of preferential logic are:

Basement slab. It is necessary to make a logical choice of whether to pour the basement slab before the superstructure above it goes up. In high-rise work the basement slab (and underslab plumbing) is often postponed until the superstructure is up several floors and has cured enough so that the shoring on the basement level can be removed. Since a building's superstructure is usually on the critical path, this results in a savings of time. However, if complicated equipment or systems are to be located on the basement level, this area could be critical.

Steel structure. When steel structure is to be used for a one- or two-story building, which comes first: structure or floor slabs? They must be in series for safety reasons. If steel procurement is a problem, perhaps it will save time to get the floor slab in first. If weather delays the floor pour, perhaps the steel could go up first and be used to enclose the slab area.

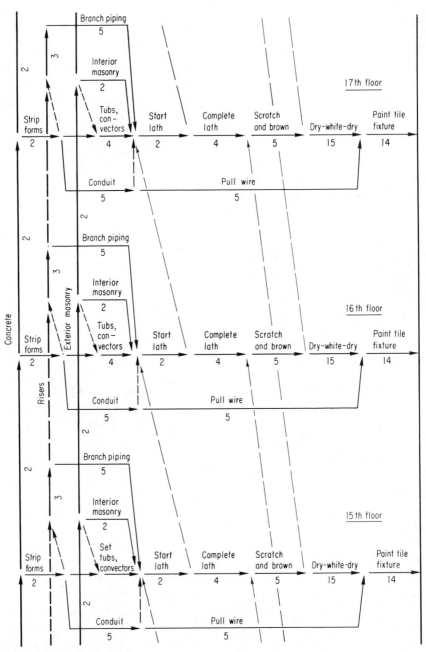

Figure 8.12 Rearrangement of summarized activities (high rise).

Glazing. When a building is to be acid-washed after masonry is erected, glazing is often deferred. However, if closing in the building is on the critical path, weeks to months can be saved by sequencing glazing between masonry and the acid wash. Glazing can also follow closely after masonry rather than waiting until it tops out.

Masonry. Usually exterior masonry starts after the superstructure is topped out. However, it is possible to gain time by hanging masonry scaffolds from intermediate levels (such as halfway or at one-third points).

Testing. This is another area where time can be gained by working sections rather than the whole building.

Plaster. In low buildings it is often usual to plaster from the top floor down so that the floors can be cleaned up from top down. However, in high-rise buildings, it is usual to plaster from the bottom up. "Bottom" in this case usually means from the second floor up, since the ground floor is kept open for handling materials and storage as long as possible.

This is of course not an exhaustive list, but it should serve to illustrate what is meant by preferential logic. The role of the CPM planner as an objective questioner is important. Preferential logic should be questioned, not accepted as a matter of routine. Often better planning can be incorporated by challenging experience-based logic. In one project the start of plastering was at first scheduled not to start until the completion of lathing on the tenth floor; this was based on a rule of thumb gained through earlier experience. In the actual project, however, this restriction was dropped because the lathing crews moved faster than the plastering crews. Accordingly, the plasterers could not catch up with the lathers and there was no need for the arbitrary restriction.

FRAGNETS

Smaller sections can be networked in more detail; this is dubbed a fragment of a network or a *fragnet*. Figure 8.13 illustrates a fragnet showing the John Doe steel erection in more detail. Figure 8.14 shows the fragnet for work on the loading dock.

PROJECT CHARACTERISTICS

Although each project plan is unique, just as each project is, there are usually certain similar characteristics present in each type of project.

1. *Hospitals.* Most hospital projects require the transfer of facilities from old to new buildings. This can be quite complicated when all or part

of the old facilities must be demolished to make way for portions of the new hospital. This is particularly true since the hospital must remain an operating entity with no loss in capabilities during the construction period. The plan must allow for the shifts of the various departments. Special equipment is necessary for the construction of operating rooms, the morgue, laboratories, etc., and delivery time is important for much of this equipment. The construction plan may also have to be broken into a number of steps or phases for funding purposes. Construction of new facilities over or beside an existing hospital building requires the use of special techniques and careful coordination. Since hospitals usually have a large area per floor, the logical breakdown of work depends upon the contractors' division of the areas.

2. *Schools.* The general construction problems here are similar to those for hospitals, but the construction of schools does not usually have the problem of new building and old being on the same site. Furnishing and moving into the new building is a phase which does require proper planning. When possible, the schedule is usually arranged to move students in by the start of a school year. In some cases the schedule is very tight and a compromise is made, high priority being placed upon finishing classrooms, with the cafeteria and then the gymnasium to follow. A knowledge of a realistic opening date is important to the school district. If the school cannot be expected to open on the desired date, the administration needs sufficient time to organize double shifts at other schools, temporary quarters, extra buses, or other stopgap steps.

3. *High-rise buildings.* These tend to develop into a typical work cycle per floor. A great advantage of CPM is the capability those using it have to try out different sequences of construction activities to determine

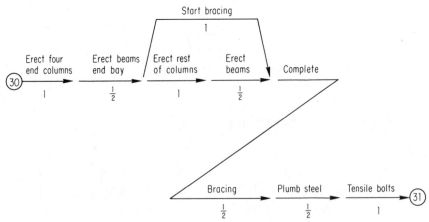

Figure 8.13 Fragnet for John Doe project steel erection.

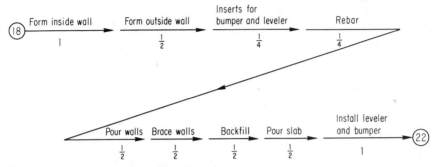

Figure 8.14 Fragnet for truck loading dock.

their potential value. Although some high-rise buildings are noncomplex, the very size of such a project requires good coordination and control of activities if a satisfactory schedule is to be met. Elevators are traditionally a critical delivery in high-rise buildings, but this can usually be avoided if the owner purchases this equipment early. In a huge civic center project, CPM highlighted the procurement of structural steel as the critical path because of the special shapes and sizes needed. As a result of this information, the owner took unusual steps to purchase the steel members months before they would normally have been procured.

4. *Process plants.*   These are particularly unique in design and construction and, thus, are good subjects for CPM planning. Equipment procurement is usually a key factor and depends, of course, on the process design phase. The foundation work, in turn, usually depends upon approved equipment shop drawings. The testing, cleaning, and starting phases of the process plant require significant time and must be carefully planned. Also, the start-up of units is usually in a specific series, which should be reflected in the sequence of completions of work on the units.

5. *Highways and pipelines.*   These projects are similar in that they call for repetitive work (similar to that shown in the network in Figure 8.1). When viewed as a whole they are like the mammoth watermelon ("I could pick it up, if I could get my arms around it . . ."). The principal problem is how to break them down into workable units. In a sense, these projects are similar to high-rise buildings in that they are noncomplex, typical operations made complex by their large size.

6. *Dams and heavy construction.*   These usually have a very definite sequence of operation. Much of the important planning in these projects involves the provision of temporary facilities to support the construction, such as living facilities for workers, a batch plant, aggregate supplies, shops, railroad sidings, craneways, cofferdams, etc.

7. *Light construction.*   Such projects as shopping centers do not usually require complex plans but can nonetheless benefit from CPM plan-

ning. Our sample John Doe project is in this class and we have seen how various considerations can affect the project plan.

8. *Other projects.*　These usually fit into descriptions similar to 1 to 7 above. For instance, a large department store would be similar to school planning, with Thanksgiving the key opening date rather than Labor Day. Space vehicle launching facilities would be similar to a combination of process plants and heavy construction.

SUMMARY

The size of a useful network is almost unlimited. Network analysis is usually a must in projects valued over $5 million; however, it can also be useful in less expensive projects. CPM often exposes previously undefined planning factors.

The current trend is to apply CPM just after the awarding of the contract. However, this is no hard and fast rule. Earlier network analysis can provide better construction schedule requirements. CPM can also be applied after construction work has started.

Phase 1 of the network preparation is the collection of information and the concurrent preparation of a rough diagram. The information collection method can be any of four approaches: conference, executive, consultant, or staff planning. The second phase of the network preparation is the rearrangement and redrawing of the rough version.

In any approach, it is vital that the CPM diagram reflect the real plans of the contractor.

Subcontractors perform many critical work functions. Their information and plans must also be incorporated into the network.

It is difficult to set definite time requirements for the preparation of a network. Familiar projects can be diagramed faster than unfamiliar ones, and noncomplex projects more quickly than those that are complex.

Planning by CPM may require more time than traditional planning because CPM provides for planning in more depth. If an arrow or arrow sequence is too broad in scope, it can be broken down into smaller sections (start, continue, etc.). If an arrow sequence has too much detail for use in calculations, it can be summarized into arrows broader in scope. On the other hand, if a time study of a specific operation, such as forming and pouring a single floor, is desired, a subnetwork can be developed. The principal benefit of a subnetwork is that it enables one to make a dependable time estimate of the work involved.

The format of the network must be logical and carefully worked out. Taking special effort to clarify the project through the layout of the network will be well worth the extra time spent to do so.

PRECEDENCE
NETWORKS

Professor John Fondahl of Stanford University, who was established in the early 1960s as an expert on noncomputerized solutions to CPM and PERT networks, was one of the early supporters of the precedence method, or PDM, terming it "circle and connecting arrow technique." Professor Fondahl's study for the Navy's Bureau of Yards and Docks included descriptive material and gave the technique early impetus, particularly on Navy projects.

An IBM brochure credits the H. B. Zachry Company of San Antonio with the development of the precedent form of CPM. In cooperation with IBM, Zachry developed computer programs which could handle precedence network computations on the IBM 1130 and IBM 360. This was particularly significant, since in 1964 C. R. Phillips and J. J. Moder* indicated the availability of only one computerized approach to precedence networks versus 60 for CPM and PERT.

The form for precedence networks was originally termed *activity on node*. The activity description is shown in a box or oval, with the sequence

---

*Joseph J. Moder and Cecil R. Phillips, *Project Management with CPM and PERT*, Reinhold, New York, 1964.

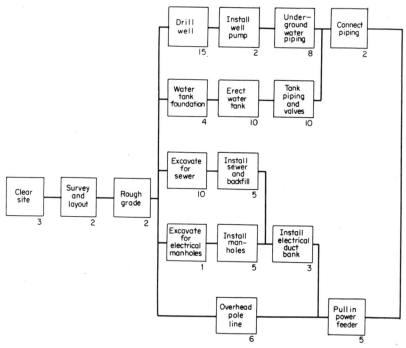

Figure 9.1 John Doe project precedence network.

or flow still shown by interconnecting lines. In some cases, arrowheads are not used, although this leaves more opportunity for ambiguous network situations.

Figure 9.1 shows the John Doe network in precedence form. There are seventeen precedence activities shown, the same number as the regular activity-oriented CPM network. However, simplicity of form is purported to be one of the advantages of precedence networks. In situations where activities have to be subdivided to show phased progress, the precedence network may result in a lower number of notations. In some cases, the reduction can be more than 50 percent, so that the precedence network can have the advantage of a simple appearance. To those utilizing precedence networks continually, their interpretation can be straightforward. However, this ability to interpret them is not as easily acquired by someone used to CPM.

PRECEDENCE LOGIC

One reason for the apparent simplicity of precedence networks is that a work item can be connected from either its start or its finish. This allows a start-finish logic presentation with no need to break the work item down.

The translation of the John Doe network into precedence form shown in Figure 9.1 consists of only one type of connection: end to start. Figure 9.2 illustrates the three basic precedence relations: start to start, end to end, and end to start. Although precedence networks are simpler in appearance than regular CPM diagrams, greater thought must be given to reading and interpreting them.

Another characteristic of PDM diagrams is the use of lead and lag factors. In CPM, lead activities can be introduced which logically delay the start of a particular activity or group of activities. (See Figure 9.3.) Assignment of a duration to the lead activity imposes a delaying factor in the CPM calculation. (This effect can be achieved in many CPM computer programs by locking in an event date to occur "not earlier than.")

Similarly, a lag activity can be imposed to direct the completion of an activity to occur some period of time after either the start or the completion of another activity. (See Figure 9.4.)

The lead/lag factors assigned to work packages in PDM can replace the multiple activities required in CPM to reflect "start-complete" or "start-continue-complete," that is, they can replace the multiple activities required in CPM to create an interim event or events, at which point(s) other activities start or conclude.

The result can be a network diagram which is apparently simpler than

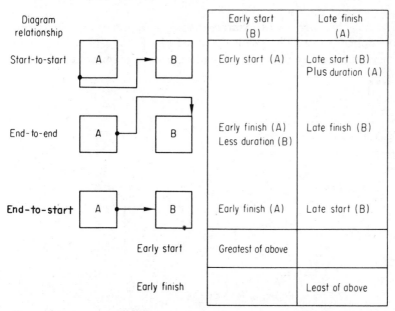

Diagram relationship			Early start (B)	Late finish (A)
Start-to-start	A	B	Early start (A)	Late start (B) Plus duration (A)
End-to-end	A	B	Early finish (A) Less duration (B)	Late finish (B)
End-to-start	A	B	Early finish (A)	Late start (B)
	Early start		Greatest of above	
	Early finish			Least of above

Figure 9.2 Typical precedence relations.

a regular CPM network, since it takes fewer work package "boxes" to describe the same set of circumstances. While the depiction appears simpler, however, it is necessary for the user of PDM diagrams to think harder to understand the logic depicted. Perhaps the greatest strength of the CPM network diagram is its ability, first, to record the logical sequence of a plan and, second, to communicate that logic. PDM, in its sophistication, takes a step backward in communications capability.

There is no doubt that PDM can be a powerful scheduling tool. Experienced schedulers using PDM on a regular basis have stated that they can fine-tune and change schedules more readily with computerized PDM. At the same time, the leads and lags make the hand calculation of PDM less practical, if not impractical. Further, time scaling of PDM is much more difficult than time scaling of CPM. And since time scaling is, in itself, a calculation, the difficulty in doing it confirms two things: first, that manual calculation of PDM is impractical; and, second, that PDM obfuscates the use of a network as a means of communicating information.

This is a very significant loss. From the earliest period of using network methods, it was clear that communication of results is vital to the effective implementation of the network-generated schedule. The network schedule itself becomes moot and meaningless if project managers are unable, or unwilling, to understand the output. CPM early on suffered from overenthusiasm, and overwhelming pages of computer printouts. As described in later chapters, though, sensitivity to the communications aspects of CPM since then has become a vital part of ensuring the effective utilization of its results.

PDM has the paradoxical characteristics of apparent simplicity and built-in sophistication. The result can make the PDM scheduler become the project guru rather than a participating project team participator.

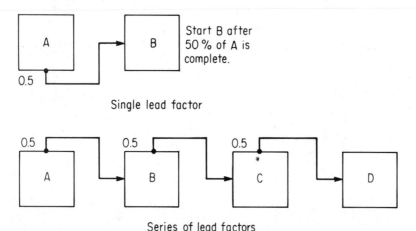

Figure 9.3 Lead factors.

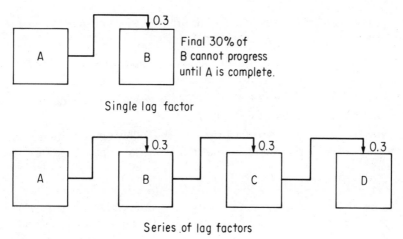

Single lag factor

Series of lag factors

Figure 9.4   Lag factors.

WORK-PACKAGE CALCULATIONS

In theory, the work-package time calculations are quite similar to the CPM event calculations. The first stage is the establishment of a work-item and duration chart. A table of relations is then constructed based upon the typical relations shown in Figure 9.2. The early start time for the first work item is 0, although a calendar start date can be inserted later. The early start time at the beginning of each of the other work items is the greatest of the paths entering the beginning of the work item. The value of these paths is computed by the following methods:

1. *Start to start.*   The early start time for the preceding work item is the early start time for the work item.

2. *End to start.*   The early finish time for the preceding work item is the early start time for the work item.

3. *End to end.*   The early finish time for the preceding work item less the duration of the work item itself is the early start time for the work item.

The longest path to the beginning of a work item determines its early start time. The early finish time for a work item is its early start time plus the duration.

By definition, the late finish time for the last work item is set equal to the early finish time for that item, which establishes a critical path. The late finish times for other work items are determined by subtraction or a backward pass from the late, or the finish, time for the terminal event.

The late finish times for other work items are the least of the paths leading into completion of the work item, as follows:

1. *End to start.*   The late finish time is the latest start time for the following work items.

2. *End to end.*   The late finish time for the work item is equal to the late finish time for the following work item.

3. *Start to start.*   The late start time for the following work item plus the duration of the work item itself determines the late finish time for the work item.

Late start time equals late finish time less duration. Float for a work item can be calculated by the same formulas as were utilized in the CPM approach. Similarly, the critical path can be identified by using the standard rules.

As noted, the introduction of lead and lag factors (easily handled by computer) makes manual calculations difficult, if not impractical.

Computer Calculation

Today, the major network calculation programs can handle either precedence or CPM. Ironically, the initial programs were a translation of PDM into a CPM format (internally in the computer program), calculation by CPM algorithm, and a retranslation back into the PDM format.

One problem in inputting the PDM diagram is the lack of event numbers. If all the activities were end-to-start, the work package numbers could be used similarly to *i-j* numbers. However, the complexity introduced by start-to-start, start-to-end, and end-to-end relationships requires a cumbersome cataloging of predecessor and successor work items.

Figure 9.5 shows the simplified PDM printout for the John Doe example. It is very similar to the CPM printout with restraints deleted. (In fact CPM outputs can have any activities, including restraints, suppressed to simplify the volume of output.) But while simple in appearance, the output cannot be used in this form to track a path through the diagram.

In a field situation, where the master net and printout were in PDM format, a CPM-oriented contractor scheduler complained that he could not match the PDM output with the diagram. The PDM project manager scheduler retorted: "Of course not, only I can do that." What the project manager really meant was that the contractor scheduler had not been given sufficient output to understand the PDM. In effect the basic output is a *scheduling directive,* and not a scheduling tool for mutual use.

Figure 9.6 shows the John Doe PDM master output with predecessors.

NETWORK REPORT
SORT BY WORK ITEM   /02

JOHN DOE BASELINE CPM SCHEDULE
PREPARED BY O'BRIEN-KREITZBERG & ASSOC., INC.

DATA DATE   PAGE   1
             01JUL87

WORK ITEM	ACTIVITY DESCRIPTION	ORG DUR	REM DUR	CNTR TYPE	WORK CAT.	SPEC SEC.	EARLY START	EARLY *FINISH	LATE START	LATE *FINISH	TOTAL FLOAT
01	CLEAR SITE	3.0	3.0	GC	1-1	0210	01JUL87	06JUL87	01JUL87	06JUL87	0.0
02	SURVEY AND LAYOUT	2.0	2.0	GC	1-2	0140	07JUL87	08JUL87	07JUL87	08JUL87	0.0
03	ROUGH GRADE	2.0	2.0	GC	1-1	0220	09JUL87	10JUL87	09JUL87	10JUL87	0.0
04	DRILL WELL	15.0	15.0	GC	1-7	0201	13JUL87	31JUL87	13JUL87	31JUL87	0.0
05	INSTALL WELL PUMP	2.0	2.0	PB	1-5	0250	03AUG87	04AUG87	03AUG87	04AUG87	0.0
06	WATER TANK FOUNDATIONS	4.0	4.0	GC	1-3	0330	13JUL87	16JUL87	14JUL87	17JUL87	1.0
07	ERECT WATER TOWER	10.0	10.0	PB	1-6	0250	17JUL87	30JUL87	20JUL87	31JUL87	1.0
08	UNDERGROUND WATER PIPING	8.0	8.0	PB	1-5	0250	05AUG87	14AUG87	05AUG87	14AUG87	0.0
09	TANK PIPING AND VALVES	10.0	10.0	PB	1-5	0250	31JUL87	13AUG87	03AUG87	14AUG87	1.0
10	EXCAVATE FOR SEWER	10.0	10.0	GC	1-1	0250	13JUL87	24JUL87	17JUL87	30JUL87	4.0
11	EXCAVATE ELECTRIC MANHOLES	1.0	1.0	GC	1-1	0250	13JUL87	13JUL87	30JUL87	30JUL87	13.0
12	INSTALL SEWER AND BACKFILL	5.0	5.0	PB	1-5	0250	27JUL87	31JUL87	31JUL87	06AUG87	4.0
13	INSTALL ELECTRICAL MANHOLES	5.0	5.0	EL	1-4	0250	14JUL87	20JUL87	31JUL87	06AUG87	13.0
14	OVERHEAD POLE LINE	6.0	6.0	GC	1-4	0250	13JUL87	20JUL87	04AUG87	11AUG87	16.0
15	INSTALL ELECTRICAL DUCT BNK	3.0	3.0	EL	1-4	0250	03AUG87	05AUG87	07AUG87	11AUG87	4.0
16	CONNECT WATER PIPING	2.0	2.0	PB	1-5	0250	17AUG87	18AUG87	17AUG87	18AUG87	0.0
17	PULL IN FEEDER	5.0	5.0	EL	1-4	0250	06AUG87	12AUG87	12AUG87	18AUG87	4.0

Figure 9.5 John Doe project PDM output.

135

JOHN DOE BASELINE CPM SCHEDULE
PREPARED BY O'BRIEN-KREITZBERG & ASSOC., INC.

WORK ITEM	ACTIVITY DESCRIPTION	ORG DUR	REM DUR	CNTR DUR TYPE	WORK CAT.	SPEC SEC.	EARLY START	EARLY *FINISH	LATE START	LATE *FINISH	TOTAL FLOAT
01	CLEAR SITE	3.0	3.0	GC	1-1	0210	01JUL87	06JUL87	01JUL87	06JUL87	0.0
02 PWI	SURVEY AND LAYOUT 01/ 0.0C	2.0	2.0	GC	1-2	0140	07JUL87	08JUL87	07JUL87	08JUL87	0.0
03 PWI	ROUGH GRADE 02/ 0.0C	2.0	2.0	GC	1-1	0220	09JUL87	10JUL87	09JUL87	10JUL87	0.0
04 PWI	DRILL WELL 03/ 0.0C	15.0	15.0	GC	1-7	0201	13JUL87	31JUL87	13JUL87	31JUL87	0.0
05 PWI	INSTALL WELL PUMP 04/ 0.0	2.0	2.0	PR	1-5	0250	03AUG87	04AUG87	03AUG87	04AUG87	0.0
06 PWI	WATER TANK FOUNDATIONS 03/ 0.0C	4.0	4.0	GC	1-3	0330	13JUL87	16JUL87	14JUL87	17JUL87	1.0
07 PWI	ERECT WATER TOWER 06/ 0.0C	10.0	10.0	PB	1-6	0250	17JUL87	30JUL87	20JUL87	31JUL87	1.0
08 PWI	UNDERGROUND WATER PIPING 05/ 0.0	8.0	8.0	PB	1-5	0250	05AUG87	14AUG87	05AUG87	14AUG87	0.0
09 PWI	TANK PIPING AND VALVES 07/ 0.0C	10.0	10.0	PB	1-5	0250	31JUL87	13AUG87	03AUG87	14AUG87	1.0
10 PWI	EXCAVATE FOR SEWER 03/ 0.0C	10.0	10.0	GC	1-1	0250	13JUL87	24JUL87	17JUL87	30JUL87	4.0
11 PWI	EXCAVATE ELECTRIC MANHOLES 03/ 0.0C	1.0	1.0	GC	1-1	0250	13JUL87	13JUL87	30JUL87	30JUL87	13.0
12 PWI	INSTALL SEWER AND BACKFILL 10/ 0.0C	5.0	5.0	PR	1-5	0250	27JUL87	31JUL87	31JUL87	06AUG87	4.0
13 PWI	INSTALL ELECTRICAL MANHOLES 11/ 0.0C	5.0	5.0	EL	1-4	0250	14JUL87	20JUL87	31JUL87	06AUG87	13.0
14 PWI	OVERHEAD POLE LINE 03/ 0.0C	6.0	6.0	GC	1-4	0250	13JUL87	20JUL87	04AUG87	11AUG87	16.0
15 PWI	INSTALL ELECTRICAL DUCT BNK 12/ 0.0C 13/	3.0	3.0	EL	1-4	0250	03AUG87	05AUG87	07AUG87	11AUG87	4.0
16 PWI	CONNECT WATER PIPING 08/ 0.0C 09/	2.0	2.0	PR	1-5	0250	17AUG87	18AUG87	17AUG87	18AUG87	0.0
17 PWI	PULL IN FEEDER 14/ 0.0C 15/	5.0	5.0	EL	1-4	0250	06AUG87	12AUG87	12AUG87	18AUG87	4.0

Figure 9.6 John Doe project PDM output with all precedence and succeeding activities.

This edit demonstrates that the purportedly simple PDM can become really cumbersome when presented in usable form.

PROJECT EXAMPLE

Figure 9.7 is a sample project network consisting of thirty-four work items. The work item identification numbers identify work items by functions. For instance, concrete items are grouped in the 300 series, and the electrical items are in the 700 series.

The networks indicate interrelations between work items and also options having to do with lag time factors. Three of the four lag time options have been included in the network. Durations for work items are shown in the small boxes under the work items.

The network indicates that the drilling of piers (work item 110) may begin after 50 cubic yards of excavation have been completed in work item 100, and this is represented by the line leading from 100 to 110. This shows that part of the duration of work item 110 may be concurrent with work item 100. The estimated quantity of work item in 100 is 150 cubic yards, so that work item 100 may start after approximately 33 percent of the excavation operation has been done, or in direct proportion, after half a day has elapsed. The top line leading from work item 100 to work item 110 indicates that the second work item cannot be completed until at least half a day after the completion of the first work item 100.

The rebar of pier 200 is shown to begin at least 1 day following the start of drilling the piers. This is shown by a lag time of 1 day on the connecting line. The relation of work items 205 and 400 to item 300 and following work item 310 is very similar to other diagraming relations showing concurrent activity.

Between work items 310 and 410, a delay of 1 day is shown. This lag permits 1 day of curing before the form stripping is started, and it could have been included by adding one more day to work item 310 or by introducing a work item 311 called *initial cure*.

The various delay and lag options shown in the precedence network can be duplicated by a CPM network, but additional arrows or activities are required.

The work item report is a listing printed in early-start sequence (Figure 9.8). In addition to the obvious descriptive material, the "PC" column shown in Figure 9.8 contains the amount of the operation completed in percentage, while the column "CAL FC HR S D" contains the hours per shift, shifts per day, and days per week or the calendar factor.

Precedence programs will accept schedule dates and therefore can produce negative slack.

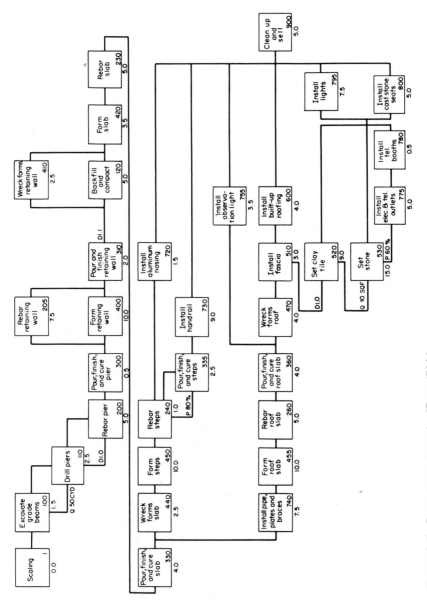

Figure 9.7 Precedence example. *(From IBM.)*

WORK ITEM	DESCRIPTION	DURATN	REMAIN DURATN	CAL FC PC HR S D	EARLY START	LATE START	EARLY FINISH	LATE FINISH	TOTAL SLACK	FREE SLACK
100	EXCAVATE GRADE BEAMS	1.5	1.5	8 1 5	4MAY	4MAY	5MAY	5MAY	.0	.0
1	WORK ITEM FOR SCALING CALENDAR	.0	.0	8 1 5	4MAY	4MAY	4MAY	4MAY	.0	.0
110	DRILL PIERS	2.5	2.5	8 1 5	4MAY	4MAY	6MAY	6MAY	.0	LAG
200	REBAR PIER	5.0	5.0	8 1 5	4MAY	5MAY	12MAY	12MAY	.0	LAG
300	POUR, FINISH AND CURE PIER	.5	.6	8 1 7	5MAY	12MAY	12MAY	12MAY	.0	.0
400	FORM RETAINING WALL	10.0	10.0	8 1 5	12MAY	12MAY	26MAY	26MAY	.0	.0
205	REBAR RETAINING WALL	7.5	7.5	8 1 5	12MAY	15MAY	22MAY	26MAY	2.5	2.5
310	POUR AND FINISH RETAINING WALL	2.0	2.0	8 1 5	26MAY	26MAY	28MAY	28MAY	.0	.0
120	BACKFILL AND COMPACT	5.0	5.0	8 1 5	1JUN	1JUN	8JUN	8JUN	.0	LAG
410	WRECK FORMS RETAINING WALL	2.5	2.5	8 1 5	1JUN	4JUN	4JUN	8JUN	2.5	LAG
420	FORM SLAB	3.5	3.5	8 1 5	8JUN	8JUN	12JUN	12JUN	.0	.0
230	REBAR SLAB	5.0	5.0	8 1 5	12JUN	12JUN	19JUN	19JUN	.0	.0
330	POUR, FINISH AND CURE SLAB	4.0	4.1	.714 8 1 5	19JUN	19JUN	24JUN	24JUN	.0	.0
740	INSTALL PIPE, PLATES AND BRACES	7.5	7.5	8 1 5	24JUN	24JUN	6JUL	6JUL	.0	.0
440	WRECK FORMS SLAB	2.5	2.5	8 1 5	24JUN	11AUG	26JUN	14AUG	33.3	.0
450	FORM STEPS	10.0	10.0	8 1 5	26JUN	14AUG	13JUL	28AUG	33.3	.0
455	FORM ROOF SLAB	10.0	10.0	8 1 5	6JUL	6JUL	20JUL	20JUL	.0	.0
240	REBAR STEPS	1.0	1.0	8 1 5	13JUL	14JUL	14JUL	31AUG	33.3	.0
335	POUR, FINISH AND CURE STEPS	2.5	2.5	8 1 5	14JUL	28AUG	16JUL	15SEP	33.3	LAG
720	INSTALL ALUMINUM NOSING	1.5	1.5	8 1 5	14JUL	14SEP	16JUL	15SEP	42.4	42.4
730	INSTALL HAND RAIL	9.0	9.0	8 1 5	16JUL	1SEP	29JUL	15SEP	33.3	33.3
260	REBAR ROOF SLAB	5.0	5.0	8 1 5	20JUL	20JUL	27JUL	27JUL	.0	.0
360	POUR, FINISH AND CURE ROOF SLAB	4.0	4.1	.714 8 1 5	27JUL	27JUL	30JUL	30JUL	.0	.0
470	WRECK FORMS ROOF	4.0	4.0	8 1 5	30JUL	30JUL	5AUG	5AUG	.0	.0
755	INSTALL OBSERVATION LIGHT	3.5	3.5	8 1 5	30JUL	10SEP	5AUG	15SEP	28.5	28.5
510	INSTALL FASCIA	3.0	3.0	8 1 5	5AUG	5AUG	10AUG	10AUG	.0	.0
520	SET CLAY TILE	9.0	9.0	8 1 5	6AUG	6AUG	19AUG	19AUG	.0	LAG

Figure 9.8 Precedence output, early-start sort (partial). *[From IBM.]*

139

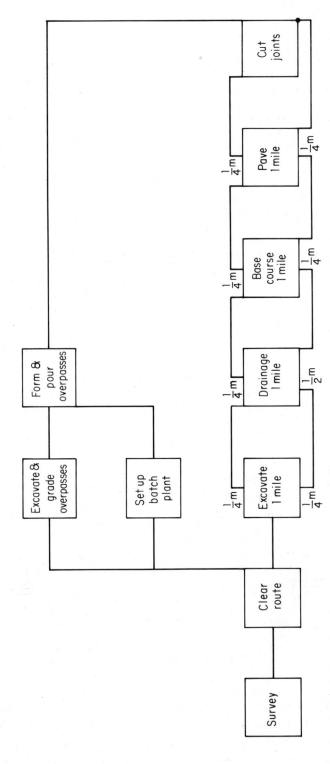

Figure 9.9 Precedence version of Figure 8.5, "Network for 1 mile of highway."

SUMMARY

While PERT has virtually disappeared from the construction scheduling scene, PDM remains a persistent participant. A more recent comer than either PERT or CPM, it offers the appeal of newness. Susceptible to ready adjustment and fine tuning, it can be readily utilized by a sophisticated scheduler.

In a recent shipyard delay claim, the scheduling consultant to one party introduced a PDM "as-built" diagram, which required a painstaking forensic review to identify what was either a blatant mistake or a deliberate lie. The more basic CPM format is not as susceptible to this type of manipulation.

Much has been claimed for the simplicity PDM offers both in regard to network diagrams and printouts (compare Figure 8.5 with the apparently simpler precedence version shown in Figure 9.9). But as in tip-of-the-iceberg cases—more is hidden than seen in many PDM schedules.

10

PROCUREMENT

Materials are involved throughout a construction project. Usually early delivery of materials cannot speed up a given activity because the progress of other activities controls its early start time. However, failure to deliver the materials for an activity can delay it indefinitely. Thus, unfortunately, the project purchasing agent or materials coordinator has a difficult problem. If he or she delivers late, the project is delayed; if he or she delivers early, the field group complains about extra handling and storage of materials. The problem reaches its most acute stage in urban areas where project supervision would like to lift materials immediately from truck or rail car to final location.

SCHEDULING PROCUREMENT OF MATERIALS

Just as subcontractors complain that the general contractor neglects their situation, most purchasing agents complain that their own companies fail to keep them informed about materials needed. Obviously, this is a problem which can be solved with CPM information. Since almost every activ-

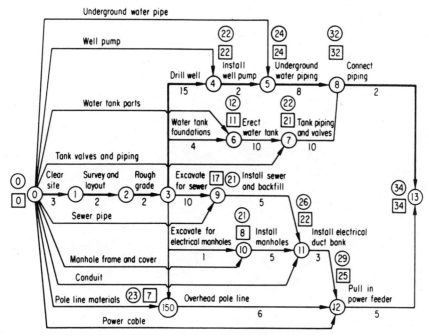

Figure 10.1 Deliveries for John Doe project site preparation, zero delivery.

ity requires materials of some sort, however, one would have to review all the activities in order to control the delivery of all their materials. A practical method of reducing this burden of work is to separate materials into two classes: commodities and key materials. Those materials which can be ordered out of stock for delivery in a week or less can be classified as *commodities*. The schedule for the first shipment of any type of commodity is useful. *Key materials* are those with long delivery times, or those which involve custom orders. Reviewing the network computer run can furnish all the necessary information about materials, particularly the order in which key materials should be requisitioned. However, by adding an arrow to the diagram for each key delivery, the necessary information about it is generated as part of the computer run.

Figure 10.1 shows the site preparation network for the John Doe project with the following delivery arrows added:

Activity		Delivery
0-4	....	Well pump
0-5	....	Underground water pipe
0-6	....	Water tank parts
0-7	....	Tank valves and piping
0-9	....	Sewer pipe

Activity		*Delivery*
0-10	....	Manhole frame and cover
0-11	....	Conduit
0-12	....	Power cable
0-150	....	Poles, crossbars, guys, insulators

Of these, well pump and water tank would definitely be key deliveries. The others could be commodities or custom items depending upon the specification to be met. If it is assumed that all materials are on hand (for instance, if the owner is furnishing them), the time duration for these activities would be zero. The computed information for the deliveries would be:

i-j	Duration, days	Description	ES	EF	LS	LF	Float, days
0-4	0	Well pump	0	0	22	22	22
0-5	0	Underground pipe	0	0	24	24	24
0-6	0	Water tank	0	0	12	12	12
0-7	0	Tank valves	0	0	22	22	22
0-9	0	Sewer pipe	0	0	21	21	21
0-10	0	Manhole frame and cover	0	0	21	21	21
0-11	0	Conduit	0	0	26	26	26
0-12	0	Power feeder	0	0	29	29	29
0-150	0	Pole line materials	0	0	23	23	23

Since materials would not usually be available at the start of the project, reasonable delivery time estimates are assigned to these delivery activities as follows:

	Activity	Assume	Duration, days
0-4	Well pump	Stock delivery, 4 weeks	20
0-5	Underground water pipe	Mechanical joint, 6 weeks	30
0-6	Water tank parts	Standard size, 6 weeks	30
0-7	Tank valves	Standard gate valves, 4 weeks	20
0-9	Sewer pipe	Terra cotta, 1 week	5
0-10	Manhole cover	Stock, 1 week	5
0-11	Conduit	Stock, 1 week	5
0-12	Power feeder	Special order, 8 weeks	40
0-150	Pole material	Stock order, 2 weeks	10

These durations are added to Figure 10.2. Event times are computed on the diagram. The activity times for deliveries are:

$i-j$	Duration, days	Description	ES	EF	LS	LF	Float, days
0-4	20	Well pump	0	20	20	40	20
0-5	30	Underground water pipe	0	30	12	42	12
0-6	30	Water tank	0	30	0	30	0
0-7	20	Tank valves	0	20	20	40	20
0-9	5	Sewer pipe	0	5	34	39	34
0-10	5	Manhole cover	0	5	34	39	34
0-11	5	Conduit	0	5	39	44	39
0-12	40	Power feeder	0	40	7	47	7
0-150	10	Pole material	0	10	31	41	31

The introduction of delivery times has increased this portion of the project from 34 days to 52 days. The critical path has shifted and is now through events 0-6-7-8-13. The old and new event times are:

Early event times			Late event times	
Old	New	Event	Old	New
3	3	1	3	21
5	5	2	5	23
7	7	3	7	25
22	22	4	22	40
24	30	5	24	42
11	30	6	12	30
21	40	7	22	40
32	50	8	32	50
17	17	9	21	39
8	8	10	21	39
22	22	11	26	44
25	40	12	29	47
34	52	13	34	52
...	10	150	...	41
Changes 7			Changes 14	

Twenty-one event times of a possible twenty-eight have changed. Using the new late-start information, the purchasing department would deliver the materials in the following order:

Activity	Description	Late start
0-6	Water tank	0
0-12	Power feeder	7
0-5	Underground water pipe	12

Activity	Description	Late start
0-4	Well pump	20
0-7	Tank valves	20
0-150	Pole material	31
0-9	Sewer pipe	34
0-10	Manhole cover	34
0-11	Conduit	39

While this list gives the order in which materials should be ordered, it has two distinct weaknesses. First, although the late start dates for ordering are important, they are extremes. If the order is placed this late, all activities following the delivery will be critical. Second, the early start times have very little value. In this example, the purchasing department could initiate nine orders the first day of the project. What, for instance, if an enthusiastic buyer orders the sewer pipe and conduit on the first project day? The conduit would arrive on site about 8 weeks before it was needed; the sewer pipe would be 7 weeks early. The field group would have a storage problem and develop a poor opinion of the office group.

These problems have often discouraged the use of CPM for the coordination of materials procurement. What is the real defect in the system noted thus far? The early start time is unrelated to the field work. Leaving

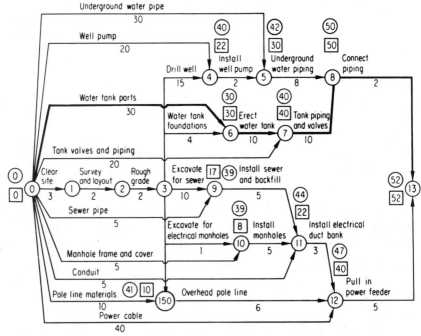

Figure 10.2 Delivery times for John Doe project site preparation.

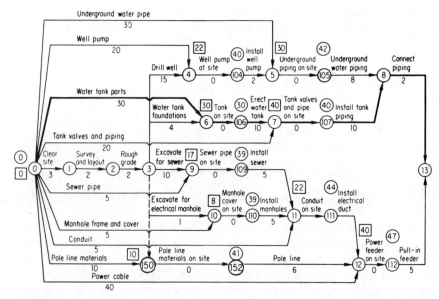

Figure 10.3 On-site delivery times.

the delivery arrows to represent delivery time, just as they were, add another set of arrows to represent the actual movement of the material from storage to the job site. These "on-site material" arrows have zero time duration and the same late finish times as the delivery arrows. Figure 10.3 shows these nine new arrows. Since they have a zero time duration, early start equals early finish and late finish equals late start. The ES, LF, and float times are:

Activity	Description	ES	LF	Float,
4-104	Well pump at site	22	40	18
5-105	Underground pipe at site	30	42	12
6-106	Water tank at site	30	30	0
7-107	Tank valves at site	40	40	0
9-109	Sewer pipe at site	17	39	22
10-110	Manhole cover at site	8	39	31
11-111	Conduit at site	22	44	22
12-112	Power feeder at site	40	47	7
150-152	Pole material at site	10	41	31

Note that the late finish times for these activities are the same as the late finish times for the delivery arrows. However, the early start times and float times are now related to the field progress.

On this basis, priority of ordering would be:

Priority	Position on first order list	Delivery as early as	Delivery no later than	Float, days
1. Water tank	1	30	30	0
2. Tank valves	5	40	40	0
3. Power feeder	2	40	47	7
4. Underground pipe	3	30	42	12
5. Well pump	4	22	40	18
6. Sewer pipe	7	17	39	22
7. Conduit	9	22	44	22
8. Manhole cover at site	8	8	39	31
9. Pole material	6	10	41	31

Note that all but two of the items are in a different position of priority on this second list.

In addition to the time required for the delivery of materials and the determination of the delivery time which should be specified on the order, there are a number of other steps in materials procurement which are time-consuming and must not be neglected. These can include approval of shop drawings, architect's review of shop drawings, resubmittal time for shop drawing corrections, review by cognizant agencies (HHFA, HFA, HRB, etc.). These steps can sometimes be accelerated for critical activities (when they are, in fact, identified as critical). However, there is a tendency to minimize the impact of these routine steps. Take care to reflect them properly on your diagram.

Figure 10.4 shows the interrelation between two material orders (hardware and door bucks) before either reaches the job site. Note that in this example the door buck delivery has 5 days float because of the additional time required to prepare hardware templates. Larger equipment may require additional time for the submission of formal bids. In Figure 10.1, the addition of nine simple delivery arrows almost doubled the network

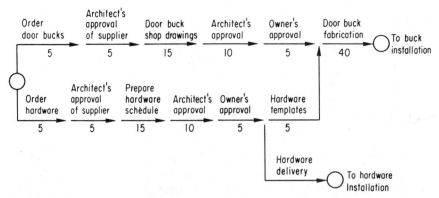

Figure 10.4 Typical material procurement cycle.

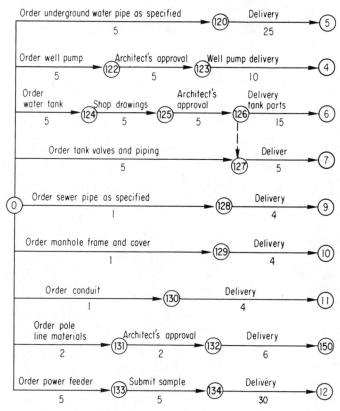

Figure 10.5 John Doe project material procurement.

size. In this network, the number of arrows showing the total materials procurement situation could easily be more than double the number of arrows showing the associated field work. Since the average project requires several separate sheets to represent its network, it is recommended that the materials procurement work be on its own sheet. This avoids confusion between the office and field functions. Of course, the "materials at site" arrows must remain with the field portion of the network. Figure 10.5 shows the materials portion of the John Doe project.

MATERIAL LEAD TIMES

Some typical material lead times for a process plant project are as follows:

	Building	
	Approval of drawings, weeks	Anticipated delivery (after approval and release), weeks
ENCLOSURE:		
Structural steel	4–6	8–13
Steel joists	2–4	8–10
Siding	3–4	13–26
MECHANICAL:		
HVAC-Fans	2–4	13–18
HVAC-Chillers	4–6	18–26
Agitators/mixers	6–8	26–32
Centrifugal blowers	4–6	20–26
Compressors (packaged centrifugal)	8–10	26–39
Compressors (Packaged Reciprocating)	6–8	26–30
ELECTRICAL EQUIPMENT		
Motor control centers	8–10	26–40
Switch gear (low voltage)	8–10	36–40
Switch Gear (High Voltage)	8–10	40–52
Transformers (Low Voltage)	6–8	30–39
Transformers (High Voltage)	6–8	40–52
Motors (to 150 horsepower)	6–8	16–26
Motors (over 150 horsepower)	6–8	26–39 (dependent on horsepower)
Turbines	8–10	40–50
Power cable (600 volt)	N/R	30–52 (dependent on quantity)
Bus duct	6–8	26–36
Cable tray	6–8	18–26
Conduit (rigid alum.)	N/R	Stock—28
Conduit (E.M.T.)	N/R	Stock—26
Emergency generators	10–12	26–30
ARCHITECTURAL:		
Hollow metal frames	8–10	12–18
Hardware	10–12	18–26
	Process Equipment	
PRESSURE VESSELS (CARBON STEEL:		
Small (non code)	4–6	18–26*
Small (code—under 20,000#)	4–6	26–36*
Large (code—over 20,000#)	6–8	36–40
Towers (w/o internals/trays)	6–8	46–50
Towers (with internals/trays)	8–10	52–60
Jacketed vessels/tanks	8–10	52–60
		*Add 4 weeks for stainless
FIELD-ERECTED TANKS:	8–10	40–52 (includes erection)
HEAT EXCHANGERS:		
Shell and tube (small)	4–6	18–20
Shell and tube (large)	6–8	36–46
Fintube	4–6	18–26
Plate type	4–6	36–40
Air-cooled exchangers	4–6	26–36

Process Equipment		
	Approval of drawings, weeks	Anticipated delivery (after approval and release), weeks
CONVEYORS:		
Pneumatic	6–8	26–30
Screw	6–8	24–30
Live roller and drag	6–8	24–28
Vibrating	6–8	26–30
Bucket elevators	6–8	26–30
Belt	6–8	30–34
PUMPS:		
Centrifugal	4–6	20–26
Centrifugal (horiz.)	6–8	26–32
Centrifugal (turbine)	6–8	24–30
Metering	4–6	20–34
Positive displacement	4–6	20–24
Vacuum	6–8	26–30
Reciprocating	6–8	26–30
DRYERS, FILTERS, SCRUBBERS:		
Instrument air dryers	8–10	24–30
Filters	6–8	20–26
Dust collectors	6–8	30–40
Fume scrubbers	6–8	20–30
Control valves	3–4	20–24
INSTRUMENTATION:		
Displacement-type flow meters	3–4	18–26
D.P. transmitters	4–5	16–22
Liquid level gauges	3–4	18–20
Transducers	3–4	14–28
Level switches	3–4	12–16
Pressure switches	3–4	16–18
Controllers	4–5	18–20
Recorders	4–5	18–20
Thermometers	3–4	14–16
Pressure gauges	3–4	16–20
Pipe, valves, flanges and fittings	N/A	Stock to 52 weeks

Materials Handling Equipment		
Monorail hoists	4–6	18–26 (dependent on capacity)
Traveling/trolley cranes	4–6	30–42 (dependent on capacity)
Fork lift trucks	4–6	26–30

JOHN DOE EXAMPLE

As noted previously, it is not usual to incorporate commodity or stock items into the CPM network. Many projects have a 3- to 9-month excavation, foundation (piles), and foundation concrete phase which has a short cycle start-up for the design mix and rebar delivery. In this typical

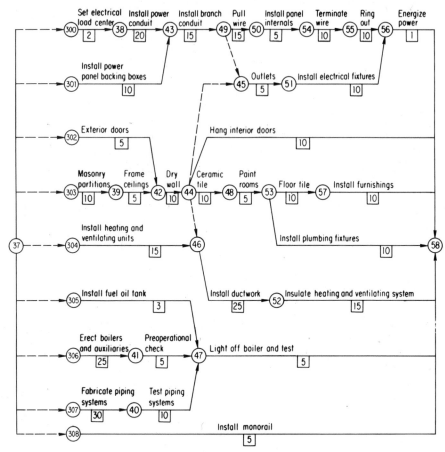

Figure 10.6 John Doe plant with added delivery points.

situation, the site and foundation work schedule has float built into it for the procurement process.

In the John Doe site example, the owner would do well to provide the water tank and well pump. Another approach would be to evaluate the requirement to provide all site services prior to event 34. If the site activities could be put in parallel with foundation work, more time would be available for site equipment procurement.

The site equipment procurement has been treated previously. To consider procurement for the balance of the John Doe project, the network should be modified to create more definitive delivery points. For instance, event 37 is a common starting point for all plant activities. Accordingly, it is not the best delivery node. Adding logic spreaders between event 37 and key delivery points will establish more definitive delivery information. This is shown in Figure 10.6.

TABLE 10.1 John Doe Procurement Activities (after site work)

Item	Starting event	Submit shop drawings, work days	Event	Approve shop drawings, work days	Event	Fabricate and deliver, work days	Event
Foundation rebar	0	10	210	10	211	10	16
Structural steel	0	20	212	10	213	40	23
Crane	0	20	214	10	215	50	31
Bar joists	0	20	216	10	217	30	33
Siding	0	20	218	10	219	40	35
Plant electrical load center	0	20	220	10	221	90	37
Power panels— plant	0	20	222	10	223	75	37
Exterior doors	0	20	224	10	225	80	37
Plant electrical fixtures	0	30	225	15	226	75	51
Plant heating and ventilating fans	0	20	227	10	228	75	37
Boiler	0	20	229	10	230	60	37
Oil tank	0	20	231	10	232	50	37
Precast	0	40	223	10	234	30	58
Packaging A/C	0	30	235	10	236	90	60

Table 10.1 lists the sequence of procurement activities (i.e., submit and approve shop drawings, fabricate and deliver) for fourteen items. These were added to the computer master file and a new computation made. The procurement portion of the John Doe project (after the site work) is listed by late start (in order of float priority) in Figure 10.7. Note that the example procurement times are in the expeditious range. If the times, especially for switch gear, were taken from the prior typical procurement time tables, procurement would control the schedule. Assuming that this would be unacceptable, the owner has two choices: either expedite (i.e., shorten) the procurement dates, or preorder (i.e., order before selecting the contractor) key equipment such as well pump, water tank, electrical switch gear, steel, and other major items.

Figure 10.8 is a sort (partial) of the John Doe project by specification section. This can be used by the purchasing department to determine the scope of work under each specification section when preparing subcontracts or purchase orders.

JOHN DOE HASELINE CPM SCHEDULE
PREPARED BY O'BRIEN-KREITZBERG & ASSOC., INC.

I NODE	J NODE	ACTIVITY DESCRIPTION	ORG DUR	REM DUR	CNTR TYPE	WORK CAT.	SPEC SEC.	EARLY START	EARLY *FINISH	LATE START	LATE *FINISH	TOTAL FLOAT
0	212	SUBMIT S/D STRUCT STEEL	20.0	20.0	—	—	0510	01JUL87	29JUL87	01JUL87	29JUL87	0.0
0	220	SUB S/D PLANT ELEC LOAD CTR	20.0	20.0	—	—	1640	01JUL87	29JUL87	10JUL87	06AUG87	6.0
0	224	SUBMIT S/D EXTERIOR DOORS	20.0	20.0	—	—	0810	01JUL87	29JUL87	24JUL87	20AUG87	16.0
0	225	SUB S/D PLANT ELECT FIXTS	30.0	30.0	—	—	1640	01JUL87	12AUG87	24JUL87	03SEP87	16.0
212	213	APPROVE S/D STRUCT STEEL	10.0	10.0	—	—		30JUL87	12AUG87	30JUL87	12AUG87	0.0
0	222	SUBMIT S/D PWR PNLS-PLANT	20.0	20.0	—	—	1640	01JUL87	29JUL87	31JUL87	27AUG87	21.0
0	227	SUB S/D PLANT HTG VENT FANS	20.0	20.0	—	—	1580	01JUL87	29JUL87	31JUL87	27AUG87	21.0
0	210	SUBMIT S/D FOUNDATION REBAR	10.0	10.0	—	—	0230	01JUL87	15JUL87	03AUG87	14AUG87	22.0
0	214	SUBMIT S/D CRANE	20.0	20.0	—	—	1430	01JUL87	29JUL87	06AUG87	02SEP87	25.0
220	221	APPR S/D PL ELECT LOAD CTR	10.0	10.0	—	—		30JUL87	12AUG87	07AUG87	20AUG87	6.0
213	23	FAB/DEL STRUCTURAL STEEL	40.0	40.0	—	—		13AUG87	08OCT87	13AUG87	08OCT87	0.0
210	211	APPROVE S/D FDN REBAR	10.0	10.0	—	—		16JUL87	29JUL87	17AUG87	28AUG87	22.0
221	37	FAB/DEL PLANT EL LOAD CTR	90.0	90.0	—	—		13AUG87	21DEC87	21AUG87	30DEC87	6.0
224	225	APPROVE S/D EXTERIOR DOORS	10.0	10.0	—	—		30JUL87	12AUG87	21AUG87	03SEP87	16.0
0	229	SUB S/D BOILER	20.0	20.0	—	—	1560	01JUL87	29JUL87	21AUG87	18SEP87	36.0
222	223	APPROVE S/D PWR PNLS-PLANT	10.0	10.0	—	—		30JUL87	12AUG87	28AUG87	11SEP87	21.0
227	228	APPR S/D PLNT HTG VENT FANS	10.0	10.0	—	—		30JUL87	12AUG87	28AUG87	11SEP87	21.0
211	16	FAB/DEL FOUNDATION REBAR	10.0	10.0	—	—		30JUL87	12AUG87	31AUG87	14SEP87	22.0
214	215	APPROVE S/D CRANE	10.0	10.0	—	—		30JUL87	12AUG87	03SEP87	17SEP87	25.0
225	37	FAB/DEL EXTERIOR DOORS	80.0	80.0	—	—		13AUG87	07DEC87	17SEP87	30DEC87	16.0
0	218	SUBMIT S/D SIDING	20.0	20.0	—	—	0740	01JUL87	29JUL87	04SEP87	02OCT87	46.0
0	231	SUBMIT S/D OIL TANK	20.0	20.0	—	—	1560	01JUL87	29JUL87	04SEP87	02OCT87	46.0
0	216	SUBMIT S/D BAR JOISTS	20.0	20.0	—	—	0520	01JUL87	29JUL87	11SEP87	08OCT87	50.0
223	37	FAB/DEL POWER PANELS-PLANT	75.0	75.0	—	—		13AUG87	30NOV87	14SEP87	30DEC87	21.0
228	37	FAB/DEL PLANT HTG VENT FANS	75.0	75.0	—	—		13AUG87	30NOV87	14SEP87	30DEC87	21.0
215	31	FAB/DEL CRANE	50.0	50.0	—	—		13AUG87	22OCT87	18SEP87	30NOV87	25.0
229	230	APPROVE S/D BOILER	10.0	10.0	—	—		30JUL87	12AUG87	21SEP87	02OCT87	36.0
230	37	FAB/DEL BOILER	60.0	60.0	—	—		13AUG87	05NOV87	05OCT87	30DEC87	36.0
218	219	APPROVE S/D SIDING	10.0	10.0	—	—		30JUL87	12AUG87	05OCT87	16OCT87	46.0
231	232	APPROVE S/D OIL TANK	10.0	10.0	—	—		30JUL87	12AUG87	05OCT87	16OCT87	46.0
216	217	APPROVE S/D BAR JOISTS	10.0	10.0	—	—		30JUL87	12AUG87	09OCT87	22OCT87	50.0
219	35	FAB/DEL SIDING	40.0	40.0	—	—		13AUG87	08OCT87	19OCT87	15DEC87	46.0
232	37	FAB/DEL OIL TANK	50.0	50.0	—	—		13AUG87	22OCT87	19OCT87	30DEC87	46.0
217	33	FAB/DEL BAR JOISTS	30.0	30.0	—	—		13AUG87	24SEP87	23OCT87	07DEC87	50.0
0	235	SUBMIT S/D PACKAGING A/C	30.0	30.0	—	—	1580	01JUL87	12AUG87	29OCT87	11FEC87	84.0
225	226	APPR S/D PLANT ELECT FIXTS	15.0	15.0	—	—		13AUG87	02SEP87	27NOV87	17DEC87	73.0
235	236	APPROVE S/D PACKAGING A/C	10.0	10.0	—	—		13AUG87	26AUG87	14DEC87	28DEC87	84.0
226	51	FAB/DEL PLANT ELEC FIXTURES	75.0	75.0	—	—		03SEP87	21DEC87	18DEC87	05APR88	73.0
236	60	FAB/DEL PACKAGING A/C	90.0	90.0	—	—		27AUG87	06JAN88	29DEC87	04MAY88	84.0
0	233	SUBMIT S/D PRECAST	40.0	40.0	—	—	0340	01JUL87	26AUG87	29DEC87	24FEB88	124.0
233	234	APPROVE S/D PRECAST	10.0	10.0	—	—		27AUG87	10SEP87	25FEB88	09MAR88	124.0
234	58	FAB/DEL PRECAST	30.0	30.0	—	—		11SEP87	22OCT87	10MAR88	20APR88	124.0

Figure 10.7 Materials by late start, computer-run.

I NODE	J NODE	ACTIVITY DESCRIPTION	ORG DUR	REM DUR	CNTR TYPE	WORK CAT.	SPEC SEC.	EARLY START	EARLY *FINISH	LATE START	LATE *FINISH	TOTAL FLOAT
		TILE-0930										
44	48	CERAMIC TILE	10.0	10.0	GC	3-7	0930	05FEB88	19FEB88	03MAR88	16MAR88	18.0
69	73	CERAMIC TILE OFFICE	10.0	10.0	GC	4-7	0930	23JUN88	07JUL88	29JUL88	11AUG88	25.0
72	80	FLOOR TILE OFFICE	10.0	10.0	GC	4-7	0930	05AUG88	18AUG88	05AUG88	18AUG88	0.0
		ACOUSTICAL-0950										
78	80	ACOUSTIC TILE OFFICE	10.0	10.0	GC	4-7	0950	05AUG88	18AUG88	05AUG88	18AUG88	0.0
		SUSPENSION SYSTEMS-0954										
77	78	INSTALL CEILING GRID OFFICE	5.0	5.0	GC	4-8	0954	08JUL88	14JUL88	29JUL88	04AUG88	15.0
		RESILIENT FLOOR*G-0965										
53	57	FLOOR TILE P-W	10.0	10.0	GC	3-7	0965	29FEB88	11MAR88	24MAR88	06APR88	18.0
		PAINTING-0990										
48	53	PAINT ROOMS P-W	5.0	5.0	GC	3-7	0990	22FEB88	26FEB88	17MAR88	23MAR88	18.0
63	80	PAINT OFFICE EXTERIOR	5.0	5.0	GC	4-7	0990	01JUN88	07JUN88	12AUG88	18AUG88	51.0
71	72	PAINT EXTERIOR OFFICE	10.0	10.0	GC	4-7	0990	22JUL88	04AUG88	22JUL88	04AUG88	0.0
		FLAGPOLES-1035										
58	80	ERECT FLAGPOLE	5.0	5.0	GC	5-7	1035	21APR88	27APR88	12AUG88	18AUG88	79.0
		FURNISHING-1200										
57	58	INSTALL FURNISHING P-W	10.0	10.0	GC	3-7	1200	14MAR88	25MAR88	07APR88	20APR88	18.0
		HOISTS & CRANES-1430										
0	214	SUBMIT S/D CRANE	20.0	20.0		-	1430	01JUL87	29JUL87	06AUG87	02SEP87	25.0

Figure 10-8 Network report sort by specification section.

SUMMARY

If procurement is ignored in the scheduling process, materials and equipment deliveries can become the controlling factors by default. In most major programs, there is enough nonmaterials-oriented front end work to allow time to order materials through the contractor. However, in special situations (renovations, overseas projects, and/or fast-track projects) it may be necessary for the owner to preorder equipment or materials.

THE CPM SCHEDULE

CPM separates planning and scheduling. With the project information collected and expressed as a network plan, and activity time estimates assigned, the CPM calculations can be made. Where does planning cease and scheduling start? The first computation marks the end of the planning phase. Once there is a project duration to compare with the desired schedule, the scheduling effort starts. The first comparison is for end date.

PRELIMINARY SCHEDULE

The owner sets the schedule for the work, utilizing advice from his or her designer and other confidants, but generally undertaking establishment of the schedule himself or herself. The typical schedule is a tight one, either intentionally or accidentally. The intentionally tight schedule is a reflection of the requirements that the project will fulfill for the owner. (Often by the time the design is completed, much of the time originally available has been utilized in the preconstruction stages.) The accidentally short construction schedule occurs when the owner is not knowledgeable or realistic about the time necessary to construct the project at hand.

Time of delivery of a construction project is a key factor to the owner. In terms of the cost of the project, it is important to the contractor also. Therefore, the contractor must have some definite opinion as to the overall length of the project in order to make a meaningful bid on it. Some of the contractor's overhead can be spread throughout the job. However, there will inevitably be additional costs to the contractor in terms of price escalation due to wages and a basic overhead cost that is tied to the length of the job rather than to the specific level of field activity the job will entail. Therefore, some contingent amount must be included in the bid to cover possible risk or exposure due to an extended contract. But if the contractor is to be the successful bidder, these contingencies cannot be extravagant.

Preconstruction Analysis

The owner who includes only the completion date in the contract has very little control during the progress of the job. In order to establish feasible schedules, many owners are turning to a preconstruction evaluation by their staff, consultants, or the construction manager, if one has already been assigned. The purpose of this prebid analysis is the development of a construction plan by knowledgeable people that can be used as the basis of the owner's schedule. The preconstruction study may well inform the owner that a reasonable contractor under normal circumstances cannot meet the owner's dates. The owner would then have a number of alternatives. One of these would be to describe the contract time as a tight one, and insist that overtime be programed into the project on a preset basis, such as 6 or 7 days a week. Another approach would be to require that the contractor work double shifts. There are, of course, severe budget impositions as a result of this type of measure. Also, such an approach would have to be evaluated in terms of area work practice. Some labor unions require a full premium for double shifts, while others impose only a nominal increase. Some areas will not work on this accelerated basis, regardless of salary premium. Another alternative is for the preconstruction schedule study team to establish a phased, projected series of dates at which parts of the project could be taken over by the owner. Often this meets the owner's true requirements. In this case, the phasing is made part of the contract, and no additional cost is programed into the project.

When a preconstruction evaluation of this type has been made, there are two basic approaches that the owner can take. One is to state that such a study has occurred, and that, therefore, there is a practicality to the dates required. This contractual clause usually goes on to state that liquidated damages are based upon reality and will be imposed. The second approach is to furnish the study or make it available to all bidders (as with soil borings).

In the first instance, the scheduling information given to the contractor is only a narrative statement. The owner does not include the results of the study as part of the contract documents. The recommended approach is to include at least a summary network and/or computer run of the network for use by the bidding contractor. This section can be marked "Information only." However, it gives the contractor a rapid method of evaluating one way in which the project can be accomplished. And when more detailed scheduling information is offered, it should be conditioned in that manner also. The inclusion of a network does not mean that the contractor *must* perform the project in this specific manner, but rather suggests that this is one way of doing it. The owner is, after all, attempting to buy the innovative thinking of the contractors as one of their basic skills.

Contractor Preconstruction Analysis

In most cases, bidding contractors do not make a serious evaluation of the contractual time requirements, unless they are unusually and obviously stringent. Twenty years ago, liquidated damages assigned by engineers were usually a "wrist slap" of $100 per day. [Compare this with the hospital that had a $200,000-per-month (or $6700-per-calendar-day) time damage.] Even today liquidated damages are generally set fairly low. The contractor who includes a condition in his or her bid response will definitely be found nonresponsive by public agencies, and may be found nonresponsive by private organizations. The bid of the contractor who has questioned or conditioned the time frame of a contract usually must be rejected. Therefore, most contractors will not do so, but may state their reservations about the projected dates after the award of the contract. Experienced contractors know that there will be unforeseen conditions and unexpected situations for which time extensions will be allowed. They also expect changes on the part of owners and anticipate that owners will either relax end dates, or that if need be, they (the contractors) will be able to successfully handle any delay claim on the part of the owners. Further, liquidated damages have traditionally been set too low by owners who are unaware that their claims for damages are limited by the liquidated damages.

Milestones

The preconstruction schedule can be used to develop something more than an end date. By means of the network evaluation, key milestone points can be identified. The analysis really tells the owner that if certain things do not occur by certain stages of the project, there is no way in which the end date can be met. Therefore, the section in the contract on scheduling can establish these milestones as specific days following the notice to proceed.

Normally the only scheduling requirement included in a contract is the end date by which the contractor agrees to complete the project. There usually *is* general language to the effect that the contractor shall keep on schedule. However, contractors, when running behind schedule, can always allege that they are going to put on more work force, will work overtime when required, or are bringing more subcontractors onto the project. There are usually no definitive means of establishing that they have failed to meet their contractual obligations.

The establishment of the *milestone* as a contractual requirement helps ensure that the owner has a means of controlling the project's progress, and gives a definitive area in which to require performance by the contractor. The contract language should include some flexibility, permitting the owner to adjust milestone dates if a contractor requests such a change and can demonstrate a realistic means of readjusting. Such requests should be in writing, and their approval should require the signed concurrence of the owner.

Typical milestone points include: completion of foundations; completion of structure; close-in and watertightness of structure; start of temporary heat; complete basic air handling system; complete permanent heat; complete lighting system. Milestone dates can also be established by area. Thus, in a hospital, certain areas may be designated for acceptance by the owner in stages. A typical initial area is the ambulatory care and staff administrative spaces. If the owner intends to take phased occupancy, the decision should be made early in the design stage, so that the layout of the facility will reflect the incremental occupancy intended. Also, the mechanical and electrical systems may require controls by local area.

END DATE EVALUATION

If the end date of the initial plan is later than the desired date, the first area to be examined is the critical path. There are two distinct methods for shortening the critical path. First, examine the path for series sequences which could be in parallel. For instance, in the John Doe project, it would shorten the critical path by 74 days if the company were able to revise their ground rule about doing the office building after the plant and warehouse. However, if this is not possible, other possible areas of overlap should be studied, such as:

1. In the foundation contract, do the pile caps (16-17) and grade beams (17-18) in parallel rather than in series. Time savings, 5 days.

2. In the foundation contract, do the underslab plumbing (19-20) and conduit (20-22) in parallel rather than in series. Time savings, 5 days.

3. Do the floor slabs (22-29) parallel with the structural steel and craneway erection (29 through 33). This would be possible by working from opposite ends of the building. Time savings, 10 days.

4. Start siding erection earlier, at event 33 instead of 35. Time savings, 5 days.

This would mean a total time savings of 25 days. The plant-warehouse area does not offer much opportunity for time savings because several paths would have to be shortened.

If this time reduction is not sufficient, the next possibility would be to reexamine the critical activities with longer durations. Perhaps by adding equipment and work force, the time for some of these could be shortened. For instance:

15-16   Shorten "excavation" from 5 to 3 days.

16-17   Shorten "pour pile caps" from 5 to 3 days.

17-18   Shorten "grade beams" from 10 to 5 days.

And so on. Take care not to shorten durations arbitrarily. There is an unfortunate tendency to be optimistic when estimating the project time required for an activity. A few people fall into the trap of using the best time they have ever experienced. Further, it is easy to overlook the time inevitably lost in coordinating many activities. Experienced estimators must include this factor in their estimates.

SCHEDULE VERSUS CALENDAR

After a suitable end date has been realized by adjusting the network, look at the practicality of the dates computed. For instance, in the John Doe networks, all foundation work is to be finished in early November. This is reasonable and allows a little room for the unexpected. In an actual high-rise project, the plumbing tests were predicted for November. They were delayed for a few weeks and the hard-freeze period set in. Then what should have been a 1-week test took 6 weeks to accomplish.

So, look at the dates computed and compare the activity with the weather you might expect at that time of the year. This is an area where you are much better equipped than the computer. What if you find that the concrete, earthwork, etc., phases are going to occur at an unfavorable time of year? First, facing up to the fact that a winter job will cost more, try a delay of the project until spring. If your end date is acceptable, set up your schedule on this basis. If you cannot afford the delay, consider applying overtime, extra crews, etc., at the start of the project to complete as much as possible before the onset of bad weather.

What do you do about that part of the work which must necessarily be done during a period of bad weather? This was perhaps best answered by a Pennsylvania Dutch concrete superintendent when asked what he would do if it rained during a big slab pour: "I'll just let it rain." If you must work through seasonal bad weather, add project time to account for lower working efficiency. This factor will vary from Canada southward, of course. You do not have to alter each time estimate to account for the weather factor. Again, this would obscure the facts of the matter. A practical method is the *weather arrow.* Assume, for instance, that the portion of the John Doe project network between events 29 and 37 was to be accomplished in January and February. The total durations for this sequence of work is 36 days. In the Middle Atlantic States we could assume an efficiency of 60 percent in this weather, that is, 3 days work accomplished for each five project days. To introduce this factor into the network, add an activity "weather factor" (29-37) with a duration of 60 days. In Montana the efficiency factor might drop to 40 percent; in Alaska it might be even lower; Texas could hit an almost normal schedule.

The Texas Department of Highways and Pennsylvania Department of Transportation (PennDOT) have published their own schedule of productive days anticipated per month for highway construction subject to weather influences. The PennDOT schedule is as follows:

Month	Work days	Cumulative work days	Conversion factor, work days to calendar days	Cumulative calendar days
Jan.	2	2	15.50	31
Feb.	2	4	14.00	59
Mar.	7	11	4.429	90
Apr.	12	23	2.500	120
May	18	41	1.722	151
June	18	59	1.667	181
July	18	77	1.722	212
Aug.	18	95	1.722	243
Sept.	18	113	1.667	273
Oct.	15	128	2.067	304
Nov.	5	133	6.00	334
Dec.	2	135	15.50	365

CONTINGENCY

Achievement of the end date desired is not necessarily an acceptable schedule. CPM has not furnished us with a crystal ball. Even though the activities and times estimates used in the network are based upon experience, a project rarely finishes ahead of its computed end date. Since weather, difficult site conditions, labor disputes, change orders, etc., are unavoidable but rather unpredictable, there is a definite tendency for the actual completion date to exceed the first CPM end date. It is, then, reasonable to allow for some contingency between the CPM end date and the actual desired completion date. How much of a contingency? There is no definite answer to this; it will vary with the specific circumstances of the project. However, if you need a 12-month period for completion of the project, set your CPM goal at about 11 months, and so forth. Some people have been reluctant to set a flat contingency at the end of the schedule. Contingency can be buried in the activity estimates, but if it is, you will not be able to separate true estimates from contingency.

Another approach is the use of contingency based upon anticipated site conditions, or any predictable problems which can be projected with some reasonableness. Then, in a fashion similar to the weather arrow, a specific contingency can be identified and assigned only to that area which it would impact. For instance, availability of space to shake out structural steel would impact during the time frame in which the structural steel is being erected; difficult site access would be solved after construction roads are in place; storage of equipment and materials would become less of a problem when foundations are ready and the equipment and materials can be set in place.

SCHEDULE MANIPULATION

Contractors may use the conversion of the basic plan into a schedule as an opportunity to manipulate the schedule in their favor. In one major hospital project ($125 million), the contractor submitted a network plan for a 4-year project which showed a very easy and extended schedule for foundations and structure which spanned more than 50 percent of the 4-year time frame available to perform the project. All of the mechanical, electrical, and finish work was crowded into less than half the time allotted for the project. To the scheduling reviewer, it was clear that the contractor intended to set up a schedule which would be easy to meet during the front end, thus keeping the project management team "off his back," while claiming that the final portions of the very complex project could be achieved in record time. The construction manager had imposed a very complete CPM specification, which unfortunately failed to establish interim milestones. This lack of milestones allowed this contractor's hybrid approach (i.e., slow start, fast finish) to meet the letter of the specification, even when clearly not meeting its spirit. Since it is important to have a baseline as-planned schedule, the CPM consultant recommended accepting the schedule, although pointing out its obvious weaknesses to the contractor. Further, it was clearly noted that if the contractor did not perform more quickly than his schedule called for during the first 2 years, there was no practical probability that he would complete the project on time.

Manipulation of a schedule, however, can be a two-edged sword, as it turned out to be in this case. The contractor did have delays during the early portion of the project, but his schedule did not support any delay impact due to changes caused by unforeseen conditions. Accordingly, he was properly denied time extensions which he might otherwise have been allowed.

In the same project, the contractor also attempted to have the network defined as 100 percent critical. Given enough time and effort, he doubtless could have succeeded in this. But what he ended up with was a network showing approximately 80 percent of the activities to be critical. From any logical viewpoint, this was clearly incorrect. In accepting the network as an as-planned baseline, the construction manager pointed out that it appeared to be resource-balanced, and that it violated the industry definition of "critical." Therefore, he also noted, it would not be an appropriate basis for determining those activities in which delays could readily be overcome by doubling relatively small work crews in special craft areas. In effect, the contractor had submitted a plan which he hoped would identify every activity as "critical," and so managed to avoid defining the truly critical activities in the project. Thus he lost a valuable tool for the evaluation of delays and the assignment of responsibility.

Another type of manipulation which is becoming more frequent is the "short schedule." In it, the contractor submits a project plan which involves a substantially less amount of time than the scheduled time frame required by the owner. The shortfall is usually substantial, often as much as a year in a 3- to 4-year project. The contractor asserts that he or she bid for the job on this basis, and that any failure on the part of the owner to completely support the "short schedule" will itself be a proper basis for delay claims. In reviewing a "short schedule," the owner should be certain that there is sufficient time allowed for shop drawing approval and other managerial reviews required in regard to specifications. Also, it is appropriate to question the considerations for weather and any other unusual conditions included in the plan. In a multiple prime project, the schedule should be reviewed to be certain that primes other than the general contractor have sufficient working time—and, for that matter, in a general construction contract that the major subcontractors have sufficient time to complete their work. The contractor submitting the "short schedule" should be required to certify that the other major primes or major subcontractors have indeed reviewed and agreed to the plan.

If the contractor submitting the "short schedule" persists in claiming it is long enough, one suggested approach has been to issue a change order at no cost, changing the end date for completion to agree with the "short schedule." However, if the owner believes that this is an unrealistically short date, such a solution to calling the contractor's bluff may have built-in legal problems.

Since the "short schedule" is becoming a much more frequent phenomenon, another way of dealing with the problem is to address it directly in the scheduling specification. The specification can state that any schedule which is substantially shorter than the required schedule (i.e., by 10 percent or more) will be considered unrealistic. It could also go on to state that the foreshortened period would be a considered scheduling contingency, and that the owner would make the best efforts to support the "short schedule," but without forgoing any prerogatives such as the mandated time for review of shop drawings or the right to review only priority shop drawings on a shorter schedule than the traditional 2 to 4 weeks.

WORKING SCHEDULE

After these adjustments, the CPM schedule is established. But is it really a schedule? The critical activities have definite start and completion dates. However, what about those activities with float? For activities having a float of 10 days or less, the CPM dates are fairly definitive. However, it is not reasonable to consider an activity with 100 days' float as scheduled. There have been a number of attempts to make the CPM schedule more definitive. One is a computer routine which allocates total float to each activity. This can be done either on a flat allocation per activity or an allocation proportioned to the activities' durations. There is nothing particularly wrong with this routine, but nothing particularly useful about it either. Since the float allocation is arbitrary, it only clouds the network information. Also, there is no judgment factor in a machine-handled allocation of float. Obviously some activities should receive a larger proportion of float than others (if the method of float allocation is to be used). Contractors usually prefer to retain all the actual float unallocated and try to work as close to early start dates as practical.

The character of the network affects its "tightness." The John Doe network would be described as very tight. This tightness, or lack of large float values, is the result of the network tying back into strong events or nodes. This results in a definitive schedule and is desirable—but don't force it. Don't introduce fake logic in order to achieve a definitive schedule, because the result will be a fake schedule.

It is entirely reasonable to introduce lead or lag arrows into float paths to schedule certain items. For instance, three activities in the John Doe

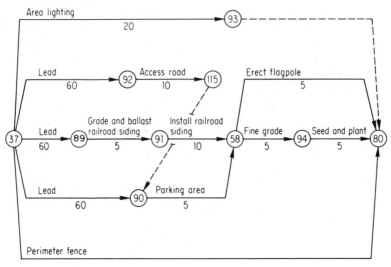

Figure 11.1 Lead and sequence arrows, site work.

site work which could start in early January are 37-91, grade and ballast railroad siding, 37-90, pave parking area, and 37-92, access road. Although these three items could logically commence at event 37, none should be scheduled in January in the northern part of the country. Since each activity has more than 12 weeks' float (37-90 has 73 days; 37-91 has 63 days; and 37-92 has 68 days), they could all obviously be scheduled for a more suitable time of year. This is easily done by introducing a lead arrow in front of each activity, as shown in Figure 11.1. The lead arrow is essentially a restraint with time added. If 12 weeks' duration is assigned to each lead arrow, the three activities will have early start times in late March. (In the MSCS program an activity can be assigned a "not earlier than" date which restrains the start. Similarly, activities can be assigned "not later than" dates, or an activity start can be locked in place.)

The fine grading and seeding could start as early as mid-April or as late as mid-August. A choice should be made whether to use a spring or fall seeding. Since a fall planting would follow the completion date, assume a spring planting. To do this, use a lag arrow after the seeding. This does not affect the early start date for seeding, but it does bring the late start date to an earlier time.

If all the available float time is assigned to either a lead or lag arrow, the activities in that chain will become critical. On some occasions it is useful to force certain paths to become critical. For instance, in a high-rise building project, concrete work was no longer critical because it had been expedited, and thus another path had become critical. Although concrete work was no longer critical for the overall project completion, how-ever, it was still critical in regard to the schedule. The roof pour was scheduled for late November, and the completion was a race against tem-perature. The concrete crew won. By completing the last slab before win-ter protection was needed, many thousands of dollars were saved. This was more than enough to pay for the overtime required to maintain a fast schedule.

RESOURCES

The CPM calculation assumes "unlimited resources," that is, enough peo-ple and equipment available as needed to do each activity. This is fairly reasonable for construction work and can usually be maintained for the critical activities. However, the superintendent must use float time as a guide in spreading out crew assignments. Although it is theoretically pos-sible to call workers out one day and lay them off the next, no sensible contractor wants this reputation with mechanics or small subcontractors. To set up the CPM schedule so that it takes this situation into account, crew scheduling arrows can be added. Looking at Figure 11.1, which shows the John Doe project site work, note the access road and parking lot. If these are to be done by the same contractor, it would be reasonable to schedule them in series rather than in parallel. This can be done by chang-ing activity 92-58 to 92-115 and then adding one sequencing arrow 115-90. This, then, will schedule the access road before the parking lot and allow the same paving equipment to be used on both activities. It also reduces total float by 5 days.

Other examples can be seen in regard to the John Doe project foun-dation work (Figure 11.2). For instance, the general contractor has to call in the plumber and the electrician for underslab work. When should they

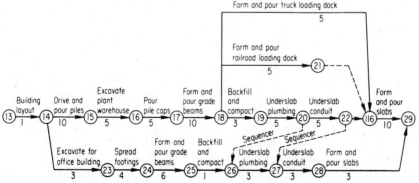

Figure 11.2 Work sequence arrows, foundation contract.

be scheduled? One reasonable method is to schedule the critical work first. To do this, a CPM computation must be made before the schedule sequence arrows are added. In this network, the plant-warehouse work is critical. So the addition of sequence arrow 20-26 will schedule the office building underslab plumbing after the critical plant-warehouse underslab plumbing. This will reduce the float in path 26-27-28-29 from 30 to 6 days.

To sequence the conduit work, don't add arrow 22-27, because this will make an illogical sequence. It will make the concrete work in the two loading docks precedent to the office underslab conduit, 27-28. Add a logic spreader to separate event 22 into two events—for instance 22-116, where 116 is the completion of the loading docks and precedes the slab pour— and 22-27 will then provide a proper crew sequence.

A useful technique in the sequencing of crews is to bar-graph the CPM output by trade or specialty, such as plastering, painting, concrete, etc. This could be quite a task if you were to attempt to bar-graph the entire CPM output. However, it is not unreasonable to do it by hand if you select only key categories. There are also methods of generating these bar graphs of the CPM output by computer (Figure 11.3). This is a task for which the computer can be very economical. Using the bar-graph "family" for a category, the best sequencing can be determined; then the schedule arrows necessary to set this sequence can be added to the network.

The use of schedule arrows can be very effective in changing CPM from a pure plan into a workable schedule. However, a strong note of caution must be introduced. Since the schedule arrows are pseudologic rather than true logic, they are more likely to go awry as the project progresses. This can produce some very illogical results, which the field group is usually the first to note. The bad impact this can have on field workers is difficult to erase. The "good news" telegram noted previously was the result of a forgotten schedule arrow which was no longer valid. The use of schedule arrows is recommended, but with discretion.

SCHEDULE CONTROL

As the schedule is updated, pressure is usually placed on the contractor by the project manager to keep the project "on schedule." The obvious way to do this is by achieving the project plan at the planned rate. Another way, however, is to manipulate the uncompleted portion of the project in a fashion which makes the project appear to be on schedule, or near schedule. This can be accomplished by shortening the activity time estimates on the critical and near-critical activities at any point after the updating date (but usually toward the end of the project), by placing segments of work which were in series in a parallel operational mode, or by a combination of both methods.

RESOURCE BAR CHART
SORT BY TRADE

JOHN DOE BASELINE CPM SCHEDULE
PREPARED BY O'BRIEN-KREITZBERG & ASSOC., INC.

DATA DATE

PAGE 1.0001
01JUL87

I NODE	J NODE	ACTIVITY DESCRIPTION	REM DUR	CNTR TYPE	WORK CAT.	SPEC. SEC.	01 JUL 87	19 AUG 87	07 OCT 87	25 NOV 87	13 JAN 88	02 MAR 88	20 APR 88	08 JUN 88	27 JUL 88	14 SEP 88
CARPENTER																
37	42	ERECT EXTERIOR DOORS P-W CP 2.0/	5.0	GC	3-6	0810	•	•	•	•	EE LL	•	•	•	•	•
39	42	FRAME CEILINGS P-W CP 4.0/	5.0	GC	3-8	0610	•	•	•	•	E LL	•	•	•	•	•
42	44	DRYWALL PARTITIONS P-W CP 2.0/	10.0	GC	3-8	0925	•	•	•	•	EELLL	•	•	•	•	•
44	58	HANG INTERIOR DOORS P-W CP 2.0/	10.0	GC	3-8	0810	•	•	•	•	EEE	LLL	•	•	•	•
53	57	FLOOR TILE P-W CP 2.0/	10.0	GC	3-7	0965	•	•	•	•	•	EEELLL	•	•	•	•
61	62	EXTERIOR DOORS OFFICE CP 1.0/	8.0	GC	4-8	0810	•	•	•	•	•	•	•	EEELL	•	•
61	68	GLAZE OFFICE CP 2.0/	5.0	GC	4-7	0880	•	•	•	•	•	•	•	EE LL	•	•
70	71	WOOD TRIM OFFICE CP 2.0/	10.0	GC	4-8	0640	•	•	•	•	•	•	•	•	EE	•
71	80	HANG DOORS OFFICE CP 1.0/	5.0	GC	4-8	0810	•	•	•	•	•	•	•	•	E L	•
72	80	FLOOR TILE OFFICE CP 1.0/	10.0	GC	4-7	0930	•	•	•	•	•	•	•	•	EE	•
78	80	ACOUSTIC TILE OFFICE CP 1.0/	10.0	GC	4-7	0950	•	•	•	•	•	•	•	•	EE	•

Figure 11.3a John Doe project bar graph output (finish work).

169

RESOURCE BAR CHART
SORT BY TRADE

JOHN DOE BASELINE CPM SCHEDULE
PREPARED BY O'BRIEN-KREITZBERG & ASSOC., INC.

DATA DATE

PAGE 1.0002
01JUL87

I NODE	J NODE	ACTIVITY DESCRIPTION	REM DUR	CNTR TYPE	WORK CAT.	SPEC SEC.	01 JUL 87	19 AUG 87	07 OCT 87	25 NOV 87	13 JAN 88	02 MAR 88	20 APR 88	08 JUN 88	27 JUL 88	14 SEP 88

ELECTRICIAN

03	12	OVERHEAD POLE LINE RES EL 7.0/	6.0 GC	1-4	0250	EE LL									
10	11	INSTALL ELECTRICAL MANHOLES RES EL 4.0/	5.0 EL	1-4	0250	EE LL									
11	12	INST ELEC DUCTBANK RES EL 6.0/	3.0 EL	1-4	0250		EE								
12	13	PULL IN POWER FEEDER RES EL 4.0/	5.0 EL	1-4	0250		EE								
27	28	UNDERSLAB CONDUIT OFFICE RES EL 4.0/	3.0 EL	2-4	1640			EE LL							
20	22	UNDERSLAB CONDUIT P-W RES EL 4.0/	5.0 EL	2-4	1640			E							
37	38	SET ELECTRICL LOD CENTER PW RES EL 4.0/	2.0 EL	3-4	1640				EE						
37	43	POWER PANEL BACKING BOXES P RES EL 2.0/	10.0 EL	5-4	0250					EEELLL					
37	93	AREA LIGHTING RES EL 2.0/	20.0 EL	3-4	1640					EEEEE					
38	43	INSTALL POWER CONDUIT P-W RES EL 1.0/	20.0 EL	3-4	1640					EEEEE					
43	49	INSTALL BRANCH CONDUIT P-W RES EL 2.0/	15.0 EL	3-4	1640						EEEE				
45	51	ROOM OUTLETS P-W RES EL 4.0/	5.0 EL	3-4	0810						EE	LL			
49	50	PULL WIRE P-W RES EL 2.0/	15.0 EL	3-4	1640						EEEE				
51	56	INSTALL ELECTRICAL FIXTURES RES EL 4.0/	10.0 EL	3-4	1650						EEE	LLL			

Figure 11.3b John Doe project bar graph output (electrical).

170

RESOURCE BAR CHART
SORT BY TRADE

JOHN DOE BASELINE CPM SCHEDULE
PREPARED BY O'BRIEN-KREITZBERG & ASSOC., INC.

DATA DATE   PAGE 1.0004
                           01JUL87

I NODE	J NODE	ACTIVITY DESCRIPTION	REM DUR	CNTR TYPE	WORK CAT.	SPEC. SEC.	01 JUL 87	19 AUG 87	07 OCT 87	25 NOV 87	13 JAN 88	02 MAR 88	20 APR 88	08 JUN 88	27 JUL 88	14 SEP 88
		IRON WORKER														
29	30	ERECT STRUCT STEEL P-W RES IR 8.0/	10.0	GC	3-6	0510	•	•	•	EEE	•	•	•	•	•	•
30	31	PLUMB STEEL AND BOLT P-W RES IR 8.0/	5.0	GC	3-6	0510	•	•	•	EE	•	•	•	•	•	•
31	32	ERECT CRANE WAY AND CRN P-W RES IR 4.0/	5.0	GC	3-6	1430	•	•	•	EE	•	•	•	•	•	•
31	33	ERECT MONORAIL TRACK P-W RES IR 2.0/	3.0	GC	3-6	1430	•	•	•	EL	•	•	•	•	•	•
33	34	ERECT BAR JOISTS P-W RES IR 11.0/	3.0	GC	3-6	0520	•	•	•	E	•	•	•	•	•	•
37	58	INSTALL MONORAIL WAREHOUSE RES IR 2.0/	5.0	GC	3-7	1430	•	•	•	•	EE	•	LL	•	•	•
58	80	ERECT FLAGPOLE RES IR 1.0/	5.0	GC	5-7	1035	•	•	•	•	•	•	EE	•	L	•
77	78	INSTALL CEILING GRID OFFICE RES IR 2.0/	5.0	GC	4-8	0954	•	•	•	•	•	•	•	E	L	•

Figure 11.3c John Doe project bar graph output (structural steel and miscellaneous metal).

171

RESOURCE BAR CHART
SORT BY TRADE

JOHN DOE BASELINE CPM SCHEDULE
PREPARED BY O'BRIEN-KREITZBERG & ASSOC., INC.

DATA DATE   PAGE 1.0009
                                   01JUL87

I NODE	J NODE	ACTIVITY DESCRIPTION	REM DUR	CNTR TYPE	WORK CAT.	SPEC. SEC.	01 JUL 87	19 AUG 87	07 OCT 87	25 NOV 87	13 JAN 88	02 MAR 88	20 APR 88	08 JUN 88	27 JUL 88	14 SEP 88
		PLUMBER														
03	04	DRILL WELL RES PB 2.0/	15.0	GC	1-7	0201	EEEE									
06	07	ERECT WATER TOWER RES PB 14.0/	10.0	PB	1-6	0250	EEE									
09	11	INSTALL SEWER AND BACKFILL RES PB 16.0/	5.0	PB	1-5	0250	EEL									
07	08	TANK PIPING AND VALVES RES PB 5.0/	10.0	PB	1-5	0250	EEE									
04	05	INSTALL WELL PUMP RES PB 4.0/	2.0	PB	1-5	0250	E									
05	08	UNDERGROUND WATER PIPING RES PB 3.0/	8.0	PB	1-5	0250	EE									
08	13	CONNECT WATER PIPING RES PB 2.0/	2.0	PB	1-5	0250	E									
26	27	UNDERSLAB PLUMBING OFFICE RES PB 4.0/	3.0	PB	2-5	1540		E	L							
19	20	UNDERSLAB PLUMBING P-W RES PB 6.0/	5.0	PB	2-5	1540			E							
53	58	INSTALL PLUMBNG FIXTURS P-W RES PB 2.0/	10.0	PB	3-5	1540						EEE				
61	64	INSTALL PIPING OFFICE RES PB 2.0/	10.0	PB	4-5	1540						LLL	EEE			
64	67	TEST PIPING OFFICE RES PB 1.0/	4.0	PB	4-7	1540								E		
73	80	TOILET FIXTURES OFFICE RES PB 3.0/	5.0	PB	4-5	1540									EL	

Figure 11.3d John Doe project bar graph output (plumbing).

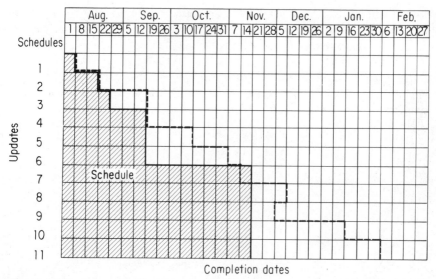

Figure 11.4 Schedule slippage over eleven updates. ── Latest date to stay on schedule; ─── projected date.

Under pressure by the owner, a scheduling consultant manipulated the schedule of the contractor working on a large water pollution control plant, applying the various methods necessary to shorten the schedule projections so that the end-date projections would meet (or appear to meet) the needs of the project. Figure 11.4 shows a series of eleven updates for the project, over which time a key milestone date actually slipped 6 months, but appeared to slip only 2.5 months because of schedule manipulation. At the time, this "schedule embezzlement" was performed with the best of intentions. It was also recorded in the narrative reports provided with the monthly schedule updates. However, the shortening and paralleling of activities were accomplished independently by the scheduling consultant and, therefore, were not truly part of the contractor's plan. Experience has taught a clear lesson that the approved schedule plan should be changed only with the permission of the project manager, and documented in the narrative update at the time the change is made. Further, the basis for the change or changes should be clearly and rationally explained (i.e., additional equipment brought in, additional crews added, or other logical reasons).

SUMMARY

The first CPM computation is a plan, not a schedule. After adjusting the project completion date by changing sequences and time estimates, an end date is determined. This date should precede the desired completion with a suitable contingency. The intermediate dates should be reviewed with the realities of seasonal weather in mind. Seasonal factors can be accounted for if necessary. The schedule at this point can still be rather loose. Lead and lag arrows can adjust float to position activities within the range of their CPM dates. Schedule sequence arrows can be used to provide a schedule using fewer crews. Scheduling arrows can add to the effectiveness of the CPM results, but one error in their use can far outweigh their benefits.

12

MONITORING PROJECT PROGRESS

How do you stay on a CPM schedule? In early CPM applications, the CPM network was left to its own devices once the project was in progress. The planners, confident that they had planned the project more carefully than ever before, did not follow up on their careful efforts. The result was similar to buying an automobile and then letting it break down because the oil was not changed.

PROGRESS STATUS

How do you determine status in regard to the schedule? The CPM network can be used as the basis for monitoring project progress. On the job, the network can be posted on an office wall and progress marked right on it. The ever-popular colored marker pens are the best way. The field usually cooperates because plotting progress seems to strike a responsive chord in most of us. Not only does this result in a current status report for the project, but the process of keeping the network up to date familiarizes the field office with the logic diagram.

An electrical contractor raised a very practical problem in regard to

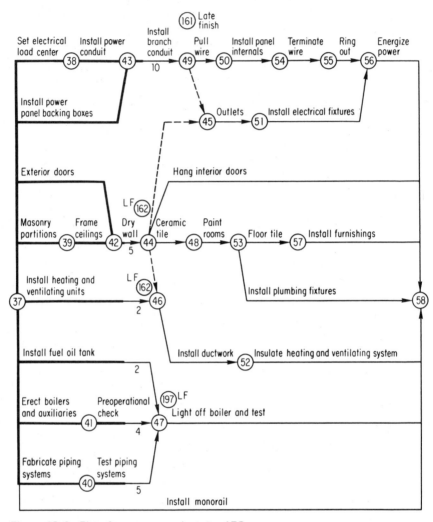

Figure 12.1 Plot of progress, project day 150.

posting the diagram on the job site. If craftspeople review the networks, however casually, some will notice the time estimates for activities on which they are to work. If the estimates are too long, there will be the tendency for the crew to take too long on the activities. If the times are too short, the CPM schedule will be seen as unrealistic. However, this problem, if anything, bears out the necessity for using a frank and realistic approach in CPM planning. The diagrams will have a big impact on field people, and some excellent comments about scheduling have been known to originate from the craft level.

Figure 12.1 is the John Doe network with progress shown by dark lines. The event times are shown for the activities in progress. The first path to check is, of course, the critical path. This status is as of project day 150; a check along the critical path shows that activity 43-49, install branch conduit, has 10 days to go and is 1 day ahead of schedule. The activities in progress with float have the following status:

i-j	Description	Time remaining, days	New float, days	Original float, days
42-44	Dry wall	5	7	13
37-46	Heating and ventilating units	2	10	23
37-47	Fuel tank	2	45	70
41-47	Boiler check	4	43	43
40-47	Test piping	5	42	33

All the float items are within the allowable CPM range. The dry wall and heating and ventilating units should be pushed so that ductwork installation can start. Figure 12.2 is another representation of the same project status. This format could be used to submit a quick weekly status report.

UPDATING

The periodic review of the CPM plan both to determine and to review the logic is termed *updating*. The object in updating the network (either with a computer or manually) is to introduce the project status as well as any logical revisions into a new computation of the completion date. To do this, all completed activities are given a duration of zero. Activities in progress are assigned the time duration required to complete them. Activities are removed, added, or assigned new event numbers to recognize any logical revisions. The first few updatings may have extensive revisions as plans are influenced by job conditions. However, after the project gets into full swing, there will be perhaps only five or ten arrow revisions per updating. The exact extent of logical revisions to be expected is, of course, unpredictable.

When the updating information has been entered in the network, a new computation is made from the present date (calendar or project day). This new run must be checked, just as the first ones were; an updating is not immune to error. After the run has been established as valid, the results are analyzed. The critical path may shift, and often does. Float activities may become near critical and must be monitored regularly. It is

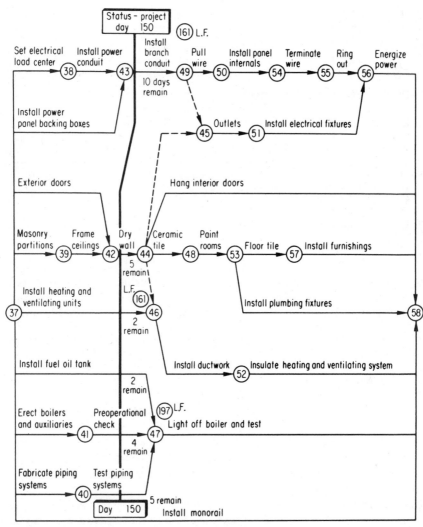

Figure 12.2 Quick status report, sample for day 150.

possible for the project to be late because of a "turtle and hare" situation. In the project race, the critical path is the hare and the float jobs are the turtle.

A key part of any competent update is a narrative report describing, at the least, the following: the critical path; activities started, in progress, complete; problems; milestone status and problem areas. Figure 12.3 is a very summary narrative report for the update described in Figures 12.1 and 12.2.

A prime advantage of CPM is that by means of it a greater amount of work can be managed "by exception" rather than "by direction." In other words, management should focus their attention on actual trouble areas, and CPM can accurately identify those areas for them.

When a New York City builder was asked to discuss the potential of CPM in his work, he responded that he had no time to do anything but check the field progress notes on his six construction projects. He left his house at 6:00 a.m. weekdays and was not home until 8:00 p.m., and on weekends he caught up on his paperwork. His reaction was, "Talk? Why, I don't even have time to think," and he was surely correct there. He was a builder who preferred field work to being in his office; but, regardless of his abilities, he could not direct six jobs by himself. Just picture any one project on the day he was "helping." He would be in and out like a whirl-wind, doing more harm than good. Here was an ideal situation for CPM. With accurate information on the critical areas of the six jobs, he would have to check only those things which needed review; the balance could be left to the superintendent's discretion. If four jobs were on or ahead of schedule, he could spend time on the jobs which were actually in trouble. Knowing the identity of the critical activities, he could offer the superintendent real assistance rather than interference.

In a multiproject company, field direction must be delegated. The best support field people can have is timely delivery of the correct materials and knowledgeable advice on construction techniques and specifics of the

JOHN DOE PROJECT

Progress Report #8
Next job meeting: March 1

ABSTRACT The project is on schedule. No unusual problems were noted. No major changes in logic or time estimates were noted.

CRITICAL PATH The critical path did not shift. It goes through events 49-50-54-55-56 and 58

MILESTONES Before next report. Boiler test—complete branch conduit—complete dry wall

DISCUSSION
1. The status information (see Figure 12.2) was collected at job site.
2. Electrical work is on schedule. However, a slight crew increase is recommended as the work spreads out.
3. Dry wall (42-44) should be pushed so that ductwork installation can begin. The prefabricated ductwork is scheduled for shipment from the shop this week.
4. The heating system will be operational in one or two weeks.

Attachments
1. Computer listing, *i–j* sort
2. Critical path listing from computer run.

Figure 12.3 Project report.

project when such advice is needed. Management can ascertain the astuteness of individual superintendents at the start of projects when they participate in the preparation of the CPM plans. These evaluations will be substantiated only through regular monitoring of the project plan.

LOGIC MAINTENANCE

Having determined its status by the logic plan, you can forecast the expected project completion date.

Experience has shown that the CPM logic will hold up very well. If so, what was wrong with the original idea of leaving the CPM schedule "on its own?" The fact is that only about 5 percent of the logical sequences will shift or change. However, the shift or addition of even one activity can delay or improve the completion date. On a school project, about 1 month before the building was to be closed in, an error was discovered. Regular glass had been ordered for glazing, whereas the specification required a special tinted glass. Although CPM was not credited with the discovery, the effect of an expected 3-month delay in delivery of the special glass was quickly evaluated by recomputing the CPM network with the extended delivery time. Since glazing was on the critical path, its delay meant the project completion date would be delayed by 2 months. This discovery occurred 5 months before the scheduled completion date; therefore, the owner was able to evaluate the relative merits of special glass versus completing the project on time. When the owner wanted both the special glass and as little delay as possible, the contractor revised his work sequence and increased crews on critical work to pick up most of the lost time. Again, CPM was used to evaluate the effectiveness of these revisions and a new schedule was agreed upon. If the CPM plan had not been reviewed periodically on this project, it would have become useless as soon as the glazing problem developed.

As noted previously, any logic changes either recommended or implemented should be documented in the narrative report accompanying the update.

UPDATING FREQUENCY

The field people should plot their progress on the CPM diagram daily and make weekly reports based upon the CPM schedule. How often should the network be recomputed? There is no single rule for setting the interval between updatings. For a refinery maintenance job, the network was updated daily. With a project duration of thirty-six shifts and an average of 400 workers per shift, close control was required. On fast-moving jobs of 6 months to 1 year, an updating every other week is recommended. On long-term jobs lasting over 1 year, monthly updatings will suffice.

The job meeting and the update should be tied together. Updating a day or two prior to the meeting is recommended. Presentation of the written report, the new run, and the summary network should be on the job meeting agenda. The CPM planner should be available during the meeting to answer questions. He or she can also give a rough evaluation of the schedule impact of proposed work sequence changes. CPM-oriented job meetings should be faster and more effective than routine job meetings.

The basis for the updating intervals given above is experience (which includes poor early CPM results when updating was not used). Looking at the updating interval in the same manner as CPM activity time estimates, most people would agree that 3 months is too long between updatings and 1 week is too short (for most cases). That would establish a range of 2 weeks to 2 months for the updating interval. Within that intuitive range, our experience factor of 2 weeks to 1 month is reasonable, with 1 month being the norm.

Any unexpected revision in work sequence, delivery, or activity estimates could be the cause for a new updating. The frequency of this type of updating is indeterminate. It is often possible to make a rough evaluation based upon the last computer run, but a new computation is necessary to confirm that evaluation.

Must the network be recomputed at each updating? There is a practical consideration: the availability of a computer. If you have your own computer facility or are using a consultant's facility, the CPM plan should be recomputed at each updating. If you are paying for each computation, the updater may decide to use the computer only when the start of any activity has fallen behind its late start time. This approach is not recommended, and when adopted on one major project effectively nullified the usefulness of CPM on that project.

Computer Update

If there are no logic changes, the progress on the project can be introduced, with the data date of the information. The result will be a status computation including an end date projection. Look at the first two pages of a computerized update 2 for the John Doe project (see Figures 12.4 and 12.5). The data date is November 1, 1987. The activity in progress is 17-18, form and pour grade beams P-W. The update indicates that 3 work days remain from the original 10-day duration.

Figure 12.4 shows the first two pages of update 2 sorted by total float. Secondary sort is by early start, so that the two pages include a chrono-

JOHN DOE UPDATE #2-STATUS DATE 11/1/87
PREPARED BY O'BRIEN-KREITZBERG & ASSOC., INC.

DATA DATE 01NOV87   PAGE 1

I NODE	J NODE	ACTIVITY DESCRIPTION	ORG DUR	REM DUR	CNTR TYPE	WORK CAT.	SPEC SEC.	EARLY START	EARLY *FINISH	LATE START	LATE *FINISH	TOTAL FLOAT
17	18	FORM+POUR GRADE BEAMS P-W	10.0	3.0	GC	2-3	0330	A 22OCT87	04NOV87	02NOV87	04NOV87	0.0
18	19	BACKFILL AND COMPACT P-W	3.0	3.0	GC	2-1	0220	05NOV87	09NOV87	05NOV87	09NOV87	0.0
19	20	UNDERSLAB PLUMBING P-W	5.0	5.0	PB	2-5	1540	10NOV87	17NOV87	10NOV87	17NOV87	0.0
20	22	UNDERSLAB CONDUIT P-W	5.0	5.0	EL	2-4	1640	18NOV87	24NOV87	18NOV87	24NOV87	0.0
22	29	FORM+POUR SLABS P-W	10.0	10.0	GC	2-3	0330	25NOV87	09DEC87	25NOV87	09DEC87	0.0
29	30	ERECT STRUCT STEEL P-W	10.0	10.0	GC	3-6	0510	10DEC87	23DEC87	10DEC87	23DEC87	0.0
30	31	PLUMB STEEL AND BOLT P-W	5.0	5.0	GC	3-6	0510	24DEC87	31DEC87	24DEC87	31DEC87	0.0
31	32	ERECT CRANE WAY AND CRN P-W	5.0	5.0	GC	3-6	1430	04JAN88	08JAN88	04JAN88	08JAN88	0.0
32	33	RESTRAINT	0.0	0.0	-			11JAN88	11JAN88	11JAN88	11JAN88	0.0
33	34	ERECT BAR JOISTS P-W	3.0	3.0	GC	3-6	0520	11JAN88	13JAN88	11JAN88	13JAN88	0.0
34	35	ERECT ROOF PLANKS P-W	3.0	3.0	GC	3-6	0340	14JAN88	18JAN88	14JAN88	18JAN88	0.0
35	36	ERECT SIDING P-W/CLOSED IN	10.0	10.0	GC	3-7	0740	19JAN88	01FEB88	19JAN88	01FEB88	0.0
36	37	RESTRAINT	0.0	0.0	-			02FEB88	02FEB88	02FEB88	02FEB88	0.0
37	38	SET ELECTRICL LOD CENTER PW	2.0	2.0	EL	3-4	1640	02FEB88	03FEB88	02FEB88	03FEB88	0.0
38	43	INSTALL POWER CONDUIT P-W	20.0	20.0	EL	3-4	1640	04FEB88	03MAR88	04FEB88	03MAR88	0.0
43	49	INSTALL BRANCH CONDUIT P-W	15.0	15.0	EL	3-4	1640	04MAR88	24MAR88	04MAR88	24MAR88	0.0
49	50	PULL WIRE P-W	15.0	15.0	EL	3-4	1640	25MAR88	14APR88	25MAR88	14APR88	0.0
50	54	INSTALL PANEL INTERNALS P-W	5.0	5.0	EL	3-4	1640	15APR88	21APR88	15APR88	21APR88	0.0
54	55	TERMINATE WIRES P-W	10.0	10.0	EL	3-4	1640	22APR88	05MAY88	22APR88	05MAY88	0.0
55	56	RINGOUT P-W	10.0	10.0	EL	3-4	1640	06MAY88	19MAY88	06MAY88	19MAY88	0.0
56	58	ENERGIZE POWER PLANT-WAREHOUSE COMPLETE	1.0	1.0	EL	3-4	1640	20MAY88	20MAY88	20MAY88	20MAY88	0.0
58	59	ERECT PRECAST STRUCT OFFICE	5.0	5.0	GC	4-6	0340	23MAY88	27MAY88	23MAY88	27MAY88	0.0

NETWORK REPORT /01
SORT BY TOTAL FLOAT

JOHN DOE UPDATE #2-STATUS DATE 11/1/87
PREPARED BY O'BRIEN-KREITZBERG & ASSOC., INC.

DATA DATE   PAGE
01NOV87   ?

I NODE	J NODE	ACTIVITY DESCRIPTION	ORG DUR	REM DUR	CNTR TYPE	WORK CAT. SEC.	SPEC	EARLY START	EARLY *FINISH	LATE START	LATE *FINISH	TOTAL FLOAT
59	60	ERECT PRECAST ROOF OFFICE	5.0	5.0	GC	4-6	0340	31MAY88	06JUN88	31MAY88	06JUN88	0.0
60	61	EXTERIOR MASONRY OFFICE	10.0	10.0	GC	4-7	0420	07JUN88	20JUN88	07JUN88	20JUN88	0.0
61	64	INSTALL PIPING OFFICE	10.0	10.0	PB	4-5	1540	21JUN88	05JUL88	21JUN88	05JUL88	0.0
61	65	INSTALL ELEC BACKING BOXES	4.0	4.0	EL	4-4	1640	21JUN88	24JUN88	21JUN88	24JUN88	0.0
65	66	INSTALL CONDUIT OFFICE	10.0	10.0	EL	4-4	1640	27JUN88	11JUL88	27JUN88	11JUL88	0.0
64	67	TEST PIPING OFFICE	4.0	4.0	PB	4-7	1540	06JUL88	11JUL88	06JUL88	11JUL88	0.0
66	67	RESTRAINT	0.0	0.0			-	12JUL88		12JUL88		0.0
67	68	LATH PARTITIONS OFFICE	5.0	5.0	GC	4-7	0910	12JUL88	18JUL88	12JUL88	18JUL88	0.0
68	69	PLASTER SCRATCH AND BROWN	5.0	5.0	GC	4-7	0910	19JUL88	25JUL88	19JUL88	25JUL88	0.0
69	70	PLASTER WHITE COATS	10.0	10.0	GC	4-7	0910	26JUL88	08AUG88	26JUL88	08AUG88	0.0
70	71	WOOD TRIM OFFICE	10.0	10.0	GC	4-8	0640	09AUG88	22AUG88	09AUG88	22AUG88	0.0
71	72	PAINT EXTERIOR OFFICE	10.0	10.0	GC	4-7	0990	23AUG88	06SEP88	23AUG88	06SEP88	0.0
72	78	RESTRAINT	0.0	0.0			-	07SEP88		07SEP88		0.0
72	80	FLOOR TILE OFFICE OFFICE COMPLETE	10.0	10.0	GC	4-7	0930	07SEP88	20SEP88	07SEP88	20SEP88	0.0
78	80	ACOUSTIC TILE OFFICE	10.0	10.0	GC	4-7	0950	07SEP88	20SEP88	07SEP88	20SEP88	0.0
80	82	PROJECT COMPLETE	0.0	0.0			-	21SEP88		21SEP88		0.0
31	33	ERECT MONORAIL TRACK P-W	3.0	3.0	GC	3-6	1430	04JAN88	06JAN88	06JAN88	08JAN88	2.0
35	37	BUILT UP ROOFING P-W	5.0	5.0	GC	3-7	0750	19JAN88	25JAN88	26JAN88	01FEB88	5.0
72	73	RESTRAINT	0.0	0.0			-	07SEP88	07SEP88	14SEP88	14SEP88	5.0
73	80	TOILET FIXTURES OFFICE	5.0	5.0	PB	4-5	1540	07SEP88	13SEP88	14SEP88	20SEP88	5.0
23	24	SPREAD FOOTINGS OFFICE	4.0	4.0	GC	2-3	0330	02NOV87	05NOV87	10NOV87	16NOV87	6.0
24	25	FORM+POUR GRADE BEAMS OFF	6.0	6.0	GC	2-3	0330	06NOV87	16NOV87	17NOV87	24NOV87	6.0

Figure 12.4 First two pages of update 2 sorted by total float.

JOHN DOE UPDATE #2-STATUS DATE 11/1/87
PREPARED BY O'BRIEN-KREITZBERG & ASSOC., INC.

DATA DATE PAGE 1 01NOV87

I NODE	J NODE	ACTIVITY DESCRIPTION	ORG DUR	REM DUR	CNTR TYPE	WORK CAT.	SPEC SEC.	EARLY START	EARLY *FINISH	LATE START	LATE *FINISH	TOTAL FLOAT
00	01	CLEAR SITE	* 3.0	0.0	GC	1-1	0210	A 01JUL87	A 03JUL87	ACTIVITY	COMPLETE	
01	02	SURVEY AND LAYOUT	* 2.0	0.0	GC	1-2	0140	A 04JUL87	A 05JUL87	ACTIVITY	COMPLETE	
02	03	ROUGH GRADE	* 2.0	0.0	GC	1-1	0220	A 06JUL87	A 07JUL87	ACTIVITY	COMPLETE	
03	04	DRILL WELL	* 15.0	0.0	GC	1-7	0201	A 08JUL87	A 22JUL87	ACTIVITY	COMPLETE	
03	06	WATER TANK FOUNDATIONS	4.0	0.0	GC	1-3	0330	A 26OCT87	A 30OCT87	ACTIVITY	COMPLETE	
03	09	EXCAVATE FOR SEWER	10.0	0.0	GC	1-1	0250	A 16OCT87	A 30OCT87	ACTIVITY	COMPLETE	
03	10	EXCAVATE ELECTRICL MANHOLES	1.0	0.0	GC	1-1	0250	A 29OCT87	A 30OCT87	ACTIVITY	COMPLETE	
03	12	OVERHEAD POLE LINE	6.0	0.0	GC	1-4	0250	A 22OCT87	A 30OCT87	ACTIVITY	COMPLETE	
04	05	INSTALL WELL PUMP	2.0	0.0	PB	1-5	0250	A 28OCT87	A 30OCT87	ACTIVITY	COMPLETE	
05	08	UNDERGROUND WATER PIPING	8.0	0.0	PB	1-5	0250	A 20OCT87	A 30OCT87	ACTIVITY	COMPLETE	
06	07	ERECT WATER TOWER	10.0	0.0	PB	1-6	0250	A 16OCT87	A 30OCT87	ACTIVITY	COMPLETE	
07	08	TANK PIPING AND VALVES	10.0	0.0	PB	1-5	0250	A 16OCT87	A 30OCT87	ACTIVITY	COMPLETE	
08	13	CONNECT WATER PIPING	2.0	0.0	PB	1-5	0250	A 28OCT87	A 30OCT87	ACTIVITY	COMPLETE	
09	11	INSTALL SEWER AND BACKFILL	5.0	0.0	PB	1-5	0250	A 23OCT87	A 30OCT87	ACTIVITY	COMPLETE	
10	11	INSTALL ELECTRICAL MANHOLES	5.0	0.0	EL	1-4	0250	A 23OCT87	A 30OCT87	ACTIVITY	COMPLETE	
11	12	INST ELEC DUCTBANK	3.0	0.0	EL	1-4	0250	A 27OCT87	A 30OCT87	ACTIVITY	COMPLETE	
12	13	PULL IN POWER FEEDER	5.0	0.0	EL	1-4	0250	A 23OCT87	A 30OCT87	ACTIVITY	COMPLETE	
13	14	BUILDING LAYOUT	1.0	0.0	GC	2-2	0140	A 29OCT87	A 30OCT87	ACTIVITY	COMPLETE	
14	15	DRIVE AND POUR PILES	10.0	0.0	GC	2-7	0230	A 16OCT87	A 30OCT87	ACTIVITY	COMPLETE	
14	23	EXCAVATE FOR OFFICE BUILDNG	3.0	0.0	GC	2-1	0220	A 27OCT87	A 30OCT87	ACTIVITY	COMPLETE	
15	16	EXCAVATE FOR PLANT WHSE	5.0	0.0	GC	2-1	0220	A 23OCT87	A 30OCT87	ACTIVITY	COMPLETE	
16	17	POUR PILES CAPS PLANT WHSE	5.0	0.0	GC	2-3	0230	A 23OCT87	A 30OCT87	ACTIVITY	COMPLETE	
17	18	FORM+POUR GRADE BEAMS P-W	10.0	3.0	GC	2-3	0330	A 22OCT87	04NOV87	02NOV87	04NOV87	0.0

JOHN DOE UPDATE #2-STATUS DATE 11/1/87
PREPARED BY O'BRIEN-KREITZBERG & ASSOC., INC.

I NODE	J NODE	ACTIVITY DESCRIPTION	ORG DUR	REM DUR	CNTR TYPE	WORK CAT.	SPEC SEC.	EARLY START	EARLY *FINISH	LATE START	LATE *FINISH	TOTAL FLOAT
18	19	BACKFILL AND COMPACT P-W	3.0	3.0	GC	2-1	0220	05NOV87	09NOV87	05NOV87	09NOV87	0.0
18	21	FORM+POUR RR LOAD DOCK P-W	5.0	5.0	GC	2-3	0330	05NOV87	12NOV87	18NOV87	24NOV87	8.0
18	22	FORM+POUR TK LOAD DOCK P-W	5.0	5.0	GC	2-3	0330	05NOV87	12NOV87	18NOV87	24NOV87	8.0
19	20	UNDERSLAB PLUMBING P-W	5.0	5.0	PB	2-5	1540	10NOV87	17NOV87	10NOV87	17NOV87	0.0
20	22	UNDERSLAB CONDUIT P-W	5.0	5.0	EL	2-4	1640	18NOV87	24NOV87	18NOV87	24NOV87	0.0
21	22	RESTRAINT	0.0	0.0			-	13NOV87	13NOV87	25NOV87	25NOV87	8.0
22	29	FORM+POUR SLABS P-W	10.0	10.0	GC	2-3	0330	25NOV87	09DEC87	25NOV87	09DEC87	0.0
23	24	SPREAD FOOTINGS OFFICE	4.0	4.0	GC	2-3	0330	02NOV87	05NOV87	10NOV87	16NOV87	6.0
24	25	FORM+POUR GRADE BEAMS OFF	6.0	6.0	GC	2-3	0330	06NOV87	16NOV87	17NOV87	24NOV87	6.0
25	26	BACKFILL+COMPACT OFFICE	1.0	1.0	GC	2-1	0220	17NOV87	17NOV87	25NOV87	25NOV87	6.0
26	27	UNDERSLAB PLUMBING OFFICE	3.0	3.0	PB	2-5	1540	18NOV87	20NOV87	27NOV87	01DEC87	6.0
27	28	UNDERSLAB CONDUIT OFFICE	3.0	3.0	EL	2-4	1640	23NOV87	25NOV87	02DEC87	04DEC87	6.0
28	29	FORM+POUR OFFICE SLAB	3.0	3.0	GC	2-3	0330	27NOV87	01DEC87	07DEC87	09DEC87	6.0
29	30	ERECT STRUCT STEEL P-W	10.0	10.0	GC	3-6	0510	10DEC87	23DEC87	10DEC87	23DEC87	0.0
30	31	PLUMB STEEL AND BOLT P-W	5.0	5.0	GC	3-6	0510	24DEC87	31DEC87	24DEC87	31DEC87	0.0
31	32	ERECT CRANE WAY AND CRN P-W	5.0	5.0	GC	3-6	1430	04JAN88	08JAN88	04JAN88	08JAN88	0.0
31	33	ERECT MONORAIL TRACK P-W	3.0	3.0	GC	3-6	1430	04JAN88	06JAN88	06JAN88	08JAN88	2.0
32	33	RESTRAINT	0.0	0.0			-	11JAN88	11JAN88	11JAN88	11JAN88	0.0
33	34	ERECT BAR JOISTS P-W	3.0	3.0	GC	3-6	0520	11JAN88	13JAN88	11JAN88	13JAN88	0.0
34	35	ERECT ROOF PLANKS P-W	3.0	3.0	GC	3-6	0340	14JAN88	18JAN88	14JAN88	18JAN88	0.0
35	36	ERECT SIDING P-W/CLOSED IN	10.0	10.0	GC	3-7	0740	19JAN88	01FEB88	19JAN88	01FEB88	0.0
35	37	BUILT UP ROOFING P-W	5.0	5.0	GC	3-7	0750	19JAN88	25JAN88	26JAN88	01FEB88	5.0
36	37	RESTRAINT	0.0	0.0			-	02FEB88	02FEB88	02FEB88	02FEB88	0.0

Figure 12.5 First two pages of update 2 sorted by i-j.

logical list of the critical path items. The milestones and their end date projections are as follows:

35-36	P-W closed in	Feb. 1, 1988
56-58	Plant-warehouse complete	May 20, 1988
72-80	Office complete	Sep. 20, 1988
80-82	Project Complete	Sep. 21, 1988

Figure 12.5 shows the first two pages of update 2 sorted by i-j sequence. In addition to the information on work remaining, the update includes information on work completed by the data date. Since the John Doe project is numbered in the traditional way where $j > i$, the low event numbers are assigned to the early activities. Accordingly, the two pages shown incorporate the early completed work. (All completed work is on page 1.)

For completed work, the MSCS (Management Scheduling and Control System) program prints out the start and finish dates under the two "early" columns and "activity completed" under the "late" columns. A capital A precedes both start and finish dates for a completed activity. It precedes only the early-start activity for an activity started but not finished. (See Figure 12.5, activity 17-18.)

The MSCS program will accept an actual date as an input. If no date is input, the dates for a started and/or completed activity are calculated by the program using the data date, the original duration (for completed work), the remaining duration (for work in progress), and the network logical sequence.

Update 2, as described by Figures 12.4 and 12.5, provides CPM calculations for all remaining work and a record of completed activities. It does not, however, necessarily measure the status of the project against its schedule. For instance, a comparison of key dates from update 2 with the original John Doe project calculation discloses the following:

i-j	Milestone	Original date	Update 2 date
0-01	Start	July 1, 1987	A July 1, 1987
35-36	P-W closed in	Dec. 28, 1987	Feb. 1, 1988
56-58	P-W complete	Apr. 18, 1988	May 20, 1988
72-80	Office complete	Aug. 16, 1988	Sep. 20, 1988
80-82	Project complete	Aug. 17, 1988	Sep. 21, 1988

The CPM update is based upon the information contained in the master file. It has no automatic cognition of the project schedule or recognition of the progress toward or projections of dates in regard to the completion of the project.

Update Compared with Schedule

In the purist sense, the update just described is the best use of CPM as a planning and scheduling tool. CPM has been used to develop a logical plan. This plan was compared with the needs of the project, weather and contingency were introduced, and a schedule was created. Update 2 gives a realistic projection of completion dates if logic and durations remain unchanged.

However, unless the milestone projections are compared with goals, update 2 would appear to acquiesce to slippage. And the printout of dates later than those called for by the contract, especially if the updating is done by the owner or the construction manager, may seem to condone the slippage.

One answer is the lock-in of the contract dates into the milestones. When this is done, a project which is behind schedule will exhibit a phenomenon known as *negative float*. If progress in the initial John Doe project up to event 3 (shown in Figure 12.6) required 12 days, since the original estimate of the time needed to get from event 0 to event 3 was 7 days, the project is 5 days behind schedule. However, the basic update does not reflect that directly. In fact, if the printout were in project days, the new completion date for the project would still be 27 project days later. But if the 12 days expended are added to that figure, it can be seen that the

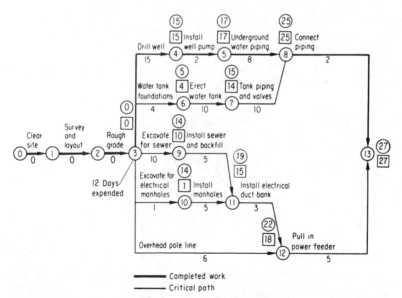

Figure 12.6 John Doe project site work progress to event 3 with initial calculation.

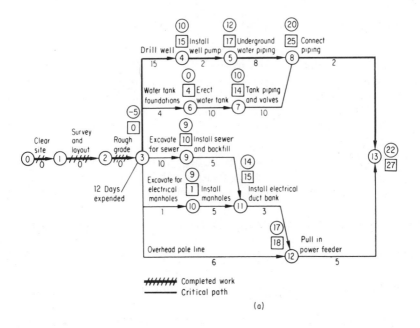

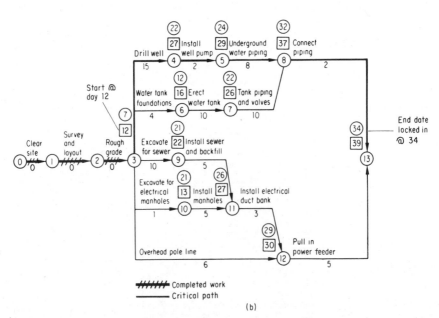

Figure 12.7 John Doe project site work progress to event 3 with (a) end date locked in at 22 days (34 − 12); (b) alternative calculation with end date locked in at 34 days.

projected time becomes 12 (expended) plus 27 (remaining) days, for a total of 39 days, or 5 days in excess of the 34 initially projected.

For this simple example, it was easy to keep track of the changes, but they were not built into the schedule calculation. To build them into the schedule, hold the latest acceptable late date at 34. The new schedule calculation (with project complete to event 3) is now shown in Figure 12.7. The figures in the squares project the earliest dates at which events can start, based upon the existing logic and durations. The figures in the circles are the latest times at which events can be completed to meet the end date, which is now *locked into* that initially calculated. Note that this locked date can be any value selected. In the example shown in Figure 12.7*a*, it is held to the original 22 days which should have concluded the project. In the example shown in Figure 12.7*b*, it is the thirty-fourth day, as initially calculated. In practice, the date used would be the contract end date.

The result appears to be illogical, with "early" dates being later than "late" dates. But the values of the "early" dates are consistent and indicate that this is the best you can do with this plan of logic and time estimates. The "late" dates now refer to the locked-in goal and indicate that this is where you *should* be in regard to that goal. Figure 12.8 shows computer update 2 with the final completion locked into Aug. 17, 1988. The negative float is -24 working days, slightly more than one month.

SUMMARY NETWORK

A useful supplement to the written report is the *summary network*. This is a simplified network used to discuss the results. In the summary network, one arrow represents a group of arrows. [For instance, in the John Doe network, the seven arrows concerned with the well (3-4, 4-5), water tank (3-6, 6-7, 7-8), and water piping (7-8, 8-13) could be represented with one arrow 3-13, install water system. This summary arrow would have a duration of 27 days.] Since this summary diagram is used for presentation purposes only, restraint arrows need not be shown. Figure 12.9 gives the summary diagram for the John Doe project. One advantage of the full CPM network, because of its size, is that it need not (and usually is not) drawn to scale. However, the summary diagram *can* be drawn to scale because the critical path is identified and can form its backbone. Figure 12.10 is the summary network drawn to time scale, with progress shown at day 150. The progress is ahead of the critical path time line, so the project is ahead of schedule by 1 day. If the progress is to the right of that vertical time line, the project is ahead of schedule. If it is to the left, the project is behind schedule.

NETWORK REPORT   /01

JOHN DOE UPDATE #2-STATUS DATE 11/1/87
PREPARED BY O'BRIEN-KREITZBERG & ASSOC., INC.

DATA DATE 01NOV87   PAGE 1

SORT BY TOTAL FLOAT

I NODE	J NODE	ACTIVITY DESCRIPTION	ORG DUR	REM DUR	CNTR TYPE	WORK CAT. SEC.	SPEC SEC.	EARLY START	EARLY *FINISH	LATE START	LATE *FINISH	TOTAL FLOAT
17	18	FORM+POUR GRADE BEAMS P-W	10.0	3.0	GC	2-3	0330	A 22OCT87	04NOV87	29SEP87	01OCT87	24.0-
18	19	BACKFILL AND COMPACT P-W	3.0	3.0	GC	2-1	0220	05NOV87	09NOV87	02OCT87	06OCT87	24.0-
19	20	UNDERSLAB PLUMBING P-W	5.0	5.0	PR	2-5	1540	10NOV87	17NOV87	07OCT87	13OCT87	24.0-
20	22	UNDERSLAB CONDUIT P-W	5.0	5.0	EL	2-4	1640	18NOV87	24NOV87	14OCT87	20OCT87	24.0-
22	29	FORM+POUR SLABS P-W	10.0	10.0	GC	2-3	0330	25NOV87	09DEC87	21OCT87	03NOV87	24.0-
29	30	ERECT STRUCT STEEL P-W	10.0	10.0	GC	3-6	0510	10DEC87	23DEC87	04NOV87	18NOV87	24.0-
30	31	PLUMB STEEL AND BOLT P-W	5.0	5.0	GC	3-6	0510	24DEC87	31DEC87	19NOV87	25NOV87	24.0-
31	32	ERECT CRANE WAY AND CRN P-W	5.0	5.0	GC	3-6	1430	04JAN88	08JAN88	27NOV87	03DEC87	24.0-
32	33	RFSTRAINT	0.0	0.0		-		11JAN88	11JAN88	04DEC87	04DEC87	24.0-
33	34	ERECT RAR JOISTS P-W	3.0	3.0	GC	3-6	0520	11JAN88	13JAN88	04DEC87	08DEC87	24.0-
34	35	ERECT ROOF PLANKS P-W	3.0	3.0	GC	3-6	0340	14JAN88	18JAN88	09DEC87	11DEC87	24.0-
35	36	ERECT SIDING P-W/CLOSED IN	10.0	10.0	GC	3-7	0740	19JAN88	01FEB88	14DEC87	28DEC87	24.0-
36	37	RESTRAINT	0.0	0.0		-		02FEB88	02FEB88	29DEC87	29DEC87	24.0-
37	38	SET ELECTRICL LOD CENTER PW	2.0	2.0	EL	3-4	1640	02FEB88	03FEB88	29DEC87	30DEC87	24.0-
38	43	INSTALL POWER CONDUIT P-W	20.0	20.0	EL	3-4	1640	04FEB88	03MAR88	31DEC87	28JAN88	24.0-
43	49	INSTALL BRANCH CONDUIT P-W	15.0	15.0	EL	3-4	1640	04MAR88	24MAR88	29JAN88	19FEB88	24.0-
49	50	PULL WIRE P-W	15.0	15.0	EL	3-4	1640	25MAR88	14APR88	22FEB88	11MAR88	24.0-
50	54	INSTALL PANEL INTERNALS P-W	5.0	5.0	EL	3-4	1640	15APR88	21APR88	14MAR88	18MAR88	24.0-
54	55	TERMINATE WIRES P-W	10.0	10.0	EL	3-4	1640	22APR88	05MAY88	21MAR88	01APR88	24.0-
55	56	RINGOUT P-W	10.0	10.0	EL	3-4	1640	06MAY88	19MAY88	04APR88	15APR88	24.0-
56	58	ENERGIZE POWER PLANT-WAREHOUSE COMPLETE	1.0	1.0	EL	3-4	1640	20MAY88	20MAY88	18APR88	18APR88	24.0-
58	59	ERECT PRECAST STRUCT OFFICE	5.0	5.0	GC	4-6	0340	23MAY88	27MAY88	19APR88	25APR88	24.0-

NETWORK REPORT   /01
SORT BY TOTAL FLOAT

JOHN DOE UPDATE #2-STATUS DATE 11/1/87
PREPARED BY O'BRIEN-KREITZBERG & ASSOC., INC.

DATA DATE   PAGE
                   01NOV87   ?

I NODE	J NODE	ACTIVITY DESCRIPTION	ORG DUR	REM DUR	CNTR TYPE	WORK CAT.	SPEC SEC.	EARLY START	EARLY *FINISH	LATE START	LATE *FINISH	TOTAL FLOAT
59	60	ERECT PRECAST ROOF OFFICE	5.0	5.0	GC	4-6	0340	31MAY88	06JUN88	26APR88	02MAY88	24.0-
60	61	EXTERIOR MASONRY OFFICE	10.0	10.0	GC	4-7	0420	07JUN88	20JUN88	03MAY88	16MAY88	24.0-
61	64	INSTALL PIPING OFFICE	10.0	10.0	PB	4-5	1540	21JUN88	05JUL88	17MAY88	31MAY88	24.0-
61	65	INSTALL ELEC BACKING BOXES	4.0	4.0	EL	4-4	1640	21JUN88	24JUN88	17MAY88	20MAY88	24.0-
65	66	INSTALL CONDUIT OFFICE	10.0	10.0	EL	4-4	1640	27JUN88	11JUL88	23MAY88	06JUN88	24.0-
64	67	TEST PIPING OFFICE	4.0	4.0	PB	4-7	1540	06JUL88	11JUL88	01JUN88	06JUN88	24.0-
66	67	RESTRAINT	0.0	0.0			-	12JUL88	12JUL88	07JUN88	07JUN88	24.0-
67	68	LATH PARTITIONS OFFICE	5.0	5.0	GC	4-7	0910	12JUL88	18JUL88	07JUN88	13JUN88	24.0-
68	69	PLASTER SCRATCH AND BROWN	5.0	5.0	GC	4-7	0910	19JUL88	25JUL88	14JUN88	20JUN88	24.0-
69	70	PLASTER WHITE COATS	10.0	10.0	GC	4-7	0910	26JUL88	08AUG88	21JUN88	05JUL88	24.0-
70	71	WOOD TRIM OFFICE	10.0	10.0	GC	4-8	0640	09AUG88	22AUG88	06JUL88	19JUL88	24.0-
71	72	PAINT EXTERIOR OFFICE	10.0	10.0	GC	4-7	0990	23AUG88	06SEP88	20JUL88	02AUG88	24.0-
72	78	RESTRAINT	0.0	0.0			-	07SEP88	07SEP88	03AUG88	03AUG88	24.0-
72	80	FLOOR TILE OFFICE OFFICE COMPLETE	10.0	10.0	GC	4-7	0930	07SEP88	20SEP88	03AUG88	16AUG88	24.0-
78	80	ACOUSTIC TILE OFFICE	10.0	10.0	GC	4-7	0950	07SEP88	20SEP88	03AUG88	16AUG88	24.0-
80	82	PROJECT COMPLETE	0.0	0.0			-	21SEP88	21SEP88	17AUG88 M	17AUG88	24.0-
31	33	ERECT MONORAIL TRACK P-W	3.0	3.0	GC	3-6	1430	04JAN88	06JAN88	01DEC87	03DEC87	22.0-
35	37	BUILT UP ROOFING P-W	5.0	5.0	GC	3-7	0750	19JAN88	25JAN88	21DEC87	28DEC87	19.0-
72	73	RESTRAINT	0.0	0.0			-	07SEP88	13SEP88	10AUG88	10AUG88	19.0-
73	80	TOILET FIXTURES OFFICE	5.0	5.0	PB	4-5	1540	07SEP88	13SEP88	10AUG88	16AUG88	19.0-
23	24	SPREAD FOOTINGS OFFICE	4.0	4.0	GC	2-3	0330	02NOV87	05NOV87	07OCT87	12OCT87	18.0-
24	25	FORM+POUR GRADE BEAMS OFF	6.0	6.0	GC	2-3	0330	06NOV87	16NOV87	13OCT87	20OCT87	18.0-

Figure 12.8 Update 2 with final completion locked at Aug. 17, 1988.

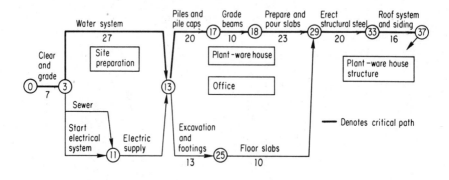

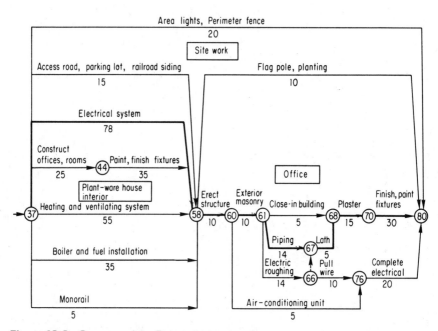

Figure 12.9 Summary John Doe project network.

Plotting activities to late dates, with float shown as a dotted line before any given activity, will result in a summary diagram which readily indicates visually the project's status. Also, late-time plots do not become obsolete as float is used—while early-time plots may.

Color coding can make the results stand out: green = completed work; red = critical activities behind schedule; yellow = float being used.

There are several graphical methods for portraying a CPM network: magnetic arrows and nodes, tracks to take activity descriptions, or even home-made devices. These are not practical for large working CPM diagrams but can be handy for a summary diagram. They take longer to prepare but may have a nice appearance. Colors can be used and the models can be photographed if copies are to be distributed.

RATE CHARTS

Figures 12.11 and 12.12 are similar charts utilized in actual project updatings. In these illustrations, the 45° line represents the track along which the monthly status falls. Relative to that track is plotted the end date projection for the updating. If the plot of the end date is vertical, or leans to the left, the project is on or ahead of schedule. If it leans to the right, then little or no progress has been made.

ADVANTAGES OF REGULAR MONITORING WITH CPM

The application of CPM to a project by an owner is in itself a positive step toward finishing the project in a timely way. It is a firm act by the owner expressing his or her genuine concern regarding the project's completion. More succinctly, the owner has put his or her money where his or her mouth is. The value of this should not be underrated. In a multimillion-dollar school project, the contractor completed what would normally have been a 20-month project in 16 months. The contractor had the added disadvantage of a midwinter start. His field forces were cooperative with the CPM consultant but not enthusiastic. The steady pressure of CPM information and updatings combined with the owner's active interest must be credited to a large extent with the outcome. (And yet do not neglect to credit the contractor: A computer cannot build a building; people must handle that task.)

Your own experience should be a factor in your CPM planning. In one high-rise apartment, elevator deliveries were shown to be critical when the updatings showed them to take longer than expected. The planner familiar with this situation would take unusual precautions. On another high rise, the owner did just that. He ordered the elevators as soon as the job funds were authorized and long before the general contract was let.

But don't let the pendulum swing too far. Don't let your experience cloud your thinking. Remember that you can't definitely identify critical work by instinct. For instance, in a 3-day concrete cycle, the superstructure was critical. However, the switch from a 3-day to a 2-day cycle was so excellent that it took the superstructure off the critical path but made

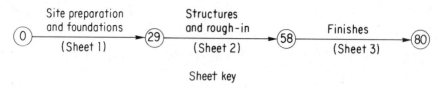
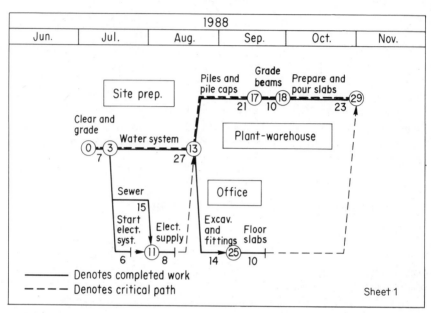

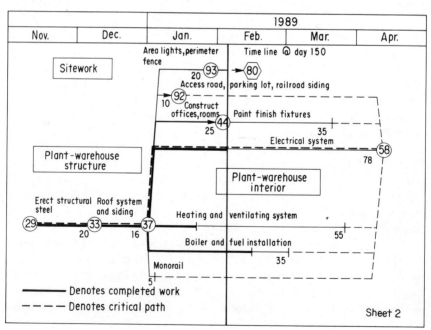

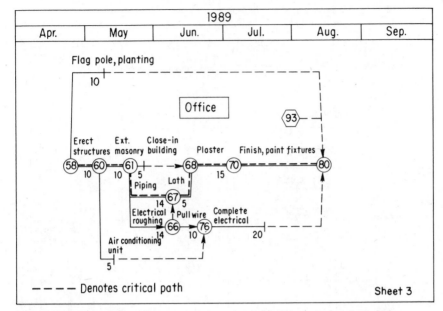

Figure 12.10 Summary diagram drawn to time scale (plotted to early times).

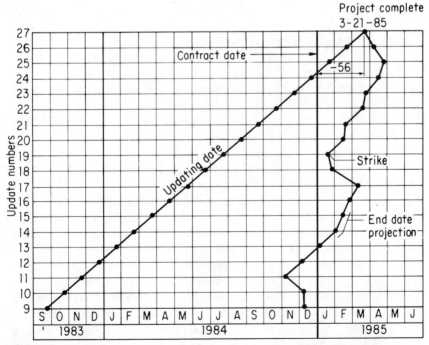

Figure 12.11 Plot of end date projection versus update numbers (between updates 9 and 27).

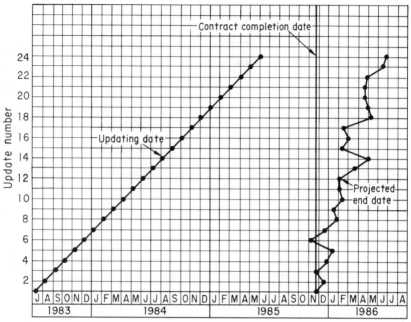

Figure 12.12   End date projections by update.

riser work critical. The field office was not reviewing the CPM update at the time and missed this until the next monthly updating.

Another advantage of updating is that it gives management an objective look at the project at regular intervals. The preparation of a weekly non-CPM report is useful to the field as well as to management because it ensures that the field office will review the project regularly. However the non-CPM report can be as indefinite as a bar graph and is, in fact, often submitted in bar-graph form. The CPM report is objective because it is based upon actual activity completions. The report is most effective when it avoids personalities, excuses, or rationalizations.

The project progress should be plotted on the field office network weekly. A weekly CPM progress report can be prepared by the field office and forwarded to all interested groups. At regular intervals, an updating should be conducted by an outside party. This can be a consultant, or someone from the contractor's or owner's office. This will add objectivity to the report and should be a cooperative effort with the field office. The updating by an outsider can help the field office view the forest instead of the trees. People close to the job often avoid adding up facts which they already know. This is not usually done deliberately, but people build up their own blind spots.

For instance, in discussing a revision to the plastering sequence for a high rise, the field office accepted a plan which would move a plastering crew up through the building, finishing each floor in 2 weeks (including drying time). The contractor planned to pump the plaster up to the floor being plastered, and the sequence would actually involve two floors at a time, the crew being busy on one floor while the floor just completed was being left to dry. At this rate of one floor per week (average time), given the size of the building, the plastering would have taken almost a year. This was the simple result of 1 week being multiplied by the number of floors, yet the field had not arrived at it. The logic of one floor requiring a week to plaster and a week to dry was correct, but the broad picture had been ignored. The answer was easy: Two more pumps, two more crews, and larger crews cut the predicted plastering time to 4 months.

SUMMARY

The best way to keep track of project progress is to plot that progress on the CPM network. This has the double advantage of keeping an accurate box score of the project while keeping the field office familiar with the network logic. Perhaps 95 percent of the original logical work sequences appearing on the network will remain unchanged through the lifetime of the project. However, the 5 percent of those that change can result in broad fluctuations of the schedule. Thus it is necessary to update the network at regular intervals. The intervals should be approximately monthly, and the updates should include written analyses of the project status as well as new computations of the network. These updatings and reports should be keyed to the project job meetings.

CPM AND
COST CONTROL

Project planning has been discussed so far in terms of the time dimension only. The original Remington Rand–Du Pont team tied money to the network in a very sophisticated fashion. However, the construction industry was not ready to assimilate two new concepts at the same time. Perhaps this was reasonable. Just as you can't learn to run until you have learned to walk, a cost system based upon CPM couldn't be useful until CPM was accepted.

CPM COST ESTIMATE

The first, and perhaps most difficult, step in using CPM for cost control is cost estimating by activity. The traditional method of estimating begins, of course, with the takeoff of material quantities from the drawings and specifications. Then material unit costs are assigned, based upon experience and suppliers' quotations. Labor costs are assigned based upon cost records. Finally, there are overhead costs, including estimates of anticipated supervision and equipment costs as well as a factored portion of the home office costs. Adding these together results in an accurate bid price. CPM does not offer a replacement for this type of cost estimate.

To use CPM in project cost control, a cost must be assigned to each CPM activity. This need be done only by the successful bidder. Since contractors can expect to be the low bidder on an average of perhaps 10 percent of the work they bid on, they can expect to have to do a CPM cost breakdown on only 10 percent of their project estimates.

One method of preparing the CPM cost estimates would be to undertake a second quantity takeoff by activity. Then the same unit costs and overhead factors would be assigned to these quantities as before. The total resulting activity costs should equal the contract price. This reestimate would cost about 50 percent more than the original estimate, though, and the adjustments required to equate it to the contract price would be an accountant's nightmare. Moreover, the method is a compromise between traditional estimating procedures and that involving project breakdown into CPM activities.

Preparing a cost estimate by CPM activity *can* be inexpensive, fast, and sufficiently accurate if done properly. Keep in mind that we know the answer which our CPM estimate must achieve. Why not start with that answer, the contract price, and work backward? Actually, this is even easier than estimating based on quantity takeoff. Almost every contract requires that the bid include a cost breakdown which, when approved by the owner, will be the basis for progress payments. The cost breakdown specified should be in categories compatible with CPM analysis. These might include:

Clearing	Room drops
Rough grading	Hung ceilings
Excavation—general	Structural steel
Excavation—utilities	Bar joists
Footings	Concrete walls
Foundation work	Siding
Grade beams	Masonry—exterior
Floor slabs	Masonry—interior
Underfloor plumbing	Windows
Underfloor conduit	Glazing
Major equipment (by item)	Doors—exterior
Ductwork	Doors—interior
Power conduit	Heating plant
Branch conduit	Water piping
Switchgear	Insulation
Wiring	Air conditioning

Plaster   Floor tile

Dry wall   Etc.

Paint

With the increasing use of the Construction Specifications Institute (CSI) 16 standard divisions for specifications, which has become a construction industry standard, a definite, industry-wide shift to a common terminology has been established. The subbreakdown of the 16 CSI divisions *MASTERFORMAT** into about 250 *BROADSCOPE** categories and an unlimited number of *NARROWSCOPE** categories provides the means to identify all estimating factors in common terms. With the increasing use of computers to write specifications, the use of MASTERFORMAT is increasing. Further, that increased use of MASTERFORMAT is resulting in an increasing number of estimates structured on the same numbering system.

Especially with computerized estimates, categories can be summarized from the standard estimating sheets without reestimates of quantities or the recalculation of costs being needed. Also the architect or construction manager can review this cost breakdown using quantities from the control estimate. Thus far the CPM cost estimate has stayed within the boundaries of usual estimating practices. Once the architect, construction manager, and/or owner have approved the broad category cost breakdown, the next phase is a further breakdown of costs. Each cost category is broken down into activity costs. This can be done in an informal manner, for example, by assigning project time to the activities. The cost assignment will be realistic and accurate enough because of the detailed breakdown afforded by the diagram.

For instance, in the John Doe project, if the cost for the category "foundation concrete" is $144,300, we can list all the activities involving foundation concrete by just sorting and listing under that code:

i-j	Description	Approximate cubic yards	Cost, $
3-6	Water tank foundation	20	3,000
11-12	Electrical duct bank	75	4,500
16-17	Pour pile caps	200	18,000
17-18	Grade beams, plant-warehouse	200	27,000
23-24	Spread footings, office	100	10,400
24-25	Grade beams, office	60	8,000
22-29	Slab, plant-warehouse	400	61,600
28-29	Slab, office	75	11,800
	Total	1130	144,300

*Copyright, Construction Specifications Institute.

The yardage breakdown by activity can be approximate. However, the total should equal the exact figure taken from the original detailed estimate. If the actual yardage for the office grade beams (24-25) was 57 cubic yards and that for the plant slab (22-29) 403 cubic yards, the effects of such differences on the total cost would be insignificant.

The breakdown of costs by activity will take additional time; and since time *is* money, the effort will be a cost to the contractor. However, with practice, this cost should become nominal.

PROGRESS PAYMENTS

Figure 13.1 shows the first sheet of the John Doe project printout with costs added for each activity. (Even when costs are in the master file, they can be excluded from the printout if the computer is so instructed.) A primary use for CPM cost data is as the basis for progress payments. Figure 13.2 shows the cost summary for one trade (electrical). CPM places progress evaluation on a well-defined basis—activity completion rather than the traditional percentage estimates. Since agreement on project status can be immediate with CPM, progress payment invoices based upon this status should be approved for payment with no delay. Figure 13.3 shows a sample CPM-based invoice for update 2.

To the contractor, faster payment of invoices represents a definite cash savings. If the approval time for invoices is shortened by 2 weeks, the savings in interest on a $300,000 invoice would be approximately $\frac{2}{52} \times 12\%$ $\times$ $300,000, or $1385. On a $9 million project, the savings would be multiplied 30 times, for a total of $41,550. It would be reasonable to expect these savings to average 0.5 percent of the project cost. An additional, intangible, savings would be the lower cost of preparing and justifying invoices.

The owner's (as well as the construction manager's and architect's) tangible savings stem from the shorter time required to approve invoices. This frees staff for other work. More important to the owner, however, is the assurance that the invoices paid represent a correct and equitable portion of the contract. While this has always been important, a recent court ruling has made it even more so. In that case, the contractor went bankrupt and the bonding company held that progress payments to date had exceeded the value of work performed. Since the bonding company had the responsibility of completing the project, it sued for the amount of overpayment.

JOHN DOE BASELINE CPM SCHEDULE
PREPARED BY O'BRIEN-KREITZBERG & ASSOC., INC.

DATA DATE   01JUL87
PAGE 1

I NODE	J NODE	ACTIVITY DESCRIPTION	ORG DUR	REM DUR	CNTR TYPE	WORK CAT.	SPEC SEC.	EARLY START	EARLY *FINISH	LATE START	LATE *FINISH	TOTAL FLOAT
00	01	CLEAR SITE CST $ 17,000/ 0/ 0	3.0	3.0	GC	1-1	0210	01JUL87	06JUL87	01JUL87	06JUL87	0.0
01	02	SURVEY AND LAYOUT $ 1,200/ 0/ 0	2.0	2.0	GC	1-2	0140	07JUL87	08JUL87	07JUL87	08JUL87	0.0
02	03	ROUGH GRADE $ 6,000/ 0/ 0	2.0	2.0	GC	1-1	0220	09JUL87	10JUL87	09JUL87	10JUL87	0.0
03	04	DRILL WELL CST $ 6,000/ 0/ 0	15.0	15.0	GC	1-7	0201	13JUL87	31JUL87	13JUL87	31JUL87	0.0
03	06	WATER TANK FOUNDATIONS $ 3,000/ 0/ 0	4.0	4.0	GC	1-3	0330	13JUL87	16JUL87	14JUL87	17JUL87	1.0
03	09	EXCAVATE FOR SEWER CST $ 13,000/ 0/ 0	10.0	10.0	GC	1-1	0250	13JUL87	24JUL87	17JUL87	30JUL87	4.0
03	10	EXCAVATE ELECTRICL MANHOLES CST $ 500/ 0/ 0	1.0	1.0	GC	1-1	0250	13JUL87	13JUL87	30JUL87	30JUL87	13.0
03	12	OVERHEAD POLE LINE CST $ 18,000/ 0/ 0	6.0	6.0	GC	1-4	0250	13JUL87	20JUL87	04AUG87	11AUG87	16.0
04	05	INSTALL WELL PUMP $ 6,800/ 0/ 0	2.0	2.0	PB	1-5	0250	03AUG87	04AUG87	03AUG87	04AUG87	0.0
05	08	UNDERGROUND WATER PIPING $ 11,000/ 0/ 0	8.0	8.0	PB	1-5	0250	05AUG87	14AUG87	05AUG87	14AUG87	0.0
06	07	ERECT WATER TOWER $ 137,000/ 0/ 0	10.0	10.0	PB	1-6	0250	17JUL87	30JUL87	20JUL87	31JUL87	1.0
07	08	TANK PIPING AND VALVES CST $ 25,000/ 0/ 0	10.0	10.0	PB	1-5	0250	31JUL87	13AUG87	03AUG87	14AUG87	1.0
08	13	CONNECT WATER PIPING $ 1,000/ 0/ 0	2.0	2.0	PB	1-5	0250	17AUG87	18AUG87	17AUG87	18AUG87	0.0
09	11	INSTALL SEWER AND BACKFILL CST $ 40,000/ 0/ 0	5.0	5.0	PB	1-5	0250	27JUL87	31JUL87	31JUL87	06AUG87	4.0
10	11	INSTALL ELECTRICAL MANHOLES CST $ 3,800/ 0/ 0	5.0	5.0	EL	1-4	0250	14JUL87	20JUL87	31JUL87	06AUG87	13.0

Figure 13.1 John Doe project printout, first sheet of *i-j*, with cost added for each activity.

COST REPORT 11J /01
SORT KEYS ARE 11J

JOHN DOE BASELINE CPM SCHEDULE
PREPARED BY O'BRIEN-KREITZBERG & ASSOC., INC.

DATA DATE   PAGE 1   01JUL87

I NODE	J NODE	ACTIVITY DESCRIPTION	REM DUR	CNTR TYPE	WORK CAT.	SPEC SEC.	TOTAL COST	PERCENT COMPLETE	TO DATE COST
10	11	INSTALL ELECTRICAL MANHOLES	5.0	EL	1-4	0250	$3,800	0	$0
11	12	INST ELEC DUCTBANK	3.0	EL	1-4	0250	$4,500	0	$0
12	13	PULL IN POWER FEEDER	5.0	EL	1-4	0250	$3,600	0	$0
20	22	UNDERSLAB CONDUIT P-W	5.0	EL	2-4	1640	$4,500	0	$0
27	28	UNDERSLAB CONDUIT OFFICE	3.0	EL	2-4	1640	$3,000	0	$0
37	38	SET ELECTRICL LOD CENTER PW	2.0	EL	3-4	1640	$18,500	0	$0
37	43	POWER PANEL BACKING BOXES P	10.0	EL	3-4	1640	$11,000	0	$0
37	93	AREA LIGHTING	20.0	EL	5-4	0250	$20,000	0	$0
38	43	INSTALL POWER CONDUIT P-W	20.0	EL	3-4	1640	$12,500	0	$0
43	49	INSTALL BRANCH CONDUIT P-W	15.0	EL	3-4	1640	$17,500	0	$0
45	51	ROOM OUTLETS P-W	5.0	EL	3-4	0810	$10,000	0	$0
49	50	PULL WIRE P-W	15.0	EL	3-4	1640	$23,000	0	$0
50	54	INSTALL PANEL INTERNALS P-W	5.0	EL	3-4	1640	$4,500	0	$0
51	56	INSTALL ELECTRICAL FIXTURES	10.0	EL	3-4	1650	$19,000	0	$0
54	55	TERMINATE WIRES P-W	10.0	EL	3-4	1640	$4,500	0	$0
55	56	RINGOUT P-W	10.0	EL	3-4	1640	$1,750	0	$0
56	58	ENERGIZE POWER	1.0	EL	3-4	1640	$1,000	0	$0
61	65	INSTALL ELEC BACKING BOXES	4.0	EL	4-4	1640	$2,000	0	$0
65	66	INSTALL CONDUIT OFFICE	10.0	EL	4-4	1640	$6,000	0	$0
66	74	PULL WIRE OFFICE	10.0	EL	4-4	1640	$6,000	0	$0
74	75	INSTALL PANL INTERNLS OFFIC	5.0	EL	5-5	1640	$3,000	0	$0
75	79	TERMINATE WIRES OFFICE	10.0	EL	4-4	1640	$4,000	0	$0
76	79	AIR CONDITIONNG ELEC CONNEC	4.0	EL	4-4	1640	$1,000	0	$0
79	80	RINGOUT ELECT	5.0	EL	4-4	1640	$1,500	0	$0
		SUBTOTAL		EL			$186,150	0	$0

Figure 13.2 Cost summary for electrical trade.

```
COST REPORT                                    JOHN DOE UPDATE #2-STATUS DATE 11/1/87                          PAGE 1
SORT KEYS ARE 11J        /03                   PREPARED BY O'BRIEN-KREITZBERG & ASSOC., INC.       DATA DATE  01NOV87
```

I NODE	J NODE	ACTIVITY DESCRIPTION	REM CNTR DUR	TYPE	WORK CAT.	SPEC SEC.	TOTAL COST	PERCENT COMPLETE	TO DATE COST
10	11	INSTALL ELECTRICAL MANHOLES	0.0	EL	1-4	0250	$3,800	100	$3,800
11	12	INST ELEC DUCTBANK	0.0	EL	1-4	0250	$4,500	100	$4,500
12	13	PULL IN POWER FEEDER	0.0	EL	1-4	0250	$3,600	100	$3,600
20	22	UNDERSLAB CONDUIT P-W	5.0	EL	2-4	1640	$4,500	0	$0
27	28	UNDERSLAB CONDUIT OFFICE	3.0	EL	2-4	1640	$3,000	0	$0
37	38	SET ELECTRICL LOD CENTER PW	2.0	EL	3-4	1640	$18,500	0	$0
37	43	POWER PANEL BACKING BOXES P	10.0	EL	3-4	1640	$11,000	0	$0
37	93	AREA LIGHTING	20.0	EL	5-4	0250	$20,000	0	$0
38	43	INSTALL POWER CONDUIT P-W	20.0	EL	3-4	1640	$12,500	0	$0
43	49	INSTALL BRANCH CONDUIT P-W	15.0	EL	3-4	1640	$17,500	0	$0
45	51	ROOM OUTLETS P-W	5.0	EL	3-4	0810	$10,000	0	$0
49	50	PULL WIRE P-W	15.0	EL	3-4	1640	$23,000	0	$0
50	54	INSTALL PANEL INTERNALS P-W	5.0	EL	3-4	1640	$4,500	0	$0
51	56	INSTALL ELECTRICAL FIXTURES	10.0	EL	3-4	1650	$19,000	0	$0
54	55	TERMINATE WIRES P-W	10.0	EL	3-4	1640	$4,500	0	$0
55	56	RINGOUT P-W	10.0	EL	3-4	1640	$1,750	0	$0
56	58	ENERGIZE POWER PLANT-WAREHOUSE COMPLETE	1.0	EL	3-4	1640	$1,000	0	$0
61	65	INSTALL ELEC BACKING BOXES	4.0	EL	4-4	1640	$2,000	0	$0
65	66	INSTALL CONDUIT OFFICE	10.0	EL	4-4	1640	$6,000	0	$0
66	74	PULL WIRE OFFICE	10.0	EL	4-4	1640	$6,000	0	$0
74	75	INSTALL PANL INTERNLS OFFIC	5.0	EL	5-5	1640	$3,000	0	$0
75	79	TERMINATE WIRES OFFICE	10.0	EL	4-4	1640	$4,000	0	$0
76	79	AIR CONDITIONNG ELEC CONNEC	4.0	EL	4-4	1640	$1,000	0	$0
79	80	RINGOUT ELECT	5.0	EL	4-4	1640	$1,500	0	$0
		SUBTOTAL		EL			$186,150	6	$11,900

Figure 13.3 CPM-based invoice for update 2 (for electrical work).

COST FORECASTING

If the costs of the activities for the first portion of the John Doe network are:

Activity		Cost, $
0-1	Clear	17,000
1-2	Survey	1,200
2-3	Rough grade	6,000
3-4	Drill well	6,000
3-6	Water tank foundations	3,000
3-9	Sewer excavation	13,000
3-10	Excavate for manhole	500
3-12	Overhead pole line	18,000
4-5	Well pump	6,800
5-8	Underground pipe	11,000
6-7	Water tank	137,000
7-8	Tank piping	25,000
8-13	Connect piping	1,000
9-11	Sewer	40,000
10-11	Electrical manholes	3,800
11-12	Electrical duct bank	4,500
12-13	Power feeder	3,600
	Total	$297,400

Time and cost dimensions can be combined to forecast the rate of spending on a project. If the project is on schedule, the contractor will earn the cost of an activity somewhere between its early finish and the late finish dates. Plot the cumulative cost of activities completed against project time: Cost against early completions will give the maximum amount of money required on any project day; cost against late finish will give the minimum amount of money required on any project day. On any project day x, the plot determines a maximum-minimum range of funds required. The actual amount will be somewhere between the two. For the contractor, this will be a forecast of his or her earning rate on the project. Working back from this, the contractor can borrow just that amount of money needed to finance the project until sufficient cash is derived from invoices to make the project financially independent. The savings to the contractor will depend upon his or her mode of financing. If the sum is being borrowed outright, a specific savings in interest will be achieved by borrowing less. If the contractor is working against a credit commitment, this approach will define the number of projects that can be handled within that amount.

The owner's savings from the cash forecast are even more definite. If financing the project from securities, the owner can liquidate at the latest time practical, and thus earn interest for the maximum length of time and maintain the principal at its largest practical value. If the owner receives the total construction fund in one lump sum, as in a bond issue, the greater portion can be scheduled for higher-interest, long-term investments, with only that part which must held for nearer-term use needing to be placed in lower-interest, short-term investments.

Figure 13.4 shows a plot of the John Doe project site preparation costs

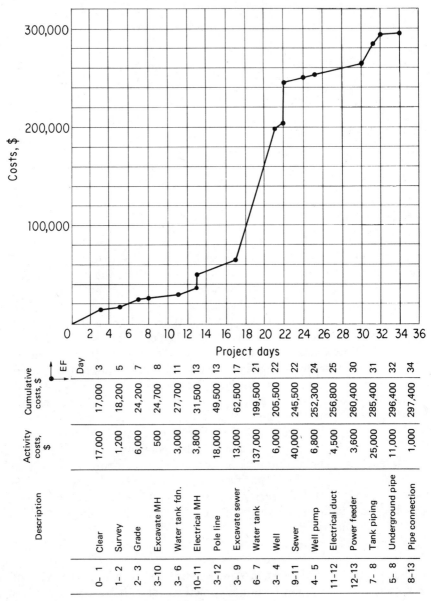

Description	Activity costs, $	Cumulative costs, $	EF Day			
Clear	0– 1	17,000	17,000	3
Survey	1– 2	1,200	18,200	5
Grade	2– 3	6,000	24,200	7
Excavate MH	3–10	500	24,700	8
Water tank fdn.	3– 6	3,000	27,700	11
Electrical MH	10–11	3,800	31,500	13
Pole line	3–12	18,000	49,500	13
Excavate sewer	3– 9	13,000	62,500	17
Water tank	6– 7	137,000	199,500	21
Well	3– 4	6,000	205,500	22
Sewer	9–11	40,000	245,500	22
Well pump	4– 5	6,800	252,300	24
Electrical duct	11–12	4,500	256,800	25
Power feeder	12–13	3,600	260,400	30
Tank piping	7– 8	25,000	285,400	31
Underground pipe	5– 8	11,000	296,400	32
Pipe connection	8–13	1,000	297,400	34

Figure 13.4 Cost versus time, early-finish basis.

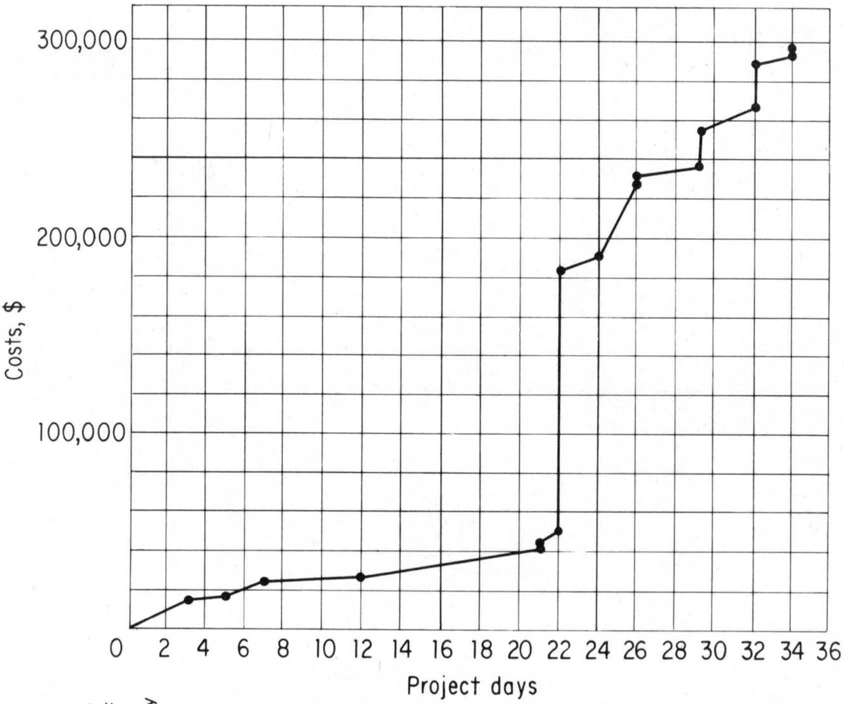

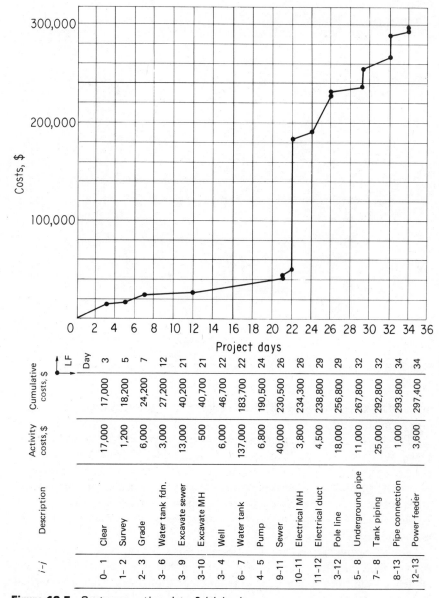

i-j	Description	Activity costs, $	Cumulative costs, $	LF Day
0–1	Clear	17,000	17,000	3
1–2	Survey	1,200	18,200	5
2–3	Grade	6,000	24,200	7
3–6	Water tank fdn.	3,000	27,200	12
3–9	Excavate sewer	13,000	40,200	21
3–10	Excavate MH	500	40,700	21
3–4	Well	6,000	46,700	22
6–7	Water tank	137,000	183,700	22
4–5	Pump	6,800	190,500	24
9–11	Sewer	40,000	230,500	26
10–11	Electrical MH	3,800	234,300	26
11–12	Electrical duct	4,500	238,800	29
3–12	Pole line	18,000	256,800	29
5–8	Underground pipe	11,000	267,800	32
7–8	Tank piping	25,000	292,800	32
8–13	Pipe connection	1,000	293,800	34
12–13	Power feeder	3,600	297,400	34

Figure 13.5 Cost versus time, late-finish basis.

based on early finish times. Figure 13.5 gives a similar plot of money versus time, but in this case based on late finish times. Figure 13.6 shows both curves on the same plot. In larger network samples, the early- and late-finish cost curves tend to parallel each other. Also, the curves are usually smooth, with very few inflection points. The time scale is usually in weeks

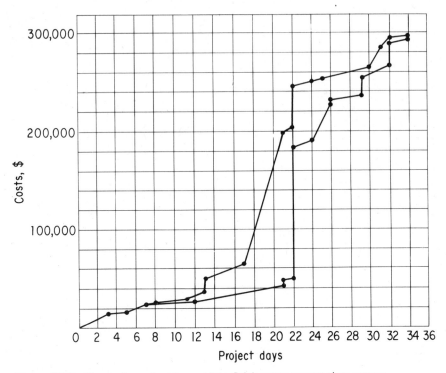

Figure 13.6 Comparison of early- and late-finish costs versus time curves.

or months since these are of more concern in the broad financial control of a project.

The cost forecast is meaningful because it is plotted to a true time scale. While the example plot was done manually, MSCS can provide computer-generated curves when the network is cost-loaded. Figure 13.7 shows the computer-generated cost forecast. As the project moves slightly ahead of or behind schedule, curves to reflect those conditions can easily be generated. The recommended updating frequency for the cost curves is about quarterly.

For an owner forecasting the finances for a fixed-price contract, time may change but the costs will not unless a change order is added to the contract. What if a major change is made or the contract is cost plus? In this case, the cost changes can be introduced just by changing the cost values for the activities affected.

The cost savings possible from CPM cost forecasting are difficult to assess. However, the uncommitted construction funds, which are 100 percent of the project cost at project day 0 and 0 percent at the end of construction, roughly average 50 percent over the life of the project. Figure 13.8 represents a project cost versus time curve. The uncommitted area

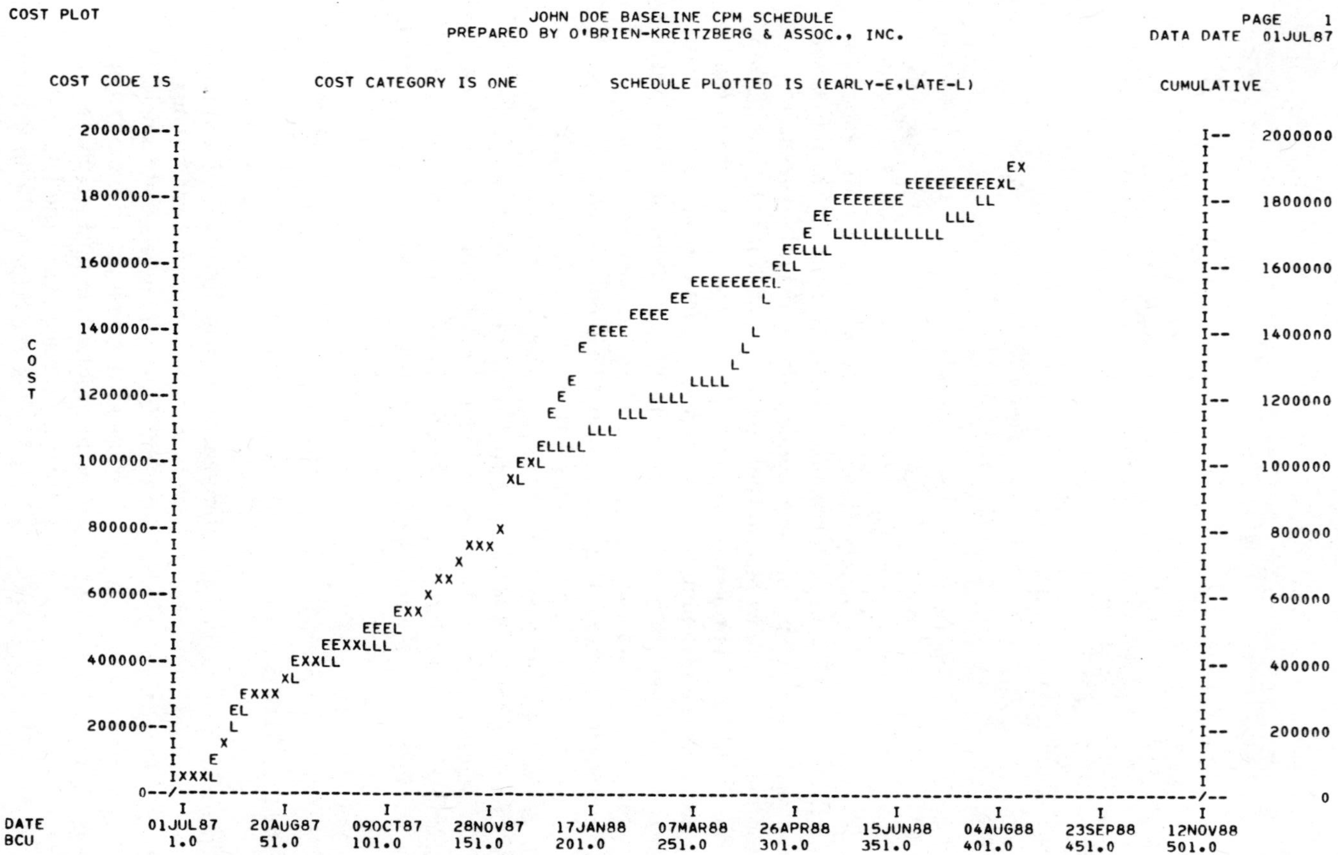

Figure 13.7 Computer-generated cost forecast, John Doe project.

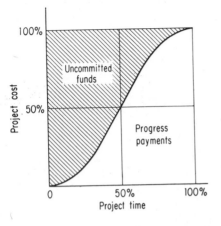

Figure 13.8 Project cost versus time curve.

(cost × time) approximately equals the money payable to the contractor. If an owner has the total construction fund at the start of the project, part of it can be invested in long-term bonds yielding about 12 percent interest. Another portion can be held in short-term notes yielding about 8 percent. Over the life of the project, an average interest of about 10 percent can be realized on the uncommitted funds (or about 50 percent of the project cost). For a 1-year project, this could amount to 5 percent of the cost. A 2-year project would be more nearly average, and the total earnings on the uncommitted funds for that period would be about 10 percent.

The use of accurate CPM cost forecast curves to predict how much money will be needed each month to pay for a project can guide the owner in investing any as yet uncommitted funds. However, the contingency cash required at any given time will be 2 to 4 percent lower because of accurate CPM cash forecasting. The additional peace of mind such accuracy will provide for the owner's investment counselor can be counted only for its intangible value.

CASE HISTORY

Figure 13.9 shows the computer-generated cash flow curves for an actual dormitory renovation project. Note the effectiveness of the visual graph compared with the tabular printout. This was a relatively small, fast project. Its total value was $343,000 and the time period for completion was 21 weeks. Note the definite point of inflection in the early cash flow curve at week 11 and the lesser point of inflection in the late cash flow curve at week 13. These seem to indicate some error in the logic or cash input. However, investigation of the critical path indicated that the delivery of special door bucks would not take place until week 12. This, in turn, would necessitate a delay in the progress of the dry wall installation. The inflection points in this case were accurate and furnished an interesting validation of the cash flow curves.

NETWORK TIME EXPEDITING

The cost assigned to each activity is the "normal" cost, that is, the cost of doing the activity with a normal crew under normal conditions. But there are cases where owners want projects completed on an expedited basis or where contractors must expedite their efforts to complete projects on schedule. The traditional approach is to put the entire project on a crash overtime basis. This is quite expensive for two reasons. First, it usually occurs late in the project when the work force is at a peak. Second, most of the work activities done on this crash basis are float jobs, the completion of which does not shorten the project by even 1 day.

Crash is defined as the shortest time within which an activity can be accomplished by using a larger crew, overtime, extra shifts, or any combination of these three. Some activities which it might appear that expediting cannot affect are "crashed" by using special techniques, such as curing concrete by using high early strength cement. By definition, normal time must be longer than crash time. (See Figure 13.10.)

In order to shorten an activity duration from normal to crash, the activity costs are inevitably increased. This increase results from premium time costs, inefficiency of larger crews, increased material costs (such as for extra forms, high early strength cement), etc. The cost associated with the crash time is known, of course, as the *crash cost*. For the John Doe site preparation network, the crash times might be:

i-j	Description	Normal time, days	Method of expediting	Crash time, days
0-1	Clear	3	Overtime	2
1-2	Survey	2	Extra crew, overtime	1
2-3	Rough grade	2	Extra crew, overtime	1
3-4	Drill well	15	Double shifts	8
3-6	Water tank foundations	4	Extra crew, overtime	3
3-9	Excavate sewer	10	Extra equipment, overtime	6
3-10	Excavate manhole	1		1
3-12	Pole line	6	Extra equipment, overtime	4
4-5	Well pump	2	Extra crew, overtime	1
5-8	Underground pipe	8	Extra crew, overtime	6
6-7	Erect tank	10	Overtime	8
7-8	Tank piping	10	Extra crew, overtime	8
8-13	Connect piping	2	Overtime	1
9-11	Sewer	5	Extra crew, overtime	3
10-11	Electrical manhole	5	Extra crew, overtime	4
11-12	Duct bank	3	Extra crew, overtime	2
12-13	Power feed	5	Third shift	2

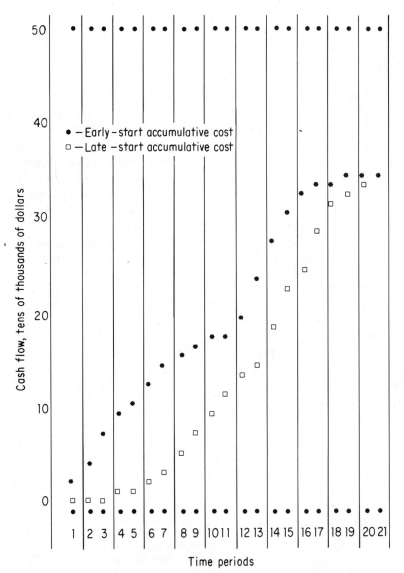

Figure 13.9 Computer-generated cash flow curves for dormitory renovation project. *(From James J. O'Brien, Scheduling Handbook, McGraw-Hill, New York, 1969, p. 173.)*

Total expenditures to date   13550.

Period	ES cost	A cost	LS cost	A cost
1	21128.	21128.	7120.	7120.
2	21116.	42244.	1600.	8720.
3	30697.	72940.	720.	9440.
4	23897.	96837.	8400.	17840.
5	12843.	109679.		17840.
6	17616.	127295.	2320.	20160.
7	14531.	141826.	10225.	30384.
8	10941.	152767.	23825.	54209.
9	11943.	164709.	16145.	70354.
10	7400.	172109.	23489.	93843.
11	5300.	177409.	19865.	113708.
12	21950.	199359.	17365.	131073.
13	35360.	234719.	9842.	140915.
14	41986.	276705.	43731.	184645.
15	31170.	307874.	39675.	224320.
16	14904.	322778.	23035.	247354.
17	7756.	330534.	41253.	288607.
18	5873.	336407.	23567.	312173.
19	3963.	340369.	9703.	321876.
20	1730.	342099.	13303.	335178.
21	400.	342499.	7321.	342499.

Figure 13.9 (*Continued*)

Figure 13.11 shows the calculation of crash event times. Note that this is just a basic CPM calculation. The normal and crash results are compared as follows:

Activity	Normal ES	Crash ES	Crash LF	Normal LF	Normal float, days	Crash float, days
0-1	0	0	2	3	0	0
1-2	3	2	3	5	0	0
2-3	5	3	4	7	0	0
3-4	7	4	16	22	0	4
3-6	7	4	7	12	1	0
3-9	7	4	17	21	4	7
3-10	7	4	16	21	13	11
3-12	7	4	22	29	16	14
4-5	22	12	17	24	0	4
5-8	24	13	23	32	0	4
6-7	11	7	15	22	1	0
7-8	21	15	23	32	1	0
8-13	32	23	24	34	0	0
9-11	17	10	20	26	4	7
10-11	8	5	20	26	13	11
11-12	22	13	22	29	4	7
12-13	25	15	24	34	4	7

Note that the total crash duration of the project is 10 days shorter than its normal duration. Also note that the critical path has shifted. Estimated crash costs are:

i-j	Normal costs, $	Description	Source of extra costs	Crash costs, $
0-1	17,000	Clear	Overtime	23,000
1-2	1,200	Survey	Second crew, overtime	2,400
2-3	6,000	Rough grade	Second crew, overtime	10,000
3-4	6,000	Drill well	Double shifts	8,100
3-6	3,000	Water tank foundations	Crew, overtime	4,500
3-9	13,000	Excavate sewer	Equipment, overtime	15,000
3-10	500	Excavate manhole		750
3-12	18,000	Pole line	Equipment, overtime	24,000
4-5	6,800	Well pump	Crew, overtime	8,000
5-8	11,000	Underground pipe	Crew, overtime	16,000
6-7	137,000	Erect tank	Overtime	150,000
7-8	25,000	Tank piping	Crew, overtime	40,000
8-13	1,000	Connect piping	Overtime	2,000
9-11	40,000	Sewer	Crew, overtime	60,000
10-11	3,800	Electrical manhole	Crew, overtime	5,000
11-12	4,500	Duct bank	Overtime	6,000
12-13	3,600	Power feeder	Third shift	6,000
Total	$297,400			$380,750

The crash cost to pick up 10 days appears to be $83,350 or $8335 per day. However, what if you do not need to expedite the completion by the full 10 days? Figure 13.12 shows a plot of normal versus crash times and costs for the activity "drill well." For a cost difference of $2100, this operation can be expedited in 7 days, which is an average extra cost of $300 per day. A linear connection between normal and crash points is generally a reasonable assumption. Minor variations tend to cancel out. How much would the drilling of the well cost if it were to be done in 11 days? The answer, from Figure 13.12, is $7200.

While the cost of expediting a particular activity is a linear function between its crash and normal costs, this assumption does not apply to the costs of expediting an overall project.

To cut 1 day off the 34-day John Doe site preparation project, cut 1 day off the critical path from any one of the following activities for the costs listed:

Critical path activity	Difference between crash and normal costs, $	Normal duration, days	Crash duration, days	Difference between crash and normal duration, days	Extra costs per day, $
0-1	6000	3	2	1	6000
1-2	1200	2	1	1	1200
3-4	2100	15	8	7	300
4-5	1200	2	1	1	1200
5-8	5000	8	6	2	2500
8-13	1000	2	1	1	1000

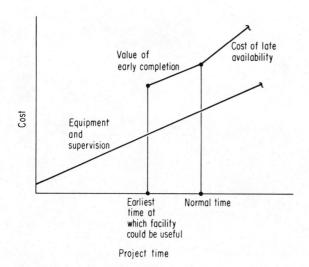

Figure 13.10 Indirect costs versus time.

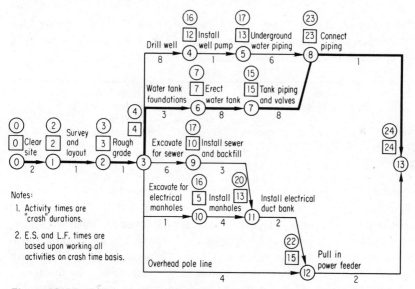

Figure 13.11 Full crash plan, John Doe project.

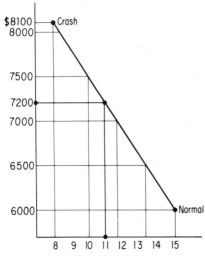

Figure 13.12 Cost-time relation for activity 3-4, drill well.

The best choice for 1 day would clearly be activity 3-4, drill well, at $300. At this point, both the well and tank paths are critical. Expediting along the tank path would cost as follows:

Activity	Difference between crash and normal costs, $	Normal duration, days	Crash duration, days	Difference between crash and normal duration, days	Extra costs per day, $
3-6	1,400	4	3	1	1500
6-7	13,000	10	8	2	6500
7-8	15,000	10	8	2	7500

If the path is to be shortened by another day between events 3 and 8, the well driller continues to be a bargain. Activity 3-6, water tank foundations, is the next best buy, since activity 6-7, erect tank, and 7-8, tank piping, are very expensive both at normal and crash costs. The minimum cost to cut two days off between events 3 and 8, then, involves activity 3-6, water tank foundations, ($1500) plus 3-4, drill well ($300), for a total of $1800.

Figure 13.13 shows the John Doe site network with the potential acceleration per activity, and the costs per day to accelerate those activities. Using that information, the optimum expediting for the initial 3 days would be:

Day 1   Drill well (3-4) .... $ 300

Day 2   Connect piping (8-13) $1000

Day 3   Survey (1-2) $1200

Thus 3 days of a possible 10 can be expedited using the logic and infor-mation at hand. The results are impressive: a 30 percent gain in time at an average cost of $833 per day versus maximum projected crash costs of $8335, for a 10:1 advantage.

Candidates for expediting the fourth through the seventh days would be:

Clear (0-1) $6000

Rough grade (2-3) $4000

Drill well (3-4) .... $ 300 ⎤

Water tank foundations (3-6) .... $1500 ⎦ $1800

Erect tank (6-7) $6500

Taking activity 3-4, drill well, and 3-6, water tank foundations, together, day 4 can be expedited for $1800. Days 5 and 6, taking activity 0-1, clear, and 2-3, rough grade, will cost an average of $5000 each to expe-dite, or more than 6 times the average cost of expediting the first 3 days. And Day 7, taking activity 6-7, erect tank, and again 3-4, can be expedited for $6500. Expediting beyond this requires consideration of the paths

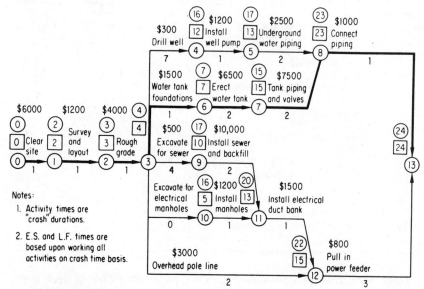

Figure 13.13 Cost/time cash planning factors for John Doe project; shown as costs per day per activity.

through the sewer, duct bank, and pole line since the normal float of 4 days following event 3 will have been used up. In summary:

i-j	Description	Normal time, days	Crash time, days	ΔT, days	$\Delta\$$	Costs/day to expedite, $
0-1	Clear	3	2	1	6,000	6,000
1-2	Survey	2	1	1	1,200	1,200
2-3	Rough grade	2	1	1	4,000	4,000
3-4	Drill well	15	8	7	2,100	300
3-6	Water tank foundations	4	3	1	1,500	1,500
3-9	Excavate sewer	10	6	4	2,000	500
3-10	Excavate manhole	1	1	—	250	
3-12	Pole line	6	4	2	6,000	3,000
4-5	Well pump	2	1	1	1,200	1,200
5-8	Underground pipe	8	6	2	5,000	2,500
6-7	Erect tank	10	8	2	13,000	6,500
7-8	Tank piping	10	8	2	15,000	7,500
8-13	Connect piping	2	1	1	1,000	1,000
9-11	Sewer	5	3	2	20,000	10,000
10-11	Electrical manhole	5	4	1	1,200	1,200
11-12	Duct bank	3	2	1	1,500	1,500
12-13	Power feeder	5	2	3	2,400	800

Expedited day	Activities expedited	Costs, $	Original path 3-4-5-8	Float used path 3-9-11-12
1.	Drill well	300	1	1
2.	Connect piping	1,000	0	1
3.	Survey	1,200	0	0
4.	Drill well/water tank foundations (300 + 1500)	= 1,800	—	1
5.	Rough grade	4,000	0	0
6.	Clear	6,000	0	0
7.	Erect tank/drill well (300 + 6500)	= 6,800		1
8.	Same activities as for day 7 plus excavate sewer (3-9) (500 + 6800)	= 7,300		
9.	Tank piping/drill well/Excavate sewer (7500 + 300 + 500)	= 8,300		
10.	Same activities as for day 9	8,300		
	Total	$45,000		

Note that this selective approach to expediting the project costs $45,000, or only 54 percent of the costs resulting from the total-crash approach ($83,350).

MINIMUM-COST EXPEDITING

Why is the owner building? Obviously to have the use of the facility. In the case of a hotel, a hospital, a manufacturing facility, a restaurant, etc., the owner can realize a definite cash payoff for every day gained in the completion of the project. This is basically a linear payoff. There can be losses in the same fashion. For instance, a school gains nothing (except considerable peace of mind) by opening early. However, if the school opens late, the cash costs can be calculated for extra buses, rented quarters, etc.

Combining the direct-cost curve with a straight-line indirect-cost curve creates a third curve, the total-cost curve. The combination is shown graphically in Figure 13.14. Note that, at some time between crash and normal, the total-cost curve dips to a minimum point. In any project, it is worth some cash outlay $\Delta\$$ to expedite the project. This will save time (ΔT) and money ($\Delta\$'$).

In the John Doe site network, assigning values to the indirect costs:

Contractor's supervision: two persons, total $2000 per week

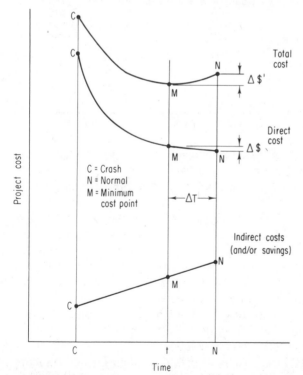

Figure 13.14 Combination of direct and indirect costs.

Equipment: Shacks, power, telephone, etc., $500 per week

Owner: Project engineer $1250 per week

Production advantage: $1000 per day

The combined indirect costs and savings per day would be:

$$\frac{\$1250 + \$500 + \$2000}{5} + \$1000 = \$1750$$

In Figure 13.15, the direct and indirect costs are shown combined.

Here is a summary of the costs for expediting, combined with indirect-cost savings:

Expedited day	Expedited activities	Construction costs, $	Total project costs,* $
	Normal time	297,400	314,900
1.	Drill well	297,700	313,450
2.	Connect piping	298,700	312,700
3.	Survey	299,900	312,150
4.	Drill well/water tank foundations	301,700	312,200
5.	Rough grade	305,700	314,450
6.	Clear	311,700	318,700
7.	Erect tank/drill well	318,500	323,750
8.	Same activities as for day 7 plus excavate sewer	325,800	329,300
9.	Tank piping/drill well/excavate sewer	334,100	335,850
10.	Same activities as for day 9	342,400	342,400

*Includes $1750 per day added project costs after day 34.

In other words, by spending $4300 to expedite the project 4 days, a net savings of $2700 can be realized. This is like having your cake and eating it too. For cost savings of 1 percent, a 12 percent time savings can be realized.

This approach is realistic, but it has not been used widely for four reasons: First, since it is CPM-based, only a company already using CPM can consider using it. Second, it requires the assignment of two costs to activities and there is a psychological barrier to the assignment of even one cost. Third, in most construction projects, it is not practical to put just certain crafts on overtime. If you do so, the other trades will usually make their objections felt in a number of ways. Fourth, only one computer program has been available for the calculation. That one, by James E. Kelley, Jr., for the GE 225 computer, is now obsolete.

The first barrier (CPM usage) is rapidly falling away. The second (cost assignment) will crumble as other CPM cost systems are adopted. It is

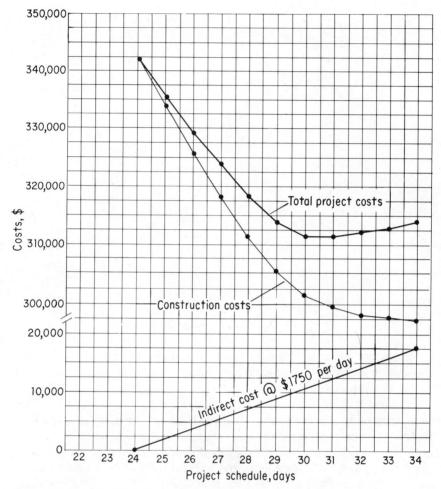

Figure 13.15 Combined direct and indirect cost curve for John Doe project.

easy to assign crash costs and times at the same time as the normal costs and times are assigned (adding perhaps 10 to 20 percent to the normal effort required to make the assignments). The third problem (not being able to put a project on partial overtime) cannot be completely overcome. However, where there is a choice, expedite in early activities, such as surveying and clearing, when the number of people involved in the project are fewer. Usually the lower costs of expediting these areas will direct the computer solution to these same areas anyway. However, the fourth barrier (the lack of a program for a currently viable computer) is significant, and will remain so until solved. This is a calculation not suitable for the manual mode.

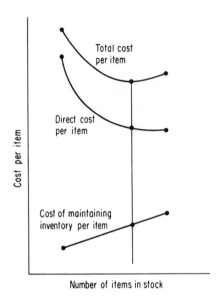

Figure   13.16 Example   of inventory optimization.

Inventory planning, as calculated by industrial engineers, offers an inspiration in regard to an expedited approach. For a given category of material, equipment, or spares, there is a minimum amount of each item which must be kept in stock. There is also some larger amount which can be purchased at a lower price. When the costs for the items in a category (such as pump impellers) are summarized, a curve similar to the direct-cost curve is achieved, which indicates that it costs more per unit to purchase fewer units at a time. Now the indirect costs of handling one item can be added in. This would be a linear relation of capital costs, including the costs for the warehouse staff, utilities, accounting, inventories, etc. When these indirect costs are combined with the direct-cost curve, a minimum-cost point can be estimated for the category, and eventually, by extension, for the entire inventory. This is demonstrated in Figure 13.16.

SUMMARY

A cost breakdown of the CPM network is best done by activity and best carried out immediately after the award of the contract. This cost breakdown should be within the framework of the bid and must also be realistic. An important use of the activity cost breakdown is for making progress payments.

Cash requirements of the project can be forecast on a time basis by computer with the use of the CPM cost estimates. These forecasts can guide owners in investing the construction funds so they realize their highest yield, and contractors in determining their financing needs and methods.

The cost of expediting a project can be accurately estimated by using a CPM-based cost system. There are even cases where a project can be completed early at a lower cost through carefully directed expediting.

The promise of cost expediting has not been fully realized, principally because existing cost collection and accounting systems do not relate directly to construction activities.

14

EQUIPMENT AND
WORK FORCE PLANNING

Time and cost dimensions have been discussed in the planning and scheduling of projects. Work force and equipment have been assumed to be available as they are needed. This is, of course, not usual. The planners, superintendents, or engineers responsible for projects keep their forces level by juggling float activities. In doing this, they must work the critical and low-float activities first, Those with more float are worked as fill-in jobs. As the project progresses, the float values will change, which makes regular updatings important in the scheduling of activities.

WORK FORCE LEVELING

Assume that phase 1 of the John Doe project is to be done overseas by Seabees; then one category (i.e., jack-of-all-trades) of work force is assigned to each activity. Also assume that equipment is available as needed:

Activity		Workers
0-1	Clear	4
1-2	Survey	5

	Activity	Workers
2-3	Grade	4
3-4	Well	3
3-6	Tank foundations	4
3-9	Excavate sewer	6
3-10	Excavate manhole	2
3-12	Pole line installation	6
4-5	Pump	2
5-8	Underground pipe	8
6-7	Tank	10
7-8	Tank pipe	6
8-13	Connect	4
9-11	Install sewer	8
10-11	Electrical manhole	6
11-12	Duct bank	10
12-13	Feeder	5

To determine the work force requirements for the project, draw the arrow diagram to scale and plot work force against time. The first step is to draw the critical path (0-1-2-3-4-5-8-13) and plot the critical work force. This must be the initial step since this portion of the work force requirements is fixed. Figure 14.1 shows this plot of critical path and associated work force. In the float paths, there is flexibility in plotting the work force. To get a planning datum of maximum needs, first plot all the float paths, starting at the early start times. The first path plotted is the low-float path (3-6-7-8). Since work force is plotted on early start, the result is an early peak of work force requirements. The peak requirement is thirty-one workers if all activities start early, and it occurs at the eleventh day.

Figure 14.2 shows a similar plot of work force based upon starting float activities and their late start dates. The peak work force requirement in this case is thirty-four workers and does not occur until the twenty-fourth day. Figure 14.3 shows both the early-start (light line) and late-start (heavy line) work force curves. Area A is common to both curves. Areas B and C are under the early-start curve only. Areas D and E are under the late-start curve only. The areas under the curves represent work force (workers × project time). Since the work force under each curve must be equal, the difference in the late-start and early-start curves must be equal. That is:

Since

$$A + B + C = A + D + E$$

then

$$B + C = D + E$$

In this case, B + C = 108 worker-days = D + E.

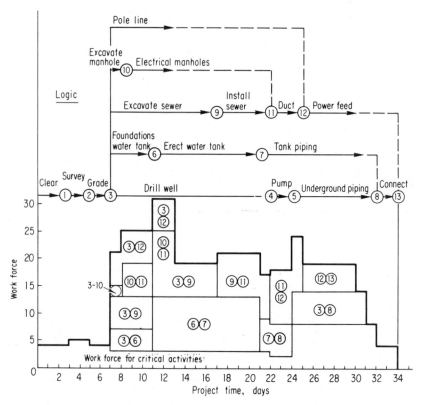

Figure 14.1   Peak work force requirements (based upon early start).

Having estimated the peak or worst cases, how can you level the work force requirements? In this simplified example, it is relatively easy. From Figure 14.3, the minimum level must be in excess of twenty workers. Since the early-start curve is the more level of the two, work from that. By shifting the 3-12 activity to a start on the thirteenth day instead of the seventh, work force can be built up slower and held under twenty-five workers. This leveling is shown in Figure 14.4. Since the estimated crew size is fixed, the job superintendent can only level beyond the graph of Figure 14.4 by further shifts of crew sizes. In shifting activities to level work force, keep in mind that the logical sequence must not be violated.

Having worked out a level work force plan for the Seabees, assume that only twenty workers will be assigned to the project. Figure 14.5 shows the plot of one solution to this problem (there is no single correct solution). This particular solution of 40 days is the minimum time in which this project can be completed with only twenty workers. In arriving at this result, a number of factors should be noted. First, there is no longer a

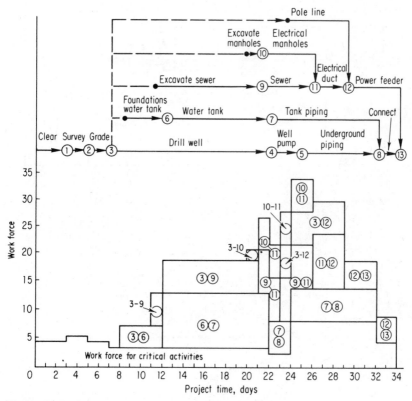

Figure 14.2 Peak work force requirements (based upon late start).

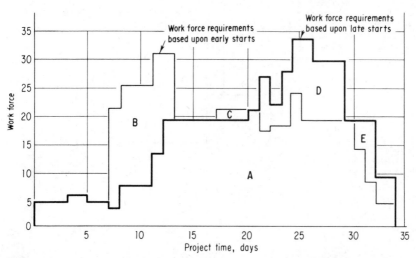

Figure 14.3 Combined peak work force requirements for both early start and late start dates.

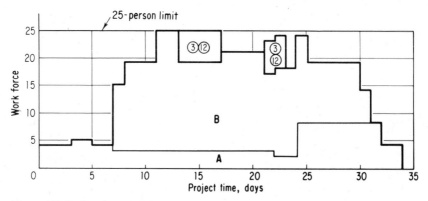

Figure 14.4 Leveled work force.

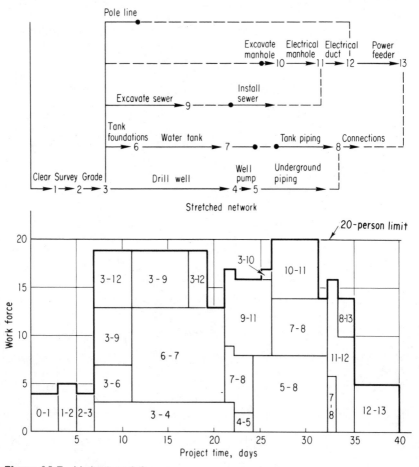

Figure 14.5 Limited work force.

critical path. Every path through the network now has interruptions during which work force is unavailable. Since there is no critical path, the critical activities do not have to be done in immediate succession.

However, the critical path is a good starting point for scheduling activities because you cannot complete this project in less than 34 days; and if you do not follow the "old" critical path you cannot complete it in 34 days. Even though there is no critical path, no activity can be started before its early start because the work must still be accomplished in the same logical sequence.

In meeting the work force restrictions, *activity splitting* is allowed. That is, you can start an activity, leave it, and come back to complete it. This occurred in activity 3-12, pole line installation. Also note that certain impractical scheduling tends to occur. For instance, activity 9-11, install sewer, follows 3-9, excavation sewer, by 2 days. Unless the climate was quite dry, the field superintendent would be unlikely to hold fast to this schedule. He or she would start installing the sewer on the seventeenth day with the seven workers available rather than the eight-person crew specified. If this were done, activity 3-12, pole line installation, would probably be delayed until the twenty-seventh day. This would still allow completion by the fortieth day with a slower build-up to the full crew.

To the advantage of having Seabee jacks-of-all-trades as workers, add one slight complication: Keeping the same total work crews, specify the number of petty officers and construction men for each activity:

	Activity	Number of petty officers	Number of construction workers
0-1	Clear site	4	0
1-2	Survey and layout	2	3
2-3	Grade	4	0
3-4	Drill well	1	2
3-6	Water tank foundations	1	3
3-9	Excavate sewer	2	4
3-10	Excavate manhole	1	1
3-12	Pole line installation	2	4
4-5	Well pump	1	1
5-8	Underground piping	1	7
6-7	Erect water tank	3	7
7-8	Tank piping	2	4
8-13	Connect piping	2	2
9-11	Install sewer	1	7
10-11	Electrical manhole	2	4
11-12	Duct bank	2	8
12-13	Power feeder	1	4

Figure 14.6 is similar to Figure 14.1 except that the work force is broken into the two categories of petty officers and construction workers. Adding the two curves together would give the same total usage requirements as Figure 14.1 (ten petty officers plus twenty-one construction workers on the eleventh day equals thirty-one, etc.).

If the twenty Seabees are made up of five petty officers and fifteen construction workers, what is the effect on the schedule? When handling more than one type of work force, the graphical plot becomes too unwieldy and another graphical approach is used to level these resources.

The first step in this method is to list all the activities in ascending order of their end event j. This list is shown in the first column of Figure 14.7 (the event numbers must be assigned in the classical order $j > i$). First on the list is the first activity 0-1, and last are the two terminal activities, 8-13 and 12-13. The others, being in order of end events, are arranged in proper logical order. If you schedule the work force in this

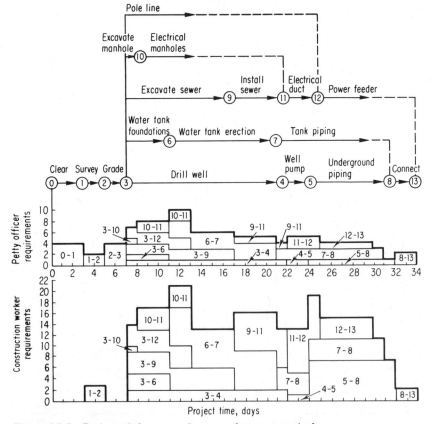

Figure 14.6   Peak work force requirements (two categories).

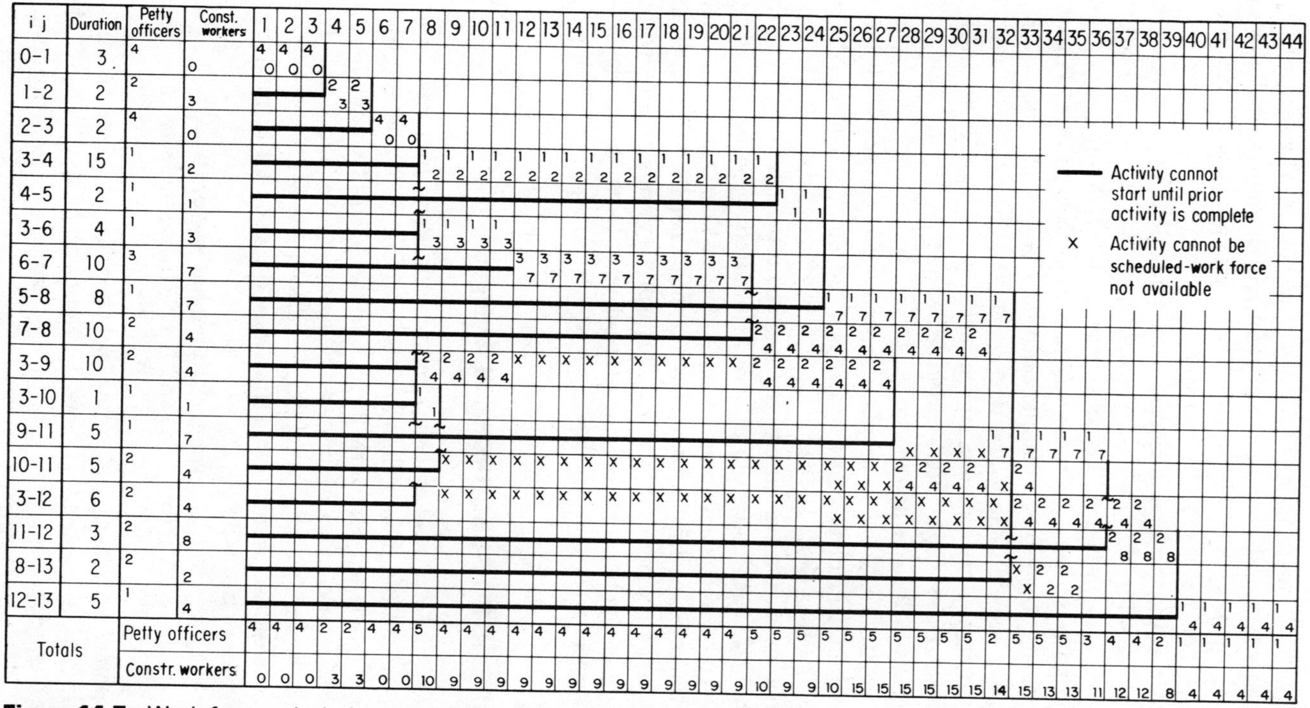

Figure 14.7 Work force calculation. Limits: five petty officers, fifteen construction workers.

Legend:

— Activity cannot start until prior activity is complete

x Activity cannot be scheduled—work force not available

i–j	Duration	Petty officers	Const. workers
0–1	3	4	0
1–2	2	2	3
2–3	2	4	0
3–4	15	1	2
4–5	2	1	1
3–6	4	1	3
6–7	10	3	7
5–8	8	1	7
7–8	10	2	4
3–9	10	2	4
3–10	1	1	1
9–11	5	1	7
10–11	5	2	4
3–12	6	2	4
11–12	3	2	8
8–13	2	2	2
12–13	5	1	4

order, you will be observing the network logical order. The second column has the activity durations. The third and fourth columns list the work force requirements. With this information, you can schedule the project without further recourse to the network.

Starting at the top line in Figure 14.7, schedule four petty officers for the first 3 days for activity 0-1. The next activity, 1-2, cannot logically start until 0-1 is completed. The heavy line represents this logical restriction. Two petty officers and three construction workers are assigned to this activity. Proceed in this manner until activity 3-9. This logically could commence at the eighth day, and does. However, on the twelfth day there are not enough petty officers, so the activity is interrupted until the twenty-second day. This interruption is represented by an X on those days when work force is not available.

The procedure, then, is simple: Consider each activity in order, and determine the logical point at which it could start. Then schedule the activity as soon as work force is available. In this example, the division of work force into two categories lengthened the project from 40 to 44 days.

While basic CPM networks of several hundred activities can easily be manually computed, such manual techniques are slow and complicated. A network of perhaps fifty activities is the practical limit for calculating work-force requirements manually. This will vary considerably with the complexity of the network and the number of different categories of skill and equipment to be scheduled.

COMPUTERIZED RESOURCES PLANNING

For most work force studies, computer analysis is much more economical in terms of time and money than manual analysis. A number of programs have been developed for work force leveling. Two of the earliest were RAMPS (Resource and Manpower Scheduling) by CEIR and RPSM (Resource Planning and Scheduling Method) by Mauchly Associates. However, these two pioneer programs were designed for computer hardware which is now obsolete.

Other major systems developed to handle resources as well as basic schedules include PMS (by IBM) and ICES (Integrated Civil Engineering Systems by MIT).

McDonnell Automation (McAuto) was part of the original PMS team and utilized that experience in its development of the McAuto MSCS (Management Scheduling and Control System) program which handles all phases of resource planning and scheduling.

The Project 2 system (Project Software & Development, Inc.) developed by Robert Daniels of the original ICES group has comprehensive resource capabilities.

MSCS and Project 2 provided the best resource capabilities during the 1970s. There were other systems, including RPC (Resource Planning and Control) by the author and MDC Systems, in development and use since 1966. RPC gives results similar to those of MSCS and Project 2, but uses resource parameter variation rather than automatic leveling. This optimizes human direction, using the computer to test results. Other systems are also available, as described later in Chapter 17, *Computer Programs and Systems.*

The systems typically have three phases: The first is a CPM normal time run; the second is a resource compilation which is called "unlimited run"; and in the third phase, the resources available are limited and two outputs are generated. One of these is a table of resources versus time. The second is the schedule needed to achieve that usage. This utilizes the logical sequence of the network but is no longer time-limited. Thus the resource-limited project duration will be greater than (or possibly equal to) the normal time duration.

A computer program's unlimited phase would generate the following usage table for the two categories of peak requirements given in Figure 14.6:

Resource Usage Table

Time	P*	C*	Time	P*	C*
1	4	0	18	5	16
2	4	0	19	5	16
3	4	0	20	5	16
4	2	3	21	5	16
5	2	3	22	4	13
6	4	0	23	5	13
7	4	0	24	5	13
8	7	14	25	5	19
9	8	17	26	4	15
10	8	17	27	4	15
11	8	17	28	4	15
12	10	21	29	4	15
13	10	21	30	4	15
14	6	13	31	3	11
15	6	13	32	1	7
16	6	13	33	2	2
17	6	13	34	2	2

*P = petty officer; C = construction worker.

A typical program can generate a schedule for this unlimited resources phase. However, it would contain the same information as the CPM output. Accordingly, the schedule is not usually printed out for this step.

In the next step, with the petty officer supply limited to five and the construction workers to fifteen, the usage table (see Figure 14.7) would be as follows:

Resource Usage Table

Time	P*	C*	Time	P*	C*
1	4	0	23	5	9
2	4	0	24	5	9
3	4	0	25	5	10
4	2	3	26	5	15
5	2	3	27	5	15
6	4	0	28	5	15
7	4	0	29	5	15
8	5	10	30	5	15
9	4	9	31	5	15
10	4	9	32	2	14
11	4	9	33	5	15
12	4	9	34	5	13
13	4	9	35	5	13
14	4	9	36	3	11
15	4	9	37	4	12
16	4	9	38	4	12
17	4	9	39	2	8
18	4	9	40	1	4
19	4	9	41	1	4
20	4	9	42	1	4
21	4	9	43	1	4
22	5	10	44	1	4

*P = petty officers; C = construction workers.

The schedule for this manpower level would be as follows:

Resource-Limited Schedule
(Based upon five petty officers, fifteen construction workers)

i-j	Duration, days	Description	Work force		Start	End
0-1	3	Clear site	4P		0	3
1-2	2	Survey and layout	2P*	3C*	4	5
2-3	2	Grade	4P		6	7
3-4	15	Drill well	1P	2C	8	22
4-5	2	Well pump	1P	1C	23	24
3-6	4	Water tank foundations	1P	3C	8	11
6-7	10	Erect water tank	3P	7C	12	21
5-8	8	Underground piping	1P	7C	25	32
7-8	10	Tank piping	2P	4C	22	31
3-9	10	Excavate sewer	2P	4C	8	11&
3-9	10	Excavate sewer	2P	4C	22	27&
3-10	1	Excavate manhole	1P	1C	8	8
9-11	5	Install sewer	1P	7C	32	36

Resource-Limited Schedule
(Based upon five petty officers, fifteen construction workers)

i-j	Duration, days	Description	Work force		Start	End
10-11	5	Electrical manhole	2P	4C	28	31&
10-11	5	Electrical manhole	2P	4C	33	33&
3-12	6	Pole line installation	2P	4C	33	38
11-12	3	Duct bank	2P	8C	37	39
8-13	2	Connect piping	2P	2C	34	35
12-13	5	Power feeder	1P	4C	40	44

*P = petty officers; C = construction workers.

This output is kept on a tape or disk so that any desired sort or listing can be furnished. The usual ones are *i-j*, start, or end. In this case, the sort is *j-i*. This is unusual, but it matches the order of activities given in Figure 14.7. Note that there is no critical path or float. This is *the* schedule which must be followed to achieve the level usage. Look at activities 3-9 and 10-11. These are split, being scheduled at two separate times. This is indicated by the ampersand.

Resource Applications

The analysis and planning of work force and equipment by a network should be preceded by the use of the basic CPM technique. In many instances the basic CPM technique is sufficient to meet all the practical needs associated with planning and scheduling a project. On the other hand, there are some applications where CPM alone is inadequate and resources must be analyzed.

In construction, this latter category includes heavy-equipment jobs such as earth-fill dams or highways. Careful scheduling of equipment across one or several projects has an immediate payoff. Contractors owning equipment are usually in a constant "rental quandary." Should they rent out their idle equipment, or will they have to rent extra equipment themselves in the near future? In heavy construction work, equipment (not time) is the limiting factor. In one highway project of 220 working days, the addition of five pieces of equipment shortened the project by 40 days. This time reduction of almost 20 percent was achieved by means of an equipment increase of less than 10 percent.

Funds can also be considered a resource. Accordingly, a number of state highway departments are considering the use of computerized fund-leveling analysis coupled with a priority system to allocate appropriated funds to specific projects. A similar method has also been tested for city budget preparation.

In a water treatment plant project, a series of resource-versus-schedule runs were made to measure the minimum number of craftspeople required per contractor. In addition to the numbers of craftspeople needed, a second concern was crowding in work areas having a high density of piping, equipment, and controls. A maximum number of tradespeople per controlling area was posed as a limit. The runs identified at least two instances where the minimum levels of craftspeople required by all the contractors together reached the cumulative population allowable for crowded areas.

Most production processes which stay on-stream for long periods of time cannot be maintained during the production cycle. When the unit is shut down, either on schedule or because of a malfunction, the plant maintenance department performs maintenance work on the unit. This work is usually pushed around the clock because downtime is costly. The time from off-stream to on-stream is usually referred to as *turnaround.* This is particularly applicable to chemical and refinery units. However, maintenance of large power generation stations, boilers, and similar plants or equipment is also in the turnaround category. Power or production plant outages are handled similarly. The payback for time savings can be tremendous. On a recent nuclear power plant outage, the cost/loss was $800,000 per day.

A utility used resource planning for the scheduled maintenance of a special superpressure turbine. Studies were carried out 2 months prior to the scheduled shutdown. One month prior to this date, the machine developed bearing noises and had to be shut down early. The company maintenance forces were committed to another turnaround which was in progress. Accordingly, the work force originally scheduled for the new turbine could not be assigned. While this unit was down, the company estimated an out-of-pocket cost of $5000 per day because of the lower efficiency of the standby units used to replace it. While the unit was in its 4-day cooldown period, new computer runs were made reflecting the reduced initial work force levels. A schedule was finally generated that retained the original maintenance project length. The computer accomplished this by shifting work which could wait to the latter portion of the project when a larger work force would be available. The project schedule was updated regularly. In the second week, subcontracted work was identified as the critical path. A work force analysis indicated that there was no need for the maintenance force to work on Easter weekend. This information resulted in a considerable money savings in addition to an earlier on-line time for the unit.

Refineries also have the problem of fixed work force and limited time to accomplish substantial turnaround assignments. Resource planning has been used to reduce downtime, but even the best schedule can achieve only a limited time reduction.

Resource planning has been applied to a number of chemical and refinery turnarounds. In one case involving a crude oil unit, an 18-day schedule was bettered by 4 days. A work force of more than 400 workers was employed. During the turnaround, the updating of the network indicated that only critical areas had to be worked over the Fourth of July holiday. Even more importantly, when another unit came down unexpectedly, the updatings gave specific dates when craftspeople could be reassigned to that second shutdown without jeopardizing the scheduled completion of the crude oil unit.

MULTIPROJECT SCHEDULING

Figure 14.8 shows five concurrent subordinate networks interconnected to produce one major NASA project network. In this case, each subordinate network is termed a *fragnet,* standing for "fragmentary network." In order to compute the major network, it would be necessary only to interconnect the nine unconnected initial networks by using nine logical restraints tied back to a starting event or node. Similarly, each of the concluding or terminating events would have to be interconnected to provide a continuous network from start to finish. Calculation could then be by basic CPM program. If the calculation is performed on this basis, there will be one critical path through the longest project, with each of the others showing float. Also, the calculation on this basis will show equivalent calendar starting dates for each project. To bring the projects into line

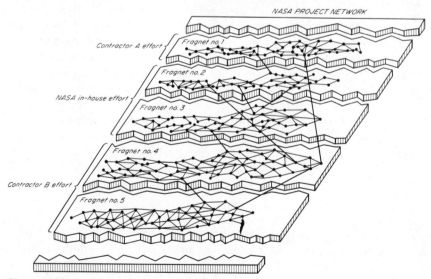

Figure 14.8   Multiproject networks. *(From NASA.)*

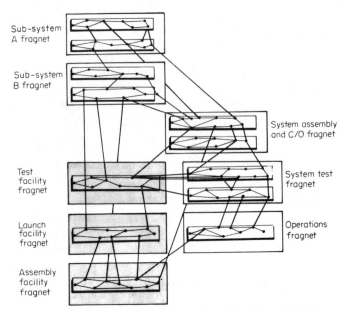

Figure 14.9 Multiproject network, functional. *(From NASA.)*

with reality, the starting restraints are assigned times to reflect the staggering of the actual project parts or fragnets. Similarly, lag or concluding time durations can be assigned so that the phasing will apply to the completion event.

To assist in the establishment of time values for lead and lag arrows (activities with no work activity but with time duration at the start of a project are termed *lead,* those at the conclusion are used to establish phasing or *lag*), the fragnets may be calculated before they are interconnected. Often, the interconnection points are dictated to some degree by the time values. That is, where there is the possibility of a choice as in preferential logic, the interface between two areas—particularly functional areas—will be established by completion time. Figure 14.9 shows more summary fragnets, but more complex interconnections.

Fragnets, or individual networks, do not have to be physically connected in order to be computed on a common basis. The connections can be made by merging nodes or adding logical restraints to the input. To interpret results, however, it is advisable to note these, at least on the summary network.

Multiproject scheduling is one of the best bases for project resource planning and scheduling, because quite often a special skill or resource must be mobilized and utilized across many networks simultaneously. Also, in multiproject network scheduling, there is often substantial concurrency of activities and often flexibility in the completion schedules of some of the subprojects. This can provide greater float opportunities, reducing peak resource projections.

Perini Construction, in an early CPM application, used multiproject resource planning to schedule special equipment for installing piling for bridge piers, each of which required 100 piles. Overall project time available for piling was less than 1 year between spring flood seasons. A total of more than 700 pilings was needed and each had to be drilled and placed to an average depth of over 200 feet at an average drilling rate of 10 feet per hour. Two special drilling rigs were designed and manufactured in France at a cost of $500,000. Each machine served several purposes: drilling holes, placing caissons, placing piles, removing caissons after placing piles (extraction). CPM was utilized to evaluate, in great depth, the placing of a set of piles. Setup and moving time was included in the calculations, and an average cycle of 36 hours was predicted and subsequently confirmed by field information. At this rate, with allowance for a 7-day week, the piling could not be completed prior to the flood season. The detailed analysis pointed out that not only was additional equipment required but that it could be a specialized caisson extractor rather than a full-fledged combination unit. The new extracting machine cost only 20 percent of the multipurpose machine and resulted in a reduction of better than 25 percent of the overall project duration.

Figure 14.10 shows three networks that make up a program for three

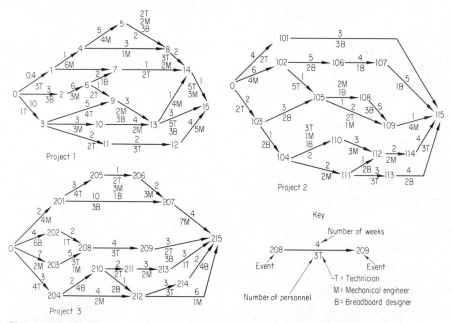

Figure 14.10 Design networks. *[Used with permission of Machine Design Magazine.]*

RPSM USAGE FOR UNLIMITED AND LIMITED MANPOWER

(a) Unlimited Manpower				(b) 10 t; 10 m; 10 b				(c) 12 t; 12 m; 12 b			
Time	b	m	t	Time	b	m	t	Time	b	m	t
1	9	10	12	1	3	10	10	1	9	10	12
2	9	10	12	2	3	10	10	2	9	10	12
3	17	12	13	3	10	6	9	3	12	12	11
4	21	15	12	4	10	10	10	4	12	11	9
5	18	15	11	5	10	10	10	5	11	12	11
6	16	18	11	6	5	9	5	6	11	12	7
7	13	13	13	7	5	5	10	7	12	12	10
8	13	16	11	8	8	10	4	8	11	12	8
9	13	12	11	9	9	10	4	9	11	11	11
10	14	8	11	10	9	9	6	10	12	8	11
11	15	9	16	11	8	10	9	11	12	11	11
12	11	9	18	12	9	10	9	12	12	11	11
13	4	11	14	13	10	8	10	13	12	8	12
14	3	11	13	14	10	5	10	14	11	1	12
15	3	12	7	15	10	4	9	15	11	6	10
16	6	14	3	16	9	5	10	16	9	12	12
17	9	7	2	17	8	4	10	17	9	11	12
18	7	7	2	18	10	6	9	18	11	11	6
19	7	4	7	19	10	7	9	19	11	11	11
20	4	3	10	20	10	9	10	20	4	10	10
21	3		5	21	10	7	7	21	3	7	5
				22	9	9	7	22		7	
				23	9	7	7				
				24	9	7	7				
				25	8	7	2				
				26	4	7					
				27		8	3				
				28		4	3				
				29		3	5				

Figure 14.11 Resource schedules. *(Used with permission of Machine Design Magazine.)*

design projects. Each has three types of design personnel: mechanical engineer m, a breadboard designer b, and an electronics technician t. The networks represent concurrent work on three different projects by one functional design area. A point to be noted is that it is not physically required for these networks to be joined by arrows but, in this case, the connection at the conclusion is by two or three lag arrows, while the common zero starting node establishes the initiation point. This calculation is to determine the minimum reasonable time span for those three projects with the use of the design work force available. Note that since these are sample networks, descriptions are not written on the activities as they normally would be. The problem was solved with the RPSM calculation and the results are shown in Figure 14.11. The first stage of calculation indicated that the projects could be completed in 21 weeks by using a maximum of twenty-one designers, eighteen mechanical engineers, and eighteen technicians. In the next step, the computer was instructed that the department had only ten people available in each class, and it therefore noted a time extension from 21 to 29 weeks. At this point, a solution was attempted by determining an optimum resource use within the basic CPM time. Part c indicates that with a 20 percent increase in work force, a 33 percent time reduction could be achieved.

TURNAROUND APPLICATION

Maintenance operations in the petrochemical industry offer one of the most typical illustrations of multiproject operations. Many individual miniprojects go on concurrently with one or more major projects. The use of CPM has been well established in preplanning these highly coordinated operations. One such turnaround was planned and implemented at Commonwealth Oil and Refinery in Puerto Rico. Key Commonwealth personnel had previously been exposed to CPM through courses, seminars, and literature. Management decided to use CPM to plan a major maintenance turnaround of the No. 2 crude distillation unit, including a catalytic cracker. Two months prior to the scheduled turnaround, the first CPM networks were prepared by the conference method. Key process, maintenance, contract, and engineering personnel for the turnaround met to discuss the work items to be included. As the scope of each work item was discussed, a network defining the logical sequence of work was developed on a blackboard, and the information subsequently transcribed onto a reproducible drawing. Normal crew sizes were assumed and time and work force estimates were added to the networks to complete the arrow diagram. The individual subnetworks were linked together to form a multiproject plan. Figure 14.12 shows a summary of CPM for the crude heater overhaul, which determined the longest major job in the turnaround. Figure 14.13 shows the typical overhaul plan for three similar units, and there were more than forty such plans for different pieces of equipment. In the Commonwealth planning, there were several major operations but the majority could occur concurrently. The establishment of a reasonable working schedule required either resource allocation or the introduction of preferential logic. In this case, computerized resource planning was utilized to establish the role of more than 400 people assigned to the 3-week operation.

During the actual turnaround, the CPM group assigned a representative to each shift, to work directly with the shift coordinator. The repre-

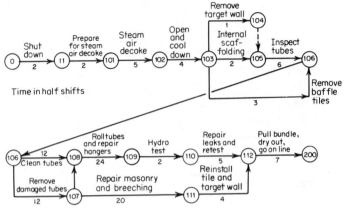

Figure 14.12 Summary plan for crude heater overhaul. *(Used with permission of Hydrocarbon Processing and Petroleum Refiner.)*

sentatives' role was to assist the coordinators in using the CPM information, and secondly to collect status information on completed work and work in progress. On a daily basis, the completed activities were noted in the project computer input deck and a new CPM and resource calculation was made. The resulting resource-usage tables forecasted work force trends, given as current work force in use.

An interesting characteristic of the trend forecast is that, for it to be

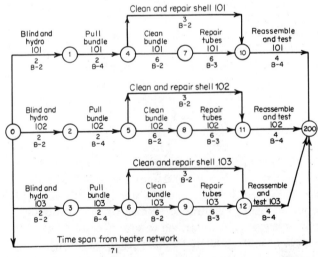

Figure 14.13 Summary plan for overhaul of three units similar to that whose plan was illustrated in Figure 14.12. *(Used with permission of Hydrocarbon Processing and Petroleum Refiner.)*

effective, the work force estimating need not be accurate, just consistent. Accordingly, if the resource computation calls for forty workers and fifty are assigned, it can be anticipated that the work force requirements will show a downward trend as the fifty gain on the work time estimated for a forty-person crew. If the daily trend holds steady, it can be inferred that the original work force requirements were too low and a crew of fifty is really the proper size. On the other hand, if the estimated crew is being used and yet work force requirements are trending downward, it can be assumed that the estimates were too conservative. In the Commonwealth project, the first several daily reports confirmed the forecasted 18-day project duration. On the sixth daily report, it was reported that a noncritical area could be completed 2 days early, and the tenth report con-

---

**STATUS REPORT FOR NO. 2 CRUDE AND
VAC. UNIT TURNAROUND:**

As a start of time unit 15, 1st shift Thursday, June 27.

DURATION:

Completion by Sat., July 13 (72 time units) is still feasible, but only if all tube repair and replacement in the vacuum-heater can be accomplished within the 18 shifts (32 units) originally allotted. A definitive re-evaluation of the tube work has not been made as yet. All other work is on schedule.

MANPOWER:

(1) Manpower computation definitely indicates that present work force is adequate to maintain schedule. (2) Further, it is doubtful that additional manpower would expedite the critical Vacuum Heater repair as working room has become limiting factor.

CRITICAL AREAS:

(1) Vacuum Heater—*(Most Critical)*
*(2) Crude Heater
(3) Insulation of Tower and vessel skirts (sandblasting scheduled for Sunday)
(4) Crude Tower Work

*Need division to go ahead with seal welding over-rolled tubes in Crude Heater. Work could start NOW.

TIME LOSSES:

(1) Without acetylene and oxygen in the critical Vacuum Heater Area for over two hours today.
(2) Chemical cleaning; not working second shift. Eight dirty bundles available.
(3) Lack of heat exchanger slings limits high pressure cleaning of heat exchangers to two a day instead of four.
(4) No ice for water cans. Time lost by people walking to other areas for water.

Figure 14.14 Turnaround analytical report. *[Used with permission of Hydrocarbon Processing and Petroleum Refiner.]*

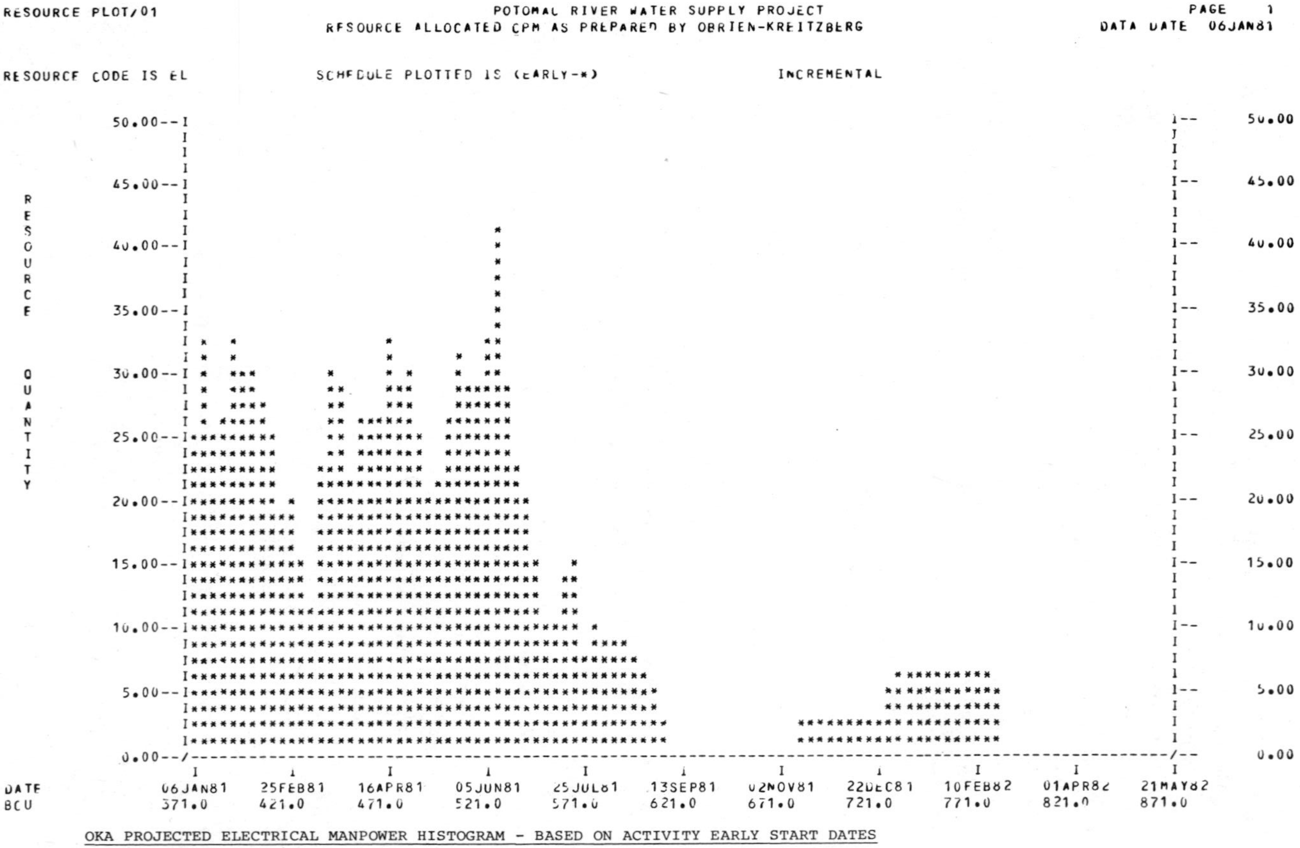

RESOURCE PLOT/01

POTOMAL RIVER WATER SUPPLY PROJECT

RESOURCE ALLOCATED CPM AS PREPARED BY OBRIEN-KREITZBERG

DATA DATE 06JAN81   PAGE 1

RESOURCE CODE IS EL   SCHEDULE PLOTTED IS (EARLY-*)   INCREMENTAL

```
                                                            50.00
                                                            45.00
                                                            40.00
                                                            35.00
                                                            30.00
                                                            25.00
                                                            20.00
                                                            15.00
                                                            10.00
                                                             5.00
                                                             0.00
```

R E S O U R C E

Q U A N T I T Y

```
50.00--
45.00--
40.00--
35.00--
30.00--
25.00--
20.00--
15.00--
10.00--
 5.00--
 0.00--
```

DATE   06JAN81 25FEB81 16APR81 05JUN81 25JUL81 13SEP81 02NOV81 22DEC81 10FEB82 01APR82 21MAY82
BCU   371.0   421.0   471.0   521.0   571.0   621.0   671.0   721.0   771.0   821.0   871.0

OKA PROJECTED ELECTRICAL MANPOWER HISTOGRAM – BASED ON ACTIVITY EARLY START DATES

Figure 14.15 Projected electrical work force histogram based on activity early start dates. *(Courtesy O'Brien-Kreitzberg & Assoc., Inc.)*

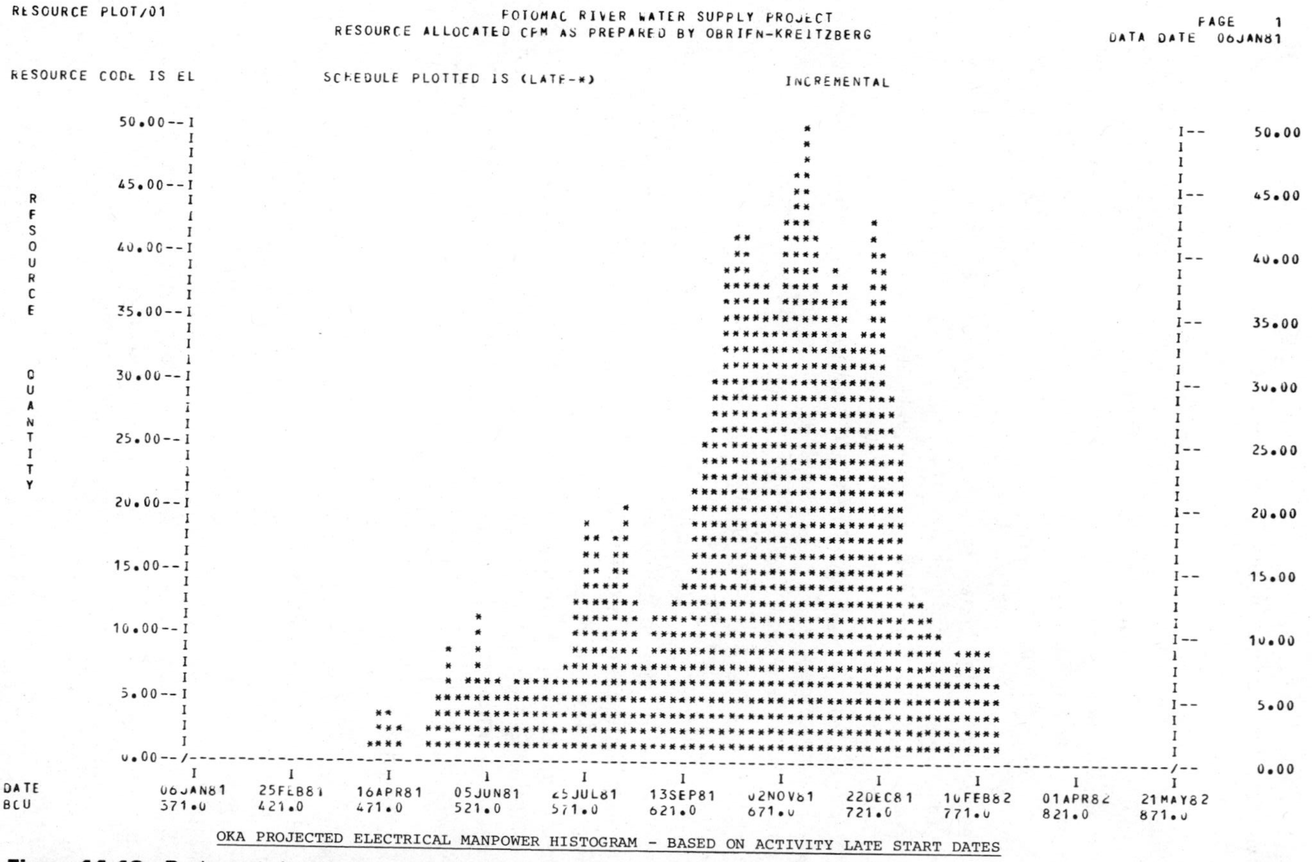

Figure 14.16 Projected electrical work force histogram based on activity late start dates. *(Courtesy O'Brien-Kreitzberg & Assoc., Inc.)*

firmed all earlier trends, which were that all work would be completed 4 days early. On the thirteenth day, the unit was turned over to process and daily reports ceased.

Thus the trend analysis method was effective. The first four reports indicated adequate work force, which was actually somewhat below the original projected requirement. On the fifth report, a downward trend was noticed. Further, it was noted that a shortage of cleaned bundles for exchangers was causing an excess of available boilermakers. And it was also evident that when bundles became available, the trend in this craft would reverse and so create a shortage of work force. On the sixth report, it was recommended that a reduction in the work force could start. The next two reports noted that the shift of some of the work force to another, unexpected, shutdown would not impede the progress of the job at hand. With further work force analysis, it was determined that on the Fourth of July holiday only critical jobs needed to be worked, which saved substantial overtime. Figure 14.14 shows an actual daily report used in the Commonwealth turnaround.

Figure 14.15 is a histogram showing projected electrical work force based on early activity starts for a project which was in its finishing stages in 1981/1982. The plot demonstrates that a leveled force of about 25 electrical workers could readily complete the project on time. However, the late-start histogram (Figure 14.16) shows that if float is used up and the electrical work is not commenced until April (a 3-month slippage), a peak force of about forty electricians would be required. Using the early-start approach and a crew of twenty electricians, the schedule was leveled and the work completed on time.

SUMMARY

Resources (work force, equipment, money, etc.) can be assigned to the CPM activities. For a simple network, maximum work force requirements can be forecast by two manual techniques. Work force can also be leveled by using these techniques. When resource limits are set in, the project duration may be lengthened.

The manual techniques are limited and cannot handle large networks. This is an excellent area for computer application.

These techniques have been used in turnarounds, highway work, naval shipyards, and other planning areas. They are practical, tested management tools.

Multiprocessing is usually the most effective way by which the resources needed for a large project can be scheduled because of the flexibility often available in terms of float for the many minor subnetworks involved. Also, the sheer numbers of activities to be accomplished provide an excellent opportunity for the computer to assist the human scheduler. In multiproject systems, such as turnarounds, the identification of the critical path is often less important than the cataloging of all the work to be done.

PROJECT SCHEDULING

In practice, and in this book thus far, the use of CPM in planning and implementing construction has been emphasized. If a project to be accomplished is considered in terms only of its construction phase, the application of CPM can save both time and money. When limited to the construction phase, the technique is being used as a control. However, many other advantages can be achieved by the earlier identification of the project as a larger universe than just its construction activities. Construction is the time when the iceberg emerges and the entire project can be viewed and understood by many people. Problems are evident, and activity is manifest. However, in most projects today, the time spent on construction is equaled by that spent on the preconstruction design phase. Further, in public projects, the administrative review cycle often equals in time both the design and construction periods. Thus, in the public or quasipublic sectors, the preconstruction project time (following identification of the project in a budget) is often twice the actual construction period. Obviously, if disciplined project control techniques are applied early, substantial time savings—and therefore, subsequent cost savings— can be achieved at a relatively low unit cost. In fact, the preconstruction phase of a project is the most probable area for the application of cost-

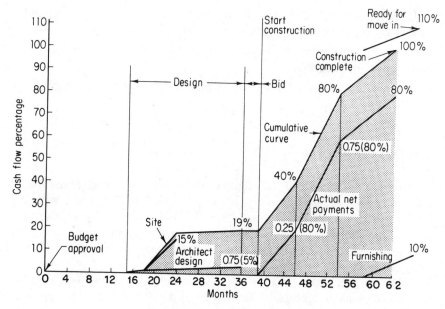

Cash flow, typical elementary school

Figure 15.1 Time-cost curve, elementary school.

optimization techniques. The input of additional funding during this phase could result in a tremendous time reduction.

Figure 15.1 illustrates the typical cash flow over 62 months between the budgeting and the opening of an elementary school. Although the school authorities on the date of budget approval might have the feeling that they have spent or committed the entire amount of money for the school, actually they will find that for the next 40 months, they will spend less than 20 percent of the overall budget. (In the example, in-house staff costs are not recognized, but should be. These would add another 10 percent or so to the cost of the project, and would be more heavily drawn on in the project's first 20 months than later, diminishing as others came in to carry the project through to its end.) The illustration points out that it is not easy to spend money, even when the decision has been reached to spend it.

The typical building project has four major phases or categories of progress:

1. *Predesign activities,* in the period between budget preparation and approval and the initiation of design, with the owner having primary responsibility for progress.

2. *Design,* with the architect, engineer, A-E, or in-house design staff primarily responsible for progress.

3. *Construction,* with the contractor or in-house construction force responsible for progress.

4. *Furnish or move-in,* with the owner or contractor having primary responsibility.

PREDESIGN PHASE

One of the least-defined, intangible, and time-consuming phases of a project is the predesign portion. During this period, the owner, with his or her technical staff and/or consultants, should be very busy with a number of important roles. Often, these are performed by omission or default, rather than carried out in a rigorous, planned manner. The seeds of many project problems are planted in this field of neglect.

Most projects seem to appear from nowhere; the result is an evolutionary manner of aggregate thinking from many sources, which gathers pressure, both political and personal, until the project has been articulated. Projects which evolve in this way include schools, hospitals, public buildings, industrial plants, highways—indeed, almost any identifiable major project. Key characteristics in their evolution are power structure and consensus. Actually, this phase of the project should go through the following stages: establishment of goals; means of accomplishing goals; decision to proceed; identification of funding source; and budget approval.

These components make up what has been termed the *Planning, Programing, and Budgeting System,* or *PPBS,* by the federal government. Operated in its best sense, PPBS uses a definition of the true needs and requirements of the organization to establish or identify the project. In order to operate PPBS successfully, needs and goals must be preestablished, preferably as policy. Projects which can be utilized to meet the goals are then reviewed against the available resources in an intuitive examination; then selections are made based upon priorities assumed or specified.

The decision to go ahead requires the identification of specific projects and the development of preliminary cost estimates. These are usually accomplished on the basis of gross estimating factors such as costs per square or cubic foot.

After a project has been given a budget and funding is available to meet that budget, the predesign phase moves on to other stages.

Site selection such as for a hospital addition or a school replacement or other finite location situations, is often part of the basic decision to go ahead with a project. However, in many cases, a new site should or must be considered. Usually the site consideration precedes the selection of a designer, since the design should be a function of the site. A number of nontechnical factors may funnel the choice of a site into a specific direction. Among the factors to be considered are:

1. *Encumbrances:* Are there tenants who will have to be relocated? Are there structures to be removed?

2. *Land cost:* What are the economic values and factors?

3. *Transportation:* Is the location adequately served, and served by media suitable to the character of the facility's needs?

4. *Utilities:* What are their availabilities? Where are the potential problems?

5. *Neighborhoods:* Is the environment suitable for the facility? Is the facility suitable for the environment?

6. *Zoning:* Does local zoning conform to the use intended?

7. *Community:* How will the community react to the facility?

8. *Subsurface conditions:* Will the foundations require unusual support? Are there unusual problems to be overcome?

There are other factors, but it is clear that in choosing between more than one site, many factors must be evaluated and considered carefully. Unfortunately, many of these factors are considered from the viewpoint of hindsight rather than at the proper time in the project.

The last predesign activity should be the development of a specific program to identify the intent of the owner regarding the functional utilization of the project. This philosophical statement is important to the designer, but is often presented only in a perfunctory, nonspecific fashion, so that the designer through the trial-and-error method ends up establishing the philosophy. It is clearly the owner's responsibility to establish these requirements and to interpret them in terms of cost impact prior to the selection of a designer. Programing is a unique talent and will probably require a combination of the knowledge and a consultant's expertise.

Functional planning requires the availability, or the assembly of pertinent information regarding the project. If the PPBS or another synthesis approach has been effective, this information will have already been made available. Demographic sources such as the U.S. Census, city planning, state planning organizations, and in-house sources should be reviewed. Information should be arranged and stored in a manner which makes it accessible for the review of future projects, or for the reconsideration of this one. Very often when the information is stored in a computer data bank, such exercises as modeling, gaming, or simulation of various alternatives can be used to test the results of different potential approaches.

The functional programing effort should be tied back to the budgetary estimate and should either reaffirm or revise it. Since the functional program incorporates the policy in regard to any project, it should be approved by the appropriate owner or authority.

A concomitant to the functional program is the architectural program, which is necessarily related to it. The architectural program may be incorporated into the schematic design phase by the architect, or may be furnished to the architect.

Typically, projects do not have formal program documents. The result is uncertainty at the beginning of the design phase. Since designers are not compensated for uncertainty, their only defense is to proceed slowly at the early stages of design, developing a program type of statement which can be confirmed or revised by their clients. Unfortunately, clients often demonstrate a proclivity for changing their minds almost constantly. From the design point of view, this is not only time-consuming, but highly expensive. Virtually the only defense designers have is the careful control of the progress of the design, not permitting it to go forward at a normal speed, but holding off every activity until a high level of definition has been achieved. This is expensive to designers, and to owners as well, since the true design work is placed into too short a period of time for economical implementation.

The predesign phase is a frustrating one for schedulers and schedules. Many factors influence the viability of a project. In most cases, timing is not the controlling factor. In a few situations, however, timing is paramount. The Bicentennial celebration in 1976 was a fixed situation that project planners had to plan against. World's fairs and Olympic games have offered similar challenges.

DESIGN

Designing a project involves a relatively complex series of activities which become increasingly detailed as the project is moved through the various design phases. These phases are: schematic development, preliminary design, and working drawings.

Schematic Development This is also called the *sketch phase,* during which "concept" plans are developed by the architect and the basic engineering system analysis is made. Design criteria are specified, and schematic drawings are prepared. A set of perspective sketches, or renderings, is usually prepared. The basic budgetary cost is confirmed, but only in very broad terms.

Preliminary Design   This phase, also called *design development,* occurs after the approval of the sketch or schematic phase. The drawings are refined to a degree sufficient to permit the development of dimensioned space layouts. Heating and ventilating systems, main feeders or ducts, electrical main feeders, and definite dimensions of the structural framework are all identified in this phase. The requirements for utilities are also defined and specific requirements are determined. A preliminary cost estimate is prepared and should be relatively firm at this stage.

Working Drawings   This phase is also termed *contract documents or final design,* and includes about two-thirds of the design work, but fewer of the decisions, as well as a disproportionate amount of the design period (usually about one-half). The design as defined in the prior stages is developed in complete detail, including dimensions so that it can be specifically priced by prospective contractors. The contract documents include both drawings and specifications.

As the project design proceeds, each change becomes more difficult and expensive to implement. Each revision requires many more reviews and changes in related items. The range of changes which can be accepted gracefully narrows down in a funnel effect, with the maximum number and size of changes being more acceptable early in the project, and more and more costly as the design phase proceeds. This is illustrated schematically in Figure 15.2.

In most cases, the design phase is essentially unscheduled and uncoordinated, even by the designer. This is partially understandable since specific interconnections between the phases and disciplines such as structural, mechanical, electrical, and plumbing are difficult to express.

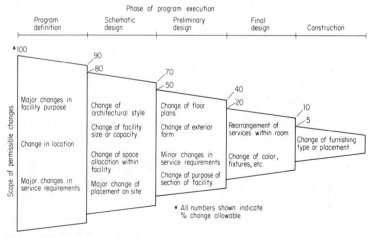

Figure 15.2   Design change funnel.

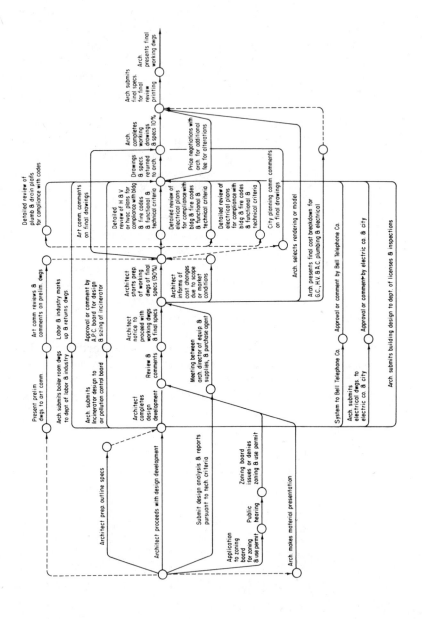

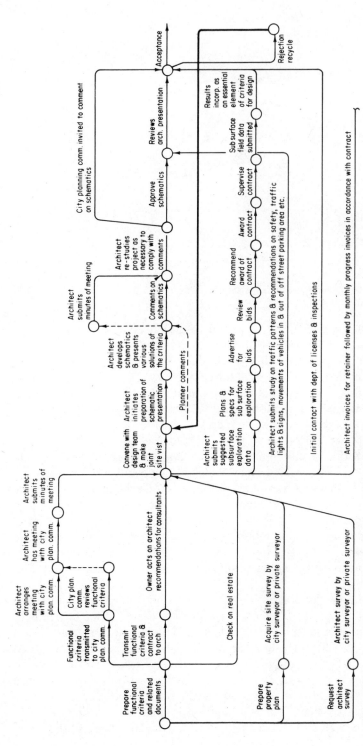

Figure 15.3 Network for John Doe project design phase.

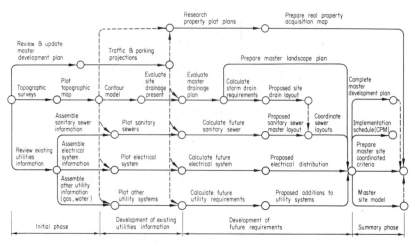

Figure 15.4   CPM plan for site development.

Nevertheless, the design phase *should* be closely coordinated and inter-connected at all stages so that the work in the field will reflect this careful coordination. To schedule this at the daily liaison level of effort could result in a fantastically large scheduling network. The usual compromise is the scheduling of concurrent activities in broader terms with an implied understanding that continual physical liaison must be carried out.

Figure 15.3 shows a network representing the design stages for the John Doe project. In this case, it is assumed that the project is located somewhere within a city limits, so that the usual agency reviews are required. Note the "rejection cycle" which is a loop and could not be com-puterized. It is shorthand to indicate that the full schematic design cycle sequence is represented (presumably with shorter durations). Since nor-mally projects such as John Doe would be placed in industrial parks, fewer reviews would probably be required—and by the state more often than by the township or county. However, the site development of an industrial park is not inexpensive and should itself be planned as illustrated in Fig-ure 15.4.

During the design stage, there is a continual interplay between the designer and the owner. The owner reviews the design at major points in its development and should be available daily for information. Quite often, the owner is furnishing or specifying special equipment which requires his or her attention. Both architect and owner are involved in various agency or company reviews. The design phase offers a tremendous potential for time gains (or losses). When an owner is handling many proj-ects concurrently, there is a substantial opportunity to utilize resource allocation of design and management staff so that the effects of the interplay between projects on the progress of all of them is calculated and structured rather than left to chance.

Just as the designer typically uses patience to wait until external pressures force a decision from the owner, the owner, assuming that the designer can work around problems without losing substantial time, typically delays decisions.

With so many people concerned about and responsible for most projects, substantial periods of time are usually spent in review and administrative planning. Often these activities are overplayed as each individual tends to see his or her own part in the project as the most important and therefore is willing to take more than a fair share of project time in arriving at this most important decision or confirmation. Also, in the early planning stages, individuals do not regard the planning time they use as really affecting the final delivery date, since that seems so far away.

In reviewing one administrative project in the Department of Labor, a network was established. As a result of this, the review cycles were reduced, and a better chain of responsible personnel was established. However, a startling fact emerged about the physical handling of the documents to be reviewed. It was found that the internal mailing system was so slow that 20 percent of the preconstruction phase of this project was taken up with mail handling by the internal mail group. Because of the importance of the project, this was changed and hand-carrying between project personnel was instituted.

Figure 15.5 illustrates the manner in which project subnetworks or

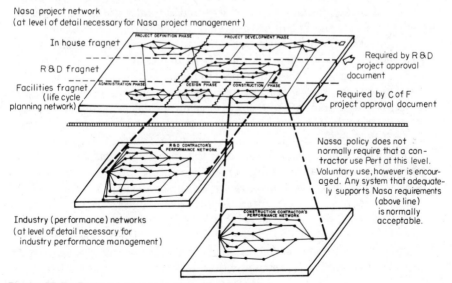

Figure 15.5 Project interconnection. *(From NASA.)*

fragnets can be tied together horizontally. Also illustrated are areas in which special phases such as R & D and construction are amplified, with only the summary information being tied into the overall project planning network. The decision to interconnect the project network at the detailed, or the semidetailed, level is an option open to the planner.

CONSTRUCTION

Construction scheduling is usually the responsibility of the contractor, and the concern of the owner. When there is a single construction contract, the contractor is the key to all scheduling problems and solutions. In certain cases, the owner is either required to or chooses to undertake contracts with several prime contractors. In that case, the owner becomes the coordinating contractor. While it would appear obvious that the owner must take positive management control steps, it usually just does not happen. In the majority of situations, the owner hopes for the best, and except in the very worst cases, the individual contractors usually accept the poor level of coordination, even though they might have legal grounds to take action because of delays caused by other prime contractors.

It is usual that the contractor does not preplan or schedule a project when he is bidding on it. The reason is economical, since contractors can expect to win only between 10 and 20 percent of the jobs they bid on, and money spent on planning jobs not acquired is totally wasted. This reality points to a very significant advantage of the construction manager (CM) approach. The CM can apply preplanning at this stage. Utilizing a preconstruction working plan can identify problems for what they are, and set an environment of thoughtfulness in regard to the construction schedule. The owner or CM can also use the same preconstruction study to establish a reasonable schedule or to develop special construction phasing, or work-arounds. Both of the latter cost more, and the owner should expect to pay more for this type of service. Of course, the final working plan and schedule are developed after the successful contractor has been determined. Very often, completion of the contract provisions is assumed to be completion of the project. However, the turnover of the facility from the contractor to the owner often includes a punch list of items remaining to be finished. These items may be trivial, or, in many cases, may involve further years of labor. The nature of the relationship between the owner and the contractor at the conclusion of a project may directly relate to the number of and difficulty in completing the items on the punch list.

FURNISH—MOVE-IN

Owners often fail to appreciate their responsibilities fully when they have taken title to their building. For one thing, personnel must be provided, who, it is hoped, have been previously selected and trained to operate the equipment in the building. Owners must be staffing and orienting personnel far enough in advance to effect a smooth takeover.

The move into the facility is often complex and should be planned carefully. For instance, moving into a high-rise building in an area such as New York City requires extensive planning, including studies of the vertical loading of elevators, dock space requirements, local permits, traffic control, security of equipment, provisions for moving personnel, waste disposal, and other factors.

Often, the final decorating has been left to the owner's discretion, but must be planned for and accomplished prior to the utilization of the building. In more complex installations, such as hospitals, special medical equipment must be ordered, which is often a long-lead series of items. The telephone system is often the owner's responsibility, whether it be Bell or a proprietary system.

The actual delivery of a building is only a milestone in the progress of the project.

PROJECT IMPLEMENTATION

From the network of a project, it is obvious that the various participants have a lot to accomplish. As the project chain is forged, inevitably some weak links occur. Some activities may be totally omitted, such as functional or architectural programing. Every project has its own graveyard of mistakes built in. In addition to having each particular task done and done well, a successful project requires good overall management and coordination of tasks. Owners must provide this continuity of management, and how they accomplish it is a matter of some import.

There are basically two types of owners, those who are familiar with the processes involved in a project and those who are not. Those who are familiar with them, and who often have substantial technical expertise of their own, may elect to use in-house project management personnel. If projects are accomplished on a continuing basis, this is desirable from an economic viewpoint. Experience by owners of this kind indicates that the costs of administering a project, including design, are in the range of 10 to 20 percent of total project costs. Since design fees are in the 4 to 10 percent range, it is obvious that the management and administrative costs are substantial, and they should be recognized as specific costs and not buried in administrative overhead.

Even owners who have an in-house technical staff often find it difficult to manage in the manner that they would like to, often because of the press of many other concurrent requirements.

The type of owner who does not understand the processes projects entail typically does not have a facilities staff, and needs assistance in managing projects. Unfortunately, these owners, not being experienced, are often not aware that they have a responsibility to manage or control their projects and that this control will require cost investment. This type of owner includes the one- or two-time project builder who usually ends the venture into the facilities field sadder but wiser and with much more understanding of what project management should be.

SUMMARY

To achieve the real benefits of logic and control through network analysis, project management should be instituted as early as practicable, preferably about the time a project is identified in a budget. Installation and implementation of CPM in the actual construction phase is of great importance, but many opportunities to save time and money will be missed if this control is instituted too late.

CPM scheduling is one of the most direct methods of controlling a project's progress. When a large number of resources are used on a single project, a computerized CPM system with resource modules can be applied. The effectiveness of resource scheduling is not as significant on a single project as it is on multiple projects or multifaceted programs.

PROJECT MANAGEMENT
INFORMATION SYSTEM—PMIS

Basic network scheduling amplified by cost and resource dimensions, applied to design as well as to construction, can generate large quantities of data. While the scheduler who assembles the information can readily understand the CPM output, more must be done to effectively deliver the significant information to management. Unfortunately, failure to distill the key ingredients of the computerized output usually results in a reaction similar to that shown in a cartoon: Two executives are looking with bewildered expressions at a computer terminal as one of them says, "What it comes down to is this thing is capable of telling us a lot more than we really want to know."

Organization of project management output into a project management information system requires additional procedures and an organized staff effort. This is particularly necessary for multiproject programs.

Broadening applications of CPM have underlined many of the factors in project scheduling and multiproject implementation, problems which were always present but often unrecognized. Project scheduling which emphasizes the needs of a single project can be handled with a system such as basic CPM or can be expanded. In multiproject situations, particularly in fixed-skill areas such as petrochemical and utility maintenance projects, basic CPM can be used with more sophisticated techniques for cost and resource control.

The basic procedures were used on many major programs during the decade 1960 to 1970, including the World's Fair in New York City, Expo 67 (Montreal), construction at New York State University campuses, the Apollo launch complex at Cape Canaveral, the San Francisco transit system, and others. This availability of tremendous amounts of project information, however important and meaningful, presented a new problem to management. Previously, although decisions were being made on the basis of sparse and limited information, the executive mind was essentially uncluttered by facts. Now, with project and resource information flowing in, managers also had to determine what information was important and what could be disregarded in order to reach or establish alternatives for their decisions. To meet this requirement, a new conception evolved, the Management Information System (MIS). Initially developed to refine the information generated by network techniques and then to display it for management consideration, MIS has now grown into an operational system which can generate its own information.

EVOLUTION OF PMIS

It would be nice to say that the idea for the Project Management Information System (PMIS) was a result of careful and reasoned study, built carefully upon the precepts and experiences of CPM, but it just isn't so. PMIS evolved in response to specific needs resulting from the use of CPM, and was channeled from the point of view of top management, and the willingness (or unwillingness) of those at the top to invest in a new management technique.

The first PMIS developments came principally from NASA, since by the mid-1960s the space program was in full swing and NASA was faced with the problem of analyzing enormous amounts of data. In most cases, the development was the result of a head-on, brute-force response to the overwhelming wave of information. Data reduction techniques were tried, and graphical outputs developed so that top management could evaluate alternatives readily. Indeed, most PMIS techniques in general have been developed in the major program areas that concerned NASA, and by established internal planning groups, the two essential components behind this usually being the need for such techniques caused by a major complex program and the availability of time and staff previously approved in the budget.

Our key consulting engineering staff combined a background in the petrochemical industry with direct experience with early CPM developers, including Catalytic Construction Company and Mauchly Associates. The Corps of Engineers district for Cape Canaveral had to analyze a tremendous volume of contractor-generated CPM information, and it used key personnel in a consulting capacity to assist it. The conversion of great amounts of project data into meaningful management information required both staff work and a summary report tool—essentially an interconnected Gantt chart—representing the CPM information. Each CPM report was analyzed and its results plotted against a time scale. The color-coded, time-scaled, wall-size, master network was used to make a weekly presentation to the Corps management staff, highlighting trouble spots as a basis for management by exception. Although the CPM reports received from the contractors were computerized, this initial summarized plot was manual.

In the words of Major General W. L. Starnes,* then in command of the Corps district for Canaveral, the application was a success:

Network analysis system gave us many correlary advantages. It provided finite information that permitted an objective schedule, enabling us to meet with NASA on an equal basis and show why a particular schedule was chosen and what had to be taken into consideration before we could revise the schedule. With constant updating, the Network Analysis System provided top management with an integrated summary picture of total progress and a projected outlook on a continuous basis.

To monitor and control the scheduling and progress of all the individual contracts at Launch Complex 39, NASA created a Site-Activation Board (SAB).

This Board was responsible for preparing and maintaining a master PERT network to provide NASA management with an up-to-date picture of the status of the project, as well as future trends and conditions based on the various networks in use, whether administered by the Canaveral District, or their own organization.

Because of the complexity of the work involved, it was considered prudent to prepare a network analysis of a construction project prior to award of the general construction and outfitting contracts. This was done to determine the feasibility of meeting NASA's required dates.

At the peak of operations, the individual networks had a total of more than 30,000 activities. Program control was achieved through the integration of the individual networks into a master PERT network with approximately 7,500 activities coded to identify systems, operations, and responsibilities. The master PERT network was updated bi-weekly and results were incorporated into a PERT analysis report.

While the Canaveral program was being developed, other consulting

---

*Major General W. L. Starnes, "CPM is a Good Investment," *Society for Advanced Management Journal,* pp. 71–77, October 1969.

personnel were working on nonaerospace projects and programs. At Columbia, Maryland, for the New Town developed by the Rouse Company, CPM plans were prepared for a series of projects whose completions were required to achieve the date set for the opening day. The PMIS program for Columbia evolved from the broad group of CPM project plans in use there, which were then summarized and presented to management in the fashion developed at Cape Canaveral—as easily read, time-scaled, management presentations. In the Columbia CPM effort, which covered a period of more than 2 years, another step in the evolution of PMIS was achieved: the development of prototypical CPM networks for key areas. These basic networks were developed and then reused repeatedly throughout the program, but customized to meet the particular requirements and conditions of given program areas. One of the most important prototype networks was for land development in a specific neighborhood. This network plan tracked land development through the various stages of land-use planning, zoning, county approvals, coordination with design, and coordination with utility companies, and finally into the actual construction process. Not only were prototypical networks being used in the Columbia system, but more recognition was given to the opportunity of achieving major time savings during the preconstruction phases of the project.

Other prototype networks included the development of streets, the interrelationship between the sanitary development and the installation of underground utilities (in particular between sewers and deep gravity flow), and the coordination of major utilities. More than 100 separate projects were planned and integrated into the PMIS for the opening year.

The next boost to developing PMIS came from the Philadelphia school system, which was initiating a $500 million program to upgrade the physical condition of their almost 270 schools, to be accomplished in concert with a revitalization of the educational program in the city. The challenge was a commanding one, with some sixty-eight schools identified as fire traps that needed replacing, and a tremendous need for additional facilities even beyond that. Although the Philadelphia district had additional engineering assistance, it decided not to use CPM for project management. This led to the next milestone in the evolution of PMIS: the development of stereotyped, or typical, CPM networks for both design and construction. While prior applications had repeated a section of typical activities within a project when necessary and then customized it, this was the first use of a completely stereotyped network as an end item. Two levels of stereotyped plans were evolved, one for design and construction progress, and the second an adaptation of the manual network or summary reporting previously developed for the Corps of Engineers. The basic network for each type of school was also used as the framework for

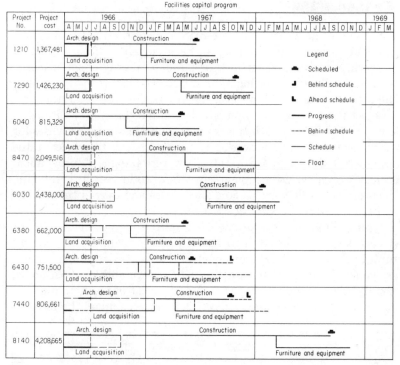

Figure 16.1 Summary of network, school board.

developing cash flow, which in turn was utilized in developing the overall budget. Figure 16.1 shows an actual example of the summary network used as part of the school board report.

In 1967, a major step forward in the evolution of PMIS occurred with the assignment of the author as a consultant to the Bureau of the Budget in New York City, for the specific purpose of developing and installing facilities-oriented Management Information Systems.

The New York City PMIS involved a basic module, which was customized for each individual department that used it. Among them were the Departments of Highways, Parks, Public Works, and Environmental Protection, the Board of Education, and the New York City Transit Authority. In most cases, operation was eventually phased over to city project management personnel. Several billion dollars in construction value were monitored with these systems and more than 2600 major projects were status-scheduled concurrently. The systems also handled portions of 50,000 minor city projects and special MIS areas such as land acquisition and tenant relocation.

T/MIS FRAMEWORK

Figure 16.2 shows the T/MIS, or time-MIS, part of the PMIS. The individual project network information can be input either from an actual CPM network, a stereotyped network, or a unilateral assignment of schedule status. Naturally, the resulting information is no better than the validity of the input. As indicated in the schematic (see Figure 16.4), the individual project network information is fed in either directly or through a *black box* method. The black box is used to generate typical activities for prototypical or stereotyped networks. The same system introduces status on projects which are in progress and which were previously programed. The black box or generator program saves time and effort by combining the typical project cycle with specific start dates and overall time allowances to produce a specific project cycle input.

The typical method of evaluating CPM output is to examine the calculated end date, compare it with the required schedule, and identify opportunities for schedule improvement if that is needed. Such evaluations are generally oriented toward the critical path and low-float areas. Since the T/MIS is by its nature a summary, most of the activities are shown as critical. An automatic analyzer is used to compare the forecast

1969	1970	1971	1972	1973	1974
69/70	70/71	71/72	72/73	73/74	

Project T-014600 Transmission line E 123rd St. to Linden Blvd. E B K L P R Status date

Project S-015200 Linden sub-station E F K L P R

Project T-015800 Transmission line 22nd St. to Maple Ave. F K L P R

Project T-015500 Transmission line 154th St. to Mark Place F K L P R

Project S-016600 West End sub-station L P R

Project S-016700 Mark Place sub-station A B E F K L P R

Activity definitions	A. Site selection B. A&E selection C. Study D. Study approved	E. Complete preliminary F. Preliminary approved G. Foundation dwgs. H. Foundation approved	I. Advertise fdns. J. Const. fdns. K. Complete final L. Final approved	M. Lead myr. N. Fiscal res. P. Construct awd. R. Construct fac.	S. Punch list T. Lead time W. Lag time Z. Restraint

Figure 16.2 T/MIS. *(From MDC Systems.)*

	J	F	M	A	M	J	J	A	S	O	N	D
101	SITE SELECTION ⊽		ESTABLISH AE START DESIGN				FINISH PRELIMINARY DESIGN					
103				ESTABLISH AE START DESIGN			PRELIMINARY DESIGN COMPLETE ○					
110				PRELIMINARY DESIGN ⊽ APPROVED								
112					SITE SELECTED ○		ESTABLISH AE START DESIGN					
113			START DESIGN ⊽		COMPLETE PRELIMINARY DESIGN ○		PRELIMINARY DESIGN APPROVED					
114				PRELIMINARY DESIGN COMPLETE ○			○ PRELIMINARY DESIGN APPROVED					
120				FINAL DESIGN COMPLETE ○		ADVERTISE AWARD CONST. CONT.						
125	PROJECT INITIATED ○ ⊽											
126				PROJECT INITIATED ○ ⊽	SITE SELECTED							
130			PRELIMINARY DESIGN APPROVED ○									
135			PRELIMINARY DESIGN APPROVED ○									
137			PRELIMINARY DESIGN APPROVED ○									
140			PRELIMINARY DESIGN COMPLETE ⊽	○ PRELIMINARY DESIGN APPROVED								
141			PROJECT INITIATED ⊽									
145		EST. ARCH. & START DESIGN		○ PRELIMINARY DESIGN								

MIS summary projects

Milestone   ○ Schedule   ▽ Achievements

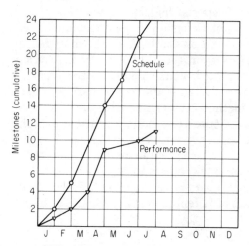

Figure 16.3 Summary MIS; milestone summary.

of end dates with the approved schedule and to print out a variance list. The variances can be adjusted with the help of a window so that the analyzer will view only a certain range or category of them.

Another output of T/MIS is the milestone summary. This curve in its simplest form is a gross listing of milestones for all projects of a given type. An example of a summary MIS chart is shown in Figure 16.3. Actual achievement is plotted below the schedule curve. With this approach, progress for all projects of a given type can be quickly evaluated. The milestone report represents the highest level of management reporting, showing status at a glance. The milestone curve can also be weighted by multiplying each milestone times project costs, so that greater weight is given to high-cost milestones. Thus far, utilization of the milestone summary has been tremendously effective, and has demonstrated realistic trends. Variations of the milestone report can be used to project 5-year budget trends and to demonstrate experience curves or trends for schedulers.

COST INFORMATION (C/MIS)

The cost portion (C/MIS) of PMIS is a cost accumulation by project, including encumbrances, cash expenditures, and projections of additional costs due to extra work. The information is collected from current sources such as controller's reports, budgets, accounting systems, and project management personnel. Calculations are direct and include establishment of percentage completed on the basis of the most recent budget figures and schedule reports from the T/MIS portion. A cost to complete the project is then generated, and included in the report to management. Information can be collected from the summarized schedule information. The summarized method is more amenable to the accounting type of cost collection systems. Figure 16.4 shows a schematic of the overall PMIS, illustrating the relationship between the C/MIS and the T/MIS portions. Invariably, cost reports lag schedule reports by several weeks, so that an offset curve is required to compare the two meaningfully. The C/MIS part can also be used to report on the accumulation of land for projects, to indicate the impact of potential cost extras, and to monitor payments to contractors.

LEVELS OF DETAIL

The use of PMIS for overall scheduling and control is indicated when techniques such as CPM are not suitable in terms of their mechanism or sufficient in their scope to correlate all the items within a program. PMIS

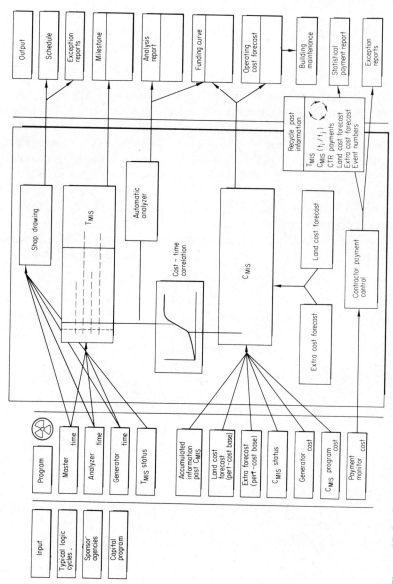

Figure 16.4 Schematic PMIS. *[From MDC Systems.]*

269

utilizes four levels of scheduling detail, originally described by NASA as levels A, B, C, and D. These are described as follows:

Level	Definition	Application
A	Overall	Top management scheduling review
B	Summary	Master project control network (T/MIS)
C	Detail level	Prototype or stereotyped networks
D	Detail	Project schedule and specific CPM

The usual input for T/MIS is the C level, while the T/MIS presentation is at the B level, which summarizes activities on a time scale. A milestone curve is an example of A-level reporting. (See Figure 16.5.)

The great capabilities of PMIS are tied to the force of networks. PMIS can handle networks at different levels of detail, summarizing automatically from the C to the B level. (Summarizing from the D to the B level is semiautomatic or manual.) PMIS furnishes a sturdy framework on which a tremendous amount of data can be imposed. As a prerequisite, the time frame should be in equivalent units.

The T/MIS reporting system does not have to have CPM input. For instance, information can be imposed or superimposed at the B level, with

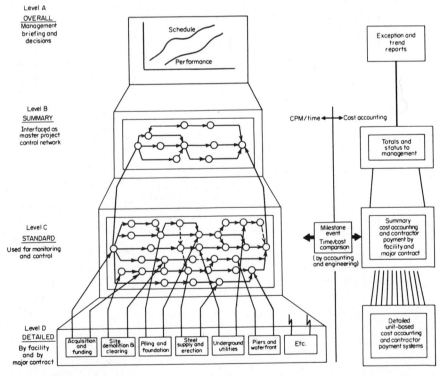

Figure 16.5 Levels of detail.

information generated in any logical (or even illogical) way. This can then be used to generate the costs of milestone trend curves without going through the time and effort of drawing up a detailed network. A mix of information can be placed in the system, with some projects being handled at the detail (or D) level, others being managed for resource purposes in a prototypical or stereotyped network, and the information for still others being made available in summary form. Combining these to give an overall picture still is valuable to management, if the information is reasonably correct.

Figure 16.6 shows a work package breakdown in an aerospace application.

RESOURCES (RPC)

The resource section of PMIS is the resource, planning, and control, or RPC, portion, which requires information to be input at the C and D levels. Dummy networks are introduced to correlate major areas such as corporate overhead, research staff, and other known but essentially intangible functions not otherwise scheduled or identified on the project network.

The RPC section can operate with any type of resource, including work force, materials, or money. The prime resource is usually the skilled work force, particularly in the engineering and design areas. While the system can just as easily handle resources at the implementation or project level, the utility of this has been limited in prior experience by other proprietary systems.

The RPC runs on an IBM 360 (or 370) with a disk operating system. The internal calculations actually have two stages, with those for the network being made first. If desired, the PMIS program can output project schedules before proceeding to RPC. In most cases the debugged schedule phase is completed before the RPC portion is run, since the RPC running time is substantially longer than that for basic CPM. The strength of the system is its ability to edit and re-sort, so that the resources that will be needed can be predicted by skills, by department, by total work force, by project area, or by a combination of these categories.

METHODS OF APPLICATION

There are three basic methods of implementing PMIS:

1. Total systems installation
2. Phase-in, horizontal.
3. Phase-in, vertical

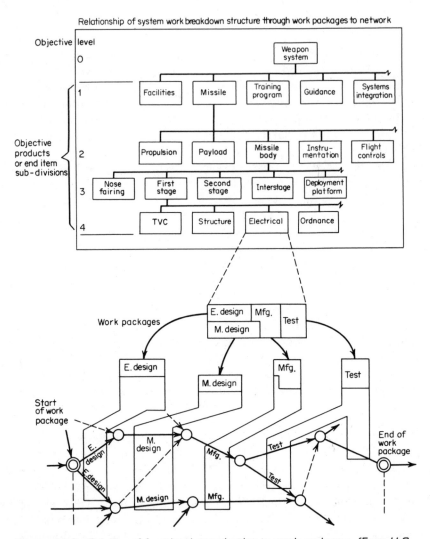

Relationship of system work breakdown structure through work packages to network

Figure 16.6 Relation of functional organization to work packages. *(From U.S. Navy.)*

The total systems method is traumatic, expensive, and generally unsuccessful. Shifting to a totally new system in one move is not only unrealistic, but doing so interrupts progress. In almost every case, experience indicates a phase-in plan would be best. The two generally acceptable plans are the phased (or sequential) implementation of PMIs horizontally and vertically.

The horizontal method is the most usual, and is initiated with a CPM treatment of a specific area. This treatment is then expanded horizontally to cover other project areas as appropriate. When successfully accomplished, more sophisticated sections of the PMIS program, such as resources, are applied in levels of great complexity and gradually expanded horizontally until layer by layer PMIS has been implemented.

The vertical approach calls for the selection of a specific area of projects or programs which require complete treatment in designing and installing a PMIS total project subsystem for that area. Expansion of a successful subsystem is done through a selected series of subprogram areas. The basic difference between the vertical and the total systems methods is in the control.

REPORTING

Although bar graphs provide a weak planning vehicle, they are an excellent reporting vehicle.

T/MIS has a computerized, machine-generated output in bar-graph form (Figure 16.2). The dark lines show progress to date, while the dashed lines represent the remaining allocated or scheduled time for activities. The system can also generate the cost output representing a proposed capital budget (Figure 16.7).

Figure 16.8 shows cumulative progress results in terms of curves of progress to date. In this case, the critical activities are slightly lagging, while the aggregate work is proceeding slightly ahead of median.

Figure 16.9 is an actual machine-generated milestone output. The ○ line represents the originally scheduled rate of activity progress. The ● represents actual progress, while the ✕'s show two projection lines, one an early projection and one from the status date. The solid-dashed line, although clearly indicating that progress is behind the original schedule, also shows a trend line, or progress per unit time, now keeping pace with the original rate of progress anticipated, and the projection shows a definite improvement in the progress of the project, moving toward closing the gap.

PURPOSE AND BENEFITS OF PMIS

The purpose of PMIS is to assist management in the decision-making process by providing:

1. Identification of activities requiring management attention
2. Sufficient information to identify and quantify the problem areas

PROPOSED CAPITAL BUDGET

Project number and description	Total est. cost	Total approp.	Total auth.	Total avail.	Project.	Current fiscal year	Proposed Budget						Required to complete
							69/70	70/71	71/72	72/73	73/74	74/75	
T-013700 Transmission line	716.1	112.0	35.4	83.7	Bal of funds	−33.4	−561.6	−9.1	0.0	0.0	0.0	0.0	0.0
					Planned budget	117.1	561.6	9.1	0.0	0.0	0.0	0.0	0.0
					Estimate	117.1	563.8	9.6	0.0	0.0	0.0	0.0	0.0

A B E F   K   L P   K   R

Schedule 00–0–0–0– – – –0– –0– – – – – –0

T-014100 Transmission line	580.9	576.0	369.2	552.0	Bal of funds	3.1	0.0	−4.9	0.0	0.0	0.0	0.0	0.0
					Planned budget	548.9	0.0	8.0	0.0	0.0	0.0	0.0	0.0
					Estimate	550.0	0.0	8.4	0.0	0.0	0.0	0.0	0.0

L P   R

Schedule 0–0–0– – – – – – –0

T-014600 Transmission line	582.8	519.0	449.6	478.5	Bal of funds	−56.8	0.0	−10.0	0.0	0.0	0.0	0.0	0.0
					Planned budget	535.3	0.0	10.0	0.0	0.0	0.0	0.0	0.0
					Estimate	534.0	0.0	10.9	0.0	0.0	0.0	0.0	0.0

K   L P   R

Schedule 0– –0–0– –0– – – – – – – – –0

Figure 16.7 Capital budget generated by PMIS. *(From MDC Systems.)*

3. A means for measuring the degree of attainment against the qualitative goals and objectives

4. Methods for measuring the effectiveness of key positions

5. An environment of achievement, within which goals or standards can be measured

The scheduling module which is the backbone of the MIS program utilizes networking to perform the following functions:

1. Illustration of the actual sequence and interdependencies of activities, specifying the order in which they will be done

2. Determining which tasks or activities are critical in terms of their effects on total time

3. Analyzing all of the activities in the total project to most effectively meet target dates and budget limitations

The primary benefits of a network-based system include:

1. Provision of a clear procedure for planning a project and then scheduling it

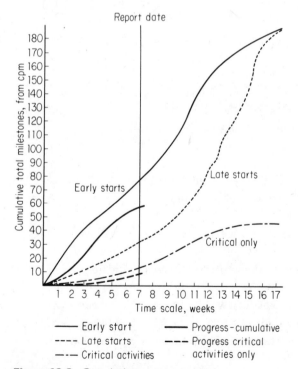

Figure 16.8 Cumulative progress report.

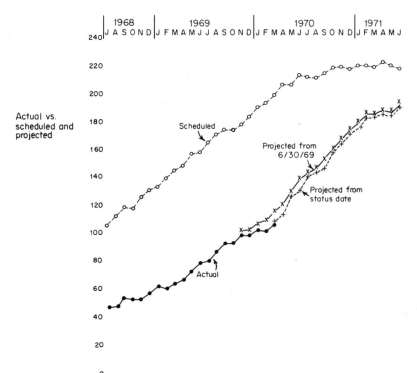

Actual vs. scheduled and projected

Sub-totals		1968	1969	1970	1971

Sub- ⎰ Scheduled 105 7 7 3 11 2 3 5 6 5 5 3 1 6 3 1 2 7 4 2 5 2 3 5 1 2 1 5 1 1 1 1 1 2 0 0
totals ⎱ Actual   46 3 3 1 5 3 1 4 3 3 6 1 3 7 2 1 5 0 2 1 4 0 0 0 0 0 0 0 0 0 0 0 0 0 0

Grand ⎰ Scheduled 105 119 133 138 149 159 163 172 175 186 193 198 204 207 213 215 217 219
totals   112 122 135 143 154 162 169 173 182 188 195 203 206 212 214 216 219 219
       ⎱ Actual   46 49 52 58 62 69 78 82 91 97 99 104 104 104 104 104 104 104 104
                         53 61 66 72 79 89 92 97 100 104 104 104 104 104 104 104 104

Figure 16.9   Milestone summary. *(From MDC Systems.)*

2. Presenting an overall picture of the total program

3. Providing a positive means of pinpointing responsibilities for activity accomplishment

4. Providing a vehicle for evaluating strategies and objectives—evaluation of alternate plans, or gaming

5. Providing a system that monitors, measures, and records the performances of the project plan

6. Providing a system that reviews all projects on a by-exception basis (although emphasis should also be placed on work accomplished)

7. Providing a system that can establish realistic projections of future requirements for projects

Unfortunately, not all PMIS attempts are successful. Failures can occur for a number of reasons including:

1. Failure to achieve top-level management involvement

2. Orientation of the system to the computer rather than the user

3. Failure to properly relate to the prime users of the system and to meet their real requirements

4. Vesting responsibility for system development and implementation in the wrong functional group

5. Inadequate explanations to the staff about the nature and purpose of the system; lack of involvement by the staff in using it

6. Underestimating the complexity of the system's design in terms of implementing resource requirements of time and/or costs

RESULTS OF USING PMIS

In regard to the effects of using PMIS, New York City's experience may be cited as an example. Former official Charles R. Morris has described the city's 1968 capital projects situation as follows*:

> . . . As many as twelve different agencies were involved in approving the plans for a single project. Harlem and Bellevue Hospitals were carried in the budget for seventeen and fifteen years, respectively, before they were finally completed. Just reviewing the final plans for a police station took almost a year. In one case, involving a number of projects, the parks department took seven years from the date that the projects were authorized before beginning design work. In 1968 more than two thousand major construction projects and fifty thousand minor ones, involving more than $3 billion, were in various stages of planning, design, or construction. A computerized project tracking system was devised to help manage the system. As a new project was authorized, a detailed schedule was fed into the computer, along with the name of the individual responsible for reporting the completion of each milestone. The computer then reported automatically on the lagging projects—a technique called "management-by-exception." Reports were kept to a minimum, and top management attention was drawn only to the projects in trouble.

These results were also documented in the New York City Budget of 1970.

---

*Charles R. Morris, *The Cost of Good Intentions*, pp. 48–49, W. W. Norton, New York, 1980.

Mayor John V. Lindsay also made these comments about New York's experience with PMIS*:

... Four years ago, the city hired a team with special experience in aerospace planning to design a system for tracking the progress of construction projects. After months of testing, they developed a Management Information System that lists every step in each project, identifies who is responsible for its completion, and estimates how much time it should take. The status of each project is regularly updated by computer. City construction officials, for the first time, know each day where each project is, where it should be and who is responsible for the lag—if any.

As a result, we have cut the average design time for police and fire projects by 47%. We have virtually doubled the number of projects in construction. We have saved hundreds of millions of dollars in cost escalation alone.

The benefits are already visible. The new Police Headquarters—stalled in the old system for 18 years—was moved through the new process in a year and a half. That's the best record in New York history. The headquarters is now well above the ground in lower Manhattan. . . .

Our outside assistants on the Management Information Systems were not members of a lay-commission asked to write a report about why construction was delayed—however valuable that might have been. They were hired to design a working system for tracking projects day-by-day. They had to work side-by-side with city officials, devising a new system, tinkering with it, getting the bugs out, making it work.

SUMMARY

PMIS is a proven project management method since it has evolved through fundamental field applications. The system offers a broad framework for either applications in depth or at the projection level, and it can also be utilized as a springboard for advanced project management techniques. PMIS marries resources to networks and maintains a disciplined cost control method. It can generate automatic or semiautomatic reports to management. PMIS can also be used for such professional project management techniques as management briefings, visibility or action rooms, management communications, decision trees, and organizational studies.

---

*Excerpt from a speech given by John V. Lindsay at the Lotos Club Public Affairs luncheon, as reported in *The New York Times*, July 17, 1970.

COMPUTER PROGRAMS AND SYSTEMS

In the 1957 to 1958 period, UNIVAC I was the only computer available for CPM computations. Since the number of users was very limited, this posed no problem. As early CPM programs were developed by General Electric (for the GE 225) and IBM, computers with programs to handle CPM became more widely available. Some of the early CPM programs were unwieldy, and a number of firms converted basic programs to suit their special needs. By 1968, however, there were more than sixty CPM programs available (Figure 17.1), and the number was probably closer to 100. Figure 17.1 is arranged in terms of the six major manufacturers of CPM-programed computers. It lists seventeen computer models produced by these manufacturers which were programed for CPM. In the majority of cases, particularly where one manufacturer was involved (such as IBM, which had nine CPM-capable computers), the program for each model was based on the same algorithm and was often reprogramed by computer to adjust for variations in equipment. Many programs were compatible with other manufacturers' equipment.

During the first decade of CPM development (1958 to 1968), therefore, computer hardware limitations were characteristic, ranging from the initial problem of finding a computer which could handle CPM computa-

Computer	Model number	Program	Capacity*	Remarks
1. Burroughs Corp.	220	CPM	400+ (A)	Activity on node
2. Control Data Corp.	G-15	CPM	850 (A)	No descriptions, noncalendar
3. General Electric	225	CPM (PROMOCOM)	2100 (A) 999 (E)	Cost optimization
4. Honeywell Corp.	200	CPM	200 to 3700 (E) (varies with memory)	Bar-graph option
5. IBM	360	CPM	5000 (A)	Many features
	650	CPM	999 (E)	LESS/cost optimization
	704	CPM	Varies	Cost optimization
	1130	CPM	2000 (A) 900 to 2000 (E) (varies with memory)	
	1410	CPM	1000	
	1440	CPM	2000	
	1620	CPM	1,600 to 5,600 (E and A)	Resources
	7090, 7094	CPM	1750 to 8000 (A)	With work force scheduling and cost optimization
6. UNIVAC	UNIVAC I, II, 1134, 1105	CPM	Varies	Cost optimization

*A = activities; E = events.

Figure 17.1   CPM program availability, 1968.

tions to the considerable variation that existed 10 years later in the capabilities of individual computer models in terms of the size of programs and number of events they could handle. And the differences in model capabilities resulted in a proliferation of software systems to accommodate the hardware.

PROJECT CONTROL SYSTEM (PCS)

The most universal CPM system in the early 1960s was MIS-LESS, which evolved from the PERT work and had Lockheed and IBM inputs. The underlying algorithm was efficient and easily customized. Then in the late 1960s, IBM developed a CPM for its IBM 1130 line. This program, dubbed *Project Control System,* or *PCS,* had replaced MIS-LESS as the available CPM baseline by the early 1970s. It is often identified with "The House that Jack Built," referring to a demonstration example used by IBM. PCS was later converted to operate under the (then) new IBM 360 (and later 370) series computers, and can support a broad range of planning and scheduling requirements applied to a single project. (PCS is described in detail in IBM's "Project Control System/360 Version 2, Program No. 360A-CP-06X," 3d ed., 1970.)

The basis, or framework of PCS is network analysis, either CPM or precedence diagrams. Either can be calculated with PCS. The network calculation is similar to most accepted CPM and precedence procedures, with the exception that work items or activities may be scheduled through the insertion of milestone schedule dates. Initially, the calculation could provide positive float only. If the insertion of the schedule date forced negative float, the item was flagged, and made critical.

To express the result of the scheduled milestones, two types of float are listed: start float and completion float. Completion float is the normal total float depending on the difference of time between the early completion and late completion dates. Start float is the amount of time between late start and early start dates and will vary because the input of milestone schedules affects the early start dates.

The PCS/360 can accept up to 100 resource descriptions for a network, with only a limited number being assigned to any single activity.

The resource output is in the form of resources required in order to achieve the network plan. The PCS does not level resources, but tabulates the amount needed for the plan. A number of special outputs are available including:

All CPM and precedence edits and sorts

Bar-chart output

Work status and progress reports

Resource assignment reports

Resource utilization reports

Lump-sum cost reports

Monthly cost reports

Milestone reports

Summary bar charts

PCS is designed to operate on an IBM 360, wtih the use of a disk operating system. Minimum memory size is 32K with two disks.

GSA-CMCS

In the early 1970s the General Services Administration (GSA) of the federal government in its Public Building Service (PBS) under Commissioner Arthur Sampson was providing a forum for the development of new systems and techniques in the construction industry. The use of CPM scheduling and value management was encouraged, as was the systems approach to construction.

One PBS office was investigating ways to develop a state-of-the-art scheduling system (based on CPM) specifically for PBS contracts. A comprehensive request for proposals was issued inviting the development of a set of criteria for the PBS system. This interim step was so complex that the author (working with Milton T. Austin of Computer Sciences Corporation) estimated a cost in excess of $200,000 to respond.

Concurrently, PBS had been developing the Construction Management (CM) approach to construction and was committed to a series of major construction programs using CM. The first CM project was at Beltsville, Maryland, and the contract required the CM program to come with its own scheduling system, including rights to the software.

The system to be furnished was described, and dubbed the *Construction Management Control System,* or *CMCS.* In effect, the PBS got its dream system "on the cheap" and dropped more sophisticated independent efforts to develop a system.

CMCS as originally delivered was a thinly disguised version of the IBM PCS. The basic time module worked well. The PBS manual for CMCS also promised a number of related cost programs. Over a number of years, PBS improved the system, first on the IBM 1130 and later on the IBM 360/370 series computers.

PBS offered the system to the construction industry at virtually no cost (only a fee for the manual and magnetic tape). It was worth the price, but little more. As one researcher noted*:

1. The package is difficult to be adapted to various user needs; there are no provisions to permit modifications of the standard reports.
2. The system is really cheap to buy ($30), but very expensive to implement and maintain (more than $5,000 for implementation and testing).
3. The overall efficiency is low; the concept is obsolete in comparison with other available packages on the market. Schedule module, purchase order, and financial module are totally independent.
4. The organization and user documentation system is below average, and there is no system to keep the user informed of modifications if any

---

*Calin Popescu, "Pitfalls of GSA-CMCS Software," *Journal of the Construction Division, American Society of Civil Engineers,* vol. 105, pp. 95–106, March 1979.

occur. This is in reference to the version dated April, 1973. Since that date there has been no news from the originators.

5. If we take into consideration for evaluation the vendor support for this package, there is none.

If a programmer is to judge this system, he/she will have the following remarks: (1) The programming quality—The I/O procedures, program documentation, and the presence of many bugs in the system (subroutine not working) give a low overall rating; (2) file organization and blocking factor create real problems in utilization because of the high cost per run; (3) the system has not been designed for an efficient usage of the IBM-370 computer resources; and (4) the internal controls, checkpoints, and backup provisions are few and may generate error messages with no meaning for a common user.

PROJECT MANAGEMENT SYSTEM (PMS)

The IBM *Project Management System,* or *PMS,* written for the IBM 360 is a major software package prepared specifically for the support of multiproject programs. It was developed by IBM with the participation of McDonnell-Douglas Aircraft Corporation and North American Aviation, Incorporated. (A complete description of the system can be found in the IBM application program description 360A-CP-04X, version I, third edition, November 1969.)

The system was intended to be a blockbuster, requiring use of large mainframe computers—specifically the (then) new IBM 360 (and later the 370 series).

PMS (version I) was originally composed of three major processors: network, cost, and report. (Resources were added later.)

The network processor performs the basic network calculations—substantially PERT-oriented, but on an activity basis. An important factor is the capability of handling multiple networks simultaneously. Subnetworks or independent networks within the overall program may be interconnected by special interface events similar to those employed in NASA-PERT C. Figure 17.2 shows schematically four fragnets involving contractors *A, B, C,* and *D.* It is not necessary for each contractor to have unique event numbers for his or her fragnet or for interface events. A common event number does not have to be used. Instead, two different event numbers in respective networks can be identified as an interface item with a separate interface number. This flexibility eliminates the necessity for coordination of the numbering of interface events. In Figure 17.2 IF-1, IF-2, and IF-3 are interface names or identifications. In contractor *A*'s network, IF-1 is event 6, but in contractor B's network it is event 1. Figure 17.3 shows a network with responsibilities divided between contractors *A*

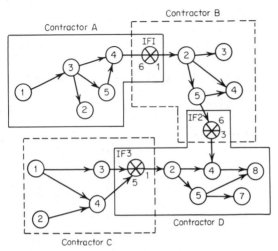

Figure 17.2 NASA-PERT II interfaces. *[From NASA.]*

and *B*. This single network can be displayed as two separate fragnets, shown in the same figure.

An additional interface card must be inserted in the network for each interface event. For an interface event between two fragnets, there are two interface cards, one associated with each interface event in each fragnet. NASA-PERT Time can of course calculate a single project also, as can all multiproject network approaches. Figure 17.4 shows a schematic of card deck input for NASA-PERT C, demonstrating the module, or interface, identification for that system.

The common processing of multiprojects permits many useful specialty-edited sorts or outputs. These include:

1. Early-start sort, with secondary on slack for all projects

2. Sort by craft or contractor, with secondary sort on early start

3. Sort by type of activity (i.e., foundations, structure), with secondary by early start

In addition, special codes can be added to highlight the use of special equipment, or identify other areas of interest common to more than one project within the network. The overall PMS program can contain up to 255 networks and subnetworks, which are termed the *master file.*

Network output can be presented in calendar form with a span of up to 15 years. A wide variation of holidays, working days, and other calendar factors may be chosen. The number of activities in an individual network or subnetwork depends upon the capacity of the computer system and may be as high as 32,000 in a 1004K 360. As the memory size shrinks, so do the limits.

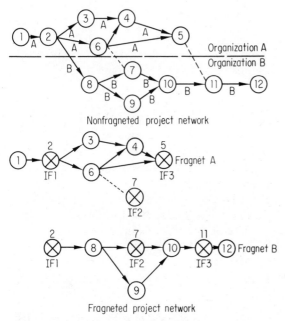

Figure 17.3 Fragnets, two contractors. *(From NASA.)*

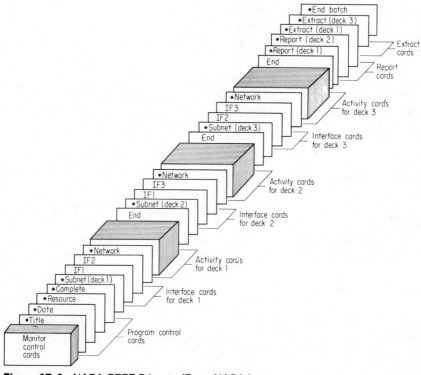

Figure 17.4 NASA-PERT C input. *(From NASA.)*

The PMS network processor accepts special conditions, such as the curing of concrete, which is a nonworking period, or the assignment of more than one activity between the same event numbers. These are essentially special conditions placed by the program designers, and have no major impact on, or variation from, basic PERT or CPM.

An important feature is the PERT ability to input schedule dates and, therefore, get secondary or schedule slack. In the calculation of multiple-project programs, this is an important feature since, without it, it is quite probable that only one or two critical paths would occur.

In performing updatings of the basic master file, any one of four actions can be performed on an activity, event, or milestone: The entire activity; events, or milestones can be added to, or deleted from, the master file; data can be completely replaced with data from the input card; or data can be modified in certain fields only.

As part of the basic calculation, the network can be summarized in two different ways:

Type 1 summarization produces reports as summary activities which are the sum of the durations of the detailed activities on the longest paths between the events of the summary activity.

Type 2 summarization produces reports that describe a summary activity by the duration of its longest path, "longest" meaning the greatest elapsed time between expected start and finish.

PMS is a large system, and was a sophisticated one for its time. The early approach, which is a functional one of computing multiple networks by merely interconnecting and running them all as a major single network, requires the recalculation and manipulation of lead and lag activities in order to lock in subnetworks and develop an appropriate schedule. Human intervention results in a much simpler process. PMS is an automatic system which can operate in a semiautomatic mode. In both modes it is complicated, and requires a large computer system.

The cost processor of the PMS is modular, and optional. It accepts cost-data input cards after the PERT/Cost descriptor card has been prepared. It is essentially PERT/Cost-oriented to relate to the multiple-project method used in the network processor section. Accordingly, since the cost processor is compatible, it will handle up to 255 subnetworks or groups. The calendar is also compatible with the network processor method. Since summaries at nine levels are possible in the network processor, the cost structure also can handle the same levels of detail, with a maximum of 32,767 charge numbers allowed at each level. Costs may be applied in terms of functioning departments, resources, or cost codes. A concomitant rate table is established which will accept multiple cost codes and up to eighteen accounting periods. Separate rates may be entered for each type of cost.

Again, the computer program is broad and quite sophisticated. It will accommodate a tremendous range of information. The basic problem with it lies less in the computer software and systems design, and more in the availability of meaningful cost information broken down in project-oriented fashion. This has always been the difficulty in the valid and effective utilization of PERT/Cost. It continues to be a problem in the PMS PERT/Cost processor, which cannot overcome the realities of normal cost accounting for each application. Inherently, the problem of properly breaking down and allocating costs is a logical but detailed application problem. Sufficient resource description and cost accounts must be available to cover all contingencies. Since the PMS network processor has many levels of available detail, and for each of these levels for each item in the network many types of cost must be available, the result is a very powerful computer system, but one which must carry a tremendous overhead whether utilized or not. This overhead is the programing required to establish the types of cost and maintain them during computation, whether used or not. PMS is modular, but only if the entire cost option is deleted will a substantial savings be realized in the computer running-time overhead.

Because of the tremendous range in numbers and levels of detail available for reports in both the network and cost processors, it is necessary to have a comprehensive means of identifying the reports required, and this is termed the *report processor*. This processor permits the selection of only those reports desired, and reduces the output to some degree, which results in concomitant savings in computer time, operating time, and paper, not to mention user's time, since the information is more carefully edited to specific needs. Typical reports include all the standard types:

1. *Time reports:* Activity time status reports, sorted as required, but including:

    Index sort (predecessor, successor)

    By value of float or slack

    By expected completion date

    By latest allowed date

    By early start date

    By department and expected dates, early or late

    Bar graph

    By summary milestones

2. *Cost reports*

    Management summary reports

    Cost category reports, summary

Category report, by rainbow of categories

Financial plan and status report by accounting period, charge number

Organization status reports, by organization, department, or charge number

Cost milestone report

Charge-number time reports

Program outlook graphs

Time versus dollars

Time versus worker-hours

This list is by no means all-inclusive. The report processor can be used to mask or edit and create other more specialized reports. This report processor is oriented toward easy reprograming to prepare these special edits.

PMS versions I and II had a conceptual resource program which was not operational. Version III had an operational resource program module capable of leveling as well as indicating the use of the critical path schedule. This was improved in version IV (Program 5734-XP4), described in IBM document GH20-0855-2.

PMS was a system developed ahead of its time. The power of brute force was used to achieve system goals subsequently attained more easily with faster, more flexible hardware. However, by that later time, PMS was too far developed to change and too much of an investment to abandon. Along the way, McDonnell-Douglas correctly analyzed the situation and dropped out of PMS development to focus on its own proprietary system (MSCS).

These comments are not intended to be unduly critical of PMS. It was used to schedule a number of major projects; lessons were learned from both its development and its use. But as in the history of some analogous computers and weapons systems, later inventions and improvements (like semiconductors replacing vacuum tubes) permitted competing systems to leapfrog ahead.

INTEGRATED CIVIL ENGINEERING SYSTEM (ICES)

The *Integrated Civil Engineering System,* or *ICES,* was developed by the Massachusetts Institute of Technology in cooperation with a number of industry representatives. One of the components of ICES is its project scheduling system, which is similar in many respects to PCS. It can be used to plan and control construction projects through CPM. It is primarily a scheduling system, but has a limited ability to deal with the areas of finances and resources.

The ICES computer effort was broad-based and provided the inspiration for the further development of many computer applications in regard to engineering/construction projects. One of the best known is STRUDL, which has become a basic for structural design. A less well known, but still significant, development was in the network field. Robert Daniels of the ICES group founded Project Software & Development, Inc., developing a network-based system based on ICES. That system (PROJECT/2) was one of the two most successful CPM/PDM workhorses in the 1970s.

PROJECT/2 was originally a mainframe (IBM 360/370) program. It is still available in that form through data center, lease, or purchase. The system has also been adapted for the Digital Equipment PDP computer and for a dedicated Hewlett-Packard minicomputer.

PROJECT/2 can process input from both activity-on-arrow (i-j) networks and activity-on-node (PDM) networks with lead-lags. Before a network can be scheduled by PROJECT/2, the *basic network processor* must analyze and store network data. This preliminary processor handles all activity data (number, description, codes, duration), precedence relationships, and calendar specifications such as the start date, work weeks, nonworking days, calendar assignments, and workday subdivisions. The basic network processor thoroughly checks all input for errors, including normal keypunching mistakes, numbering and logical inconsistencies, duplication, and invalid dates. A loop detector prints out a list of all loops.

Throughout PROJECT/2, codes are used to provide flexible and powerful output control. Three 9-digit code numbers can be assigned to each activity. These code numbers allow selection, sorting, subdivision and labeling, and the summarizing of reports.

When repetitive networks must be developed, the *network generator* facility eliminates the need for duplicate input coding and keypunching. Basic subnet data are reproduced internally. Activity numbers, descriptions, and durations vary according to instructions. The network generator is ideally suited to multiple-unit or high-rise construction projects and to transmission/distribution projects in the utilities industry.

Error messages explain on the printout the exact nature of any input mistake. PROJECT/2 checks the network logic, pointing out such errors as numbering inconsistencies, invalid dates, precedences to nonexisting activities, and a wide variety of data entry mistakes. All loops are detected in one computer run and are clearly identified in the output.

PROJECT/2 offers a choice between more than 50 types of reports. Output can be produced on the line printer in tabular format as bar charts or curves, or on the plotter as network diagrams or bar charts.

The numeric and alphanumeric coding fields in PROJECT/2 allow reports broken down by department, responsibility, location, cost account, etc.

The PROJECT/2 *report writer* creates custom reports.

Complex projects usually require more than one work calendar. Engineering and construction may follow different schedules; offices in different parts of the country may observe different holidays. The *multicalendar* feature of PROJECT/2 can define up to 100 different work calendars for any project. Within each calendar the work week may vary. For example, you might want to schedule engineering activities 5 days a week, and construction activities 6 days a week during the spring and summer but only 5 days a week during the fall and winter.

After a current schedule has been calculated, it may be compared by the *target processor* with a variety of other benchmark or *target schedules*. Up to fifty user-defined target schedules may be retained and compared to the current schedule, either by activity or by summary group. Target schedules may be produced in tabular or bar-chart formats. The target processor also produces a list of activities targeted for action as of a specified date.

The *cost processor* handles all data related to the input, calculation, and output of project costs. It generates cash-flow histograms and cumulative S curves over the project schedules based upon estimated and actual costs. It can compare the latest revised costs to the project budget in detailed or summarized forms. The cost processor can also produce earned value reports based upon progress and a payments schedule.

The *resource allocation processor* assigns resources to activities and distributes resources over schedules. An activity can have any number of resources assigned to it, and a resource may be assigned to any number of activities. Resource allocation reports may be generated project-wide, by activity or by resource. Distributed resource usage (cumulative or time interval) is output in tabular and/or graphical format. Activity budget estimates can be developed by automatically pricing resources, based on their escalated costs.

The *resource constraining processor* computes and saves schedules based upon resource limitations, time constraints, and activity resource allocations. The scheduling is performed via a user-controlled rule-of-thumb procedure resulting in an economical use of computer time. There is also an optional special report available, which illustrates the procedures and decisions used. *Resource schedules* can be displayed on most reports or saved as target schedules.

Other features of PROJECT/2 resource-constrained scheduling include: activity splitting; emergency resource availabilities; priority assignments for scheduling activities; debugging and bottleneck reports showing what resources and activities are causing delay in meeting the schedule; combined time and resource constraints; consumable resources; and resource-constrained "windows."

MANAGEMENT SCHEDULING AND CONTROL SYSTEM (MSCS)

In the 1950s, McDonnell-Douglas Aircraft Co. realized that with the advent of the first generation of computers, some of its scheduling requirements could be solved. An automated scheduling software tool was needed to facilitate the planning, scheduling, and control of the company's manufacturing lines along with its research and development projects.

At first McDonnell-Douglas was involved in developing the PMS system, but then dropped out of that work to concentrate on its own comprehensive scheduling system, the *Management Scheduling and Control System*, or *MSCS*. The predecessor of MSCS, was the *Management Control Systems* or *MCS*, which was written in Autocoder and originally run on an IBM 1401. But large core requirements resulting from the addition of the FORTRAN-based, resource allocation section forced the move to a larger machine: the IBM 7094. Then in 1967 MSCS was first tested, with its initial commercial use following in 1968 by contract with Smith Kline and French Laboratories in Philadelphia. Redesign and rewrite occurred later with the introduction of the IBM 360 series of computers in order to take advantage of newer machine technology and a more economical core.

MSCS employs CPM network analysis techniques in project planning, scheduling, and control.

Data input into MSCS falls under two primary categories: control and activity. Control data is used to direct processing, define the calendar framework, and provide general constraints to the resource scheduling process. Activity data describes each activity in the network diagram and defines its interrelationships. Resource and cost information can be included with activity data.

MSCS maintains this information in a single, central data store containing project calendar and activity, cost, resource, and dictionary information.

MSCS performs network analysis to determine if the activities input are logical and continuous in their relationships. If the system detects a network logic problem, it will inform one of illogical activity relationships and/or activities not properly identified as beginning or ending events.

If the CPM network is logical, the system considers external, conditional, and mandatory dates and then calculates early and late schedule start dates for each activity, the remaining duration of started activities based on current status, and activity criticality.

MSCS permits the entry of multiple beginning, ending, and network-independent activities, as well as of objective dates. In addition to tracking project status, MSCS network calculations assist in identifying contractual milestones; determining if a project can be completed within a desired time frame; and verifying when subcontractors, materials, and special equipment will be needed on the job.

MSCS allocates resources within project time and resource constraints. It can determine the schedule impact of limited resources, schedule available resources for optimum use, and identify resource requirements over time.

MSCS allows assigning an activity to any one of eight calendars for scheduling and reporting purposes. Designed with complex international projects and unique plant shutdown/turnaround situations in mind, MSCS can define multiple calendars involving Gregorian, Arabic, Jewish, Moslem, or any other type of time frame to the level of detail desired. Each calendar may have its own time unit definition, work or nonwork periods, and special holiday schedules. MSCS also offers many options for representing external dates at either input or report time.

MSCS generates a comprehensive set of standard reports which supply the following types of project information: activity scheduling, resource allocation, costs, turnaround and work orders, status, and/or slippage.

An application report request language, MSCS's *selection criteria*, modifies standard reports by selecting activities to be printed out, based on their specific characteristics. For example, a report page can contain only activities with common characteristics. Or activities with certain characteristics can be printed or suppressed from the report. Standard activity codes or user-defined fields can be used for activity classifications.

MSCS offers many options in report content and format: It can limit reports generated to only certain time periods or activities, summarize into a single report entry scheduling information that pertains to a group of activities, vary title and subtitle information, control the selection and placement of schedule information and slippage calculations in target reports, and mask from a report certain fields or characteristics associated with an activity.

Over time, MSCS has been enhanced. Additions of target reporting and slippage analysis were major strides toward satisfying user needs. In 1980 multiple calendar capability for the scheduling needs of internal projects was introduced. Serial allocation techniques expanded user control over the allocation process and further improved efficiency.

In 1981, to increase the system's hardware compatibility, MSCS was rewritten to conform with ANSI's COBOL language. Execution environments now include the original IBM OS/VS under MVS, IBM VM/CMS, and the VAX/11 family.

And in 1982 an on-line option was introduced that improved and upgraded the user's interface with MSCS, making batch mode no longer the sole mode of operation. The on-line option offers immediate access to master and transaction files, prompt search and find features, and a flexible screen facility for customizing screens and the terminology used. It enhances MSCS network scheduling efficiency by reducing transaction update inaccuracies and performing data verification and diagnostic error checking before system processing begins. In addition, it permits on-line data entry, transaction and master file review and maintenance, on-line or batch execution, report review, and storage and retrieval of frequently used control and network transactions.

CPM examples discussed in this book were run on the MSCS system.

COMPARISON OF CURRENT SYSTEMS

MSCS and PROJECT/2 continue as leaders in the CPM software field. In 1978, the Project Management Institute (PMI) conducted a survey of software programs and published the results. This survey was updated in 1982 for PMI by Dr. Larry A. Smith and Dr. Joan Mills of Florida International University. That survey was summarized in the PMI *Project Management Quarterly*** and the information from it included here is used with permission.

Summary of Major Project Management Network Programs Currently Available

This is an updating of an earlier comparison by L. A. Smith and Peter Mahler of 20 major network programs. Currently available commercial software programs have taken advantage of the increased capability of computer hardware to reduce many of the earlier constraints on data and data manipulation. Many of the programs evaluated here have indicated either no upper limit or significantly high (nonbinding) constraints on the size of projects they can handle.

Forty computer software programs were evaluated by means of questionnaires, phone calls, and published and readily available company literature, as well from information to be found in published articles. Sub-

---

*L. A. Smith and Joan Mills, "Project Management Network Programs," *Project Management Quarterly*, vol. XIII, no. 2, pp. 18–29, June 1982.

jective judgments were sometimes applied when indicating the existence or nonexistence of particular characteristics.

In terms of whether the systems are arrow diagram or precedence the following was found:

	Number of programs	Percentage of total
Arrow diagram	35	87.5
Precedence	32	80.0
Both	26	65.0

The size and detail of the projects that are being planned, scheduled, and controlled with the aid of networks are:

Activities per network	Number of programs	Percentage of total
0–10,000	12	30
10,001–20,000	2	5
20,001–30,000	3	7.5
30,001–40,000	8	20
40,001–50,000	0	0
Over 50,000	15	37.5
Total	40	100

Fifteen (37.5 percent) of the forty programs have the capability of handling over 50,000 activities per network. Several programs indicate that there is no upper bound on the size of the networks they can handle.

All of the forty programs surveyed have some form of internal calendar that allows the user to select from a shop calendar, a fiscal calendar, or some combination of both. Their flexibilities range from a standard fiscal calendar to customized project calendars containing holidays, nonworking days, standard work weeks that range from 1 to 7 days, etc.

Thirty-nine of the forty programs provide a graphical representation by activity or work versus time. Some depict, using various notations, critical activities, free float, total float, activities in progress, activities completed, etc.

One of the options that can be valuable to a user is a program's ability to specify the type and format of reports. These include management summary reports, time-related reports, cost-related reports, and resource-related reports. Thirty-four of the forty programs indicate various degrees of report generator flexibility.

Projects vary in their degree of required cost control, from a simple comparison of actual costs versus budgeted costs to more complex plots of cash flow, cumulative cash flow, budgeted cost of work scheduled

(BCWS), actual cost of work performed (ACWP), budgeted cost of work performed (BCWP), monies committed, etc. Thirty-nine of the forty programs claimed to be able to handle some form of cost control.

All of the programs allowed the option of developing a plan and cost resource program with the constraint of meeting predefined milestones and completion dates.

One of the options many project managers require is the ability to sort activities according to such user specifications as cost accounts, responsibility, active jobs, finish jobs, late jobs, amount of float, etc. Most of the programs surveyed provided at least a limited amount of this type of flexibility.

Resource allocation, leveling, and balancing is an important option, especially in a multiproject environment. It is the most important technique available when attempting to prioritize the allocation of resources. In its simplest form it allows the user to see a histogram of resources required and to make changes accordingly. In its most useful format, resource allocation balances resources and simultaneously adjusts the schedule. In the survey, thirty-four programs indicated they had some capability of allocating resources.

Once the logic has been developed and the interrelationships of activities evaluated, it may be beneficial to have the network plotted. Because of the development in plotting techniques and graphics, there has been an increase in the availability of this type of option.

Table 17.1 evaluates the forty programs in terms of thirteen major characteristics that a project manager should first evaluate. (The names of the companies producing those programs are given in the table, and the addresses of the companies are listed starting on page 305.) This selection is only a small subset of characteristics available in most of the programs assessed. An "×" indicates the characteristic is available in that program, an "L" indicates limited availability, "No" indicates that it is not available, and three dots or an empty cell indicates that its availability is not known. The characteristics are discussed in the next section.

Definitions of Characteristics

1. *System capacity.* Indicates the number of activities and/or number of subnetworks that may be used.

2. *Network schemes.* The network schemes are activity diagram (AD) and/or precedence relationship (PRE).

3. *Calendar dates.* An internal calendar is available to schedule the project's activities. The variations and options of the different calendar algorithms are numerous.

4. *Gantt or bar chart.* A graphical display of the output on a time scale is available, if desired.

5. *Flexible report generator.* The user can specify within defined guidelines the format of the output.

6. *Updating.* The program will accept revised time estimates and completion dates and recompute the revised schedule.

7. *Cost control.* The program accepts budgeted cost figures for each activity and then the actual costs incurred and summarizes the budgeted and actual figures on each updating run. The primary objective is to help management produce a realistic cost plan before the project is started and assist in the control of the project's expenditures as work progresses.

8. *Scheduled dates.* A date is specified for completion of any of the activities for purposes of planning and control. The calculations are performed with these dates as constraints.

9. *Sorting.* The program lists the activities in a sequence specified by the user.

10. *Resource allocation.* The program attempts to optimally allocate resources using one of many heuristic algorithms.

11. *Plotter availability.* A plotter is available to plot the network diagram.

12. *Machine requirements.* This is the minimum hardware memory requirement for the program (in units of bytes).

13. *Cost.* Indicates whether the program is sold and/or leased and the purchase price and/or lease price (if known).

Other programs listed in a Smith-Mahler work in 1978* but not included in the 1982 group of forty programs are:

Program	Company
CPM System	Canadian General Electric Information System
Data line	Dataline
Fasnet	University Computing
Mini-PERT	International Business Machines Corp.
MSCS	McDonnell-Douglas Automation Co.

---

*L. A. Smith and Peter Mahler, "Comparing Commercially Available CPM/PERT Computer Programs," *IE Magazine,* pp. 37–39, April 1978.

PERT/TIME	Control Data Corp.
Project Network	
Analysis (PNA)	NCR Corp.
PROCON 3	Nichols and Co.
PROMIS-TIME	Burroughs Business Machines
PROSE	Construction Industry Computer Consultants, Ltd.
SPRED	Computer Science Corp. (Infonet)

Other programs listed in the 1978 PMI Survey, but not in the 1982 survey, are:

Program	Company
ASA PMS	ASA (SIPOS)
CPM	Technical Economics, Inc.
Event Scheduling System	Sheppard Software Company
PCM (Project Cost Model)	Project Software Ltd.
PPS IV	CISCO
Project Reporting System	Adderfer Associates
PROSYS/80	Call Data System
QUICK-TROL	Quality Data Products
READINET	Educational Data System
RESMAN	Rarmit
T/A 2 Network Analysis and Control	Time/Audit Ltd.
TIMETABLE	United Computing Systems Inc.

Some of the programs discussed in the 1978 survey, such as MSCS, are known to be still available. Others appear to have been renamed. Some of the companies listed in the 1978 report are no longer offering CPM software. Some other companies not incorporated into either PMI survey that have advertised CPM software include T & B Computing (INTACT 50/ TRACK 50), Sun Information Services Company (SUNPLAN II), Dynamic Solutions, Inc. (PERT 6, MICROPERT 6), Trimag Systems (CO$TIME), Translog Services (PROMAC/M), and PMA Software (SPAN). And there are others.

The increasing availability of microcomputers is leading to programs for those high-powered, low-priced units. Garland Publishing offers PATHFINDER, which it says can operate on twelve currently available computers including Apple III and the H.P. 125. Other firms offering

TABLE 17.1 Program Characteristics

Program name, company	Sys. cap.	Network schemes	Cal. dates	Gantt or bar chart	Flex. report gen.	Up-dating	Cost cntrl.	Sched. dates	Sorting	Res. alloc.	Plotter avail.	Mach. Req'ts.	Cost
1. AIIE Industrial Engineering Activities & Management Systems	100	AOA	X	X	X	X	X	X	X	X	X	16K TRS 80 Level II or Apple II	$30 for audio tape
2. APECS Eval. & Control System ADP Network Services	64,000	AD PRE	X	X	X	X	X	X (yes on PERT version)	X	X	X	Only through ADP	Variable based on usage and fixed price, lease available
3. ARTEMIS Metier Management Systems, Inc.	32,000	AD PRE	X	X	X	X	X	X	X	X	X	Hewlett Packard 1000 with 200Mbyte disk drive	Purchase and rental
4. ASTRA General Electric Information Services	1920; graphics included	AOA	X	X	X	X	X	X	X	X	X	Through GE info. services GE Mark III series	
5. Accuratech, Inc. United Computing Systems	165,000 Cray 1, 42,000 batch, 5000 timesharing	AD PRE	X	X	X	X	X	X	X	X	X	Cray 1 and through United Computing Systems Cyber series	
6. CM-4	Unlimited	AOA	X	X	X	X	X	X	X	X	No	Available on request	Available on request
T. L. Sutton Assoc.													
7. CM4	2000	PRE	X	X	X	X	X	X	X	X	X		
8. CMS	3000	X		X	X	X	X	X	X	X		
9. CM6	5000	X	X	X	X	X	X	X	X	X		
10. "CONSTRUCT" Construction Information Systems, Inc.	Unlimited	AD PRE								X	In planning stage	Prime information computer; no minimum hardware configuration	Purchase only, $7000

#	Name	Capacity	Type									Machine/Compiler	Terms
11.	CPM Gnomon, Inc.	1000 and 750 events	AD	L	X	X	X	X	no	no	no	MK III disk	Various royalties; $1500/year lease; $8000 purchase
12.	CPMIS Glenn L. White Co.	30,000	AD	X	No	X	X	X	X	No	X	IBM 360/30 with 4 tapes, 22314, 5 and 25 core	Lease $40/mo.; license $25,000 TGL expenses
13.	GRAM E.S.I.	5000 to 10,000	AD	X	No	X	X	X	X	X	X	Dec 20, Dec 10, CDC 3300, CDC, Cyber 74, Burroughs	Time sharing lease, purchase
14.	CUE Gilbert/Commonwealth	32,000	PRE AD	X	X	X	X	X	X	X	X	HPC 3000 series 3, 30, & 33, 44 PRIME, all models Fortran	Lease of perpetual lease
15.	Kaiser Engineers, Inc.	32,000, graphics	PRE	X	X	*	No	X	X	No	No	OS/360-370	Ties in with other packages that do budgeting
16.	MAPPS Structural Programming	5000		X	X	X	X	X	X	X	X		
17.	MCS—MARK II Hill International, Inc.	32,760	PRE AD	X	X	X	X	X	X	X	X	Batch or on-line, any Fortran IV	Lease, license or service bureau.*Lease, $650/mo.; license, $38,000
18.	MCS/90	100,000	AD PRE	X	No	X	X	X	X	No	X	VS/9,05/3	
19.	MICROPERT Computerline, Ltd.	Maximum of 5000	AD PRE	X	X	X	X	X	X	X	X	Tandy Model II or software for various machines	License
20.	MINI 4	300	AD PRE	X	X	X	X	X	X	X	X	Dec-vax II or Wong V5	
21.	MISTER Shirley Software Sys.	Unlimited procedures 1200 different reports in a file format	X	X	No	X	X	X	X	X	X	Any 1966 Fortran compiler	Purchase, $14,500 to $39,500; lease, $500 to $1500 per mo.

TABLE 17.1 Program Characteristics (*Continued*)

Program name, company	Sys. cap.	Network schemes	Cal. dates	Gantt or bar chart	Flex. report gen.	Up-dating	Cost cntrl.	Sched. dates	Sorting	Res. alloc.	Plotter avail.	Mach. Req'ts.	Cost
22. MPM Florida Power Corp.	Unlimited Graphics	AD	L	X	X	X	X	X	X	X	X	GE Mark III	Use basis on GE Mark III, no upfront costs
23. N5500 Program Nichols and Company	36 6 X	AD PRE	X	X	X	X	X	X	X	X	X	Tape, disk, online, batch	Time sharing or purchase
24. Optima	11,000	AD PRE	X	X	X	X	X	X	X	X	X	1100 CPV line printer	$660/mo.
25. OSCAR On-Line Systems, Inc.	Unlimited	AD PRE	X	X	X	X	X	X	X	X	X	Any	Time sharing or purchase
26. PAC MACRO International Systems	Unlimited	AD PRE	X	X	X	X	X	X	X	X	X	Disk storage to support files	Purchase, $26,000 to $40,000
27. PACE	Limited only by machine	PRE	L	No	No	X	X	X	X	No	X	Dec 10	Information available on request
28. PMS	8,160,000	AD PRE	X	X	X	X	X	X	X	X	No	Any OS machine	Monthly lease
29. Point 4 Data Corp.	Unlimited	AD	X	X	X	X	X	X	X	X	X	DG Nove-type 64K	Purchase, $6,000
30. PREMIS K & H Computer Sys., Inc.	64,000	AD PRE	X	X	X	X	X		X	X	X	IBM 500K, IBM-compatible peripherals	Leased or sold, $30,000; monthly rental, $2700
31. PROJAC IBM Corporation	32,000	AD PRE	X	X	X	X	X	X	X	X	No	DOS or OS in virtual environment	Monthly lease
32. PROJECT/2 Project Software and Development, Inc.	32,500	AD PRE	X	X	X	X	X	X	X	X	X	IBM 370 43-41, or 43, 31 and UNIVAC 1100 and digital vex	$3000/mo. lease or pay-as-you-use plan; price varies with machine and time used

#	Program / Company	Capacity	AD/PRE									Computer / Requirements	Pricing / Availability
33.	Project Control/70 Atlantic Software	Unlimited	PRE	X	X	X	X	X	X	X	X	On-line, batch, full screen	Batch, $25,000; on-line, $35,000
34.	PRO MAC/90 Promacon, Inc.	32,000	AD PRE	X	X	X	⋯	X	X	X	X	256K core, Fortran compiler disk pack and spindle, high-speed 132 minicomputer	$35,000–$50,000 purchase; $1750/mo. lease
35.	PROMINI/ PREMINI K & H Computer Sys., Inc.	32,000	AD PRE	X	X	X	X	X	X	X	X	64K, any machine with a Fortran compiler	Leased or sold, $36,000; monthly rental, $1200
36.	Proplan Control Data Corp.	14,000	PRE	X	X	X	X	X	X	X	X	Most any line printer; graphics interfaced from EZ PERT package	
37.	SNAP (Sharp Network Analysis Program) I. P. Sharp Assoc.	500 sub networks each containing 500 activities	AD PRE	X	X	X	X	X	X	X	X	Sharp ADL	Purchase or time-sharing in 350 cities internationally
38.	Vepco—PICS Virginia Electric and Power Company	32,000	PRE	X	X	X	X	X	X	X	X	IBM 43XX, 303X, 370, 360	Service bureau purchase
39.	VISION EZ PERT (only a graphics program must be interfaced with a scheduling system) Systonetics, Inc.	32,000	AD PRE	X	X	X	X	X	X	X	X	Prime 150 through 850	Software starts at $25,000 up to $110,000
40.	VUE National Information Sys.	3000	AD PRE	X	X	No	X	X	No	X	X	Any CRT or line printer	$15,000–$22,500

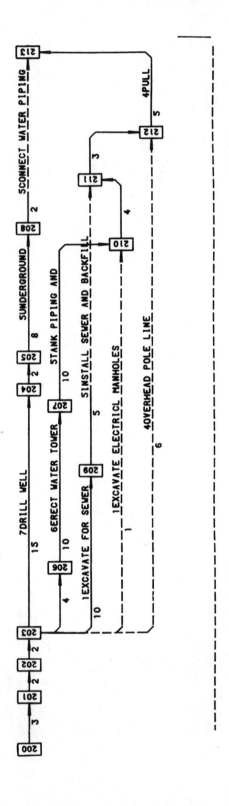

302

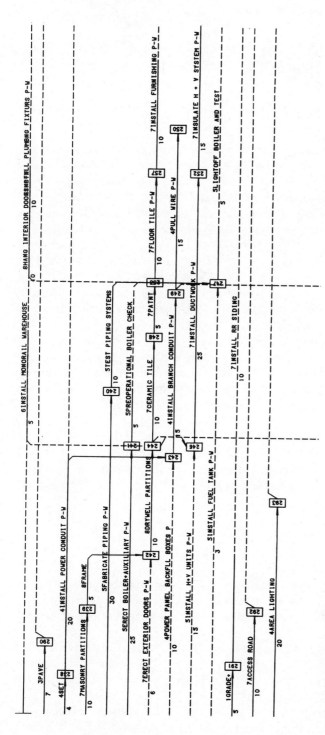

Figure 17.5 T-MAPS sample.

micro programs include MicroSym, Primavera Systems, Inc., P.P.M.C.S., FD Consulting, and North America Mica, Inc.

GRAPHICS

As noted in the PMI survey, most of the software packages can generate a graphical output. This may be the bar-graph format described in Chapter 7. Most bar graphs generated are on standard computer paper, with repeated page breaks—both horizontal and vertical. To assemble the bar graph, the sheets must be trimmed and taped together. This can be avoided if the computer center has an x-y plotter such as a Calcomp drum or flat bed unit.

The more sophisticated programs can produce a plotted network. The Systonetics EZPERT program, in fact, is designed solely to provide the interface between basic CPM output and the plotter. Project Software & Development, Inc., has a package QWKNET which can either create a PDM network or display the network result.

CM Associates has an in-house program to machine-generate all of its schedules. Turner Construction Co. created a network generator named T-MAPS, which is available to MCAUTO users and which can produce a network from various network calculating systems, including MSCS. Figure 17.5 shows part of the John Doe network generated by T-Maps driven by MSCS.

The development of computer-aided design (CAD) has resulted in multicolor plotters which can provide multicolor networks.

Bar-graph generation does not require special network organization. Some network generator programs require special numbering, in addition to the basic unique i-j number.

SUMMARY

Early CPM software was closely tied to hardware capabilities. Language development made it easier for computer software to be utilized on different computers. This reduced the need for a large number of unique software systems.

Evolution in computer hardware into the third generation (IBM 360/370) made many of the early programs obsolete. Comprehensive software developed in the 1970s for mainframe computers resulted in three major systems: MSCS, PROJECT/2, and PMS.

The 1980s, following the evolution from vacuum tube to transistor to semiconductor to chip technologies, have been characterized by a virtual explosion in hardware capabilities. CPM systems are again being tailored to hardware, but now in terms of greater capabilities rather than limitations. Listed below are companies producing CPM software.

ASA
104 E. 40th Street
New York, NY 10016

Accuratech Inc.
United Computing Systems
2525 Washington
Kansas City, MO 64108

Atlantic Software
320 Walnut Street
Philadelphia, PA 19106

Burroughs Business Machines Ltd.
980 St. Antoine Street
Montreal, Quebec
Canada, H3C 1AB

CISCO
810 Thompson Building
Tulsa, OK 74103

Call Data Systems, Inc.
20 Crossways Park North
Woodbury, NY 11797

Canadian General Electric
  Information Services
2001 University Street
Suite 1120
Montreal, Quebec
Canada, H3A 2A6

Computer Sciences Corp., Infonet
650 N. Sepulveda Boulevard
El Segundo, CA 90245

Computerline, Ltd.
118 Church Road
Addleston, Weybridge
Surrey, UK
(0932) 55757

Computing and Information Sciences
  Corp.
810 Thompson Building
Tulsa, OK 74103

Construction Industry Computer
  Consultants Ltd.
(CINCOM)
620 Dorchester Boulevard West
Montreal, Quebec
Canada, H3B IN9

Construction Information Systems, Inc.
Box 484
Mill Valley, CA 94941

Construction Management Systems
P.O. Box 90
Haddonfield, NJ 08033

Control Data Corp.
P.O. Box 0
Minneapolis, MN 55440

Control Data Corp.
2200 Berkshire Land North
Minneapolis, Mn 55441

Dataline
40 St. Clair Avenue, West
Toronto, Ontario
Canada

Dynamic Solutions Incorporated
50 Lytton Avenue
Hartsdale, NY 10530

E.S.I.
P.O. Box 35244
Minneapolis, MN

Educational Data Systems
1682 Langley Avenue
Irvine, CA 92714

Evaluation & Control System
ADP Network Services
175 Jackson Plaza
Ann Arbor, MI 48106

FD Consulting
4233 Spring St. #71
La Mesa, CA 92041

Florida Power Corp.
P.O. Box 14042
St. Petersburg, FL 33733

Garland Publishing
136 Madison Avenue
New York, NY 10016

General Electric Information
Services
401 N. Washington Street
Rockville, MD 10880

Gilbert/Commonwealth
P.O. Box 1498
Reading, PA 19603

Gnomon, Inc.
P.O. Box 30169
Cincinnati, OH 45230

Hill International, Inc.
Garden Plaza Building
P.O. Box 397
Willingboro, NJ 08046

Honeywell Information Systems
800 Dorchester Boulevard, West
Montreal, Quebec
Canada, H3B 1X9

IBM Corporation
1133 Westchester Avenue
White Plains, NY 10604

Industrial Engineering Activities
& Management Systems Department
University of Central Florida
P.O. Box 2500
Orlando, Fl 32816

International Business Machines
IBM France
Program Product Center
36 Avenue, Raymond Poincare
75116 Paris, France

International Systems
890 Valley Forge Plaza
King of Prussia, PA 19406

International Systems, Inc.
150 Allendale Road
King of Prussia, PA 19406

K & H Computer Systems, Inc.
P.O. Box 4
Sparta, NJ 07871

Kaiser Engineers, Inc.
300 Lakeside Drive
P.O. Box 23210
Oakland, CA 94623

McAuto
Dept. KBR-500
Box 516
St. Louis, MO 63166

McDonnell-Douglas Automation Co.
500 Jefferson Building
Suite 400
Houston, TX 77002

Metier Management Systems, Inc.
Suite 100
10175 Harwin Drive
Houston, TX 77036

MicroSym
512 West Lancaster Avenue
Wayne, PA 19087

NCR Corp.
Dayton, OH 45479

National Information Systems
20370 Town Center Lane
Suite #245
Cupertino, CA 95014

Nichols & Co.
1900 Avenue of the Stars
Los Angeles, CA 90067

North America Mica, Inc.
11772 Sorrento Valley Road
San Diego, CA 92121

On-Line Systems, Inc.
115 Evergreen Heights
Pittsburgh, PA 15229

PMA Software
Software Marketing Coordinator
P.O. Box 1368
Ann Arbor, MI 48106

P.P.M.C.S.
Project Planning Management
& Control Systems
1309 East 132nd Street
Burnsville, MN 55337

Point 4 Data Corp.
2569 McCabe Way
Irvine, CA 92714

Primavera Systems, Inc.
29 Bala Avenue, Suite 224
Bala Cynwyd, PA 19004

Project Software and Development,
    Inc.
14 Story Street
Cambridge, MA 02138

Promacon, Inc.
P.O. Box 96
Maple Glen, PA 19002

Quality Data Products Inc.
N417 Argonne
Spokane, WA 99206

Rarmit Associates
385 Rountree Glenn
Escondido, CA 92026

I. P. Sharp Associates
145 King Street West
Toronto, Ontorio
Canada, M5R 1J8

Sheppard Software Company
Calaveras Business Park
558 Valley Way
Milpitas, CA 95035

Shirley Software Systems
1936 Huntington Drive
Pasadena, CA 91030

Sperry UNIVAC
P.O. Box 500
Blue Bell, PA 19424

Structural Programming
83 Boston Post Road
Sudbury, MA 01776

Sun Information Services Company
280 King of Prussia Road
Radnor, PA 19087

T. L. Sutton Associates
P.O. Box 84
Snug Harbor Station
Duxbury, MA 02332

Systonetics, Inc.
600 N. Euclid Street
Anaheim, CA 92801

T & B Computing, Inc.
3853 Research Park Drive
Ann Arbor, MI 48104

Time/Audit Ltd.
P.O. Box 403
Willowdale, Ontario
Canada, M2N 521

Translog Services, Inc.
600 North Jackson Street
Media, PA 19063

Trimag Systems
9918-101 Street, Suite 1701
Edmonton, Alberta
Canada, T5K 2L1

Trimag Systems
4141 Sherbrooke St., W.
Suite 255
Montreal, Quebec
Canada, H3Z 1B8

United Computing Systems, Inc.
2525 Washington
Kansas City, MO 64108

University Computing Co.
1930 Hiline Drive
Dallas, TX 75207

Virginia Electric and Power
   Company

1 James River Plaza
Richmond, VA 23219

Glenn L. White, Co.
2560 Huntington Avenue
Alexandria, VA 22303

18

APPLICATION AND ADVANTAGES OF CPM

How does the construction manager, contractor, owner, or designer apply CPM? Even more important, what advantages can be anticipated by doing so?

CONTRACTOR CPM PREPARATION

In a fixed-price contract, the contractor is not identified until the contract is awarded. With the exception of a few special situations, a bidder does not plan the implementation phase of a project until the contract is in hand. Contractors have to invest enough in bidding for the 50 to 90 percent of the proposals for which they will not receive contracts, so it is only after—although immediately after—the contract award that the successful contractor should start the CPM plan, with the help of either staff planners or a CPM consultant. This assistance is only needed to translate the contractor's *own* plan into arrow-diagram terms. The CPM plan must be the plan the contractor expects to follow; otherwise, CPM becomes an exercise of little value.

Through the discipline of CPM, the contractor can achieve better planning. By means of it, the contractor's people can better concentrate their thinking and apply their experience to all phases of the new project. CPM helps to accomplish much of this because the CPM planner can commit ideas to graphical form, and is thus not burdened with a tedious memory chore.

The initial CPM plan should be prepared, with a schedule computed, in 4 to 6 weeks. On one large project this initial CPM plan-preparation phase took more than 9 months. This was an extravagant planning exercise consuming 35 percent of the project's life. To provide the best results, CPM planning must be timely.

Contractor's CPM Schedule

Review of the CPM schedule can indicate the need, if any, to expedite the project. If this need is present, the early stages usually offer the best bargain in terms of least cost to expedite. When doing foundation work in pleasant spring weather, it is difficult to view the close-in of the building with the proper gravity. But the use of CPM can help one achieve this perspective.

The CPM plan can assign priorities to material and equipment acquisition. The first part of the critical path is often through equipment deliveries. When the critical deliveries have been pinpointed, it may be possible to improve the dates by arranging for better delivery times or by having the material or equipment shipped in smaller lot sizes.

If the owner has specified a special item whose delivery will be difficult, the CPM diagram and schedule may provide logical reasons for requesting a suitable substitute. However, CPM is a two-edged sword. Owners and architects usually regard such requests with a jaundiced eye, and they may well use the contractor's network to prove that the delivery could logically be made at a later event.

Whatever the situation, foresight is much more acceptable than hindsight. The contractor may uncover areas requiring revisions in design or time extensions. The earlier these problems are discovered, the less the panic that will result.

CPM in the Field

When the basic schedule has been prepared, what next? The contractor can go into specialized cost and work force studies. However, these are usually not employed until the contractor has developed a considerable experience and confidence in the use of the basic CPM technique. The next step is usually the transmittal of the schedule to the field office. In this area, the smaller contractor has an advantage, being directly in charge in the field or at least in close touch with the field people working on the project.

Larger contractors can experience problems in transmitting the CPM schedule to their field group. This can be the result of a staff planning group preparing plans for the field, which is an easy trap for a large company to fall into. Not only will field people be unfamiliar with plans made by others, but often they are unfamiliar with the CPM technique itself. The adequate training of both field and office personnel in the use of CPM is a continuing need, but also a continuing problem because of fairly rapid turnover. This problem has diminished as CPM use continues to broaden, but contractors themselves could help solve it if they offered adequate CPM familiarization courses to their workers (these can be given in 1 or 2 days) and/or allowed the field group to learn about CPM through participating in the preparation of the initial diagrams for their projects.

Advantages to the Contractor of Using CPM

Scheduling requires effort, but there are immediate payoffs. First, the field becomes an integral part of the operation. Second, through CPM, the office and field develop a new medium of communication unique to their project. Both factors can be effective in developing a genuine project team spirit.

The graphical character of CPM offers several advantages to the contractor. First, all interested parties can review the planned work sequences. Mistakes made on paper are much easier to correct than those made on-site. Second, if the management of a project has to be changed in midcourse, the CPM plan can help expedite the transfer. Third, the CPM graphical plan is dynamic rather than static. New ideas or changes can be evaluated rapidly. This area of evaluation includes proposed field change orders.

CPM results in an improved plan. But how much improved? Ten, twenty, thirty percent? These figures sound reasonable, but 30 percent of *what?* You cannot measure planning, so no one can accurately quantify the advantages of CPM in regard to planning.

CPM can, and usually does, shorten a project's duration through better planning and control. But how much time can you expect to cut off that duration with CPM? One contractor says 20 percent. The president of a major consulting firm says 30 percent. Again, these figures seem reasonable, but 30 percent of *what* time? Frankly, there is nothing to prevent the CPM estimate from *extending* the expected duration of a project. However, since traditional time estimates are usually conservative, the more accurate CPM estimate can usually pinpoint a shorter duration. As CPM comes into more common use, there will not be as many "long" project estimates to reduce. The best estimate is the one which matches the actual result.

OWNER CPM APPLICATION

If the contractor is using CPM, can the owner expect to automatically reap the advantages of that use? Absolutely not. Since contractors do not apply their CPM planning until the contract price is set, all cost savings accrue to them. (However, it is true that, in the long run, CPM can make the quality contractors more competitive, and the lower bid prices that result represent broad-based savings to owners. In turn, the prime contractors that use CPM should themselves be able to obtain better subcontract prices.)

How about the time savings which contractors can realize through CPM? Owners cannot expect to obtain these gratis. Like many other something-for-nothing deals, this concept can be an expensive *mis*conception. Contractors may use CPM defensively to obtain time extensions. At best, their CPM plans will be oriented to their own benefit rather than to the benefit of owners. This is as it should be. If CPM is to be effective for contractors, it must reflect the project as seen through their eyes. In most cases contractors are interested in early completions. However, in some situations they may achieve a cost savings by delaying work. For instance, delaying plastering until warm weather may save thousands of dollars per month in temporary heating costs. Contractors could use CPM to justify such a delay. Also, they may prefer to shift key personnel and equipment to suit the needs of their many other projects rather than to suit those of a particular owner's one project.

Owner Input into the Working Plan

If owners want to be assured of timely project completions through CPM, what can be done? They can prepare CPM plans of projects themselves and monitor progress by means of them. Since there are more ways to plan a project than one would care to count, however, this system tends to be ineffectual. But it is an approach and has been used—the Titan site monitoring system (TRACE) was an example.

A better way is for owners to directly subsidize contractors' planning efforts. This is done by furnishing qualified CPM planning and computer services to assist the contractors in preparing their arrow diagrams. In this approach owners rate more of a voice in the planning of their projects. This does not mean the right to interject ideas into the working plans.

Working plans must remain under the control of contractors as their plans of attack for the work they are doing. However, the presence of an objective and knowledgeable observer in the planning effort of a project does help both owner and contractor. The contractor, in describing the plan to an outsider, often sees flaws in the planning as it is described. In other cases, the consultant can sometimes point out the broad plan when the contractor cannot see past the details. An owner, for his or her part, has the advantage of an objective evaluation of the contractor's approach. A consultant can also point out areas where the owner can assist in moving the project along. And when extra work or changes are being considered, both owner and contractor can get a better evaluation of the effects those alterations will have on the project's schedule since the consultant, having no ax to grind, can often get better information from subcontractors than either of them. One caution, though: To be effective, the consultant must be frank; the owner cannot afford a CPM yes-person.

Contractors are often reluctant to update their CPM plans. They may try to move a project back onto the original or last schedule computation. This can mask the actual status; but making the project fit an obsolete plan can lead into traps. The updating of any project on a regular and objective basis is a key factor in maintaining its progress. And while the schedule updating is itself of prime importance, there are two intangible side benefits to regular CPM reevaluations. First, the effort on the part of the owner in using CPM to ensure timely completion of a project actively demonstrates the owner's desire to get the job done. Second, the regularity of the updating in itself helps to emphasize the passage of time.

The comments thus far have been directed more or less toward fixed-price single contracts. But they would also be appropriate for two other types of contract: fixed-price separate primes and negotiated.

In the construction project owner-architect-engineer-contractor-subcontractor relationship, a tremendous amount depends upon good faith. CPM cannot supplant that good faith; as a method, on the contrary, it cannot work without it. On a separate prime contract job there will usually be some honest differences of opinion. CPM can evaluate those differences in terms of project time. In keeping problems to specifics CPM can help to maintain good working relationships among all the parties concerned. However, CPM is a tool. It cannot ensure perfect coordination, any more than a dictionary can write a novel.

Negotiated contracts are based upon either an owner's need for rapid construction or the special capabilities of a particular contractor. As a result, there usually exists a definite owner-contractor rapport which can provide an excellent basis for CPM use. CPM information in turn is best accepted and utilized in this positive atmosphere.

Special CPM Techniques of Use to Owners

The owner may need to use resource leveling to accomplish turnaround or maintenance work with in-house workers and/or equipment. In contracted work, however, the owner is usually not concerned with this. But there are notable exceptions. For projects in remote areas such as Kwajalein, the owner often is responsible for the transportation, housing, and meals of contractor personnel. In such cases, the owner has a definite interest in a level work force.

Preliminary or Prebid CPM Study

The preliminary, or prebid, CPM plan is prepared when the architect's working plan is available. It is also practical to develop the prebid CPM plan from the architect's preliminary plans if those are definitive. Since this CPM plan is prepared prior to the selection of a contractor, the CPM planner must have construction experience in order to develop a practical plan.

The requirement that a CPM plan must reflect the contractor's actual plan if it is to be useful has been emphasized. Since there is no contractor at this point, then, what is the usefulness of the prebid CPM plan? The primary purpose of the prebid plan is the establishment of a reasonable construction period. In the past, the construction completion requirements specified in the request for bids have usually been prepared in one of two ways: Either by a plain country guess or by allowing the needs of the owner to dictate the construction dates specified. And many responsible owners and architects (who normally handle all financial matters with considered care) have treated this important matter of the allowable construction period in the most casual manner. There was, of course, a good reason for this—traditional planning methods did not afford a reliable method for setting a reasonable construction period.

On the receiving end of the specification, the contractor was almost as casual. The estimator reviewed the plans and specifications and took off the quantities in great detail. Little attention was given to the construction period. The problem was to get the job, then to figure out how to do it. There were also other reasons for this nonchalance. First, most owners had no real teeth in their specifications in regard to enforcing completion dates. If liquidated damages were specified at all, they were small.

Set by engineers or architects, the liquidation damage figure of $100 per day was almost a custom of the trade for years. The thought often expressed was, "Let's not scare off any bidders." Furthermore, especially in the public sector, it was usual to waive liquidated damages by granting a time extension equal to the time overrun.

Today there is a much greater awareness of the cost of time. For one thing, the litigious decade of the 1970s found contractors pressing claims like $1000 to $10,000 per day of delay. Also, it is now well understood that delays by even one of the subcontractors or separate prime contractors might well inflict costs and delay upon other contractors, as well as upon the owner. Moreover, while folklore in the trade thought liquidated damages to be unenforceable without a matching bonus clause, this has long been untrue. A court found against a contractor named Wise who claimed that the liquidated damages clause was not enforceable. The court said that "there is no sound reason why persons competent and free to contract may not agree upon this subject as fully as upon any other ..." [*Wise vs. United States,* 239 U.S. S 361 (1919)].

A second reason for contractor nonchalance was the expectation that, at worst, job conditions would provide a way out of any time overruns. That is, if unforeseen conditions did not provide a bona fide excuse, the owner would oblige by breaching the contract. This, in turn, would relieve the contractor of being subject to the liquidated damages clause.

Today, with costs of delay well recognized (and typical liquidated damages in the range of $1000 to $5000 per day), contractor and owner alike are no longer casual about the contractual performance period.

Through a prebid CPM analysis, realistic time requirements can be determined. If the owner's desired dates cannot be met by working the job in a practical manner, it is better for the owner to know this before going out for bids. Contractors will recognize a very tight schedule, and their bids accordingly will be higher. If by those high bids the owner is advised that the time requirements are stringent, either the time constraints can be relaxed to avoid paying a premium or the basic cost estimate can be adjusted to reflect that premium.

It is more usual for owners not to require tight schedules in order to avoid the risk of premiums. This conservative outlook can result in substantial overallowances for construction time, overallowances which are costly to owners. Contractors in such cases do not gain either since, in accord with Parkinson's law, the work (and overhead) expand to fill the time available.*

The goal of the prebid CPM plan is analogous to another Parkinsonian conception: "The Short List, or Principles of Selection." In the chapter of his book on this subject, Professor Parkinson discusses in his humorous fashion several methods of selecting personnel, the basic problem being: How do you select from a number of qualified candidates? While all the

---

*By permission from C. Northcote Parkinson, *Parkinson's Law,* Riverside Editions, Houghton Mifflin Company, Boston, 1957.

methods are interesting and worthy of study, Professor Parkinson's "perfect" solution is of particular interest. He suggests that the perfect want ad would attract only one qualified person. He gives an example similar to the following:

> WANTED: Tight rope walker to cross wire 200 feet above raging furnace. Two performances daily, three on Saturday. Salary $70.00 per week. No fringe benefits. Apply in person.

He points out that only qualified people would dare apply, so there would be no need to request qualifications or experience. On the other hand, the salary requirement must be such that only one person would apply. If the salary offer were too high, there would be too many applicants. If it were too low, there would be none. The problem is, what salary would you quote to achieve this result?

The selection problem in regard to writing a want ad is similar to the problem of specifying a construction schedule: What schedule can be specified which will produce the project in the least time at the desired cost? There is only one exactly correct answer. Unlike the example of the help-wanted ad, we can never know just how close we have to come to that correct answer. But prebid CPM gives the best opportunity to select the best construction schedule, and it can also be a basis for deciding on amounts to set for liquidated damages.

The prebid CPM plan is not intended to replace the postbid working plan. Owners should never impose the prebid CPM plans on contractors' postbid planning. First, owners can thereby well make themselves liable for any difficulties which the contractors encounter in trying to meet those imposed plans. Second, owners are buying the knowledge and experience of the contractors they hire. Nothing should restrict contractors in using their ingenuity and applying their experience to projects.

This should not prevent an owner from including the prebid CPM plan as part of the specification. However, it should be clearly stated by the owner that this is only one way in which the project can be constructed. CPM-oriented contractors have found preliminary CPM studies useful as a fast way to become familiar with projects. They are also useful as checklists. They are *not* sufficiently detailed to provide the basis for the preparation of bids, however.

In a number of cases, contractors have filed claims or entered suit in regard to prebid CPM plans. In one instance, the prebid plan showed the building work in great detail—sufficiently enough to qualify as a working plan. However, the CPM planner had not recognized how difficult it could be to relocate required utilities before the work on foundations could proceed. The relocation required blasting several deep cuts through rock. The prebid CPM showed it taking 6 weeks, while it actually took more than 6 months.

This experience suggests that the prebid CPM plan must be carefully reviewed with the architect and with engineers to be certain that the prime factors in the project have been considered. Although offered as an aid to contractors in preparing their bids, prebid CPM plans incorrectly drawn up can do more harm than good. In this sense, they are similar to the results of site surveys and soil borings. Fearing either misinterpretation of or mistakes in the findings, architect-engineers often note that the information is available, but offer it to bidders with the disclaimer that there is no warranty of its correctness.

The typical preliminary CPM plan takes less than half the time to prepare than the working plan does. However, the study and research that have gone into the specifications and plans will usually shorten the time required for preparation of the postbid working plans. The prebid diagram should be about one-third the size of the working diagram, and the level of its detail should be about the same as that shown in the sample John Doe network.

Preconstruction Phase

Many years ago, only conceptual drawings were required for the construction of all parts of a structure except special fixtures and appurtenances. The architect and craftspeople worked out details as the building progressed. But the advent of fixed-price contracts and the displacement of the old craftsperson concept by new work techniques have complicated the role of the architect. Working drawings and specifications must now describe every detail of the project and must be complete before actual construction commences. Funding often involves one or more governmental agencies. The function of the buildings themselves has become complex. Structures housing such exotic entities as cyclotrons and space test facilities have become commonplace. Design is subject to review by numerous committees and agencies. These conditions often combine to make the preconstruction or paperwork period of a project longer than its construction period. Unfortunately, delays in paperwork are more difficult to pinpoint than construction delays, which are obvious even to "sidewalk superintendents." The preconstruction phase is often almost devoid of planning—and yet it is an area to which CPM can readily be applied.

One large industrial corporation follows the usual preconstruction phase routine. When a new process or facility is suggested by the research or production departments, engineering does a conceptual design study. A cost estimate is prepared. This estimate goes to the corporate staff, where marketing and economic studies are made. The corporate review may take from 1 to 20 months. When the project is approved, the company wants it "built yesterday." In the specific case of a new research laboratory, corporate approval took 9 months and was announced in the spring of the year. At that point, working drawings were started. The piping systems required were fairly sophisticated and the bid package was not ready until August even though the team preparing it worked overtime. Management was now interested in having the facility as soon as possible. Therefore, the bidders had to take into consideration that they would be laying the foundation during wintertime, and their prices went up accordingly. This could have been predicted by a CPM preconstruction plan. An obvious time-saving move would have been to start the working drawings early. This could have been as soon as the basic concept was approved but before construction funds were available. If the situation could have been presented to corporate management in an objective manner, they probably would have agreed. The major problem here was communications.

In a hospital-medical school project valued at over $50 million, CPM was used to control the preconstruction phase. With more than ten separate but interrelated agencies and architects planning the ten distinct projects involved, rigorous and disciplined planning was necessary for months, even years, could have been lost. The factors considered included land acquisition, urban renewal procedures, street and sewer development, conceptual design, working drawings and specification preparation, interproject coordination, federal funding requests (to three separate agencies), school approvals, parking studies, and—finally—phasing of the

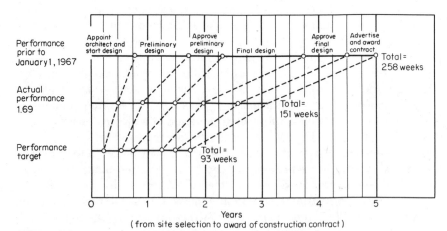

Figure 18.1 Preconstruction results, PMIS. *(From New York City 1969–1970 Budget.)*

construction itself. The results were excellent, although CPM uncovered as much bad news as good. This is healthy since the first step in solving a problem is the recognition that it does, in fact, exist.

Figure 18.1 summarizes the results of 2 years of applying PMIS techniques to preconstruction phases of projects in New York City.

REACTIONS TO CPM

CPM technique is logical and based upon common sense. People often are not. It is not surprising that "people problems" are the most difficult obstacles to successfully applying CPM. The response will vary from top management to the working level of organizations that use it. However, a natural desire to maintain the status quo manifests itself throughout all levels. Anticipation and appreciation of these reactions will aid in the application of CPM.

People agree that good planning is a project requirement. But they differ about the definition of good planning and particularly on how much should be paid for it. A first reaction many people have is that planning costs nothing. And in regard to CPM, they think it is fine for someone else, but not for them.

Management Reactions

This group includes the top-level management (owners, prime contractors, architects). A common reaction on their part is: "We get jobs done with few problems. Why do we need CPM?" One reason for this response is the lack of problem flow upstream to the front office. Also, top management personnel often have the impression that they are already getting a CPM quality of planning. This group usually does not want to be isolated in an ivory tower. The ivory tower is fabricated by subordinates who do not want to disturb the boss. CPM can offer top-level personnel the means of keeping in touch with projects, yet participating directly only when their attention is needed. This is "management by exception" at its best.

Top managers display another interesting twist. As a group they are often reluctant to delegate authority, yet when CPM is to be used, they sometimes put it on a "let's vote" basis. This is like the general asking a sergeant, "Should we attack?" Once management has evaluated CPM and elected to try it, *try it;* don't vote on it. This is a situation where managers must manage if they expect to get good results. Of course, it is reasonable to have key subordinates evaluate the potential of CPM before management decides to try it. Also, lower-echelon personnel should be oriented and trained in CPM if it is going to be used.

Middle Management

This group includes engineers, supervisors, office managers, and others between the top level and the field. Depending on the company structure, it may include field managers and project superintendents. This is the group which the tool (CPM) most competes with. That is, this group usually generates the plans, schedules, bar graphs, and S curves which CPM replaces. As a group they usually do not regard CPM as a competitor. While this is good, they often display a companion attitude which is somewhat defeatist. They recognize the potential of CPM but declare, "Management won't buy it, and if they do, the field won't use it." In this sense, they are *really* in the middle.

This is the group whose evaluation and advice will often be sought prior to the decision made by top management to utilize CPM. It is also a group which can be readily trained in CPM techniques and which will be instrumental in its application.

Public and in-house courses to train middle management in CPM use are available. The original courses required 5 days for a good exposure to CPM. About half of this time was spent on an actual CPM problem furnished by the students. Substantial coverage was given to the mathematical basis for the technique. However, this was not useful to the average user because it dwelt on the problem of transferring human common sense into computer language. It often did more harm than good because it implied that the CPM user has to have a good academic background in mathematics, whereas actually addition and subtraction will suffice.

The original courses also had difficulty in getting across the idea of the arrow-diagram representation of activities. Today, however, most students have been exposed to arrow diagrams through professional literature, orientation seminars, etc. Where early students did their first sample problems by bar graph, today most of them use an arrow diagram without the benefit of instruction. When twenty out of a class of twenty-four people at an in-plant course did this, we almost folded our tent and left. However, even though they could draw simple diagrams, most lacked confidence in their do-it-yourself approach. All were interested in instruction, direction, and ideas on the application of CPM.

By dropping the fancy mathematics and cutting down on the introductory material, a good course can be given in 2 or 3 days. This includes work on sample problems, review of sample computer outputs, instruction on the advanced techniques, open discussion time, and a short team project. A streamlined version of this can be given in about 6 hours of classroom time. This is a workshop session that omits student plans and provides only a limited discussion of advanced techniques and limited time for questions.

Field Reactions

Field superintendents have usually learned their jobs the hard way. They are somewhat like the army topkick who got his stripes and rockers by drive, talent, and initiative. The sergeant likes the work but it does rankle to be training an endless procession of second lieutenants on their way up the army ladder. The newly graduated engineer is the construction second lieutenant, and it is understandable if the field person is reluctant to have his or her brain picked by a newcomer. With CPM, field people have a double threat to contend with. Not only does this technique tend to bring more engineers into their lives, but now the intruders drag a computer with them.

The answer is orientation and training to get across the message that the system is based on common sense and the computer is capable of no hocus-pocus. Beyond that, the active assistance of the field supervisers must be enlisted. Without that help, CPM is a crippled duck and can operate at only half power.

Training for the field group should be on the same level as for the various levels of management. In fact, it is strongly recommended that classes be a mixture of management and field personnel. In government groups, we have noticed that some students are reluctant to ask questions in the presence of their bosses, and vice versa. However, this situation usually thaws out. Also we have noted that construction people are not usually so inhibited. Members of mixed groups develop a rapport during the course of the classes that can be invaluable in their future work together. These mixed classes are often made up of a very interesting cross section of people. In a typical in-house course for a small- or medium-sized company, there may be top-level managers, engineers, field superintendents, subcontractor personnel, accountants, estimators, and even secretaries. The class reaction to CPM has been unfailingly good.

The value of training must be emphasized. Two field workers, both graduate engineers, returned from a 6-month assignment at a PERT-run TRADEX project on Kwajalein. They had had no PERT training prior to the job and saw no value in the PERT plan furnished to them during it although they were required to make weekly progress reports based upon the PERT schedule. When asked how they had been able to do this without utilizing the PERT plan, they said they had kept two sets of books—one to build by, the other to report by. Both were capable engineers. Their negative reactions to PERT techniques stemmed from not having participated in the plan preparation and from a lack of training in PERT.

Owners' Reactions

The reactions of owners to CPM are usually favorable. One refinery manager noted that his own people always furnish straight answers—if *he* asks the right questions. Through CPM he got comprehensive daily CPM reports during a turnaround. Without CPM, owners usually get very little useful progress information. One has said that job meetings without CPM are long on talk and short on information. *With* CPM, however, he noted, the trend is completely reversed, primarily because CPM helps guide the discussion to specific real problems instead of allowing it to drift toward generalities. This particular owner is an unusually capable administrator and has learned much about problems in practical school construction methods. He used a CPM consulting service to monitor the progress of the CPM plan on one project. However, he kept in daily touch with the project, CPM computer run in hand. He expected good information from CPM but he did not see it as a panacea for all the problems the project might generate.

In the early days of CPM application, it was often dismaying to find computer runs left unopened in the owner's office. Owners have become more conversant with CPM since those days, and CPM consultants have matured too. It is now realized that it was not enough to furnish raw computer runs to the owner. A natural step in management by exception is for the CPM planner to analyze each computer run, summarize its results, and prepare a narrative report that is supplied to the owner.

One owner questioned the value of updating when, for 6 months, CPM just confirmed that his project was on schedule. Then in the seventh month he delayed deciding on the color of the brickwork. Since masonry was on the critical path, the owner himself was now delaying the project. His decision, and the delivery of the off-shade brick he chose, took 5 weeks. This was a clear-cut delay. Now that the CPM shoe was on his own foot, he developed a better appreciation of the meaning of the term "critical path." He also found that delays on the critical path cannot be buried when the project is being monitored regularly.

At a job meeting for another project, the contractors let out a good-natured whoop when the CPM consultant (retained by the owner) announced that the owner and the architect had moved onto the critical path. (The decision required from the owner and shop drawings needed from the architect were delivered posthaste.)

The chief of construction for a nationwide corporation declined to discuss using CPM with the author and his associates. He said that he had his own method of meeting completion dates which had never failed. We were intrigued about this method, of course. He confided that he started each project 1 year earlier than he thought he had to. While this may ensure timeliness, it is certainly an expensive approach which we do not believe will displace CPM as a planning and scheduling technique.

Contractors' Reactions

One macho construction superintendent on a Chicago high rise said that CPM was probably okay for planning anything "except sex and construction." Other, more progressive contractors, have been willing to use new tools to meet the challenges of construction, recognizing that the planning techniques of the early 1900s do not suit the competitive needs of today's construction industry. And still many others have backed into an acquaintance with CPM. Some were forced to use CPM or PERT on government projects. Others originally agreed to use CPM as a form of status symbol to demonstrate their progressiveness. However, as CPM has become better known through publications and orientation courses held by organizations such as the Association of General Contractors (AGC), there has been less need for contractors to come to CPM through the back door.

At the end of a project it is difficult to identify exactly how much CPM has improved its completion dates or reduced its costs. It is also difficult to speculate objectively what you might have done wrong in the course of it. But once you have established the best approach to a project through CPM, the plan will be sensible and realistic. It may well be the same plan you would have followed without CPM. However, without CPM, any plan will be made week to week, and long-range decisions and orders for materials cannot be based upon it. Planning *with* CPM is like forecasting a company's annual budget so that, based upon the predicted cash flow, policy decisions can be made. Planning *without* CPM is like running a company with no budget or planned financial policy—it operates out of its checkbook, and if that should run dry because of an unnecessary peaking of expenses, the company is out of business.

One general contractor who has a medium-sized company, after 20 years of pushing projects in the field, has changed his outlook. While he still appreciates that the actual construction of a project is of prime importance, he now realizes that his profit is made or lost in the office support of the field effort. He has moved inside to coordinate material, equipment, and subcontracts for the projects his company undertakes. He sees CPM as the tool that enables him to exercise close control over more projects with greater effectiveness.

Architects' Reactions

Architects play a significant role in much of the nation's construction work. What has been their reaction to CPM? Many architects have nothing to react to; that is, they are not familiar with the technique. CPM's beginnings in the petrochemical industry and PERT's military beginnings may originally have acted as buffers between architects and the techniques. But this situation is reversing and architects are becoming increasingly involved with CPM. In most cases, this involvement has resulted from owner-furnished CPM services on particular projects. In others, the architect has been the leader in bringing CPM into the project picture.

PROBLEMS RELATED TO APPLYING CPM

During the early PERT years, the federal government established a PERT coordinating group. In the government's words: "The PERT coordinating group has been established to both develop and continuously improve a PERT system that is uniform and promotes better decision-making processes." The group was made up of representatives from the major federal departments, with particular emphasis on the Department of Defense and NASA, and was a committee type of operation vested with no official powers but wielding considerable power informally. The group issued, with considerable candor, a discussion of the problems associated with implementing and operating both the PERT and PERT/Cost systems. As many of those problems also relate to nonaerospace systems, including CPM, the following six problems cited in regard to implementation are listed here:

1. Lack of management support and participation
2. Failure to organize for PERT/Cost implementations
3. Faulty interpretation of PERT/Cost guidance documents
4. Failure to integrate existing systems fully with PERT/Cost
5. Narrow scope and slow pace of PERT/Cost implementation
6. Incompatibility of contract items with program elements

EXTENT OF CPM UTILIZATION

PERT has been used on, and in fact had its inception because of, major construction programs. After the Polaris project, many of the major NASA missile programs leading to the Apollo launch used PERT, and eventually CPM.

An early (1965) survey on CPM and PERT use by the magazine *Building Construction* reported on 500 firms, among which were (although not in equal numbers) architects, engineers, contractors, and package designer-builders. About 25 percent of the architects were using CPM to plan their projects and another 25 percent were seriously considering its use. Half of the engineers were currently using CPM or PERT to plan work and another 25 percent were expecting to use CPM sometime. Among the contractors, about 60 percent were currently using CPM, many in combination with their standard bar-graphing techniques. All parties to the survey agreed that more systematized specifications and standards for CPM use would be helpful. The consensus was that better planning could result in a time savings averaging between 5 and 7 percent during the construction phase of projects.

An even earlier survey concentrating on 500 contractors was conducted by *Construction Equipment and Materials,* but a correlation of CPM use by contractors between that survey and the one conducted by *Building Construction* was not readily apparent. Only a small percentage of the 500 contractors indicated they were using CPM currently, and only 25 percent were interested in a better means of planning. The difference between the results of the two surveys was probably due to the fact that 89 percent of the 500 firms questioned in the first survey were doing less than $1 million per year each in business. Thus those that did indicate CPM use were in the minority percent-wise but they may well have been performing the majority of construction work throughout the country. Among the contractors indicating they did use CPM, 65 percent were generally satisfied with it as a planning technique and 25 percent were very satisfied. Only 10 percent were in any way dissatisfied.

Still a third survey was conducted in 1970 by the Harvard Business School, and its results again did not exactly correlate with either of the other two surveys. Some typical comments furnished as concomitants to the Harvard survey included:

"CPM—excellent in owner, architect, contractor teamwork to produce a finished product. CPM can be abused by any one of the three by either lack of understanding or superior ability in use of this method."

"CPM is excellent. We used it on a large complicated structure after the construction started. It assisted us in rescheduling certain trades to complete the building on schedule. It primarily forces the individual to think through the processes and set up reasonable time factors."

"CPM applied to a large terminal project brought to our attention several critical points which had been overlooked in bar graph scheduling."

"If management takes the pains to develop a reasonably accurate CPM network before a project is well under way, and then files it in the wastebasket, they have already gained two-thirds of the benefit to be derived from CPM. This is true simply because they had to think out the project to draw the network. . . ."

SUMMARY

Most of those owners, contractors, engineers, and architects who have used CPM find it a definite advantage. A key factor in all successful applications is personnel training from field worker up to company president. CPM does provide the means to better planning. This is most evident just after the initial working plan has been pulled together.

CASE HISTORIES

After more than 25 years of experience with CPM, there are thousands of case histories which could be recounted. Many are unavailable because of the proprietary nature of the information involved. In the past decade, the increase in construction litigation has dampened the willingness to release scheduling data.

Some of the case histories memorialize early network applications. In the first 10 years of network use, successful case histories were like foundation stones in building the credibility of the approach.

In one application, the Bureau of Labor utilized networks to plan the publication of annual statistical results. The first computation of the plan showed a critical path of 420 days, which was 50 percent longer than the target schedule. A study of the critical path indicated that more than 25 percent of the time was absorbed by the interdepartmental mail system. Through revisions in planning (and upgrading of the internal mail delivery system) a 269-day work schedule was achieved.

CHICAGO CIVIC CENTER

The Chicago Civic Center was completed in the mid-1960s at a cost of $87 million, of which $64 million was spent on construction. It benefited from several CPM applications. The owner prepared a CPM master plan to determine schedule feasibility, and this plan estimated that a general contract award on the date scheduled could not be completed on schedule unless steel was provided to the general contractor. By acting on this prediction, the field work did top out on time.

CHICAGO COURT HOUSE

Network planning was used by Paschen Contractors, Inc., in the building of a $32 million court house and federal office building in Chicago (Paschen had also used PERT in its work on the foundations of the Chicago Civic Center). The company worked with seventeen major subcontractors to develop the basic network for the court house. The immediate benefit was a better understanding on the part of the subcontractors about their responsibilities. An example of the effectiveness of the planning involves the elevators and the power transformers needed for them. The power company had planned to use the elevators to hoist the power transformers to the roof; meanwhile, the elevator company was depending on the same transformers already being installed in order to operate the elevators. It also became apparent from an analysis of the network that while steel erection was on the critical path, pouring the concrete floors was only 2 weeks behind that activity on a near critical path. Accordingly, any time gained in steel erection had to be carefully compared with the progress in floor pouring. The planning group made up a detailed network for carrying out structural work on the basement and nine of the thirty floors in the building, and that was sufficient to provide detailed plans for the remaining twenty-one floors.

TIMES TOWER

The total renovation of the historic New York Times building for use by the Allied Chemical Corporation was performed with the use of a detailed CPM plan consisting of 1200 separate activities. Allied decided to remodel a 60-year-old building rather than build a new one since, under the New York City building and zoning regulations, a new building on the site would have been limited to twelve stories rather than the existing twenty-three. The total renovation consisted of a complete strip-down to the basic steel framework and then a rebuilding, retaining many of the famous features of the landmark. The contractor, Crow Construction Company, made direct use of CPM planning. Construction equipment, workers, materials, and all work-vehicle flow had to operate without interrupting the steady flow of pedestrians and city traffic at one of the busiest intersections in the world. CPM was a factor in the timely completion of the project.

TELEPHONE EXPANSION

AT & T required CPM planning for constructing many of its relay stations across the country. The actual CPM plan was prepared by the individual contractor for each relay station, and AT & T was able to utilize the similarities between the plans to evaluate the feasibility of each schedule, as well as to point out problems common to many of the projects.

SAN FRANCISCO REDEVELOPMENT

The Golden Gate redevelopment project in the heart of San Francisco included nine major structures, and many town houses and parking areas as well. The work was done in four 22-month phases and was under the direction of Perini Construction Company, which was represented on both the ownership and the construction teams. The overall development was initially planned with the aid of CPM. Detailed studies were made of certain specific work areas such as the roles that would be played by climbing cranes, special formwork, and precast elements.

Using the plan, Perini was able to deliver a floor about every fifth day, the key to the overall progress being the availability of four special tower cranes which were worked concurrently. Since the site had almost no storage space available, material was scheduled to be picked right off delivery trucks and hoisted to the proper site location. There was almost no backlog of either delivery trucks or major stored material.

In a more recent redevelopment project, the George R. Moscone Convention Center (originally started as the Yerba Buena Redevelopment Project), Perini was again one of the contractors. This $130 million project used CPM networks to plan and monitor the work of many contractors during its two-phase development. Networks were on two levels, one for lead prime contractors, and the other for the overall construction manager, Turner Construction Company. The city used O'Brien-Kreitzberg & Associates (OKA) as the project manager to monitor networks at all levels.

AIRPORT CONSTRUCTION

Highway and pipeline projects depend upon the effective utilization of resources for timely completion. Building projects, on the other hand, rely more on the sequencing of work activities within the confined areas of the building(s) being constructed. Airports offer problems in both areas and CPM has been utilized very successfully in regard to them.

During the early 1970s, many major airport construction programs made use of network analysis and control in one form or another, including both the Philadelphia and Pittsburgh International Airports. Another successful application had to do with the expansion of a runway for the Allegheny County Airport in Pennsylvania. The 2-year period project was completed in 18 months, not only because of the effective use that was made of CPM to identify opportunities for saving time, but also because of the contributions to the CPM plan made by the balanced team of owner, contractor, and project manager and their thoughtful use of the CPM results.

The project consisted of a 1000-foot extension to the main runway, complicated by the presence of a four-lane highway, three railroad tracks, and a ravine more than 100 feet deep in the path of the extension. A rigid-frame, concrete underpass, 144 feet wide by 828 feet long, was constructed to house the highway and the railroad tracks. Approximately 1 million yards of embankment were used to fill in the ravine area. The general contractor, W. P. Dickerson, actively cooperated in the CPM planning and the implementation of the CPM plan, cooperation that was most important to the success of the operation.

CPM established a target date of December 9 for completion of the underpass, with actual completion occurring on December 23. This completion was a key activity since its success ensured that work on the project could continue through the winter. The second most critical activity was the relocation of four phases of the Union Railroad track, which was completed 5 days ahead of the CPM target date. Then, utilizing CPM, the CM and the contractor were able to coordinate the manufacture and delivery of precast, prestressed, concrete beams after an initial analysis indicated that construction would be delayed by the lack of those beams. The contractor studied his precast plant facilities and indicated a willingness to expand them if the county would pay for the inventory of the beams. The county agreed that having the beams available to meet the schedule requirements was important, and underwrote the inventory costs so that the supplier was indeed able to meet the construction schedule.

CPM was also utilized to evaluate the effects on meeting the schedule of a number of other considerations including relocation of a graveyard, securing additional foundation material, substituting foundation materials, and a strike. In some cases the CPM analysis indicated how measures to expedite could be undertaken, while in others it pointed out that a slower timing than originally hoped for would have to be accepted.

The major vertical structural members of the tunnel required bracing during curing and prior to the pouring of the tunnel's roof. CPM was used to plan the entire forming, pouring, and stripping sequence of activities, and to evaluate special bracing equipment required to expedite the entire operation and ensure its completion on time. Following the information on bracing that CPM provided, the contractor ordered additional braces, which permitted the pouring of the tunnel's roof to proceed as originally scheduled. In the end, the contract was completed fully 6 months early.

The contractor hired to install a new fueling system at JFK International Airport in 1963 was required by the New York Port Authority to use CPM in planning the project. But the construction application was dropped when the CPM consultant to the Port Authority advised that the contractor's CPM plan did not match the field realities. The same consultant later employed CPM to reconstruct an as-built schedule which was used to settle major delay claims (see Chapter 22 for a discussion of "as-built" plans).

CPM was used extensively in the expansion of the Philadelphia International Airport that was undertaken from 1969 to 1976. It also figured in claims and litigation regarding delays in the project.

CPM was also used in the expansion of the Atlanta, Denver, Tampa, and Orlando airports.

At the San Francisco International Airport, the final $200 million phase of the current Modernization and Replacement (M & R) Program involves demolishing some outdated terminal facilities, remodeling others, and building new terminal facilities while the airport operates at full capacity.

The M & R Program consists of seven major construction contracts each in the $10 to $40 million range, and approximately 60 small construction contracts, each costing less than $5 million. The small projects include demolition, apron paving, and setting up interim facilities for various airlines. The larger projects include new aircraft boarding areas, a new international terminal with customs facilities and a control tower, a new terminal connector building with roof-top parking, and the remodeling of two-thirds of the existing terminal complex.

The work is under the direction of Jason G. Yuen, AIA (Administrator, Bureau of Terminal Construction), and OKA is providing CPM scheduling, both for the prebid stage and during construction.

HIGH-RISE CONSTRUCTION

High-rise contractors have utilized CPM both to study the activities required on a single typical floor, and to correlate this in summary fashion for work to be carried out on all the floors. The Chicago Marina City Towers constructed by the James McHugh Construction Company used CPM in planning and constructing the two sixty-story towers, including twenty commercial and parking floors. Initially a detailed critical path diagram was developed for a typical floor. This was used to study what the rest of the project would require, and it was decided to complete the first few floors at the rate of one per week, later accelerating to two and a half floors per week in the east tower and two per week in the west. The complete activity range was regenerated at the detailed level for all of the project, and resulted in a network of 9600 activities, which was used successfully.

The use of CPM for Detroit's twin Lafayette Towers permitted a schedule improvement of 1 month despite a 7-week strike shutdown. This twin twenty-two-story apartment building used tower cranes placed in the elevator shafts, and supplementary hoisting equipment as indicated by the CPM plan. A 4-day cycle for each floor was developed by means of the CPM study. The contractor, A. J. Etkin, estimated the job time was reduced by 20 percent and the direct payroll by 5 percent by following CPM recommendations.

In another high-rise building in the Bronx, the superstructure was on the critical path, which is a usual situation. Through intensive coordination, the contractor was able to achieve a 3-day pouring cycle per floor. As the project progressed, this cycle was cut to an almost unbelievable 2 days. However, in concentrating the supervision on this reduction of time spent on superstructure work, the plumbing riser work which followed became critical. CPM highlighted the need to push the riser work, and if this had not been noted, the 2-day cycle achieved for superstructure work would have had little effect upon the completion date since the riser work cycle was still at 3 days.

In Phoenix, Arizona, the Mardian Construction Company has used CPM scheduling for all its projects, but in particular for apartment buildings. One of the projects was a twenty-two-story Executive Towers apartment building in which concrete framing was completed in less than 88 days, with the superintendent contributing much of the success to CPM planning. The prime factor was the development of a feasible forming system and the choice of a tower crane as a result of early CPM planning. One floor was scheduled in great detail, and then the information was recycled for the rest of the high rise. Close monitoring of the project resulted in a reduction of the basic floor cycle from 4 to 3 days, but the CPM plan demonstrated that the shoring required to continue this phase was uneconomical, so the 4-day schedule was reinstated.

In Philadelphia, the Arthur A. Kober Company, a developer-builder, collaborated with OKA to develop a CPM schedule for its $35 million Academy House Condominium.

This thirty-seven-story high rise, including three subsurface levels for parking, was built on a congested urban site. The structure was of reinforced concrete, with a brick exterior. The foundation work was complicated by the need to underpin and brace adjoining structures including the historic Academy of Music.

The upper thirty floors were residences, and apartment color and material selections were coordinated with the construction schedule.

The public areas, except for the condominium service portion, were shelled, and the work leapfrogged up the structure into the living units. Every tenth floor housed temporary shops, and two cranes were utilized.

NASA

Network analysis was used in all the major contracts awarded for work on and at the Apollo launch complex at Cape Canaveral, and for similar space-project contracts awarded earlier and later.

The level of detail used in those network systems varied, as did the forms of the networks. One of the major applications was under the direction of the Corps of Engineers, Canaveral District, and included the review of independent contractors' networks and the correlation of this information into a master analysis network for the Vertical Assembly Building (VAB) and related facilities used for the Saturn program.

The approach was to require both systems and construction contractors to provide network schedules. In turn, both NASA and the Canaveral District Corps of Engineers (under Major General W. L. Starnes) used network-based PMIS systems to monitor and evaluate the network input from the contractors.

In the Saturn program, an unused launch complex control room was turned into a war room (later dubbed the "moon room") displaying the many contractors' networks at various levels of detail.

The use of networks to plan and control space programs has become routine procedure for most projects, including the space shuttle.

HOUSING

CPM was used by the Rouse Company to plan the engineering and site development phases in the building of the new town of Columbia, Maryland. Activities relating to grading, sewers, water, electrical service lines, and paving were coordinated to deliver entirely developed areas ready for housing construction to major contractors for the construction and eventual sale of individual houses. CPM was also used to plan the building of the town center, an engineered lake, and the sewer and water utility connections to service the first completed part of the town.

CPM was credited with the on-time delivery of 300 duplex housing units for a Navy housing project at the naval station in Rota, Spain. The CPM diagram was developed by considering more than 3100 required operations, including not only the prefabrication of the housing units, but the distribution of available work force and equipment resources, as well as activities relating to site preparation, utilities, roads, and foundations. The plan included a sewage station and distribution system and was used to determine the basic field crew size needed to erect prefab units most efficiently. The crew size decided upon was 12 workers, including a superintendent, a crane operator, a rigger, an electrician, and a plumber. The study also helped in the selection of equipment such as air-powered hammers (the need for which was determined after it was pointed out that 5000 nails per duplex would be used). Stateside fabrication speeded up operations by premanufacturing 80 percent of the buildings.

MANUFACTURING FACILITIES

Butler Manufacturing used network techniques for planning the construction of a 95,000-square-foot plant in Knoxville, Tennessee, which had to be completed within 20 weeks. The preplanning by the owner indicated that deliveries from a sole source would materially shorten the implementation period, and used this as a basis for justifying the sole source purchase of the Butler building. Complete sections of the building were prefabricated and organized as units and zone-delivered to the site. The design development identified the need for twenty-six cranes, and these were added without a delay of even 1 day.

Another major systems facility delivered for partial occupancy within 6 months was a 300,000-square-foot building in Georgia developed for use by Lockheed in constructing its C5A transport plane. The design was carried out by the Atlanta-based firm of Heery and Heery, which had previously used CPM to complete the Atlanta Braves stadium on time. In this case, a different form of preplanning was utilized. The architect-engineers drew on the preplanned Inland modular systems' design which had been developed as part of the School Construction System Development (SCSD) in California. The system was based on a predesigned 4-foot-square horizontal module including structural and ceiling lighting systems.

IBM has required the use of CPM techniques in the planning of its various manufacturing and office facilities for many years. IBM's facilities management group, located in Westchester County, New York, has used CPM planning to plan and monitor the company's building programs nationwide for more than 15 years.

CBS Records was proceeding with design of a plant at a new site to manufacture and distribute records and tapes. Because of the close integration needed between the manufacturing/processing and storage equipment to be used at the facility with the plant's construction requirements, CBS Facilities Engineering decided to develop a CPM network covering the various equipment development/design/procurement lead times and decision points. A detailed CPM network illustrated the various actions required and their interfaces with the design process for constructing the facility by the outside designers.

General Electric's aerospace division at Valley Forge, Pennsylvania, used CPM plans to monitor the performance of developers and contractors in the delivery of more than twenty facilities at the height of this nation's aerospace programs. In addition to requiring contractor networks, facilities manager John D. Orr had in-house training seminars for his facilities engineering staff. (Organizations such as Corning Glass, Celanese, and many others have used the in-house seminar approach either to introduce or to revitalize CPM planning for facilities.)

CPM PREPARATION TIME

Experience in time versus size of networks cannot be considered a definitive guide as to how long it might take to prepare a network. Nor does quantity ensure quality. However, case histories are useful for reference:

CASE A: NASA MISSILE LAUNCH SITE UTILITY SYSTEM
          COST: $10 million
          CONSTRUCTION TIME: 6 months
          CLIENT: Contractor (prebid) who was concerned about the short construction period and the high liquidated damages ($5000 per day)
          PLANNING APPROACH: Executive (contractors, estimator, project engineer, and CPM consultant)
          RESULTS: A network of 900 arrows. The preparation for the computation phase took about 70 hours of team time. This was a produc-

tion of about thirteen arrows per hour. However, this particular network was deliberately condensed in portions so that work force studies could be applied. In perhaps 80 hours, a 1600-activity network could have been developed.

CASE B: CONSTRUCTION OF A NEW HOSPITAL AND DEMOLITION OF THE OLD HOSPITAL
COST: $5 million
CONSTRUCTION TIME: 24 months
CLIENT: General contractor who wanted a good construction schedule to ensure completion on time
PLANNING APPROACH: Executive (contractors, superintendent, project engineer, and CPM consultant)
RESULTS: About 104 team-hours were used in preparing a 1200-arrow network. This was an arrow production of about thirteen arrows per hour.

CASE C: HIGH-RISE APARTMENT (FORTY STORIES)
COST: $16 million
CONSTRUCTION TIME: 14 months
CLIENT: Owner-builder
PLANNING APPROACH: Executive (owner's assistant, superintendent, and CPM consultant)
RESULTS: 1500-arrow diagram was completed in 5 weeks, a production rate of about eight arrows per hour. Here is a case where the fallacy of an arrow production rate is evident. The diagram for the forty similar floors was based upon a detailed study of a typical floor. This typical floor had 150 activities and connections. Multiplied by forty floors, this could easily have been converted into a 6000-arrow network. This would have been a nominal arrow production rate of thirty arrows per hour. However, the resulting information would have been overwhelming in its detail.

CASE D: HIGH SCHOOL
COST: $5 million
CONSTRUCTION TIME: 16 months
CLIENT: School Board
PLANNING APPROACH: Executive (CPM consultant worked directly with the major contractors' superintendents to prepare networks)
RESULTS: The 1200-arrow diagram was prepared in 4 weeks, a production rate of about eight arrows per hour.

CASE E: AIRPORT FUEL DISTRIBUTION SYSTEM
COST: $15 million
CONSTRUCTION TIME: 24 months
CLIENT: Owner
PLANNING APPROACH: Contractors' staff planning group
RESULTS: Diagram of about 3200 activities took more than 16 weeks to prepare. The arrow production rate was five arrows per hour. In this case, the results unfortunately did not justify the deliberation implied in the slower network preparation time.

CASE F: CITY PLANNING STUDY
          COST: $900,000
          PROJECT TIME: 24 months
          CLIENT: City Planning Group
          PLANNING APPROACH: Conference (group of six to eight key people and
             CPM consultant)
          RESULTS: The 400-arrow diagram took about 10 team-days to pre-
             pare. The rate of five arrows per hour does not give an indication of
             the excellent results achieved through the conferences.

CASE G: OIL REFINERY TURNAROUND
          COST: $2 million
          DOWN TIME: 7 weeks
          CLIENT: Refinery
          PLANNING APPROACH: Conference (group of about ten people when
             discussing boiler overhaul; the group was reduced to six when dis-
             cussing more routine overhaul work)
          RESULTS: The 1200-arrow diagram took about 3 team-weeks to pre-
             pare. This was a production rate of ten arrows per hour. The careful
             planning resulted in less equipment downtime.

CASE H: COLLEGE
          COST: $10 million
          CONSTRUCTION TIME: 18 months
          CLIENT: Owner
          PLANNING APPROACH: Consultant (this network was prepared in the
             pre-award period to establish realistic completion date)
          RESULTS: 600-arrow diagram required 5 weeks to prepare, a rate of
             three arrows per hour.

In comparing arrow production rates, do not lose sight of their significance. The preparation of the initial network falls into two phases. The
first is the collection of information and the preparation of the rough diagram. The second is the conversion of the rough diagram into smooth
form and the review of this finished diagram. The conference members
are needed primarily in the first phase. To achieve an overall arrow rate
of ten arrows per hour means averaging twenty per hour in the first phase
and a like rate in the second phase. Figure 19.1 shows a plot of arrow
production versus network size for the case histories given above.

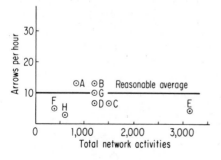

Figure 19.1 Arrow production versus network size. A, NASA utilities; B, hospital; C, high-rise apartment building; D, high school; E, airport fuel distribution system; F, city planning; G, oil refinery; H, college.

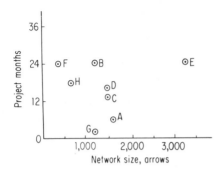

Figure 19.2 Project life versus number of arrows. A, NASA utilities; B, hospital; C, high-rise apartment building; D, high school; E, airport fuel distribution system; F, city planning; G, oil refinery; H, college.

The following general observations can be made:

1. An arrow production rate of ten arrows per hour is a reasonable average rate.

2. As the level of detail in the network increases, the arrow production rate tends to increase.

3. For research work or unusual projects, the arrow production rate tends to decrease.

4. The arrow production rate is unrelated to the network size.

Figure 19.2 shows a plot of calendar time for the case histories given above versus their network sizes which indicates no relationship between network size and project duration. However, it should be noted that there *is* some relationship—it is just obscured by other factors.

SUMMARY

The size of a useful network is almost unlimited. Network analysis is usually a must in projects valued over $5 million; however, it can also be useful in less expensive projects. CPM often exposes undefined planning factors. The trend is to apply CPM after the award of contract. However, this is not a hard and fast rule. Network analysis done prior to award of contract can provide better construction schedule requirements, and CPM can also be applied profitably after construction work has started.

Phase 1 of the network preparation is the collection of information and the concurrent preparation of a rough diagram. The information collection can be made by any of four approaches: conference, executive, consultant, or staff planning. The second phase of the network preparation is the rearrangement and redrawing of the rough version into a smooth form.

In any approach, it is vital that the plan reflect the real plans of the contractor.

Subcontractors perform many critical work functions. Their information must also be incorporated into the network.

It is difficult to set definite time requirements for the preparation of a network. Familiar projects can be diagramed more quickly than unfamiliar ones and noncomplex projects more quickly than complex ones.

CPM *seems* to require more time than traditional planning, but only because with CPM techniques planning is done in more depth.

20

SPECIFYING CPM

Specification of a service, such as CPM, is usually the owner's problem. If a contractor decides to use CPM, but is not required to, there is no question of specification if the contractor can provide the service. However, most contractors find the use of outside assistance cost-effective. And when they do employ consultants, they stand in the shoes of the owner in terms of needing a means of describing the scope of the service. Furthermore, if a general or prime contractor decides to use CPM, the contractor again assumes the role of owner as described in this chapter.

STANDARD REFERENCES

The easiest way to specify the use of CPM would be to invoke standard references of the type prepared by ASTM (American Society for Testing and Materials) or ANSI (American National Standards Institute). And since ASTM, as its name implies, deals with testing and materials, ANSI would be the more likely source. The British counterpart of ANSI has published a standard on networks. Moreover, two separate ANSI subcommittees have worked on a similar project over a long period of time and draft material has been published. However, the usefulness of the British standard or the draft material as a reference for specification would be limited because they provide an even-handed description of networks— so much so that they do not select or specify one single method of application. And even the use of this book as a standard would suffer from the same characteristic of providing a broad description of various alternative routes to the implementation of CPM rather than concentrating on any one preferred method (unless reference was limited to Chapters 1 through 7).

One book which was written with a single focus can serve to describe or specify CPM as used by the general contractor: *CPM in Construction: A Manual for General Contractors.* This 127-page work, first published in 1965, was authored by Glenn L. White under the direction of an Associated General Contractors of America (AGC) committee, and was published by AGC. It provided a clear description of CPM theory and technique and stopped short of describing methods and philosophies of application of the technique. Accordingly, it provided a good common reference.

The Use of CPM in Construction, again authored by Glenn L. White and published by AGC in 1976, combined White's *CPM in Construction* and a later work, *Cost Control and CPM in Construction.* This 192-page volume added a discussion not only of cost but also of more advanced applications, different network techniques, and application philosophies. It is inherently AGC-oriented, but is basically even-handed. It should be noted that the glossary of the 1965 work defined the term "total float" but the glossary of the 1976 book omits that very important term while introducing a new one described as "relative float."

Another standard which has evolved is the U.S. Army Corps of Engineers reference regulation ER-1-1-11, titled *Network Analysis System,* which is used by the Corps as a reference standard when they specify network scheduling. This document has evolved over 20 years. It describes network theory and technique and leaves the method of application to the particular specification.

CPM BY CONTRACTOR

Federal agencies set the pattern for specifying the application of CPM by the contractor. Since this approach is essentially purchasing scheduling services from the contractor, the owner must carefully and completely spell out the scope of what is wanted. The Corps of Engineers has incorporated the requirement of using CPM for many projects into a specification section in the Special Provisions part of its regulation; this section often reads similarly for all projects, but can be tailored specifically to each one. One such example is given here:

SP-4.   CONTRACTOR-PREPARED NETWORK ANALYSIS SYSTEM:
The progress chart to be prepared by the contractor pursuant to the General Provisions entitled "Progress Charts and Requirements for Overtime Work" shall consist of a network analysis system as described below. In preparing this system the scheduling of construction is the responsibility of the contractor. The requirement for the system is included to assure adequate planning and execution of the work and to assist the Contracting Officer in appraising the reasonableness of the proposed schedule and evaluating progress of the work.

a. *An example* of one of the numerous acceptable types of network analysis systems is shown in Appendix I of Corps of Engineers Regulation ER-1-1-11 entitled "Network Analysis System," single copies of which are available to bona fide bidders on request. Other systems which are designed to serve the same purpose and employ the same basic principles as are illustrated in Appendix I will be accepted subject to the approval of the Contracting Officer.

b. The system shall consist of diagrams and accompanying mathematical analyses. The diagrams shall show elements of the project in detail and the entire project in summary.

(1) Diagrams shall show the order and interdependence of activities and the sequence in which the work is to be accomplished as planned by the contractor. The basic concept of a network analysis diagram will be followed to show how the start of a given activity is dependent on the completion of preceding activities and its completion restricts the start of following activities.

(2) Detailed network activities shown on a detailed or sub-network diagram shall include, in addition to construction activities, the submittal and approval of samples or materials and shop drawings, the procurement of critical material and equipment, fabrication of special materials and equipment and their installation and testing, and delivery of Government-Furnished Property primary priority by scheduled late delivery and secondary priority by scheduled early delivery. The network diagrams shall contain a minimum of one activity showing scheduled dates (early and late) for each delivery of major elements of Government-Furnished Property (GFP) listed in Section 1B of these specifications, properly located to reflect the logical restraints to on-site activities. The description of each GFP delivery activity shall include the drawing reference, quantity of GFP items required for the activity and an adequate word description. All activities of the Government that affect progress, and contract required dates for completion, shall be such that duration times of activities will range from 3 to 30 days with not over 2 percent of the activities exceeding these limits. The selection and number of activities shall be subject to the Contracting Officer's approval. Detailed networks, when summary networks are also furnished, need not be time scaled but shall be drafted to show a continuous flow from left to right with no arrows from right to left. The following information shall be shown on the

diagrams for each activity: Preceding and following event numbers, description of the activity, cost, and activity duration. *The critical path shall be determined and shall be clearly indicated on the diagram.*

(3) Summary Network: If the project is of such size that the entire network cannot be readily shown on a single sheet, a summary network diagram shall be provided. The summary network diagram shall consist of a minimum of fifty activities and a maximum of one hundred. Related activities shall be grouped on the network. The critical path shall be plotted generally along the center of the sheet with channels with increasing float placed towards the top or bottom. The summary network shall be time scaled using units of approximately one half inch equals one week or other suitable scale approved by the Contracting Officer. Weekends and holidays shall be indicated. Where slack exists, the activities shall be shown at the time when they are scheduled to be accomplished.

(4) The mathematical analysis of the network diagram shall include a tabulation of each activity shown on the detailed network diagrams. The following information will be furnished as a minimum for each activity:

(a) Preceding and following event numbers. (Numbers shall be selected and assigned so as to permit identification of the activities with bid items.)

(b) Activity description.

(c) Estimated duration of activities (being the best estimate available at time of computation).

(d) Earliest start date (by calendar date).

(e) Earliest finish date (by calendar date).

(f) Scheduled or actual start date (by calendar date).

(g) Scheduled or actual finish date (by calendar date).

(h) Latest start date (by calendar date).

(i) Latest finish date (by calendar date).

(j) Slack or float.

(k) Monetary value of activity.

(l) Responsibility for activity (prime contractor, subcontractors, suppliers, Government, etc.).

(m) Manpower required.

(n) Percentage of activity completed.

(o) Contractor's earnings based on portion of activity completed.

(p) Bid item of which activity is a part.

(5) The program or means used in making the mathematical computation shall be capable of compiling the total value of completed and partially completed activities.

(6) In addition to the tabulation of activities the computation will include the following data:

(a) Identification of activities which are planned to be expedited by use of overtime or double shifts to be worked including Saturdays, Sundays and holidays.

(b) On-site manpower loading schedule.

(c) A description of the major items of construction equipment planned for operations of the project. The description shall include the type, number of units and unit capacities. A schedule showing proposed time equipment will be on the job keyed to activities on which equipment will be used and will be provided.

(d) Where portions of the work are to be paid by unit costs, the estimated number of units in an activity which was used in developing the total activity cost.

(7) The analysis shall list the activities in sorts of groups as follows:

(a) By the preceding event number from lowest to highest and then in the order of the following event number.

(b) By the amount of slack, then in order of preceding event number.

(c) By responsibility in order of earliest allowable start dates.

(d) In order of latest allowable start dates and then in order of preceding event numbers and then in order of succeeding event numbers.

c. Submission and approval of the system shall be as follows:

(1) A preliminary network defining the contractor's planned operations during the first 60 calendar days after Notice to Proceed shall be submitted within 10 days. The contractor's general approach for the balance of the project shall be indicated. Cost of activities expected to be completed or partially completed before submission and approval of the whole schedule shall be included.

(2) The complete network analysis consisting of the detailed network mathematical analysis (on-site manpower loading schedule, equipment schedule) and network diagrams shall be submitted within 40 calendar days after receipt of Notice to Proceed.

d. The contractor shall participate in a review and evaluation of the proposed network diagrams and analysis by the Contracting Officer. Any revisions necessary as a result of this review shall be resubmitted for approval of the Contracting Officer within 10 calendar days after the conference. The approved schedule shall then be the schedule to be used by the contractor for planning, organizing and directing the work and for reporting progress. If the contractor thereafter desires to make changes in his method of operating and scheduling he shall notify the Contracting Officer in writing stating the reasons for the change. If the Contracting Officer considers these changes to be of a major nature he may require the contractor to revise and submit for approval, without additional cost to the Government, all of the affected portion of the detailed diagrams and mathematical analysis and the summary diagram to show the effect on the entire project. A change may be considered of a major nature if the time estimated to be required or actually used for an activity or the logic of sequence of activities is varied from the original plan to a degree that there is reasonable doubt as to the effect on the contract completion date or dates. Changes which affect activities with adequate slack time shall be considered as minor changes, except that an accumulation of minor changes may be considered as a major change when their cumulative effect might affect the contract completion date.

e. The contractor shall submit at intervals of 30 calendar days a report of the actual construction progress by updating the mathematical analysis. Revisions causing changes in the detailed network shall be noted on the summary network, or revised issue of affected portions of the detailed network furnished. The summary network shall be revised as necessary for the sake of clarity. However, only the initial submission or complete revisions need be time scaled. Subsequent minor revisions need not be time scaled.

f. The report shall show the activities or portions of activities completed during the reporting period and their total value as basis for the contractor's periodic request for payment. Payment made pursuant to the General Provision entitled "Payments to Contractor" will be based on the total value of such activities completed or partially completed after verification by the Contracting Officer. The report will state the percentage of the work actually completed and scheduled as of the report date and the progress along the critical path in terms of the days ahead or behind the allowable dates. If the project is behind schedule, progress along other paths with negative slack shall also be reported. The contractor shall also submit a narrative report with the updated analysis which shall include but not be limited to a description of the problem areas, current and anticipated, delaying factors of their impact, and an explanation of corrective actions taken or proposed.

g. Sheet size of diagrams shall be 30″ by 42″. Each updated copy shall show a date of the late revisions.

h. Initial submittal and complete revisions shall be submitted in 6 copies.

i. Periodic reports shall be submitted in 4 copies.

j. The contractor shall maintain on the job site as part of his organization, a staff trained in the use and application of scheduling systems whose sole responsibility will be the monitoring of progress and providing computer input for updating the mathematic analysis and revising logic diagrams when necessary. The size of this staff will be subject to the approval of the Contracting Officer and will be supplemented at no additional cost to the Government if additional personnel are required by directive of the Contracting Officer.

k. When modifications in the work are found to be necessary, and Notice to Proceed with the changes must be issued prior to settlement of price and/or time to avoid delay and additional expense, the Contracting Officer will furnish the contractor, promptly thereafter, suggested changes in the network logic and/or duration time of all activities affected by the modifications. The contractor shall use the suggested logic and/or duration changes in updating network diagrams and machine printouts in subsequent required submittals; provided, however, that if the contractor has objections to any of the suggested logic and/or activity duration time changes he shall advise the Contracting Officer promptly, in writing, of such objections fully supported by his own counterplan; and provided further, that if the contractor does not submit such written objection and counterplan within thirty (30) days after the date of the Notice to Proceed with the modifications, the contractor will be deemed to have concurred in the Contracting Officer's suggested logic/duration time changes, which changes then will be the basis for any required equitable adjustment of the time for performance of the work.

l. Float or slack is defined as the amount of time between the early start date, and the late start date, or the early finish date, and the late finish date, of any of the activities in the NAS schedule. Float or slack is not time for the exclusive use or benefit of either the Government or the contractor. Extensions of time for performance required under the Contract General Provisions entitled, "CHANGES," "DIFFERING SITE CONDITIONS," "TERMINATION FOR DEFAULT—DAMAGES FOR DELAY—TIME EXTENSIONS" or "SUSPENSION OF WORK" will be granted only to the extent that equitable time adjustments for the activity or activities affected exceed the total float or slack along the channels involved.

m. In order to provide specific information for planning purposes, network analysis systems will clearly indicate the scheduled completion dates for the items of work listed below:

(At this point, the specification goes on to list project milestones.)

CPM BY CONSULTANT

CPM planning done through a consulting service requires an additional specification describing the scope of work to be accomplished by the CPM consultant. The scope proposed by the consultant is often incorporated as an appendix to the contract between the consultant and the owner. This practice is appropriate. In the early CPM period, many owners, at the suggestion of the consultants, used the same consultant-generated scope of work as the scheduling section of the construction contract. However, the consultant-authored scope of work is typically a very positive statement, appropriate between owner and consultant but definitely inappropriate between owner and contractor. It places the owner in the position of promising to provide definite services to the project, which means promises to provide the services to the contractor(s). If during the contract performance the owner decides for any reason to reduce or discontinue the CPM coverage, the change can be viewed as a breach of contract on the owner's part. Such a situation has been claimed in a number of claims/litigation cases. Clearly, the incorporation of the consultant's scope of work into the main contract between owner and contractor exposes the owner to a needless risk.

In some cases, the owner will issue a "Request for Proposal" (RFP), which includes a request for a description of the proposed scope of work. The following example is a CPM consultant scope-of-work specification issued by the federal General Services Administration (GSA) for a medical facility:

SCOPE OF SERVICES
A. General: CPM consultant services under this contract are requested for:
Construction Contract No. GS-OOB-01331,
Lister Hill National Biomedical
Communications Center, N.I.H., Bethesda,
Maryland.
Estimated Construction Completion Time: 900 calendar days

1. The Critical Path Method (CPM) consultant shall prepare and furnish a Postaward Construction Network Analysis including arrow diagrams and computer-produced schedules. Prebid services are not required in this contract. The CPM consultant shall develop a network plan indicating complete fulfillment of all proposed construction contract requirements. I-J technique shall be utilized. The principles and definitions of the terms used herein shall be as set forth in the associated General Contractors of America (AGC) publication "CPM in Construction, A Manual for General Contractors," Copyright 1965.

2. The CPM consultant shall:

a. Have a staff of two or more employees regularly engaged full time and skilled in the application of network techniques to construction projects valued at $1 million or more;

b. Possess or have access to a library of computer programs for production of schedules and cost reports;

c. Have computer facilities or access on short notice to computer facilities, and

d. Submit with his detailed price proposal the names, education and experience of the personnel he proposes to employ on the project. No subsequent substitution of personnel approved by the Government will be made without the written authorization of the Contracting Officer.

3. All consultation between the CPM consultant and the constructing contractor concerning the preparation of the construction network analysis including monthly updates shall be accomplished at the construction site. The CPM consultant shall work directly with the construction contractor at the construction site during the formation and finalization of the arrow diagram, and compilation of the arrow diagram supporting data as well as for each subsequent monthly update. Review and subsequent approval of the proposed plan and schedule as required by Paragraph C "Review and Approval," also will be performed at the construction site.

4. Within 2 months after the date of construction contract Notice to Proceed, the Critical Path Method (CPM) consultant shall prepare and submit for the Contracting Officer's review a Postaward Construction Network Analysis including arrow diagrams, computer-produced schedules, and computer-produced report sorts. The CPM consultant shall develop a network plan demonstrating the construction Contractor's plan for complete fulfillment of all construction contract requirements and keep the network plan up to date in accordance with the requirements of this contract.

B. INITIAL SUBMISSION: The CPM consultant shall submit for the Contracting Officer's review an arrow diagram describing the activities to be accomplished by the construction contractor and their dependency relationships together with a computer-produced schedule in accordance with the requirements listed below, showing starting and completion dates for each activity in terms of the number of days after receipt of Notice to Proceed. All completion dates shown shall be within the period specified for the contract completion.

1. Arrow Diagram Requirements. The arrow diagram shall show the sequence and interdependence of activities required for complete perfor-

mance of the construction contract. In preparing the arrow diagram, the CPM consultant, with assistance from the construction contractor, shall break up the work into activities of a duration of no longer than 15 working days each, except as to nonconstruction activities (such as procurement of materials, delivery of equipment, and concrete curing) and any other activities for which the Contracting Officer may approve the showing of longer duration. The diagram shall show not only the activities for actual construction work for each trade category of the project but also such activities as the construction contractor's work of submittal of shop drawings, equipment schedules, samples, coordination drawings, equipment schedules, samples, coordination drawings, templates, fabrication, delivery and the like, the Government's or Architect-Engineer's review and approval of shop drawings, equipment schedules, samples and templates, and the delivery of Government furnished equipment or partition drawings, or both. Activities related to a specified physical area of the project shall be activities grouped on the diagram for ease of understanding and simplification. Activity duration (i.e., the construction contractor's single best estimate, considering the scope of the activity and the resources planned for the activity) shall be shown for each activity on the diagram.

2. Arrow Diagram Supporting Data

a. The CPM consultant shall obtain from the construction contractor and furnish the following supporting data with the arrow diagram:

(1) Cost estimate for each activity which cumulatively equals the total contract cost. Estimated overhead and profit and the cost of bonds shall be prorated throughout all activities.

(2) Other data such as the proposed number of working days per week, the planned number of shifts per day, the number of hours per shift, and the usage on the site of major construction equipment.

b. The CPM consultant shall furnish with the arrow diagram, and each revision thereto, which affect contract time, cash flow curves in a suitable scale indicating graphically the total percentage of activity dollar value, scheduled to be in place based on both early and late finish dates.

c. Computer-Produced Schedule Requirements

(1) The CPM consultant shall furnish with the arrow diagram, and each revision thereof, a computer-produced schedule showing the following minimum data for each activity:

(a) Activity beginning event number
(b) Activity ending event number (optional with I-J techniques)
(c) Activity description
(d) Activity duration estimate
(e) Cost estimate
(f) Trade code
(g) Early start date—by calendar date
(h) Early finish date—by calendar date
(i) Late start date—by calendar date
(j) Late finish date—by calendar date
(k) Total float
(l) Status: critical or noncritical

(2) As a minimum, the following computer-produced report sorts of the basic activity data shall be supplied with clear identification on the first page of each report:

    (a) Activity listing by number sequence

    (b) Activity sort by total float

    (c) Activity sort by late finish date

C. REVIEW AND APPROVAL: Within ten calendar days after receipt of the initial arrow diagram and computer-produced schedule, the Contracting Officer shall meet with the construction contractor and the CPM consultant for joint review, correction, or adjustment of the proposed plan and schedule. Within five calendar days after the joint review, the CPM consultant shall revise the arrow diagram and the computer-produced schedule in accordance with agreements reached during the joint review and shall submit two copies each of the revised arrow diagrams and computer-produced schedule to the Contracting Officer. The resubmission will be reviewed by the Contracting Officer and, if found to be as previously agreed upon, will be approved. An approved copy of each will be returned to the CPM consultant. After the CPM consultant has received the approved copy of the arrow diagram and computer-produced schedule, he shall immediately substitute calendar dates on the computer-produced schedule in lieu of the number of days from the date of Notice to Proceed and shall furnish three copies each of the computer-produced schedule as thus revised and the arrow diagram to both the Contracting Officer and the construction contractor. The arrow diagram and the computer-produced schedule generated therefrom, as approved by the Contracting Officer, shall constitute the construction contractor's project work schedule until subsequently revised in accordance with the requirements of this contract.

D. PROGRESS REPORTING CHANGES:

1. Once each month (except for any month in which no changes have arisen) the CPM consultant shall meet with the construction contractor to obtain the information necessary for the CPM consultant to prepare and submit to the Contracting Officer within thirty working days after such meeting a revised arrow diagram showing all changes in network logic, including but not limited to changes in activity duration, revised activity cost estimates as the result of contract modifications, changes in activity sequence, and any changes in contract completion dates which have been made since the last revision of the arrow diagram. Where the Contracting Officer has not yet made a final decision as to the amount of time extension to be granted, and the construction contractor and the Contracting Officer are unable to agree as to the amount of the extension to be reflected in the arrow diagram, the CPM consultant shall reflect that amount of time extension in the arrow diagram as the Contracting Officer may determine, in his best judgment, to be appropriate for such interim purpose. After the Contracting Officer has made a final decision as to any time extension, the CPM consultant will revise the arrow diagram prepared thereafter in accordance with such decision.

2. Once each month, prior to the date specified by the Contracting Officer for submission of the updated computer-produced calendar-dated schedule, the construction contractor and the Contracting Officer shall jointly make

entries on the preceding computer-produced calendar-dated schedule to show actual progress, to identify those activities started and those completed during the previous period, to show the estimated time required to complete each activity started but not yet completed, and to reflect any changes in the arrow diagram approved in accordance with the preceding paragraph. After completion of the joint review and the Contracting Officer's approval of all entries, the CPM consultant shall submit an updated computer-produced calendar-dated schedule, in the detail specified herein under Computer-Produced Schedule Requirements, to the construction contractor and the Contracting Officer within three working days after such joint review but not later than the twenty-fifth day of the month.

3. In addition to the foregoing, the CPM consultant shall submit to the construction contractor and the Contracting Officer a narrative report once each month at the same time as the updated schedule required by the preceding paragraph in a form agreed upon by the CPM consultant and the Contracting Officer. The narrative report shall include a description of the amount of progress during the last month in terms of completed activities in the plan currently in effect, a description of problem areas, current and anticipated delaying factors and their estimated impact on performance of other activities and completion dates, and recommendations on corrective action for the construction contractor's consideration.

The construction specification section on scheduling should identify the fact that CPM will be used and clarify the role of the CPM consultant. The following example is taken from a New York State Dormitory Authority contract. Note that the contract language refers to an "Owner's Representative," which gives the owner the flexibility to utilize a CPM consultant, a design professional, a construction manager, or staff members to fulfill the owner's role.

.01 GENERAL

A Critical Path Method (hereinafter referred to as CPM) shall be used to schedule the progress and time fixed for completion of the work. This system shall be implemented by the Owner or the Owner's Representative. All work shall be done in accordance with CPM planning and scheduling and each contractor shall cooperate fully with the Owner's Representative.

.02 PRELIMINARY CPM PLAN AND SCHEDULE FOR CONSTRUCTION

A preliminary schedule for the Work, consisting of an arrow network diagram, is included in the contract for two (2) purposes:

A. To illustrate a feasible plan and schedule for completion of the Work on or before the completion date.

B. To provide bidders with an example of an arrow network diagram and computer printout schedule as an introduction to the CPM.

.03 PRE-BID MEETING

A pre-bid meeting shall be held approximately two (2) weeks prior to the bid date. The Owner or the Owner's Representative shall attend the pre-bid meeting and shall explain to all prospective bidders how CPM shall be implemented, shall answer questions about the planning and scheduling system and shall outline the cooperation that shall be required of the successful bidder in the development of the working CPM plan and schedule.

.04   PROJECT WORKING PLAN AND SCHEDULE

A. After the Contract has been executed by the contractor or a Notice to Proceed has been given to the contractor, whichever occurs first, the Owner or the Owner's Representative shall meet with the contractor to develop a comprehensive and detailed project working plan and schedule.

B. The project working plan and schedule shall be developed by the Owner or the Owner's Representative in the form of a CPM arrow network diagram. The contractor shall supply all information required by the Owner including but limited to the following: work activity descriptions; sequence of work; time estimates for the placing of orders for materials, submission of shop drawings, delivery of materials; all activities in connection with the work.

C. The arrow diagram shall represent the contractor's plan for the project. The contractor shall insure that all of the contractor's work is described by the arrow diagram and that the arrow diagram represents the sequence in which the contractor plans to do said contractor's work and the time in which the contractor expects to do said work.

D. Upon completion of the arrow diagram, the Owner's Representative shall make a computer calculation to forecast the duration of work under the contract. In the event the calculation indicates that the schedule exceeds the completion date required by the contract, the estimates used to develop the diagram shall be reviewed and revised. Additional computer calculations shall be made when necessary to adjust the arrow diagram to the completion date required by the contract.

E. When completed, the project plan and schedule shall be submitted by the Owner's Representative to the Owner for approval. The computer printout thereof shall show: job identification; job duration; job description; calendar dates for early start, early finish, late start and late finish for each job; the total float and the jobs critical to the completion of the work on schedule.

F. The contractor shall supply all information required by the Owner and Owner's Representative for the completion of the CPM plan and schedules no later than thirty (30) days after receipt by the contractor of Notice to Proceed or execution of the contract by the contractor, whichever comes first.

.05   PROJECT CONTROL AND UPDATING

A. The contractor shall be required to attend all scheduled meetings as directed by the Owner or the Owner's Representative for the purpose of expediting the work.

B. A computer calculation shall be made by the Owner's Representative to show how the changes or delays will affect the scheduled completion of the work. All corrective action to keep the work on schedule shall be performed immediately by the contractor as directed by the Owner or the Owner's Representative.

C. If it appears that the time of completion required by the contract shall not be met, then the sequence of the work shall be revised by the contractor and the Owner or the Owner's Representative until the schedule produced indicates that the time of completion required by the contract shall be met.

.06   TIME OF COMPLETION

Notwithstanding the implementation of the CPM, it is the sole responsibility of the contractor to complete the work within the time of completion required by the contract.

COMBINED APPROACH

The contractor preparation approach provides for the maximum contractor involvement in CPM planning. However, it also produces greater limitations and problems in the updating phase. The consultant preparation approach, conversely, produces good updating control, but involves less contractor input to the basic network.

The following was prepared by O'Brien-Kreitzberg & Associates for a city project as an example of how to maximize contractor input to the basic network while providing for good control in the updating phase.

PROGRESS PAYMENT AND PERFORMANCE SCHEDULE

DESCRIPTION

The contractor shall be responsible for the development of a construction schedule which shall provide a practical work plan under which the project shall be completed within the contractual time period, in accordance with the special sequences of work described in the Section "Summary of Work and Work Sequence" (including attached table).

The schedule must demonstrate the order and sequence of all significant work activities, including the interdependence between work activities. In addition to construction activities, the schedule must demonstrate recognition of the procurement of critical materials and equipment, fabrication of special materials and equipment, and provide a schedule of submittals of samples and/or shop drawings for equipment or materials which could have a schedule impact.

The schedule submitted shall be of a level of detail to assure adequate planning and execution of the work, and such that in the judgment of the Director it provides an appropriate basis for approval of the proposed schedule, and monitoring and evaluation of the progress of the work.

NETWORK ANALYSIS SYSTEM

The schedule, when submitted for approval, shall be in activity-on-arrow network analysis form. The specific networking procedures will be determined by the City, but will generally be in accordance with "CPM in Construction—A Manual for General Contractors" published by the AGC.

As described above, the contractor is responsible for the schedule content, and shall provide in a timely and convenient fashion all information regarding work operations, sequence of work, breakdown of the work into individual activities, and time estimates for these individual activities. The contractor shall also furnish a cost by activity. The contractor may use bar graphs, networks, sequence charts, and other graphic material to transfer information on schedule to the City.

The City will prepare the draft of the schedule for approval, and will also perform all data takeoff and computer operations.

After the Notice to Proceed has been given to the contractor, the City will meet with the contractor to start preparation of the network representation of the contractor schedule. It is anticipated that it will be necessary for this work to proceed concurrently with the contractor's finalization of his scheduling and cost information.

The network will show the sequence and interdependence of activities as planned by the contractor, and will be drafted to show a continuous flow from left to right, and will provide a logical representation of the work to be accomplished. It is anticipated that the work breakdown into activities will be such that the average activities will range from 3 to 30 days. Activities on the network will consist not only of the actual construction operations, but will also include shop drawing submittal, procurement of materials and equipment, installation and testing of major and/or critical items.

Within 30 days after Notice to Proceed, the contractor shall be responsible for the submittal of a preliminary performance schedule. This will be prepared from the same base material as the detailed schedule, and shall show the contractor's general approach to the overall project, with a detailed plan of mobilization, procurement, and construction during the first 90 calendar days. Preparation of the preliminary plan shall not be allowed to delay the development of the detailed plan and schedule.

When the arrow diagram representing the detailed plan has been completed in draft form, it will be provided to the contractor for review and comment. Concurrently, the City will make a calculation to determine the dates of completion which would be achieved under that plan. (This calculation shall not be considered a precedent to the contractor reviewing and commenting upon the draft network.)

If the projected schedule indicates a work plan which will not deliver the program in accordance with the contractual schedule, it shall be the contractor's responsibility to indicate means of reducing the work plan by concurrency of operations or reducing critical work spans; and/or a combination of both so that the contractor schedule can reflect compliance with the contract.

When the appropriate changes and adjustments have been made to the arrow diagram so that it is within the contractual requirements and describes all the contractor's work, the contractor shall so certify in writing on the face of the arrow diagram drawing, and submit same to the Director for approval.

This submission of a network-based schedule in approvable form shall be made no later than 60 days after Notice to Proceed.

The City reserves the prerogative of limiting the number of activities on the network, with the understanding that the contractor may make any reasonable request to add additional activities, particularly where the additional activities would more appropriately describe the cost breakdown for progress payment purposes.

Prior to approval, the contractor will be provided with several sets of draft network and/or computer information, as appropriate to proceed with the scheduling effort. Upon approval by the Director, the contractor will be furnished five sets of the arrow diagrams, and ten sets of the computer output. The computer output will include the following sorts:

1. I-J Sort
2. Total float Sort
3. Sort by Major Trade Contractors
4. Sort by Major Work Areas

The contractor may request the City to provide different sorts than those above, if deemed to be more useful. The computer printout will include job identification; activity description; activity duration; calendar dates for early start, early finish, late start and late finish for each activity; total float by activity; and identification of critical activities.

PROGRESS REPORTING, PAYMENTS AND SCHEDULE UPDATING

The CPM network diagram shall, at all times, represent the actual history of accomplishment of all activities as well as the contractor's current projected plan for orderly completion of the work. The contractor shall, at monthly intervals, evaluate work progress with the City by review of actual accomplishments since the previous update. The network diagram shall be jointly reviewed by the City and the contractor to identify all changes in the network logic, work item sequence and duration including delays, cost estimates and/or dollar value redistribution as the result of activities changes, or contract changes, and any changes in milestone interface completion dates projected since the previous update. Data furnished to the City shall include a description of the problem areas, current and anticipated delaying factors and their impact, and an explanation of corrective action to be taken or proposed.

Upon completion of the monthly progress evaluation, the City (at no expense to the contractor) will revise the network diagram to incorporate all current and projected schedule and program data and revise the computer mathematical analysis based on the current updated information. One copy of the revised network diagram and the computer mathematical analysis will be furnished to the contractor for his use in evaluating his progress for the following months partial progress payment. (This revised network diagram and computer mathematical analysis will agree with the changes made in the joint review by the City and the contractor during the work progress evaluation.)

The City reserves the prerogative to limit the size of the monthly computer reports. This will be accomplished in either of two methods: first, project history which will be maintained in the data file will not necessarily be printed out. Secondly, work more than 6 months in the future, other than long lead procurement items, may be printed out in summary form. Neither of these approaches to abbreviating the size of the monthly output will change the schedule; if a change is agreed upon in the schedule, the monthly output will reflect that change. At the time of any major change or revision to the schedule, a complete output will be made. Similarly, monthly issues of the network diagrams will be limited to those sheets which have active progress, and/or which have changes.

PROGRESS PAYMENTS

Monthly progress payments shall be based on the total value of activities completed or partially completed, as mutually agreed to by the contractor and the City.

Such payments will be in an amount equal to 90 percent of the value of the work completed since the previous evaluation, but in no event shall progress payments at any time total more than 90 percent of the certified contract amount. The accumulated retainage will be shown as a separate item in the payment summary. This clause applies to the 50 percent progress point.

If the contractor fails, or refuses, to participate in the progress evaluation with the City, the contractor shall not be deemed to have provided the required progress data, and shall not be entitled to progress payments.

RESPONSIBILITY FOR WORK COMPLETION

The contractor agrees that whenever it becomes apparent from the current monthly progress evaluation and updated schedule data that any milestone interface completion dates and/or contract completion dates will not be met, the contractor will take some or all of the following actions at no additional costs to the City.

1. Increase construction manpower in such quantities and crafts as will substantially eliminate, in the judgment of the City, the backlog of work.

2. Increase the number of working hours per shift, shifts per work day, work days per week or the amount of construction equipment, or any combination of the foregoing sufficient to substantially eliminate, in the judgment of the City, the backlog of work.

3. Reschedule activities to achieve maximum practical concurrency of accomplishment.

The effect of the contractor's planned corrective action shall be incorporated into the next updated computer mathematical analysis to determine whether or not the planned action can achieve the original schedule. If the original schedule cannot be achieved, additional corrective actions will be taken by the contractor until the original schedule is projected by analysis or until all possible alternatives are exhausted.

The submission of an amended schedule will not relieve the contractor of the responsibility to notify the City in writing of all anticipated potential delays in the prosecution of the work.

ADJUSTMENT OF CONTRACT OR MILESTONE INTERFACE COMPLETION TIME

1. Contract or milestone interface completion times will be adjusted only for causes specified in this contract. In the event of a request for an extension of any milestone interface completion date and/or contract completion date,

the contractor shall furnish such justification and supporting evidence as the City may deem necessary to determine whether the contractor is entitled to additional time under the provisions of this contract.

2. Each request for change in any milestone interface completion date and/or contract completion date shall be submitted by the contractor within seven (7) calendar days after the beginning of the delay for which a time extension is requested (unless the City grants a greater period of time). No time extension will be granted for a request which is not submitted within the foregoing time limit.

3. After receipt of a request for a time extension the City shall make its finding of facts and its decision thereon and shall advise the contractor in writing.

4. If the City finds that the contractor is entitled to extension of any milestone interface completion date and/or contract completion date under the provisions of the contract, the City's determination of the total number of days extension shall be based upon the current computer mathematical analysis for the schedule and upon all data relevant to the extension. Such data shall be incorporated in the next monthly update of the performance schedule.

5. The contractor acknowledges and agrees that delays in activities which, according to the computer mathematical analysis, do not in fact actually affect any milestone interface completion dates or contract completion date shown on the CPM network at the time of the delay will not be the basis for a change thereto.

SANCTIONS

The discussion of specifications is a proper place to identify those actions which will be taken if the CPM schedule and method are not properly applied. The most common sanction is a refusal to make progress payments unless the CPM schedule has been submitted and approved, or to limit progress payments to the first 3 months or some other reasonable time frame.

An example taken from the Dade County specifications for its metro system spelled out the following sanctions:

FAILURE TO SUBMIT NETWORK ANALYSIS: Failure of the Contractor to submit the network analysis or any required revisions thereto within the time limits stated, shall be sufficient cause for certification that the Contractor is not performing the Work required by this Section, or that the Contractor's personnel directly responsible for planning, scheduling, and maintaining progress of the Work are not performing their work in a proper and skillful manner, or both. The Engineer may withhold approval of the Contractor's invoices for progress payment until such delinquent submittal is made.

Dade County in its general contracts has one of the strongest sections on sanctions used to date by anyone or any organization:

A. The Contractor shall prosecute the Work in accordance with the latest approved network analysis. In the event that the progress of items along the critical path is delayed, the Contractor shall revise his planning to include additional forces, equipment, shifts or hours as necessary to meet the time or times of completion specified in this Contract. Additional costs resulting therefrom will be borne by the Contractor. The Contractor shall make such changes when his progress at any check period does not meet at least one of the following two tests:

1. The percentage of dollar value of completed work with respect to the total amount of the Contract is within ten percentage points of the percentage of the contract time elapsed, or

2. The percentage of dollar value of completed work is within ten percentage points of the dollar value which should have been performed according to the Contractor's own network analysis previously approved by the Engineer.

B. Failure of the Contractor to comply with the requirements under this provision will be grounds for determination that the Contractor is not prosecuting the work with such diligence as will ensure completion within the time of completion specified in this Contract. Upon such determination, MDC may terminate the Contractor's right to proceed with the Work, or any separate part thereof. . . .

SUMMARY

CPM as a theory needs a specification to bring it into contractual reality. The availability of an acceptable reference standard can make this easier. There are at present no ANSI or ASTM standard references to fill this role. The 1965 AGC book can fill the role even-handedly. The 1976 AGC effort does so less even-handedly. (The first seven chapters of this text could also be invoked.)

The balance of the chapter offers examples of various modes of scheduling specification.

21

CPM COSTS

If you approach the application of CPM with a penny-wise-pound-foolish outlook, you will doubtlessly get a poor bargain. If you hope to find something for nothing in CPM, you would be well advised to forget it. CPM is not a get-rich-quick scheme. It is, rather, an investment which will return substantial and regular dividends.

CONSULTANT OR STAFF APPLICATION

A number of factors are involved in the cost of CPM. One consideration is whether the application is done by a consultant or your own staff. It is recommended that a qualified CPM consultant be involved in all major CPM efforts. This involvement should be in inverse proportion to the ability of your technical staff to handle CPM and their direct previous experience with it. Qualified consultants have encountered and solved a variety of CPM pitfalls. Basic CPM has not changed since its first usage but the technique of applying it has come a long way. There have been a number of innovations in its use. Some have been ingenious, but many are just plain wrong. It is both uneconomical and time-consuming for new users to follow a trial-and-error path when experience is available.

To evaluate roughly the ability of your own organization to handle CPM, score yourself on the following questions. Mark the suitable percentage in the "yes" column. If the answer is "no," mark an X in that column.

Condition	Yes	No
1. Do your have your own technical staff? (Credit 10 percent.)		
2. Do you have people on your staff with construction experience? (Credit 5 percent.)		
3. Is your staff large enough to handle additional assignments? (Credit 5 percent.)		
4. Does your staff have practical experience in the actual application of CPM? (Credit 2 percent for each actual application up to a maximum of 20 percent.)		
5. Are your field personnel trained and experienced in CPM? (Partial credit up to 10 percent.)		
6. Do you have a computer available?		
7. Does your computer center have the following programs (credit as indicated):		
a. Basic CPM program? (4 percent.)		
b. Input error check for open activities and events? (1 percent.)		
c. Error check for loops?(2 percent.)		
d. Resources program? (2 percent.)		
e. Cost forecasting? (1 percent.)		
8. Can your computer center give you immediate service or must you wait your turn? (Partial credit up to 5 percent.)		
9. Is the project a type which you have done many times before? (Partial credit up to 10 percent.)		
10. Considering the number of sources to be used, is project information readily available? (Partial credit up to 10 percent.)		
11. Is ample time available for construction? (Partial credit up to 10 percent.)		

Total _____

A maximum "yes" score of 100 percent would indicate no need for consultant assistance. This scoring is, of course, an oversimplification and suggested for discussion purposes only. Each project must be considered in terms of its own characteristics.

The fees for consulting will vary. Most CPM consultants will work on a fixed-fee basis. Generally speaking, the cost per unit of work will be lower for larger contracts.

The cost for staff CPM planning will be high if your company uses CPM only intermittently. But if you can justify a continuing volume of

CPM planning work, it may be useful to set up your own staff planning group. Remember the cautions about staff planners mentioned previously, however. If they lose their sense of perspective, they will have the earth going around the moon instead of the moon around the earth. Whether done by consultant, staff planner, or a mixture of those, applying CPM will cost about the same. This is not immediately obvious since consulting costs can be readily identified while a large portion of the staff planning costs are buried in overhead.

COST OF CPM

In broad terms, the cost of a complete CPM application should be 0.5 percent of the overall project cost. This figure is subject to many kinds of qualifications, but it does establish the size of the ball park and is approximately correct in the general value range of $10 to $50 million projects. For projects costing over $50 million, either a slight percentage reduction in CPM costs is noted or the large project actually breaks down into a number of discrete smaller projects. For the scope covered by the 0.5 percent figure, a reasonable breakdown might be:

	Consultation, %	Computer, %	Total, %
Preliminary (prebid) plan	0.04	0.01	0.05
Working plan	0.11	0.04	0.15
Updating	0.20	0.10	0.30
Totals	0.35	0.15	0.50

For a $10 million project, the cost of CPM would be about $15,000 for setting up the initial schedule and $30,000 for the updating phase. As the project size goes down to about $1 million, the percentage cost jumps sharply to about 1 percent or even higher, although the breakdown by category of task and technique remains proportionately the same. For projects costing less than $500,000, CPM can be very useful but the project cannot support a full CPM treatment.

The breakdown given above did not include special extensions and techniques. If these are used, the approximate additional costs might be:

	Consultation, %	Computer, %	Total, %
Preconstruction plan	0.04	0.01	0.05
Resources planning	0.04	0.16	0.20
Cost control—forecasting	0.04	0.06	0.10
			0.10
Cost expediting	0.04	0.06	
Totals	0.16	0.29	0.45

Note that computer costs make up the larger portion of the overall costs of the advanced techniques. This is the reverse of the cost breakdown for basic CPM. However, do not lose sight of the fact that these are extensions of the basic work and not independent applications.

SAVINGS THROUGH BASIC CPM

Intuitively, everyone recognizes the value of good planning. To be against good planning is like being against motherhood. You must always consider the potential cost of not using good planning. However, someone in business cannot invest two dollars to save one. In broad terms, you must consider the *reasonable* savings that can be realized from CPM.

Through planning the preconstruction phase of a project, an owner should be able to cut at least 20 percent from the time a non-CPM-planned preconstruction period would take. There is no proof to offer for this statement; none exists. However, from experience in this type of work the figure could actually be closer to 50 percent. Note that the reduction is in terms of the time which would really be consumed without such control, *not* in terms of the desired preconstruction period (which is usually ridiculously optimistic). But even a single month saved in the preconstruction period means that the owner can use the building one month earlier, and this has a value. One school administrator said that each month's delay in the delivery of a new high school would cost $30,000 in bus costs, rental space, interest, etc., which amounted to about 0.5 percent of the value of the school. This meant that the school would pay for itself in 200 months. Assume a savings of 20 percent off the preconstruction period times 0.5 percent per month. For a 20-month preconstruction period initially, a savings of at least $20\% \times 20 \times 0.5\%$, or 2 percent, could be realized. The potential savings are even greater, but this will do for a rough figure.

Prebid CPM analysis results in either shorter or more realistic construction periods. Our experience has been that the reduction in time is about 10 percent. For a 30-month construction project, the owner can get the facility about 3 months earlier if CPM is used. Using the relation from the previous paragraph, this results in three additional months of usage to the owner, valued roughly at 0.5 percent per month, or 1.5 percent. The contractor, in turn, also realizes a savings in supervision costs and the costs of certain equipment and facilities through the three-month reduction. If the contractor's overhead on this 30-month project averages 1 percent per month for supervision and equipment, he or she can expect to save only part of it by shortening the project's length. However, a savings of 50 percent on that overhead would amount to $50\% \times 1\% \times 3$, or 1.5

percent. This is very significant when the contractor's projected profit is 5 to 7.5 percent.

Preparation and monitoring of the project CPM plan is the heart of the CPM system. This planning is somewhat analogous to flight insurance. After a safe ride, the one-trip policy has served its purpose and the cost is charged off to peace of mind. Although CPM can be considered a form of "project completion insurance," management must look for a way to pay the "premiums." New York State officials estimate the cost of adequate monitoring of field progress to be 1.5 to 2 percent of total project costs. A more realistic figure lies in the 2 to 5 percent range. With CPM, the net cost of this monitoring can be reduced while its effectiveness is increased. These savings would accrue to the owner, and their order of magnitude would be about 0.5 percent. But intangible savings would also accrue to the contractor.

Summarizing the savings available through basic CPM:

CPM phase	Cost, %	Savings to contractor, %	Savings to owner, %	Net savings, %
Preconstruction	0.05	0	1.0	0.95
Prebid	0.05	1.0	1.0	1.95
Working schedule	0.45	0	0.5	0.05
Totals	0.55	1.0	2.5	2.95

There are several cautions that should be voiced in regard to this attempt to enumerate the quantitative savings available through using basic CPM techniques: It is an order-of-magnitude view but the savings are not guaranteed. CPM is an information system. The savings occur when that information is used effectively by effective contractors.

CLAIMS AVOIDANCE

While positive savings of 3 percent of total project costs are a reasonable expectation when CPM planning is used, claims avoidance through project management is, perhaps, the greatest incentive for the use of functional project controls. Claims by contractors *equal* to the total contract price are not unusual, and the principal cost factor is delay. At the apogee of interest and inflation rates in the early 1980s (i.e., when inflation was at 12 percent and interest rates at 22 percent, for a combined time-cost factor of 34 percent) the time crunch on contractors was obvious. But there are other direct costs for contractors that are related to time and delay. These include:

Field overhead	
Supervision @	8%
General conditions @	8%
Home office—overhead @	4%
Bond @	1%
Equipment @	4%
Total	25%

Thus, on a 30-month project, if overhead is 25 percent of the project costs, then the costs of an overrun in time amount to almost 1 percent per month. Interest costs and lost profits can increase this figure.

SAVINGS THROUGH ADVANCED TECHNIQUES

The extension of the basic CPM techniques can also result in definite savings. By the use of cost forecasting, owners can realize a savings of between 0.25 and 1 percent through a better return on investments. Assume on the average owners see a 0.5 percent savings in this way. Then too, faster progress payments, a companion of this same technique, could save contractors 0.24 percent. And in addition, intangible, but very definite, savings can result to owners and contractors from these methods.

Planned expediting of a project has resulted in a savings in time of 12 percent and in net costs of 1.2 percent. An assumed cost savings of 1 percent when this technique is used may be considered conservative. And since a mutual effort between owner and contractor is required to achieve the savings, divide it between both. A 10 percent time savings is a reasonable expectation when a project is expedited, and this would accrue to the owner. Using a 24-month example of project time and the 0.5 percent value per month of project time, a reasonable value for this savings in time would be $10\% \times 0.5\%$, or 1.2 percent. By combining this with the percentage of cost savings, planned expediting can conservatively be estimated to be worth 1.6 percent in savings to the owner and 0.6 percent to the contractor.

Another area is resources planning, where considerable savings are possible through the rigorous scheduling of equipment use. In the highway example cited earlier, a 20 percent time savings resulted from a 10 percent equipment increase. In this case well over 50 percent of the project's costs went to pay for the equipment and its operators. This equaled equipment (including labor) costs times the project's length in days, or equipment × time according to the initial plan. Using the resources-leveled plan, however, this would mean (1.1 times the amount of equipment originally scheduled) × (0.8 times the amount of time originally estimated to complete the project), or (0.88 times the original estimate of equipment required) × time. Since equipment × time made up at least 50 percent of project overall costs, the savings overall would be at least 50% × (1.00 − 0.88), or 6 percent. This does not seem to be an unreasonable expectation, but cut it in half and forecast only 3 percent. The savings in plant maintenance realized would go to the owner; the savings in construction costs would go to the contractor.

Summarizing the additional savings possible through the use of advanced CPM techniques:

	Cost, %	Savings to contractor, %	Savings to owner, %	Net savings, %
Resources planning	0.20	3.00	. . .	2.80
Cost control forecasting	0.10	0.25	0.5	0.65
Cost expediting	0.10	0.60	1.6	2.10
Totals	0.40	3.85	2.1	5.55

The use of advanced CPM techniques thus tends to offer a greater return in terms of savings than does the use of basic techniques. This is reasonable since the advanced techniques are applied only in specific cases where they are especially valuable. But it is very doubtful that all three would be applied to a single project. If they were, they could still achieve their results, but the results of each might tend to counteract the results of the others.

PAYMENT FOR CPM

There are a number of methods and procedures for the payment of CPM services. However, to paraphrase an old saying: the owner always pays. Since through the use of CPM the owner can expect to realize a combined time and cost savings on the order of 2½ times what the contractor will realize, the owner should expect to pay the freight. The contractor makes other contributions in the way of cooperation, time, interest, attitude, and enthusiasm. A contractor using CPM at the owner's insistence is much like a trucker being directed to use a new turnpike by the shipper. The shipper wants to save time, and perhaps knows that the trucker will save enough on gas, tires, and vehicle upkeep to more than offset the cost of tolls. Nonetheless, the shipper would be well advised to pay the toll the first time or two out.

In certain building construction situations, the owner has no authority or funds for the purchase of CPM consulting services. These are usually owners who also lack a technical staff. There are several ways to handle this situation. One is to include the CPM planning in the construction specification, stating that the consultant, who shall act for the owner and direct the contractor in setting up the CPM plan, shall pay a specific amount (i.e., an allowance) to the contractor for providing these services. The specification should clearly indicate that the service is to be oriented to the needs of the owner. Further, it should state that in the event of any dispute, claim, or litigation, the CPM consultant shall represent the owner. The fee can include retroactive payment for prebid work. Through this approach the owner has the advantage of knowing the exact scope of CPM coverage, the consultant, and the cost of drawing up the CPM plan, while the contractors have a set fee to include in their bid, which avoids any bid spread due to CPM. The primary disadvantage of the approach is the reluctance owners often feel to specify the sole source for a consulting service. But since CPM consultation can be classified as a professional service, this would appear to be a paper dragon.

Owners *can* specify the CPM service required even if they choose not to specify the sole source. There are a number of problems in this approach. First, there is no standard CPM specification available. With specification writers still using two or three pages for the specification of 3000 pounds of concrete, how many pages would be required to describe adequately a new planning technique? Second, there is the problem of establishing the qualifications of CPM consultants. CPM experience and professional background are relevant here.

The owner may specify the scope of CPM services required, leaving the choice of consultant or staff planner to the discretion of the contractor. The owner's specification in this case must be even more complete. Where the contractor does have a true CPM capability, there would seem to be the possibility of mutual savings. In that case, either the contractor should get a credit for the CPM capability or the owner should be able to spend less money for the service.

One approach in this vein is to bid CPM as an alternative. In practice, this has not worked too well. If there are six bidders, five may bid a reasonable fee for the service while the sixth may sandbag with a high price. If the sixth is the low bidder for the overall contract, he or she may well be the contractor most in need of CPM assistance. At this point, the owner faces a self-made dilemma.

A better approach if the contractor has CPM capability is to allow a credit. This can be written into the CPM consultant's contract. The consultant, for a reduced fee, will evaluate the results of the contractor's CPM plan for the owner. This is an area which the government ignored in the early days of PERT use. Reams of PERT data were sent to people who did not have the experience or training to evaluate them. Consulting help would have been very worthwhile.

The basic CPM application during the construction phase has a cost split of about 33 percent for the initial preparation of the schedule and 67 percent for updating it. One cost savings option would be to hold a monthly review of the CPM schedule status, but require a computerized update only quarterly. However, this has proven ineffective for several reasons. First, it precludes the use of CPM as a basis for progress payments. Second, a quarterly update is at least twice as difficult to carry out as a monthly one—thus diluting the savings provided by the option. Finally, the interval between updates is too great and the discipline of a regular schedule review is lost. The lesson: If CPM is worth doing, then it is worth doing right.

SUMMARY

Although the decision whether to use a consultant or to do the CPM planning with your own staff is important, the cost of application is about the same in either case. In broad terms, the cost of applying CPM will be about 0.5 percent of the project's total costs. But the potential savings it offers are several times the cost of using it. Advanced techniques cost more but offer greater returns in terms of savings if properly applied.

Payment for CPM planning is usually assumed by the owner, who stands to gain the most, in terms of time and money savings, when CPM is used.

CPM IN CLAIMS
AND LITIGATION

An important function of scheduling in the construction industry, both for the owner and those doing the construction, concerns claims which may evolve out of the failure to meet schedules. CPM can affect claims in two ways. First, the establishment of a realistic schedule through prebid CPM planning can furnish a legal basis for the enforcement of damages, while perhaps even more importantly, CPM can be utilized to evaluate actual claims situations through the reconstruction of a project's history or the use of an existing CPM plan to indicate the effects of changes on the original schedule.

In an early instance, a contractor, a consortium, was asked by a bridge authority to show cause why it should not be pressed for $550,000 in liquidated damages. Actually, the authority felt the contractor had done a good job, but because of the public trust involved, the authority also felt that it needed tangible proof of this good performance. To respond, the contractor used a construction CPM plan to demonstrate the effects of three different unforeseen circumstances: unusually bad weather, loss of special equipment by fire, and time lost in doing work claimed as extra. The presentation demonstrated the combined effect of the three causes (which, of course, was less than the serial effect) and the effects of any one or two of them alone and together. Thus, if any one or two of the factors had been deemed unacceptable, the effect of the remaining factor or factors was still quantified. On the basis of this finite presentation, the bridge commission did not press for the liquidated damages.

In a complex multimillion-dollar suit and countersuit back in 1966, the owner, an airport authority, used a detailed CPM to evaluate realistically the overall effects of the changes which both the owner and the contractor had imposed on the project. This network, set up on a historical basis, could be run so as to consider the combined effect of the changes as well as the separate effects of individual changes. Information from daily, weekly, and monthly field reports was utilized in preparing the historical CPM network, and the calculated results were quite interesting—and they were invaluable to the owner's engineer for preparing a factual testimony. The pretrial and trial periods extended over a number of years, and without this historical network, factual testimony would have become almost impossible.

In negotiating extra work, contractors have often neglected the effects the change order will have on working time, so that either they have requested no time extension or an extension equaling the total period they estimate the additional work will require. Generally speaking, however, extra work on a project affects float areas, and any time extension granted should be less than the total incremental time needed to complete the additional work. At Cape Canaveral, the combined emphasis on time and public pressure for completion of projects reversed this situation. Contractors recognized more clearly the time-money relationships and usually made substantial requests for additional time as well as for extra money to implement changes. The Corps of Engineers and NASA required network analysis for the basic work on most of the major projects undertaken there. Thus most of the contractors prepared network-oriented fragnets to demonstrate the effects that additional work would have on scheduling. Although there were abuses, in the long run CPM was used by both parties to evaluate requests for time extensions fairly, and many claims were settled without the drudgery of formal legal suits.

Also at Cape Canaveral, a new type of claim evolved, a claim for acceleration charges. Contractors would often accept extra work items and agree to perform them in the originally allotted time span. To balance this obvious inequity of additional work but no time extensions, a fee for work acceleration would be charged to compensate for the costs of overtime and other problems that arose such as the inefficiencies generated by the overstaffing of particular areas of work.

The type of contract originally signed for a project has an impact on whether or not there is a potential for easy resolution or settlement of claims should they arise. Claims relating to construction management and negotiated contracts in the private sector can often be resolved by means of an objective report, based upon schedules and other factual information. Such objective evalution is important not only in regard to the legalities of the settlement proceedings, but as documentation for proving to both plaintiff and defendant that a proper settlement has been reached. However, claims in the public sector are usually not so easily settled, and increasingly disputes there are running the full course of litigation.

DELAY

The principal dimension measured by schedules is delay. In years past, delay in the completion of construction used to be a mutually accepted condition; even the courts on occasion recognized that delay was a normal situation in the construction process.

Today, however, with tight budgets on the part of owners, who usually want to expend their funds right up to the limits of their budgets but no further, and the real costs contractors encounter in staying on a job longer than planned—delay is a very problematic area. When delays occur during construction, the parties involved attempt to shift the costs that result onto each other. If litigation results after negotiating fails, the lawsuits are between two (or more) losers all of whom are attempting to mitigate their losses. There are no winners in delay.

To the private owner, delay can mean a loss of revenues through the resulting lack of production facilities and rentable space, as well as through a continuing dependence on present facilities. To the public owner, it can mean that a building or facility is not available for the use to which it needs to be put at the proper time. The service revenues lost through delay can never be recovered. To the contractor, delay means higher overhead costs that result from the longer construction period, higher prices for materials resulting from inflation, and escalation costs due to labor cost increases. Further, working capital and bonding capacity are tied up so that other projects cannot be undertaken.

Responsibility for Delay

The assignment of responsibility for delay after the fact is usually difficult, and the courts have often remarked that delay should be anticipated in any construction project. Traditionally, the courts have protected owners more than contractors. Until recently, no-damage-for-delay clauses have often been enforced, with the contractors receiving only time extensions when delays occurred. However, the granting of time extensions avoids another owner-oriented remedy for problems connected with delay: liquidated damages. Even with courts that are inclined to consider recovery of damages for owner-caused delays, the burden is on the contractor to prove active interference on the part of the owner in order to receive a favorable decision.

There are four general categories of responsibility:

1. Owner (or owner's agents) responsible
2. Contractor (or subcontractors) responsible
3. Neither contractual party responsible
4. Both contractual parties responsible

In cases where the owner (or owner's agents) has (have) caused the delay, the courts may find that the language of the contract, in the form of the typical no-damage-for-delay clause, protects the owner from having to pay damages but requires a compensatory time extension to protect the contractor from having to pay liquidated damages. If the owner can be proven guilty of interfering with the contractor's progress on the project or has committed a breach of contract, however, the contractor can probably recover damages from the owner.

If the contractor (or subcontractors) causes (cause) the delay, the contract language does not generally offer the contractor protection against litigation on the part of the owner to recover damages.

If the delay is caused by forces beyond the control of either party to the contract, the finding generally is that each party must bear the brunt of its own damages.

If both parties to the contract contribute to the delay or cause concurrent delays, the usual finding is that the delays offset one another. An exception to this would occur in those instances where the damages can be clearly and distinctly separated, although the courts are not quick to allow such distinctions.

Types of Delay

There are three basic types of delay: classic, concurrent, and serial.

Classic delay occurs when a period of idleness and/or uselessness is imposed upon the contracted-for work. In *Grand Investment Co. v. United States*, 102 Ct. Cl. U.S. 40 (1944), the government issued a stop order by telegraph to the contractor that resulted in a work stoppage of 109 days. The contractor sued for damages caused by the delay, basing the suit on a claim of breach of contract. The court found that the stop order was not justified and thus resulted in a breach of the government's obligations in the contract. The court allowed, among other things, a damage due to the loss of utilization of equipment on the job site, finding: inability to utilize equipment on the job site, stating:

When the government in breach of its contract, in effect, condemned a contractor's valuable and useful machines for a period of idleness and uselessness . . . it should make compensation comparable to what would be required if it took the machines for use for a temporary period.

Johnson v. Fenestra, 305 F. 2d 179, 181 (3d Cir. 1962), also involved a classical delay: Workers were idled by the failure of the general contractor to supply materials. This type of delay, to be legally recognized as such, must be substantial, involving an essential segment of the work to be done, and it must remain a problem for an unreasonable amount of time.

Generally, if two parties claim *concurrent delays,* the court will not try to unravel the factors involved and will disallow the claims by both parties. In *United States v. Citizens and Southern National Bank,* 367 F. 2d 473 (1966), a subcontractor was able to show delay damages caused by the general contractor. However, the general contractor in turn was able to demonstrate that portions of the damages were caused by the factors for which he was not responsible. In the absence of clear evidence separating the two claims, the court rejected both, stating: "As the evidence does not provide any reasonable basis for allocating the additional costs among those contributing factors, we conclude that the entire claim should have been rejected."

Similarly, in *Lichter v. Mellon-Stuart,* 305 F. 2d 216 (3d Cir. 1962), the court found that the facts supported evidence of delay imposed upon a subcontractor by a general contractor. However, it also found that the work had been delayed by a number of other factors including change orders, delays caused by other trades, and strikes. The subcontractor had based its claim for damages solely upon the delay imposed by the general contractor, and both the trial court and the appeals court rejected the claim on the basis that:

> Even if one could find from the evidence that one or more of the interfering contingencies was a wrongful act on the part of the defendant, no basis appears for even an educated guess as to the increased costs . . . due to that particular breach . . . as distinguished from those causes from which defendant is contractually exempt.

It should be noted, however, that in recent decisions, the courts increasingly have demonstrated a willingness to allocate responsibility for concurrent delays.

Serial delay is a linkage of delays (or sometimes of different causes of a delay). Thus, the effects of one delay might be amplified by a later delay. For instance, if an owner's representative delays reviewing shop drawings, and the resulting delay causes the project to drift into a strike or a period of severe weather resulting in further delays, a court might find the owner liable for the total serial delay resulting from the initial incremental delay.

Force Majeure Causes

These include what are known as "acts of God." The general contract usually provides a list of such events: fires, strikes, earthquakes, tornadoes, floods, and similar unforeseen circumstances. Should they occur, the contract provides for a mutual relief from demands for damages due to delay and the owner is obligated to provide a reasonable (usually a day-for-day) time extension.

In the case of weather-related delays, usually only those occurrences shown to be beyond the average weather conditions expected for the area based upon past records can be considered as a reason for time extensions. However, this can vary with contract language. A number of states and cities allow a day-for-day extension (noncompensable) for all bad weather.

Many contracts have clauses stating that time extensions for delay caused by "acts of God" shall be granted only to those portions of the projects that are specifically affected by such events. Thus, a severe downpour after a site has been graded and drained and the building closed in may cause no actual delay, so that claims for time extensions because of it would not be accepted even though it would qualify under other methods of evaluation as a *force majeure* act.

AS-PLANNED CPM

CPM can be useful in establishing the facts, and also the intentions, of the parties to a contract. The most important part of the CPM work in this respect is the initially approved CPM network, because it describes the manner in which the contractor intended to meet the requirements of the contract at the start of the project. The network can be used by the owner to demonstrate areas of failure on the part of the contractor, and can be used by the contractor to demonstrate points of interference on the part of the owner (or owner's agents).

A project involving regular (usually monthly) reviews or updatings of the CPM plan should provide a good basis, through the CPM reports, for evaluating the progress of the work done on it. Unfortunately, many such projects have only a collection of CPM diagrams and computer runs to show for those reviews. The CPM reports are far more valuable if each updating is accompanied by a comprehensive narrative. These narratives, which should be normal portions of the project documentation, are prepared in the normal order of business—and therefore can be accepted later at face value, with due weight given to their origins.

It is not unusual for the CPM scheduling team to periodically readjust the schedule of a project to attempt to maintain the end date or to accommodate problems and unexpected situations. When looking at those periods of rescheduling, it can appear that the project was either on schedule or had not fallen further behind schedule, while in reality the dates were being revised in terms of the overall plan but did not necessarily reflect the true progress on the project.

A first step in utilizing CPM to analyze what happened on a project is to set up the initially approved plan in network form. If the original network was small (1000 or fewer activities), it is merely recomputerized to confirm the initially scheduled dates. If the network was larger, particularly in the range of 5000 to 10,000 activities, milestone points should be identified and a summary of activities prepared. A summary CPM network of 1,000 or fewer activities equivalent to the detailed major network should then be developed. Finally this equivalent summary network should be computerized to confirm that it gives the correct initial dates, and that it is, indeed, equivalent to the original, larger network.

In addition to the above steps, the network should be redrawn to a time grid. A typical scale would be 2 inches for each month, so that a 3-year project would be represented by a 6-foot-long diagram. The vertical dimension is a function of the arrangement of the schedule, and the number of activities. If a more convenient size is preferred, the larger network can be shot down by Xerox techniques to half size, or a scale of 1 inch equal to each month can be utilized. But note that too small a scale precludes the opportunity to use the as-planned network for demonstrating the effects of schedule changes.

AS-BUILT CPM

When the activities on the as-planned network have been identified, work can start on an as-built network. This second network should include the same activities as the first, for comparison purposes, but be based upon actual performance dates. These dates are researched from the updatings of the original CPM plan, the progress reports, and any other documentation available. Sparse or faulty project documentation makes development of an accurate as-built network difficult. (For this reason, CPM updatings should plug in actual dates for all activities as they start and are completed.) The as-built network is drawn to the same time scale, and organized in the same arrangement, as the as-planned network. The two can now be compared directly.

The work involved in preparing these two schedules will vary with the input information available, its organization, and the information on the levels of the work provided by the client and/or the client's attorney. From two to five people will be needed to work on them, over a period of 1 to 3 months. The work should be under the direction of a CPM scheduling professional who is qualified to testify in regard to the final products.

CAUSATIVE FACTORS

With the completion of the as-planned and as-built schedules, a uniform format for the evaluation of the causative factors in the delay is now available. (Even before the completion of the networks, a separate group under the direction of the scheduling professional can begin that evaluation.) The identity of most of the causative factors should be readily apparent, but the specific impact of different factors may not be as obvious.

One of the first areas to be identified is *force majeure.* The most common areas for this in construction projects are strikes and bad weather. Strikes should be documented in terms of their lengths, the remobilization time it takes when they are over, and the trades and areas of work affected by them. Most contracts provide for time extensions due to strikes, but not for compensation. In the case of a contractor making a claim, it would be important to be able to demonstrate that a strike had little or no impact on the critical path of a project, so that other compensable factors could be shown to be the cause of the damages being claimed. Conversely, an owner defending against claims should be able to demonstrate that strikes did, indeed, cause the delays, and other problems were, at worst, concurrent.

Change orders are evaluated in terms of the specific impacts they have on the progress of a project. This is done in two ways. First, a determination is made at what point in the network a particular change order impacted on the field work. In addition, activities are identified which were preparatory for implementing the change order, such as change order proposals, the ordering of material, mobilization, and any other preimplementation factors. Next, the change order's impact is identified in terms of the amount of labor power required to accomplish it. The size of a typical work crew can be derived either from standard estimating sources or from the labor portion of the work activity being evaluated if it is identified either in the bid estimate or approved progress payment breakdown. The worker-hours involved in implementing the change are then determined by multiplying the typical crew size by the number of hours it took to complete the work item.

A separate evaluation is done for every change order in the project. In addition to identifying the basic impact each has had on the plan, it is necessary that the analysis also identify the times of issue of the individual change orders' Notices to Proceed. In each case, if that is later than the late start date of the affected activity, it is obvious that the change order had the potential to delay the project. And in fact, it probably did delay it unless there were methods to work around the change—methods that must themselves be demonstrated to have been used.

Another area to be researched is stop orders or suspensions. These are applied to a network in the form of actual dates, or as activities inserted in the stream of activities affected.

TIME IMPACT EVALUATIONS

When all the causative factors have been identified, a time impact evaluation (TIE) is prepared for each one. The information is assembled as described previously, and prepared in a format such that the impact of each factor on the as-planned network can be determined and applied to it. When the impacts of all the causative factors have been correctly determined and applied, the result should be an approximation of the as-built network. Then the impacted, as-planned network should be compared with the as-built one, and any major disparities between them should be examined to identify whether TIEs were incorrectly applied, or whether there were additional causative factors not identified.

The theoretical effects of the impacting factors on the as-planned network must be explainable in terms of the as-built network, or the proposed analysis is probably incorrect. Some professionals take a different position, however. One well-known scheduling consultant expounds the theory of the "500 bolts": If an owner is to provide 500 bolts, and has delivered only 499, in the consultant's opinion the activity involved will be impacted until that 500th bolt has been delivered. But it appears more logical to examine the function of the 500th bolt. For instance, if it is a spare or there is a readily acceptable substitute which permits construction to proceed, then it is not, theoretically speaking, proper to claim that the as-planned network has been impacted by its absence.

Another position, often taken by schedulers who conduct impact analyses on as-planned networks for contractor evaluations, is that all float belongs to the contractor. This has been a continuing argument in the profession. In fact, some recent owners' specifications, in order to counteract such claims, outright state, "All float belongs to the owner." Neither position is tenable, however. Float is a shared commodity. Like a natural resource, it must be used with common sense. The owner should be permitted to use float for order changes, shop drawing reviews, and other owner-responsible areas. On the other hand, it is obvious that owners should not use float excessively to the point that the entire project becomes totally critical. This would be an overreach on the part of owners. Conversely, contractors should be expected to utilize float only to balance their work forces and to work efficiently, in order to complete projects on time and at the optimum budgets.

When all of the TIE information has been imposed on the as-planned network, a standard CPM calculation is made. This calculation should correlate, as discussed previously, with the as-built network. When such a correlation is observed, the TIEs are selectively zeroed out by category. For instance, the *force majeure* changes are zeroed out, and a run made to determine the overall impact of their absence on the network. Similarly, contractor-related TIEs are zeroed out, and whatever further improvement their absence makes in schedule is noted. Then the owner-related TIEs, involving changes and any hold orders, etc., are zeroed out, and this final result should bring the network back to its as-planned status.

Since the various categories of changes are each zeroed out concurrently, the effects of concurrency due to combined impacts can be observed from the results of the three separate runs. This can provide an arbitrator or a court with the means to allocate delay damages and impacts caused by the various parties.

One of the first applications of this approach was in regard to a major airport project. The airport authority had contracted for the installation of a $15 million underground fueling system. The contractor for the work, who was the low bidder by several million dollars, prepared a construction CPM plan that was never accepted by the owner and all the milestone dates were completely missed. The airport authority took under advisement the matter of whether or not to enter suit for delay damages due to losses in interest on money and in airport operating efficiency, as well as for other direct delay damages. But when the contractor filed a $6 million delay suit against the authority, the authority promptly filed a counterclaim and litigation ensued.

In the absence of a mutually acceptable CPM plan representing what actually happened, the owner directed that one be prepared to evaluate the real causes of the delays. The daily, weekly, and monthly reports, as well as personal observations by the owner's field team and the CPM consultant, were utilized in developing this comprehensive plan. It contained milestone points reflecting actual dates of accomplishment for various activities. Between the milestone points, the estimates for the time that the work should have taken were inserted, and the CPM team then divided the delay proportionally by its causes. The causes were either by: contractor, owner, combined, or neither. The first computer run of the network showed the actual dates for all the events. The next computation established the amount of delay due to the contractor alone. The third established the amount of delay due to the owner alone. The fourth identified the amount of delay due to both. But this total delay was less than what the combined total was when the amounts caused by the owner alone and the contractor alone were added together.

Using this very specific information, the managing engineer for the owner was able to direct efforts toward an out-of-court settlement that took more than a year to negotiate. (Part of the willingness to negotiate on the part of the owner's management personnel arose out of a recognition of the very real delays caused by slow shop drawing review. Many of these delays were due to the high work load that the owner's engineering department was carrying at the time, but many were also identified as coming from attempts by the owner's engineers to redesign the shop drawing submissions, a common mistake made in the course of many shop drawing reviews.)

AS-SHOULD-HAVE-BEEN CPM

While it is best to start with an as-planned network, there are situations where a good as-planned network did not exist, or in which the one utilized had flaws or was inadequate. In those cases, one approach is to produce an as-should-have-been network.

In some cases, the as-should-have-been network has a bar graph to utilize as a guideline.

In one major project, the new Library of Congress building (James Madison Memorial Library), it was recognized by both the owner, the Architect of the Capitol, and the contractor, Bateson Construction Co., that there would be delay claims as a result of certain delay problems in the project. It was mutually agreed that it would be advantageous to convert the contractual as-planned bar graph into a CPM network which would be more useful in evaluating the effects of delay impacts. The contractor's scheduling consultant, A. James Waldron, converted the network into a CPM diagram and printout. This was reviewed for the Architect of the Capitol by O'Brien-Kreitzberg & Associates (OKA), and after some adjustments a mutually agreed upon baseline was stipulated. The network was useful to both sides in determining the responsibility for delays and the costs resulting therefrom.

Usually the use of an as-should-have-been network is more of an uphill situation. Lacking the agreement by both parties to a previously approved as-planned network, those producing the as-should-have-been network must be prepared to provide a foundation for it, and to justify the use of same.

In one such application, a state department of transportation specification had an elaborate narrative description of the sequencing required for the implementation of a project. Unfortunately, the state did not then require CPM planning (although it does now). The contractor, a major heavy construction contractor, submitted a totally inadequate bar graph that used fewer than 25 activities to describe the work to be accomplished. The contractor also proceeded to work in a fashion that produced a large amount of excavation spoil which was to be used on and/or sold to other projects. While the economic plan made sense, the logic did not. OKA utilized experienced highway engineers to develop an in-depth, as-should-have-been network some 24 sheets long in its logic, and made up of over 4000 activities. The computer run demonstrated the impropriety of the initial actions on the part of the contractor, and also served to illustrate his lack of planning in regard to the project.

TIE EXAMPLE

Take the 34-day CPM plan for the initial portion of the John Doe project as a schedule, and use it to measure delays or impacts. If, for instance, the well pump required a 6-week delivery time, the equivalent number of working days would be 30. The impact area is measured by adding an activity starting at 0 and going to event 4. The activity would be titled "late delivery of well pump," and adding it would produce the result shown in Figure 22.1, the time scale version of the initial part of the John Doe project. Since the well work was on the critical path, the delay would force the late start of activity 4-5, install well pump, to await the delivery of the well pump. In this example that would be 30 minus 22, or a delay of 8 working days. Of course, it is necessary to view the entire contractual universe. For instance, if there were a 2-week delay in the Notice to Proceed for reasons other than the pump delivery, then the pump delivery delay would be better represented by disconnecting the initial or *i* end of the delay arrow from the 0 event and bringing it into the network as a new starting point with a specified date. Thus, if there were a 2-week *force majeure* delay imposed on the start of the site work, the additional time needed for delivery of the well pump would become concurrent delay.

Figure 22.2 shows a TIE form describing the delay in the delivery of the well pump. Figure 22.3 shows a TIE form describing a 60-day delay in the delivery of steel. This is applied to the phased construction network, which incorporates both design and procurement phases with the construction phase, and procurement, in this case, is the owner's responsibility. (The owner, in turn, may have a claim against the construction manager, or the architect-engineer, if the fault for late delivery lies with either of those parties.) When the two problems are imposed upon the overall network, it is seen that the critical path as shown in Figure 22.4 now goes through procurement of the structural steel, and even with the

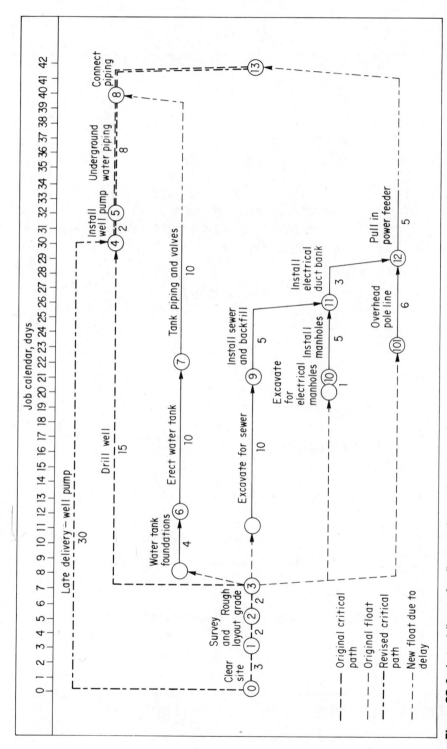

Figure 22.1 Late delivery of well pump, time scale.

TIME IMPACT EVALUATION

PROJECT: _John Doe_   TIE #: _1_
PREPARED BY: _J. J. O'Brien_   DATE: _9/15/83_

DESCRIPTION: LATE WELL PUMP DELIVERY – DELIVERY WAS SIX WEEKS AFTER CONTRACTOR NOTICE TO PROCEED. CONTRACTOR WAS READY FOR PUMP AT DAY 22.

ACTIVITIES AFFECTED:

4-5 "INSTALL WELL PUMP"

TYPE OF IMPACT:

INCREASED DURATION: _____   AMOUNT: _____

DELAYED DATE/SUSPENSION OF WORK: DELIVERED @ DAY 30

FRAGNET:

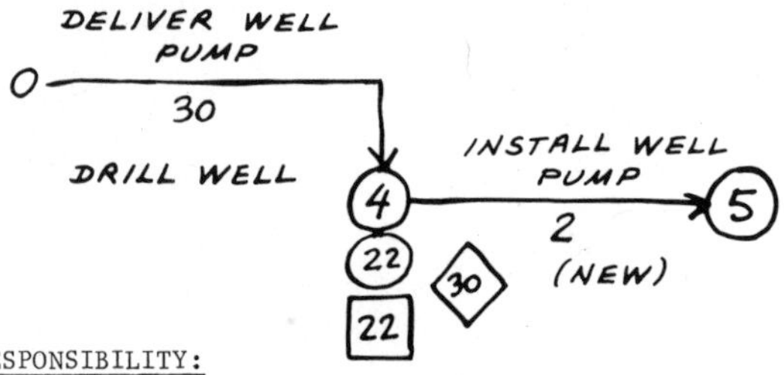

EVALUATION/RESPONSIBILITY:

L.S. OF 4-5 WAS 22; ACTUAL START 30, THEREFORE 8 WORK DAYS DELAY ON CRITICAL PATH

RESPONSIBILITY: A-E (FAILED TO DELIVER SPECIFICATIONS)

Figure 22.2 Time impact evaluation (TIE) describing delay of well pump.

Figure 22.3 TIE for 60-day delay in delivery of structural steel.

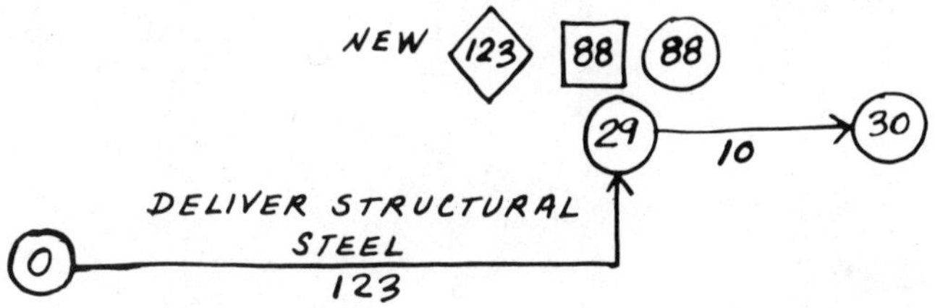

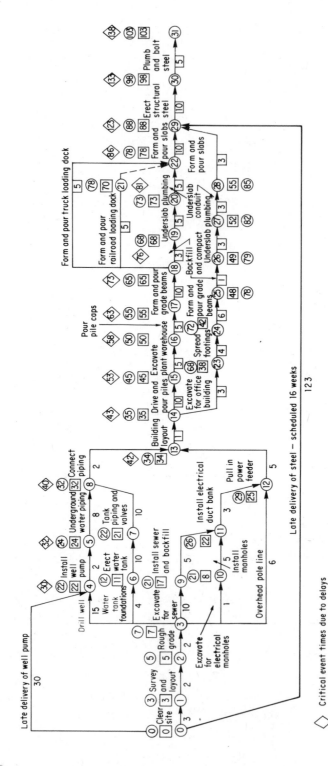

Figure 22.4 Time scale network showing steel delay.

382

slow delivery of the well pump, the initial site work network now has float as shown in Figure 22.5. There are, however, an additional 8 days of float in the early activities prior to the installation of the well pump. The 8-day differential in float along the well drilling path is still imposed by the late delivery of the well pump. However, there is no impact upon the overall project because the late steel delivery takes precedence.

To determine the cumulative effect of all delays, all TIEs should be developed and impacted against the network simultaneously. To evaluate the impact of any one category, just the TIEs representing that category (i.e., owner's responsibility, *force majeure,* contractor responsibility, etc.) should be applied to the network.

EVIDENTIARY USE OF CPM

During the 1960s, CPM schedulers, technicians, and engineers anticipated that Critical Path Method would be utilized as a tool in construction claims and litigation at some point in time. In fact, as early as 1962 to 1965, consultants to the litigants on both sides of a case involving the Atomic Energy Commission utilized CPM to prepare their positions, although a case citation is not available, and no wide exposition of the results was made. (The firm providing consultants to both sides was Mauchly Associates.)

In the 1970s, CPM techniques were used in presenting, and defending, delay claims cases in many instances. In no case where OKA was involved was the use of CPM questioned by opposing counsel or the court. Some of these cases include the following (dates are approximate):

- IBM vs. Henry Beck Construction; Federal Court, Florida, 1973

- Somers Construction vs. H. H. Robertson; Arbitration, Philadelphia, 1973

- E. C. Ernst vs. City of Philadelphia; Eastern Federal District Court, Philadelphia, 1976

- Arundel vs. Philadelphia Port Corp.; Commonwealth Court, Pennsylvania, 1979

- Buckley vs. New York City; New York State Court, 1979

- Federal Construction vs. Blake Construction; Federal District Court, Washington, DC, 1980

- Kidde-Briscoe vs. University of Connecticut; Connecticut State Court, 1980–1982

- Keating vs. City of Philadelphia; Eastern District Court, Philadelphia, 1981.

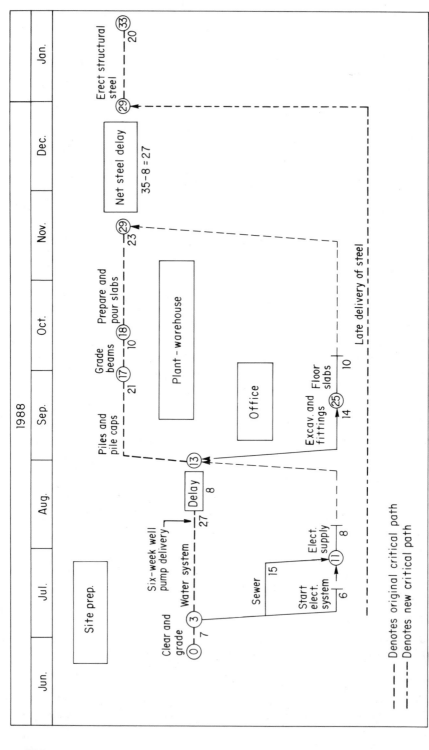

Figure 22.5 Overview showing relative float created in site work because of late deliveries.

- Glasgow vs. Commonwealth of Pennsylvania; Commonwealth Board of Claims, 1982–1983

- PT & L Construction vs. NJDOT: New Jersey State Court, 1983.

On many more OKA cases which had been entered and were en route to trial, CPM was a factor in settlement.

In early 1970s, several lawyers researched the question of CPM as an evidentiary tool. A series of articles and presentations followed, a number of which used the same thread, starting with the article "The Use of Critical Path Method Techniques in Contract Claims," by Jon M. Wickwire and Richard F. Smith in the *Public Contract Law Journal* of October 1974. Extracts from that article follow*:

> Judicial acceptance of CPM analyses as persuasive evidence of delay and disruption has been slow to develop, primarily due to technical errors in the analysis submitted or a failure of a presentation to realistically portray the work as actually done. In spite of the early reluctance to accept CPM presentations, the current state of the law is that use of CPM schedules to prove construction contract claims has become the standard, rather than the exception. Scheduling techniques which cannot display activity interrelationships are not favorably regarded as evidence of delay and disruption.
>
> "In Minmar Builders, Inc., GSBCA, 3430, 72-2 BCA ¶ 9599 (1972) the General Services Administration Board of Contract Appeals commented upon Minmar Builder's construction schedules (bar charts) which were offered to show project completion delay due to government's failure to timely issue ceiling change instructions:
>
> "Although two of Appellant's construction schedules were introduced in evidence, one which had been approved by the government and one which had not, neither was anything more than a bar chart showing the duration and projected calendar dates for the performance of the various contractual tasks. Since no interrelationship was shown as between the tasks the charts cannot show what project activities were dependent on the prior performance of the plaster and ceiling work, much less whether overall project completion was thereby affected. In short, the schedules were not prepared by the Critical Path Method (CPM) and hence are not probative as to whether any particular activity or group of activities was on the critical path or constituted the pacing element for the project."
>
> The greatest difficulty encountered by contractors using CPM techniques in claim presentation is the requirement for the presentation to be thoroughly grounded in the project records. The failure of contractors to properly document CPM studies has been held controlling in many board decisions. . . .
>
> Guidelines for the use of CPM presentations were set forth in the General Services Administration Board of Contract Appeals decision in Joseph E.

---

*Permission to quote courtesy the *Public Contract Law Journal*.

Bennett Co. (GSBCA 2362, 72-1 BCA ¶ 9364 (1972)) which . . . affirms the need to properly update a CPM and support the study with accurate records. The contractor's claim in this appeal was founded on a letter from the contracting officer ordering completion of the work by the contract completion date. The contractor argued this requirement was an acceleration order, which was denied by the contracting officer because of a lack of meaningful evidence. The contracting officer rejected the accuracy of the contractor's critical path method construction plan on the basis of errors in the interrelationships of activities.

At the board, the appellant presented a computer analysis of the CPM used on the project to isolate the delays caused by government activities. The board held that the usefulness of this analysis was dependent upon three things: 1) the extent to which the individual delays are established by substantial evidence—this requirement is concerned with the project records and evidence available for the appellant to show the underlying causes of delay; 2) the soundness of the CPM system itself—this requires the contractor to demonstrate the logic of the CPM and show that its theoretical and scheduling analyses are sound; and 3) the nature of and reason for any changes to the CPM schedule in the process of reducing it to a computer program—this relates to the exactness and accuracy with which the appellant has reduced the CPM network to a computer analysis and how effectively this analysis can be used in a claim presentation.

As expected, the appellant in Bennett argued that the CPM was the proper basis for any analysis of the project since the plan was submitted by the appellant and approved by the government.

However, the board rejected the appellant's CPM analysis because it: 1) contained numerous mathematical errors; 2) failed to consider foreseeable weather conditions; 3) changed the critical path and float times without reason; and 4) was prepared without the benefit of any site investigation and after the project was already completed. . . .

The gradual acceptance of CPM presentations when properly documented is demonstrated in the case of Continental Consolidated Corp. ENG BCA 2743, 2766, 67-2 BCA ¶ 6624 (1967). . . .

In this case a claim was submitted for extra costs due to suspension of work and subsequent acceleration directed by the government. The appellant alleged it was entitled to time extensions due to government delay in approving shop drawings. The government's failure to grant time extensions for these delays made the work appear to be behind schedule as of certain dates when in fact, if proper time extensions had been granted, the appellant would have been on schedule. As a result, government directives to work overtime and/or extra shifts would have been unnecessary. . . .

The contract set completion dates for various elements of the work which in effect required a critical path for each element within an overall work plan. With the use of the appellant's CPM analysis, the board was able to separate out the delay costs due appellant and the additional costs incurred due to a compensable acceleration order. This evidentiary tool allowed the board to identify the periods of delay and actual progress on the job and thereby determine when an acceleration order was properly issued from that point in time when such an order was compensable because the contractor was back on schedule.

Thus the boards have recognized the value of a CPM developed contemporaneously with the work or subsequent to the work so long as it based upon the relevant records available.

The records may include daily logs, time sheets, payroll records, diaries, purchase orders.

While the boards have accepted the CPM as an evidentiary tool, this tool cannot rise above the basic assumptions and records upon which it is founded. The board can accept the theoretical value of a CPM presentation, but reject its conclusion for failure to base the analysis on the actual project records. (See C. H. Leavell & Co., GSBCA 2901, 70-2 BCA ¶ 8437 (1970); 70-2 BCA ¶ 8528 (1970) [on reconsideration] where the contractor failed to establish the accuracy of the input data for its computer analysis of delays due to design deficiencies.)

Where the board has received persuasive evidence that the CPM network is either logically or factually inaccurate, incomplete or prepared specifically for the claim, the board will discount its evidentiary value. A CPM must be linked to the job records, as a CPM analysis is primarily concerned with visually portraying the job records to establish the cause of delay or disruption.

The extent to which a CPM presentation may be used to document a claim can be seen in Canon Construction Co. (ASBCA 16142, 72-1 BCA ¶ 9404 1972) where the contractor gained total acceptance of its CPM schedule to establish a delay claim. In this opinion, the board recognized the underlying logic and evidence presented in the appellant's original CPM schedule and the value of CPM techniques to prove extended overhead costs.

In Canon, the contractor was awarded his overhead costs determined by the difference between the actual date of completion and the date the contractor would have completed the work absent government fault and performance of changed work. But the recovery for extended overhead costs was held to be limited by either the extended period of performance time or the aggregate net extent of delays caused by government fault or changed work, whichever is the lesser. Using this formula the board recognized that the contractor was not entitled to recovery for the group of excusable but noncompensable delays including weather delays, reasonable suspensions of work, etc. . . .

The Canon decision is extremely important since it shows that a properly prepared and presented CPM schedule will be accepted by the board as the basis for computing project delays. In this regard it is noted that the board clearly indicated that it was "relying principally on the CPM chart and only using the witness' testimony to ascribe an aspect of reasonableness to the chart."

The Canon decision is also significant since it provided further guidance as to the application of CPM principles to claims. For example, the board acknowledged that delays incurred off the critical path would not delay ultimate performance. Further, the board found that where the sequence established by the network was violated, costly start and stop operations would result and implied that the contractor's planned network operations need not be the only way to accomplish the work shown, but must be shown to be economical in both cost and time. (Reference: Stagg Construction Co., GSBCA, 2664, 69-2 BCA ¶ 7914 (1969); 70-1 BCA ¶ 8241 (1970) [on reconsideration]).

In 1975, co-authors Paul J. Walstad, Jon M. Wickwire, Thomas Asselin, and Joseph H. Kasimer wrote a book titled *Project Scheduling and Construction Claims, a Practical Handbook,* which is published by A. James Waldron Enterprises. On page 14-1 the authors note*:

> There was reluctance at first to accept the use of CPM analysis as evidence of delays and disruption. Of paramount concern were possible technical errors in the system or a failure of the system or analysis to realistically portray the work as actually done. *See e.g., A. Teichert & Sons, Inc.,* ASBCA No. 10265, 68-2 BCA ¶ 7151 (1968)....
>
> This concern no doubt stemmed from early presentations which based CPM analysis to a great extent on speculation, inferences, or innuendo rather than hard, documented facts. Thus, even though the CPM has become recognized as a competent source of evidence ... its usefulness in providing a claim has been held dependent upon at least four factors:
>
> 1. The soundness of the CPM schedule itself.... This requires proof of the reasonableness and feasibility of the schedule so as to show that on a theoretical basis the scheduling was sound;
>
> 2. The extent to which any individual delays can be established by substantial evidence. This goes to the basic records and evidence available to the claimant to show the underlying causes of delay or disruption;
>
> 3. The nature of any changes to the CPM schedule made during the claim analysis process. This relates to the exactness and accuracy with which the claimant has analyzed the project scheduling in making his presentation;
>
> 4. Proof that the work sequence shown was the only possible or reasonable sequence by which the work could be completed on time.

In the late 1970s and early 1980s, *Engineering News-Record* has presented a series of professional seminars in regard to claim and litigation. Paul J. Walstad, Esq., has been a leader in the formulation and presentation of a number of these. The comments on evidentiary value of CPM continue as previously described. By 1980, Walstad had added the following in this regard†:

> In *Blackhawk Heating & Plumbing Co., Inc.,* GSBCA No. 2432, 75-1 BCA, the contractor claimed 403 days as a result of ductwork design deficiencies.

---

*Permission to quote courtesy A. James Waldron.

†See Page 269 of Material on ENR's "Advanced Course on Construction Claims," Arlington, VA, May 1 and 2, 1980. Permission to quote courtesy *Engineering News-Record,* copyright McGraw-Hill, Inc., and Construction Education Management Corporation.

The Board found the deficiencies were the fault of the Government. However, the Board indicated the main question was whether the ductwork delay had extended contract completion; the Government contended a delay involving electrical fixtures was the critical item.

In support of its position, the Government produced its own CPM analysis, which had been prepared after the delays had occurred. The Government CPM showed the ductwork design problems were not on the critical path; the activities which the contractor had contended were delayed actually had "float" time remaining even after the delay was considered, and the critical path ran through the electrical fixture approval, delivery and installation cycle.

The Board carefully analyzed the Government's CPM, and found it . . . established a sound network diagram and computer run showing just how the project was actually constructed up to the date of substantial completion on December 7, 1970. . . .

After reviewing the delay analysis set forth in the Government CPM, the Board further concluded it had provided "a sound basis upon which to evaluate various project delays." Based upon the finding the electrical fixture delay was the factor which delayed ultimate completion, the Board then proceeded to allocate responsiblity for the fixture delays. Upon reconsideration, the Board refused to modify its original decision, indicating the as-built CPM was the best evidence of delay.

The use of CPM as an evidentiary tool in claims and court proceedings is not confined to administrative boards. In the *Brooks Towers Corporation vs. Hunkin-Conkey Construction Company,* 454 F. 2d 1203 (10th Cir. 1972), the owner claimed delay damages from the contractor. The Tenth Circuit Court of Appeals affirmed an award in favor of the contractor, and in so doing placed great weight on the CPM analysis provided by an expert witness:

"The testimony of Richard N. Green, a Construction Consultant, is corroborative of Ratner's grant of some 185 days extensions and significant in relation to the 'clockwork' scheduling of work components required to accomplish the original contract completion schedules. Green's study took into consideration the plans and specifications, *the computerized Critical Path Scheduling program,* all Bulletins, formal Change Orders, related correspondence, Daily Progress Report and Monthly Pay Requests. He computed some 394 days involving requests for extensions. He eliminated those of an 'overlapping' nature and those which were not critical. He did not consider delays resulting from labor disputes or severe weather conditions. He arrived at a total of 180 days extension of time to which the Contractor was entitled."

In its decision of July 18, 1983, the General Services Administration Board of Contract Appeals (GSA BCA) complained about the misuse of CPM schedules in the presentation of a claim by Welch Construction, Inc. Welch filed a claim for damages as a result of owner delay in the modification of a geological survey center. Presenting its claim, Welch utilized

CPM diagrams which purported to present as-planned and as-built schedules. In its opinion, GSA BCA, denying the claim, stated:

> Candor compels us to admit that we may not have figured out what it was that Appellant thought its exhibits would show. If so, Appellant has only itself to blame.... [One] of the surest ways of losing a case for lack of proof is submitting complex exhibits to a tryer of facts with no attempt to explain what they show or how they relate to the other evidence in the record.

The Board believed that the schedules used in presenting the claim ignored both contractual and actual completion dates.

SUMMARY

The use of CPM in claims and legal cases has increased dramatically in the 1970s and 1980s as parties to construction contracts have come increasingly to rely upon litigation to settle disputes. The as-planned network, preferably approved by the owner, the contracting officer, or the construction manager, is a keystone in the process of claims evaluation. The best approach to such evaluation is the TIE, or Time Impact Evaluation, which applies all the delay factors to the as-planned schedule in order to determine how they impacted on it. If there was no as-planned network or it was inadequate, an as-should-have-been network can be substituted.

A detailed, as-built network, compressed rather than impacted, can be used to evaluate a situation if a good as-planned network is not available. The as-built network can also be compared with the impacted, as-planned network, or the impacted, as-should-have-been network, to validate the evaluation of what impacts the delay factors had.

Examples of the impact approach were given. Experience in the 1970s and 1980s underscores the receptiveness of the courts to network analysis.

GLOSSARY OF TERMS

ACTIVITY: The work item which is the basic component of the project.

ACTIVITY TIMES: Time information generated through the CPM calculation which identifies the start and finish times for each activity in the network.

ARROW: The graphical representation of an activity in the CPM network. One arrow represents one activity. The arrow is not a vector quantity and is not necessarily drawn to scale.

ARROW DIAGRAM: See Network.

CPM: Critical Path Method.

CRITICAL PATH: The longest route through the CPM network.

DURATION: The time required to accomplish an activity.

EARLY EVENT TIME: The earliest time at which an event can be started.

EARLY FINISH: The earliest time at which an activity can be completed.

EARLY START: The earliest time at which an activity can be started (equal to early event time).

EDIT: A computer sort by i-j, total float, code, or early or late dates.

EVENT: A point in time representing the intersection of two or more arrows. The event has no time duration.

EVENT TIMES: Time information generated through the CPM calculation which identifies the start and finish times for each event in the network.

EXPECTED TIME: The activity duration for a PERT activity.

FREE FLOAT: Activity float which identifies the scheduling flexibility which will not delay the early start of any succeeding activities if used. While this would appear to be a useful value, it has not proved so.

HARDWARE: In computers, this term refers to the equipment as delivered by the manufacturer.

HORIZONTAL EVENT NUMBERING: Assigning event numbers in horizontal order.

INPUT: The data which must be introduced into the computer before it starts a computation.

LAG: An arrow introduced into the CPM network after a series of activities to schedule them at an earlier time.

LATE EVENT TIME: The latest time at which an event can be reached without extending the length or duration of the project.

LATE FINISH: The latest time at which an activity can be completed without lengthening the project.

LATE START: The latest time at which an activity can start without lengthening the project.

LEAD: An arrow introduced before a series of activities to schedule them at a later time.

LOGICAL LOOP: A circular connection of arrows which is illogical and cannot be computed.

LOGICAL RESTRAINT: An arrow connection which is used as a logical connector but which does not represent actual work items. It is usually represented by a dotted line. Sometimes called a *dummy* because it does not represent work, it is an indispensable part of the network.

MATRIX: A grid system used in the graphical solution of mathematical problems. It was used in the manual solution of CPM in the early period but has been outmoded (in CPM) by later techniques.

MILESTONE: A significant event.

MONITORING: Following the progress of the project. This phase follows the preparation of the CPM plan and schedule.

MOST LIKELY TIME: Project duration estimate (PERT terminology).

NETWORK: The connected sequence of arrows representing the project. This is the basis of CPM and PERT. The network must have one start point and one terminal point.

OPTIMISTIC TIME: In PERT, the earliest time in which an activity can be completed.

OUTPUT: The results of the computer computation.

PESSIMISTIC TIME: In PERT, the slowest time in which an activity can be completed.

PERT: Originally Program Evaluation Research Task, now Performance Evaluation and Review Technique.

PLAN: The sequence in which the project is to be done. This is independent of the schedule.

PRECONSTRUCTION CPM: A plan and schedule for the concept and design phase preceding the award of contract.

PRELIMINARY CPM PLAN: CPM analysis of the construction phase made before the award of contract to determine a reasonable construction period.

PROJECT: The overall work being planned. It must have one start point and one finish.

PROJECT TIME: The time dimension in which the project is being planned. It must be consistent and is a net value (less holidays).

RESOURCE: Work force, equipment, etc., required to implement the project.

SCHEDULE: The specification of the plan in terms of project time.

SCHEDULED EVENT TIME: In PERT, an arbitrary schedule time which can be introduced at any event, but is usually only used at certain milestones or the last event.

SLACK: In PERT, the scheduling flexibility available for an activity; equivalent to total float in CPM.

SOFTWARE: The programs and systems prepared to utilize computer hardware.

SUBNETWORK: The amplification of a section of the CPM network to study a special sequence or establish a difficult time estimate.

SUMMARY NETWORK: A summarization of the CPM network for presentation purposes. This network is not computed.

TOTAL FLOAT: The measure of scheduling flexibility available; it is a shared commodity.

UPDATING: The regular review, analysis, evaluation, and recomputation of the CPM schedule.

VERTICAL EVENT NUMBERING: Assigning event numbers in vertical order.

LIST OF SYMBOLS

a: optimistic PERT activity time
b: pessimistic PERT activity time
E.E.T.: early event time
E.F.: early finish
E.S.: early start
F.F.: free float
i: starting event, typical activity
j: finish event, typical activity
L.E.T.: late event time
L.F.: late finish
L.S.: late start
m: most likely time, PERT
MSCS: Management Scheduling and Control System (McDonnell Automation)
PCS: Project Control System (IBM)
PMIS: Project Management Information System
PMS: Project Management System (IBM)
PPBS: Planning, Programming, and Budgeting System
R&D: Research and development
SPO: Special Project Office (Navy)
t_e: PERT activity time, equal to $\dfrac{a + 4m + b}{6}$
T_E: E.E.T.
T_L: L.E.T.
T_S: scheduled event time

INDEX